The Search for World Democracy

The Search for World Democracy

W. E. B. DU BOIS AND THE
POLITICS OF SPACE

Adam Dahl

THE UNIVERSITY OF CHICAGO PRESS
CHICAGO AND LONDON

The University of Chicago Press, Chicago 60637
The University of Chicago Press, Ltd., London
© 2026 by The University of Chicago
All rights reserved. No part of this book may be used or reproduced in any manner whatsoever without written permission, except in the case of brief quotations in critical articles and reviews. For more information, contact the University of Chicago Press, 1427 E. 60th St., Chicago, IL 60637.
Published 2026
Printed in the United States of America

35 34 33 32 31 30 29 28 27 26   1 2 3 4 5

ISBN-13: 978-0-226-84675-0 (cloth)
ISBN-13: 978-0-226-84677-4 (paper)
ISBN-13: 978-0-226-84676-7 (ebook)
DOI: https://doi.org/10.7208/chicago/9780226846767.001.0001

Library of Congress Cataloging-in-Publication Data

Names: Dahl, Adam, author.
Title: The search for world democracy : W. E. B. Du Bois and the politics of space / Adam Dahl.
Description: Chicago : The University of Chicago Press, 2026. | Includes bibliographical references and index.
Identifiers: LCCN 2025038021 | ISBN 9780226846750 (cloth) | ISBN 9780226846774 (paper) | ISBN 9780226846767 (ebook)
Subjects: LCSH: Du Bois, W. E. B. (William Edward Burghardt), 1868–1963—Political and social views. | Democracy.
Classification: LCC E185.97.D73 D34 2026
LC record available at https://lccn.loc.gov/2025038021

♾ This paper meets the requirements of ANSI/NISO Z39.48-1992 (Permanence of Paper).

Authorized Representative for EU General Product Safety Regulation (GPSR) queries: **Easy Access System Europe**—Mustamäe tee 50, 10621 Tallinn, Estonia, gpsr.requests@easproject.com
Any other queries: https://press.uchicago.edu/press/contact.html

Contents

Preface vii

CHAPTER ONE
"No True Inter-Nation"
Imagining World Democracy · 1

CHAPTER TWO
"The Fourth Dimension of Color"
Interracial Utopianism in the Age of Empire · 40

CHAPTER THREE
"Unusual Returns"
Transnational Whiteness and the Dividends of Empire · 85

CHAPTER FOUR
"The Voice of Colonial Peoples"
Constructing a Global Majority · 125

CHAPTER FIVE
"The Habit of Democracy Must Encircle the Earth"
Constellations of Democratic Peace · 167

CONCLUSION
Democracy Out of Empire · 213

Acknowledgments 229
Bibliography 233
Index 253

Preface

This book offers a conceptual genealogy of "world democracy" in the work of W. E. B. Du Bois by placing his unique approach to democratic theory in the context of transatlantic debates about the transformation of European imperial order in the twentieth century. While it focuses on a singular political thinker and adjacent intellectual and political networks, I also treat Du Bois's archive—his published books and articles as well as a vast array of unpublished speeches, essays, and correspondence—as a source that can illuminate a broader conceptual history of global democracy itself. For readers immediately interested in my conceptualization of "world democracy," my underlying interpretive framework, and an outline of the argument, I encourage you to turn to chapter 1. For those interested in my approach to the historical and archival research for this book, I hope that this brief preface will suffice.

In seeking to reconstruct what I call the "spatial grammars" that underpinned Du Bois's vision of world democracy, my goal is to apprehend his transnational democratic thought as a response to the problems that a global and increasingly interconnected world made by centuries of European imperialism posed to the global emergence of democratic practices and institutions. In undertaking this work of political theory, I will heavily focus on archival sources, which will bring to light a number of neglected, virtually unstudied, and unpublished documents that illuminate the distinctively transnational and spatial features of his democratic theory. In turning to the archive, my purpose is not to add to the endless compendium of details and particularities about Du Bois's life already well documented by historians and biographers. It is instead to use these particularities to recontextualize Du Bois's thought and to illuminate possibilities for new histories of core concepts in democratic theory such as peoplehood, citizenship, the color line, democratic peace, constituency, industrial democracy, and majority rule. Specifically, this book draws on archival research in the Du Bois Papers at the University of Massachusetts Amherst and related collections at Fisk University; the Schomburg Center for Research in Black Culture in Harlem, New York; the Library of Congress; and Howard University in Washington, DC.

The vast archival materials at these sites reveal Du Bois to be a thinker deeply invested in practical projects, one whose notion of what world democracy means and requires is constantly being shaped by epochal changes in the imperial world order throughout his life. To uncover the meaning of "world democracy" as a response to a specific set of political challenges, it is not enough to rely on analysis of canonical texts. At this point in the twenty-first century, there is no question that Du Bois is a canonized social and political theorist whose primary texts—namely, *Souls of Black Folk* (1903), *Darkwater* (1920), *Black Reconstruction in America* (1935), and *Dusk of Dawn* (1940)—repeatedly appear as the subject of undergraduate syllabi, graduate school reading lists, and vast troves of secondary interpretation alongside such canonical texts as Thomas Hobbes's *Leviathan* or Niccolò Machiavelli's *The Prince*. And in the discipline of sociology, Du Bois is now widely considered to be among the foundational figures of modern social theory alongside Karl Marx, Max Weber, and Émile Durkheim. This is certainly a welcome development. But it is also the case that canonization brings its own blinders, limiting the interpretive practices we bring to familiar figures. While I do attend to some of these canonical texts, I position them alongside extensive analysis of his speeches, unpublished essays, memoranda, personal correspondence, and less studied books such as *Color and Democracy, Colonies and Peace* (1945), *The World and Africa* (1947), and *In Battle for Peace* (1952). The purpose of this juxtaposition is not simply to use archival sources to better contextualize canonical texts. Instead, I pose a more radical turn toward treating the archive as itself a privileged site of theoretical and conceptual reflection for a political actor whose thought was continually shifting and responding to changing historical conditions. In this regard, it can be the archive more than the canonical text that contains the recorded deposits of a mind in motion, what Patchen Markell calls the "kinetic activity of thought and writing."[1]

In fashioning this interpretive work as a conceptual genealogy, and in using terms such as "imaginary" and "spatial grammar," I invoke the influence of a range of diverse figures including Michel Foucault, Quentin Skin-

---

1. Patchen Markell, "Education, Independence, and Acknowledgement," in *Debating Moral Education: Rethinking the Role of the Modern University*, ed. Elizabeth Kiss and Peter Euben (Duke University Press, 2009), 194.

ner, J. G. A. Pocock, Cornelius Castoriadis, and Reinhardt Koselleck on my own understanding of the history of political thought. But I have also taken a methodological cue from Du Bois himself. In his 1961 autobiography, Du Bois reflected on his own practice of life writing, casting his own book more as a soliloquy of a man in his twilight than as an authoritative textual source:

> Autobiographies do not form indisputable authorities. They are always incomplete, and often unreliable. Eager as I am to put down the truth, there are difficulties; memory fails especially in small details, so that it becomes finally but a theory of my life, with much forgotten and misconceived, with valuable testimony but often less than absolutely true, despite my intention to be frank and fair. . . . What I think of myself, now and in the past, furnishes no certain document proving what I really am. Mostly my life today is a mass of memories with vast omissions, matters, which are forgotten accidentally or by deep design. . . . In *Dusk of Dawn* I wrote much about my life as I saw it at the age of 70, which differs much from what I think at the age of 91. One must then see these varying views as contradictions to truth, and not as final and complete authority. This book then is the soliloquy of an old man on what he dreams his life has been as he sees it slowly drifting away; and what he would like others to believe.[2]

In these statements, Du Bois explicitly loosens interpretive authority over his own autobiography so as to invite debate over the meaning of his life and ideas. The fragmented temporality of his own recollections is here reminiscent of Foucault's description of discourse as "a fragment of history, unity and discontinuity in history itself, laying out the problem of its own limits, of its ruptures, of its transformations, the specific forms of its temporality rather than its abrupt upheaval in the midst of the complicities of time."[3] Understood in these terms, the idea of world democracy is recoverable not as a coherent "doctrine" but only as a series of fragments that span across a vast intellectual career and that are surrounded by a series

---

2. W. E. B. Du Bois, *The Autobiography of W. E. B. Du Bois* (Oxford University Press, 2007), 4. For further exploration of autobiographical writing as a distinctive form of political theory, see Nolan Bennett, *Claims of Experience: Autobiography and American Democracy* (Oxford University Press, 2019).

3. Michel Foucault, *Archaeology of Knowledge and the Discourse on Language* (Pantheon, 1972), 117.

of archival elisions that "are forgotten accidentally or by deep design" yet nevertheless provoke theoretical curiosity.[4]

Research by Phillip Luke Sinitiere demonstrates that Du Bois exercised a certain degree of curatorial control in the collection, composition, and organization of the papers and documents that would become the Du Bois archive. As Sinitiere puts it, Du Bois developed an "artifactual imagination" in engaging in practices of archiving and self-documentation of his own life's work.[5] If so, then this sense of the tenuous authority of the biographical author can and should be extended to the archive. If Du Bois was deeply and self-consciously involved in the construction of his own archive, then authorial intention certainly matters for any interpretation. But this also signals that intentionality is a partial and incomplete guide to his own life and thought, leaving the reader to piece together the shattered fragments and "surplus of meaning" that exceed what the author "really meant."[6] To be honest, conceiving of Du Bois's own assertion of a lack of interpretive authority over his ideas in this way has provided an odd degree of comfort. The difficulty of interpreting Du Bois lies not just in his voluminous body of work (not to mention the astronomical amount of secondary literature). It lies, more so, in the multiplicity of Du Boises, the fact that every text resides within a multiplicity of contexts.[7] My goal is not to adjudicate the tensions emerging from this multiplicity. Rather, in taking a genealogical approach, I seek to piece together fragments from the archive while rejecting any attempt to reconstruct a systematic or totalizing philosophy of global democratic politics.

My reading of Du Bois's own practice of loosening his interpretive authority over his own archive dovetails with the inspiration I have found in feminist theorists of the archive such as Kathy Ferguson and Kathi Weeks. For Ferguson, the archive is a center without boundaries and without periphery, proliferating temporal and spatial connections both from within

---

4. For instance, see Zachariah Mampilly, "The Du Bois Doctrine: Race and the American Century," *Foreign Affairs* (September/October 2022): 156–67.

5. Philip Luke Sinitiere, "'An Impressive Basis for Research:' Arna Bontemps' Co-Creation of the W. E. B. Du Bois Collection at Fisk University," *Black Scholar* 52, no. 2 (2022): 51–52; Philip Luke Sinitiere, "'There Must Be No Idle Morning': W. E. B. Du Bois's Legacy as a Black Radical Intellectual," *Socialism and Democracy* 32, no. 3 (2018): 207–30.

6. Mary Dietz, "Between Polis and Empire: Aristotle's Politics," *American Political Science Review* 106, no. 2 (May 2012): 277.

7. Robert Gooding-Williams, "Philosophy of History and Social Critique in *The Souls of Black Folk*," *Social Science Information* 26, no. 1 (1987): 99.

and from without. While they are "misleadingly solid, clearly framed spaces," archives have "no clear borders" and thus offer "unspecifiable possibilities." "Archives," Ferguson continues, recounting her own experiences in the Emma Goldman papers, "are like multiple skeins of yarn, wound at different angles and degrees of tightness around a common spool. Tug on the civil liberties thread and a chain of signifiers unfolds linking Goldman to Roger Baldwin, the Free Speech League, and the American Civil Liberties Union. Tug on the birth control thread and follow the possible links to Margaret and William Sanger, the early eugenics movement, and the contested medicalization of reproduction." Archival interpretations are inherently partial and incomplete because there "is always one more dusty file to read, one more surprising government document to investigate, one further historical connection to another unanticipated figure." It is the "dense particulars and interpretive possibilities," Ferguson clarifies, "that are the gift of the archive."[8]

The gift of the archive, perhaps, is less to settle interpretive disputes than to proliferate them, to pose new kinds of questions and problems by placing familiar thinkers in new historical contexts. What does Du Bois's conceptual understanding of democracy look like when we find out about his disputes with Andrew Carnegie and the broader US peace movement, his debates with John Foster Dulles over the idea of domestic jurisdiction in international law, or his seat at the deathbed of H. G. Wells, one of the most important novelists and global thinkers of the twentieth century? In asking these questions, we find much less that, as Ferguson says of Goldman, Du Bois was "ahead of his time" and more so that he was very much of his time. But other quirks and turns of the archive suggest a different notion of time, one that is composed of an interlaced network of multiple temporalities, or one that is seemingly cut short and buried in the past with no hope of resurrection.[9] What should we make of the fact that his most systematic and developed work of democratic theory is an unpublished manuscript that reads as part epistolary novel and part travel memoir and that lies literally fragmented in the archive (chap. 1)? How do we account for letters and other unpublished papers that unsettle received interpretations of specific periods (such as a 1935 essay that questions black separatism in favor of transnational democracy)? What do we do with those loose archival threads that end abruptly, such as his unfulfilled plans for a

---

8. All Ferguson quotations are from Kathy Ferguson, "Theorizing Shiny Things: Archival Labors," *Theory & Event* 11, no. 4 (2008): https://muse.jhu.edu/article/257578.

9. Ferguson, "Theorizing Shiny Things."

collected anthology of anticolonial petitions, resolutions, and manifestos in the twentieth century (chap. 4)? The point of posing these questions is not to settle on an objective interpretation. To the extent that the archive reveals unknown possibilities, it suggests a temporal disposition of unexpected anticipation for a future when, as Ferguson quoting Jacques Derrida puts it, "anyone, anything, might happen or arrive."[10]

This temporal disposition of anticipation for unexpected possibilities—of searching for those thoughts, dreams, and elisions "which are forgotten accidentally or by deep design"—also suggests something of the untimeliness of an approach to the history of political thought that prioritizes the archive rather than the canon as the primary domain of interpretation. In clarifying this distinction, Weeks proposes the archive as an alternative to the canon (and related notions of tradition) to grasp theoretical continuities over time without homogenizing differences in context. Unlike notions of canon or tradition, which often take on a sacral guise, the archive acknowledges its own profanity, its constructed and contingent character. What makes an object archival is the process by which it is selected and curated. "Archives," Weeks suggests, "are not so much discovered as they are invented; consequently, exclusions are as constitutive of every archive as are the various unconscious or unaccounted for complicities also generated from their never-immaculate conception."[11] Rather than adhere to "the diachronic trajectory" of canon or tradition, archives are organized in avowedly nonlinear ways, resembling more of a "synchronic composition" than an object developing seamlessly through time.[12] The archive is thus inherently genealogical in the way it reorders the temporal relationship between the elements it collects and composes. The generativity of the archive comes not from coherence and uniformity but from the resonances of its discordant elements.[13] In this way, it enables distinctive ways through which to reimagine the relationship between past, present, and future. What this all amounts to, simply put, is that the archive is not simply a place that houses a collection of documents; it is more saliently a constitutive frame of historical interpretation and temporal understanding.

What the archive further shows is that Du Bois, or any other figure with such a vast collection of both primary and ephemeral material, was not just

---

10. Ferguson, "Theorizing Shiny Things."

11. Kathi Weeks, "Scaling-Up: A Marxist Feminist Archive," *Feminist Studies* 47, no. 3 (2021): 5.

12. Weeks, "Scaling-Up," 14.

13. Weeks, "Scaling-Up," 16.

of his time but of many conflicting and contrasting times. Indeed, one of the things I have been most struck by is the way that forgotten ideas, discourses, recollections, and turns of phrase have reappeared in his writings across the span of several decades, albeit in diverse historical contexts. Sometimes even, material is wholly reproduced and repurposed across the expanse of decades and deployed to particular political purposes. For instance, what do we make of the recurring characterization of the global color line as akin to "the fourth dimension" of space-time, deployed in such disparate contexts as the imperial ascendance of the United States in the 1890s and the consolidation of the liberal international order in the 1940s (chap. 2)? What about the recurring use of the financial languages of shares and dividends to theorize the economic and psychological benefits of transnational whiteness across decades (chap. 3)? Or what about the repeated attribution of the inability of white pacifists and racial liberals to grasp the interconnections of race, war, and democracy to "race provincialism" (chap. 5)? The recurrence of these aspects of political language—what I call "spatial grammars"—suggests not only a degree of continuity in Du Bois's transnational democratic thought but also that these recurrences arise in distinctive contexts.

Because of these convoluted recurrences in political language, the book is not organized in a linear manner. Rather, it drops the reader into the 1930s, stretches back to the 1890s, and then fast-forwards to the 1940s and 1950s, with several other jumps, twists, and turns in between. Framed as a conceptual genealogy, the organization of the book largely rejects a historical approach that prioritizes linear intellectual development or that attempts to parse Du Bois's thought into specific phases such as a middle or late period, or, most prominently, a radical break from liberalism in the 1930s. I have become convinced that notions of an epistemological break in Du Bois risk obscuring more than they illuminate, casting aside precisely those recurring and untimely elements of the archive hinted at previously. None of this is to say that Du Bois's thought does not change. He was an eminently dialectical thinker who self-consciously confronted the challenges of thinking amid ever-shifting historical conditions. It is, rather, to say that rigidly positing such breaks as the basis of historical and theoretical interpretation impedes the ability to grasp the tangle of continuity and discontinuity in the play of political ideas, discourses, and languages. My aim is thus less to trace the linear development of Du Bois's thought than it is to connect a set of recurring albeit disjointed and fragmented themes across his published work, correspondence, speeches, and unpublished essays.

Before diving into the argument, the purchase of this approach can be quickly sketched by considering the perpetually shifting spatial scale of

Du Bois's thought, which is a central concern of this book and constitutive of the meaning of world democracy. When I started this project, I was initially interested in the way the spatial scale of democracy was constantly expanding throughout the long arc of Du Bois's political thought and activism, moving from the town meeting of Great Barrington, Massachusetts, to the challenges of national agitation with the National Association for the Advancement of Colored People (NAACP) and all the way up to the international organs of the United Nations. These shifting spatial scales are neatly captured in the 1952 book *In Battle for Peace*, wherein Du Bois proclaimed, "As, then, a citizen of the world as well as of the United States of America, I claim the right to know and think and tell the truth as I see it. I believe in Socialism as well as Democracy."[14] Du Bois then turns from this articulation of worldly citizenship to a discussion of perhaps the first site of democratic deliberation he was exposed to—that is, the New England town meeting. As biographer Manning Marable notes, it was through the town meeting of Great Barrington, where citizens would meet every spring to discuss public expenditures and infrastructure maintenance, that the black scholar received his "first lessons in democracy."[15]

The shifting spatial scale of democratic politics is a persistent theme in Du Bois's transnational democratic thought, moving back and forth between the microinstitutional settings of board governance to the national institutions of constitutional democracy, up to international institutions of global governance. One way to read this worldly invocation of multiple sites of democratic practice is to view it as a unidirectional process of scaling democracy up from the local and national to the world. In this view, the expanding spatial scale of democracy is narrated through a quasi-teleological form of development from the local to the national to the global in which Du Bois gradually inhabits a wider global consciousness throughout his career, culminating in proclamations of world citizenship in the 1950s. This teleological narration is also bound up with a linear account of Du Bois's intellectual development in which his growing concern with the global dimensions of democracy slowly arises out of his heightened attention to the limits of achieving racial justice from within domestic politics. In crucial respects, this teleological narrative of Du Bois's intellectual development mimics common conceptual histories in which the spatial scale of democracy moves in an almost foreordained way from the small scale of the city-state to the nation-state to the higher form of the cosmopolis.

14. W. E. B. Du Bois, *In Battle for Peace* (Oxford University Press, 2007), 114.

15. Manning Marable, *W. E. B. Du Bois: Black Radical Democrat* (Twayne, 1986), 5.

Yet such interpretations miss the multidirectional way that Du Bois continually moves across and against these multiple spatial scales. In proclaiming himself a "citizen of the world" alongside his turn to "democratic town meeting" as "an effective tool of local government," he cues attention to the scalar interconnection of democracy across discrete spatial sites. Indeed, rather than evidence of the persistent possibility of democracy in America, the eclipse of the democratic town meeting alongside the dedemocratization of national politics is a symptom of the fact that "the nation is ruled by the more or less hidden concentration of power in the hands of an industrial oligarchy." Against the assumption that the size of territory and population are the primary alibis for the failure of both national and international democracy, Du Bois turns to the fact that democracy at the local level of the town, ward, and city has almost completely atrophied. The oligarchic control of power at all levels of government is indicative not of the inherent normative limits of democracy at ever-larger scales but of the fact that the "business interests" that dominate national politics are "today in control of a huge oligarchy striving to belt the world."[16] The oligarchy that belts the world moves not just horizontally across geographic contexts but also vertically from institutions of national and international politics down to town government.

What is at stake in the expression of world citizenship, for Du Bois, is much less a form of cosmopolitan belonging in supranational forms of political association that supersede local forms of political membership. Rather, such proclamations of world citizenship alongside national and local citizenship articulate what I will elaborate in chapter 1 as a "transscalar democratic imaginary," in which Du Bois brings his sense of worldly belonging to bear on the critical reconstruction of US citizenship and grapples with the interconnection of democracy at the national and international levels. Instead of an attempt to bring the obligations of cosmopolitan and national citizenships in line with one another, as if to close the gap between a series of nested concentric circles representing varying scales of obligation, Du Bois enacts transscalar practices of citizenship that move across and in turn destabilize the boundaries between sites of democratic practice (i.e., the local, national, and international).[17]

---

16. Du Bois, *Battle for Peace*, 114–16.

17. Lawrie Balfour, *Democracy's Reconstruction: Thinking Politically with W. E. B. Du Bois* (Oxford University Press, 2011), 130–31. For a similar take on transscalar democracy, see Melissa Williams, "Deparochializing Democratic Theory," in *Deparochializing Political Theory*, ed. Melissa Williams (Cambridge University Press, 2020), 201–29.

This all suggests a much more complex spatial orientation than that captured by teleological narratives, but it also points to a persistent problem shaping Du Bois's engagement in world politics: the fact that any transformation of the United States into a multiracial democracy is impossible without an equal transformation of the global imperial order. Whether it is the provincialism of racial liberalism and white pacifism in the United States, the constricted visions of labor solidarity plaguing various forms of socialist internationalism, or the construction of "domestic jurisdiction" in international law, the dilemma of political scale posed a structuring "problem-space" to Du Bois's transnational democratic thinking.[18] But I hope to accomplish more than an illumination of the specific historical conjunctures and political problematics into which Du Bois intervenes. As explored in the conclusion and throughout the book, problem-spaces are not simply given to political thinkers and actors by historical conditions. They are also mapped and remapped by political thinkers deploying spatial grammars to chart the interconnections of democratic struggles across multiple spatial scales.[19] This deployment of spatial grammars suggests that problem-spaces do more than passively shape the context within which a given political thinker and actor operates. It is suggestive of a politics of actively remapping the spaces in which problems arise as problems at all. The purpose of this exploration, therefore, is not to call for a recovery of Du Bois's normative vision of world democracy as a solution to contemporary global problems but instead to cue attention to its style of posing and remapping the terrain of specific problematics that revolve around the scalar and spatial constructs that govern the emergence of democratic possibilities.

18. David Scott, *Conscripts of Modernity: The Tragedy of Colonial Enlightenment* (Duke University Press, 2004), 4.

19. I define a *spatial grammar* not by its inclusion in domains of discourse typically concerned with questions of space (e.g., geometry, physics, geography) but rather by its political use as a means of reorienting the scale and boundaries of politics.

[CHAPTER ONE]

"No True Inter-Nation"
Imagining World Democracy

In 1936, William Edward Burghardt Du Bois set off on a journey from New York that would take him on a world tour in search of an idea. As usual, his world travels were a mix of business and pleasure. In this particular case, however, his goal was to write a popular book about the possibilities and perils facing democracy throughout the world. Taking the form of an epistolary novel, the almost completed yet unpublished manuscript was titled "A World Search for Democracy." When he returned from his trip around the world in February 1937, he addressed a letter to Alfred Harcourt (who had only two years before published *Black Reconstruction in America*) soliciting interest in the publication of the novel. On the one hand, Du Bois pitched the project as a study of comparative politics—specifically, the multiple efforts of political regimes to govern according to popular will and deal with the new economic problems of mass democracy involved in organizing work and distributing wealth and income. On the other hand, he moved beyond a comparative view and placed the problems of democracy in world-historical perspective by proposing to study how the dominant political ideologies of the age such as liberalism, fascism, and communism drew into their orbit and addressed "the colored peoples of the world; the people of China, Japan, and India, and the peoples of Africa."[1]

As his main theses, Du Bois proposed several points. First, he held that true democracy entails not simply the regulation of industry but the

---

1. Du Bois to Alfred Harcourt, February 11, 1937, in *The Correspondence of W. E. B. Du Bois*, vol. 2, *1934–1944*, ed. Herbert Aptheker (University of Massachusetts Press, 1976), 173. I am deeply indebted to Lisa McLeod, who has provided the most sustained scholarly treatment of the novel: Lisa McLeod, "Du Bois's *A World Search for Democracy*: The Democratic Roots of Socialism," *Socialism and Democracy* 32, no. 3 (2018): 105–24. The first significant discussion of the manuscript is from Nahum Chandler, "A Persistent Parallax: On the Writings of W. E. Burghardt Du Bois on Japan and China, 1936–1937," *CR: The New Centennial Review* 12, no. 1 (Spring 2012): 291–316.

extension of democratic self-rule from the political to the economic realm. Reflecting his deepening engagement with Marxism in the 1930s (as well as his lifelong inclination toward socialism), the novel fostered the view that substantive democracy required both the extension of the suffrage to excluded populations and the consolidation of popular control over industry.[2] From this perspective, the dominant ideologies of modern politics were differences over how to deal with the problems of wealth, work, and wages. From this initial thesis, Du Bois ventured an even bolder hypothesis: the extension of democratic control to the economic realm within domestic political systems was intricately connected to the colonial exploitation of labor in the imperial system. Du Bois wrote, "The world is too near unity to leave colored labor and the wishes of colored peoples out of the equation."[3] The search for democracy required a worldview that saw distinct spaces of democratic politics in nation-states, local municipalities, industrial firms, and even nongovernmental organizations (such as the National Association for the Advancement of Colored People, or NAACP) as parts of a structured whole. Reflecting a theme that would become central to his work with the United Nations (UN) in the 1940s, this worldview cast the problems of colonialism and racism as central obstacles to the global proliferation of democratic practices, institutions, and culture.

To explore these themes, Du Bois structured the novel as an exchange of letters between Abraham Lincoln Jones, a professor on leave from a black college in the South, and his friend and love interest, Jane Kent.[4] While Jones visits and writes on politics in England, France, Germany, Russia, Japan, and China, Jane focuses her letters on democracy in America and the problems of war, labor exploitation, and colonialism in Africa. Each character exemplifies not just a specific geographic perspective but also conflicting political perspectives through which Du Bois speaks. If Jones is largely ignorant of the colonial world and praises the Soviet Union, Jane embraces an explicitly anticolonial perspective and is highly critical of Soviet Russia. Moreover, while Jones writes from a social scientific perspective and in empirically descriptive prose, Jane embodies Du Bois's theoretical and poetic

---

2. On Du Bois's lifelong inclination toward socialism, see Michael Saman, "Du Bois and Marx, Du Bois and Marxism," *Du Bois Review* 17, no. 1 (Spring 2020): 33–54; Andrew J. Douglas, "Du Bois and Marx's Influence: Black Reconstruction," in *The Oxford Handbook of W. E. B. Du Bois*, ed. Aldon Morris et al. (Oxford University Press, 2022).

3. Du Bois to Harcourt, 173.

4. Reflecting Du Bois's own use of names in the novel, I refer to the characters as Jones and Jane.

voice. Indeed, Jane serves as Jones's theoretical muse on his trip, constantly reminding him to consult the political theory of Aristotle, Thomas More, G. W. F. Hegel, Karl Marx, H. G. Wells, Harold Laski, and Vilfredo Pareto to tie his empirical observations together. The result of this epistolary structure is a transnational form of democratic theory that resists the tendencies of comparative methods to bind isolated cases as discrete and disconnected from one another.[5] The exchange of letters between Jones and Jane exemplifies the transnational character of Du Bois's political thought—the way in which he envisions the economies of exchange between democratic practice and struggles across the boundaries of race, nation, and empire.

Considering the epistolary structure of the novel requires taking the spatial dimensions of Du Bois's democratic thought seriously. The novel begins with a student in Jones's class asking, "Professor, just what is Democracy?" In an impulsive response that he felt was both trite and distasteful, Jones responded with his namesake's classic formulation of democracy as government by, of, and for the people. Sensing the unease of his professor, the student immediately retorted, "Is there any such thing as democracy anywhere today?" After a long pause and admission of uncertainty, Jones affirmed his commitment to democracy even though he was unsure where exactly it could be said to exist. "I know it exists," Jones responded, "but where and in just what form—that I do not know, and I want to find out," at which he point he committed to undertake a "new search—a sort of voyage of discovery."[6] Jones joked with his students that such a journey would require traveling to Russia and China to see where democracy was hiding. As he further discussed his plans with Jane, his friend encouraged him, "Go to England and then to France, and so round the world and just snoop. Just look at the scene and say: What is this world order? How far does it spring from popular demand; how far is it serving the real interests of people? How far are the people running it themselves? And above all who are the people, so-called?"[7]

Several things are remarkable about this episode. The first is that Jane

---

5. See Micol Seigel, "Beyond Compare: Comparative Method After the Transnational Turn," *Radical History Review*, no. 91 (Winter 2005): 62–90; Jurgen Kocka, "Comparison and Beyond," *History and Theory* 42, no. 1 (February 2003): 39–44; Michael Werner and Bénédicte Zimmermann, "Beyond Comparison: *Histoire Croisée* and the Challenge of Reflexivity," *History and Theory* 45, no. 1 (February 2006): 30–50.

6. Du Bois, "A World Search for Democracy" (n.d.), unpublished manuscript, box 225, p. 1, Special Collections and University Archives, University of Massachusetts Amherst Libraries (hereafter cited as Du Bois Papers).

7. Du Bois, "World Search," Du Bois Papers, box 225, p. 5.

encourages Jones to ask the most basic questions of democratic theory (i.e., what is popular control, what are popular interests, and who are the people?) by couching his search in a broader inquiry about the nature of world order. As Jane indicates, any inquiry into these basic questions requires simultaneous attention to the world-system within which democracies exist. But perhaps more importantly, this question of the relationship between democracy and world order flows out of a shift in the first and most basic question of democratic theory that prompts Jones to undertake his search. In shifting the line of inquiry from "what" to "where" democracy is, the student moves from a definitional question of substance and classification to a spatial question of location and scale. On one level, this is simple: can any country on earth be classified as democratic? But on a deeper level, this shift points to trickier questions not of regime classification but of the scale and space of democracy, background conditions that are often taken for granted as the subject of democratic debate and deliberation in their own right.

Du Bois's inquiry in the novel entails not simply a search for the place or location of democracy in discrete spatial sites. It is a cartographic charting of the modern world-system to understand how entangled dynamics in one spatial site of democratic struggle affect another. One of the remarkable features of the book concerns the perpetually shifting spatial boundaries of Jones's inquiry. His search takes him across national and regional contexts from the United States, Britain, and Germany to Russia, Japan, and Africa. At the same time, his perspective shifts back and forth across various institutional scales. He and Jane are of course concerned with democracy at the national level. But in considering international politics alongside the practical organization of democracy in municipal government, committees, economic firms, and boards of trustees, their perspective is at once microscopic and telescopic. In its focus on connections between these scalar sites and on the connection of domestic to international politics, the book could have just as easily been called "A Search for World Democracy." In reality, Du Bois initially wrote the novel with a simpler, unmodified title—"A Search for Democracy." It appears that the modifier *world* was introduced by the publisher.[8] In any case, it is hardly necessary. As the scale and spatial location of democratic politics constantly shifts throughout the book, it is clear that a world perspective was always at the center of Du Bois's political thought and practice.

I begin with this seemingly inconsequential speculation about the

---

8. McLeod, "Du Bois's *A World Search for Democracy*," 105.

title of an unpublished novel because it cuts to the core concerns of this book: namely, the spatiotemporal grammars and transnational imaginaries that underpin Du Bois's democratic theory. Titling the book "A Search for World Democracy" would not have been out of the ordinary. The discourse of "world democracy" emerged in international politics during the "Wilsonian moment" of World War I in the midst of debates over the meaning of self-determination and as President Woodrow Wilson announced his international mission to make "the world safe for democracy."[9] With US entry into World War I, several black activists and intellectuals embraced these invocations of the worldwide spread of democratic forms through US police power as a means of fighting for domestic political inclusion. In protest of discrimination and segregation within the military, a 1918 meeting of activists and NAACP officials in New York issued a statement declaring, "as our country is the professed champion of world democracy based upon justice, fellow feeling and equality, that its first and most binding obligation is to safeguard every man within its own domain—black and white alike."[10] At the same time, the phrase was a staple among transatlantic socialists and militant labor activists, who employed it as a means of internationalizing working-class struggles over control of industry, culminating in the establishment of the International Labor Organization in 1919 under the League of Nations. Yet the term was by no means an uncontested banner of struggle for international communists. In his 1917 tract *Imperialism*, Vladimir Ilyich Lenin cast the idea as fatally pegged to the bourgeois internationalism of Wilson by lampooning "the utter falsity of social-pacifist views and hopes for world democracy."[11]

In seeking to reconstruct the spatial imaginaries that underpinned these invocations, the aim of this book is to provide a conceptual genealogy of the problem of "world democracy" in Du Bois's transnational political thought. For now, however, I wish only to convey that its meaning was a contested language and part of a broader series of ideological conflicts over

---

9. Erez Manela, *The Wilsonian Moment: Self-Determination and the International Origins of Anticolonial Nationalism* (Oxford University Press, 2007); Woodrow Wilson, "Address to a Joint Session of Congress Requesting a Declaration of War Against Germany: April 02, 1917," American Presidency Project, https://www.presidency.ucsb.edu/node/207620.

10. Chad Williams, *Torchbearers of Democracy: African American Soldiers in the World War I Era* (University of North Carolina Press, 2010), 89.

11. V. I. Lenin, "Preface to French and German Editions," in *Imperialism: The Highest Stage of Capitalism: A Popular Outline*, July 6, 1920, Marxists Internet Archive, https://www.marxists.org/archive/lenin/works/1916/imp-hsc/pref02.htm.

the connected dynamics of war, racism, empire, colonial exploitation, and class conflict in the twentieth century. Throughout his career, Du Bois repeatedly entered the fray of this ideological conflict, constantly invoking "world democracy" as a protean political vision that moved beyond, across, and against the boundaries of the multiple spatial scales such as the nation-state, international order, and industrial organization. In certain moments, Du Bois upheld the Wilsonian view by declaring that racial discrimination domestically undermined US claims to global leadership and democracy promotion. In the wake of World War II and amid the emerging contours of Cold War politics, he proclaimed, "If America is to accept a role as leader for true world democracy it cannot afford to maintain the present status of Negro-White relationships."[12]

Yet, in the same moment, Du Bois would often challenge US claims for global leadership by linking segregation and discrimination against African Americans to imperial domination in European colonial possessions. In this view, racial oppression within the United States was part of a broader colonial problem that impeded the creation of a democratic international order. In the midst of the emergence of the UN, Du Bois pronounced, "I want to indicate today that because of the colonial situation, democracy is not being practiced among most people; and without worldwide democracy applied to the majority of people, it is going to be impossible to establish a universal peace."[13] This idea that colonialism was the central impediment to the proliferation of democratic habits and the establishment of universal peace stretches back to one of his earliest usages of "world democracy" in his 1915 essay "The African Roots of War," which biographer David Levering Lewis rightly calls "one of the analytical triumphs of the early twentieth century."[14] For Du Bois, the abolition of imperialism and the establishment of democratic self-rule in European colonies were a vital

---

12. Du Bois to Earl Jackson, 22 September 1947, Du Bois Papers, box 114, p. 1. In his 1945 book *Color and Democracy, Colonies and Peace*, Du Bois similarly wrote, "The Negro problem forces the United States to abdicate its natural leadership of democracy in the world and to acquiesce in a domination of organized wealth which exceeds anything elsewhere in the world"; W. E. B. Du Bois, *Color and Democracy*, in *"The World and Africa" and "Color and Democracy,"* ed. Henry Louis Gates Jr. (Oxford University Press, 2007), 297.

13. Du Bois, "Colonialism, Democracy, and Peace After the War," in *Against Racism: Unpublished Essays, Papers, Addresses, 1887–1961*, ed. Herbert Aptheker (University of Massachusetts Press, 1985), 236.

14. David Levering Lewis, *W. E. B. Du Bois: A Biography* (Henry Holt, 2009), 327.

means of establishing peace and international cooperation: "We must extend the democratic ideal to the yellow, brown, and black peoples.... We shall not drive war from this world until we treat them as free and equal citizens in a world-democracy of all races and nations. Impossible? Democracy is a method of doing the impossible." As a method of doing the impossible, this vision was an avowedly utopian project of transcending the global color line and establishing a "new peace and a new democracy of all races: a great humanity of equal men."[15]

At this point, I present these passages not to settle the meaning of "world democracy" but only to show that it is a persistent term that appears across Du Bois's oeuvre and that connects him to a series of debates in international and transnational political thought concerning the shifting relationship between democracy and empire in the twentieth century. As these brief references illustrate, the worldview exemplified in his epistolary novel is a central feature of his democratic vision. Through original archival research, this book places Du Bois's unique approach to democratic theory in the context of transatlantic debates about the transformation of European imperial order in the twentieth century. More specifically, I trace the recurring discourse of "world democracy" in Du Bois's intellectual career from his early sociological work in the first decade of the twentieth century to his work on world peace and anticolonialism with and against the UN in the 1940s and 1950s. I argue that "world democracy" comprises a *transnational political imaginary*, a way of envisioning the spatial scale of democratic politics that situates struggles for popular control, industrial democracy, decolonization, and racial enfranchisement in their crosscutting, polyspatial contexts. It names less a specific model of global governance than a politics of space and scale, a mode of perpetually contesting the boundaries between domestic and international politics by linking local sites of democratic struggle within and against the global color line. My purpose is not simply to reiterate the by now well-worn insight that Du Bois was a global political theorist who moved beyond domestic contexts to imagine complex forms of post-Westphalian political association. Rather than fix the analysis on a single political scale such as the local, national, or international, my aim is to show how Du Bois imagined transscalar modes of democratic engagement that move across and against multiple scales, and in doing so contested spatial boundaries imposed on and around democratic struggles.

15. W. E. B. Du Bois, "The African Roots of War," *Atlantic Monthly*, May 1915, 712, 714.

In this effort, I join a substantial range of interpreters who have established Du Bois as a central democratic thinker of the twentieth century.[16] Yet for much scholarship that gives explicit focus to the concept of democracy in Du Bois's work, the constitutional nation-state often remains the taken-for-granted container of democratic thought and practice even as Du Bois's internationalism is foregrounded.[17] For instance, in a recent philosophical exploration of democracy in Du Bois's "Of the Ruling of Men," Derrick Darby writes, "And while Du Bois's political thought also addresses imperialism, exploitation, and racism, which are global problems not limited to democratic societies, questions of democracy loom large for him."[18] In invoking an implicit separation between "global problems" and "questions of democracy" that at times overlap, Darby leaves aside central

---

16. Lawrie Balfour, "Unreconstructed Democracy: W. E. B. Du Bois and the Case for Reparations," *American Political Science Review* 97, no. 1 (February 2003): 33–44; Elvira Basevich, "W. E. B. Du Bois's Socialism: On the Social Epistemology of Democratic Reason," *Philosophical Topics* 48, no. 2 (Fall 2020): 23–50; Arash Davari, "On Democratic Leadership and Social Change: Positioning Du Bois in the Shadow of a Gray To-Come," in *A Political Companion to W. E. B. Du Bois*, ed. Nick Bromell (University Press of Kentucky, 2018), 241–70; McLeod, "Du Bois's *A World Search for Democracy*"; Joel Olson, *The Abolition of White Democracy* (University of Minnesota Press, 2004); Melvin Rogers, "The People, Rhetoric, and Affect: On the Political Force of Du Bois's *The Souls of Black Folk*," *American Political Science Review* 106, no. 1 (February 2012): 188–203.

17. I am not arguing here that scholars neglect the role internationalism and transnationalism in Du Bois's thought, only that explicit theorizations of democracy often remain within the nation-state. There are some notable exceptions that I engage with throughout the manuscript. Manning Marable has characterized Du Bois as a "black, radical democrat" for whom international concerns were central. As a biographer, Marable extensively catalogs Du Bois's various political positions on international issues yet doesn't attend as much to the theoretical dimensions; see Manning Marable, *W. E. B. Du Bois: Black Radical Democrat* (Twayne, 1986). Lawrie Balfour has covered these intersections through briefer interpretations of *Darkwater* and *The Suppression of the African Slave Trade*: see Lawrie Balfour, "*Darkwater*'s Democratic Vision," *Political Theory* 38, no. 4 (August 2010): 537–63; Balfour, *Democracy's Reconstruction*, 115–40. Most significantly, my work builds on but departs from that of Inés Valdez's in two ways. First, my focus is on theories democracy rather than justice. Second, I trade Valdez's overt celebration of anachronism that enters conversation with neo-Kantian cosmopolitanism for a more textured historical analysis of the changing political predicaments Du Bois confronted and the various intellectual currents informing his responses to those problems. Cf. Inés Valdez, *Transnational Cosmopolitanism: Kant, Du Bois, and Justice as a Political Craft* (Cambridge University Press, 2019).

18. Derrick Darby, "Du Bois's Defense of Democracy," *Democratic Failure: NOMOS LXII*, ed. Melissa Schwartzberg and Daniel Viehoff (NYU Press, 2020), 209.

questions regarding the possibility of a democratic world order that might arise out of the ruins of modern imperialism. Moreover, such a bifurcation neglects the possibility that the central dilemmas of democracy in the twentieth century are not ones to be resolved from within the singular scale of the constitutional nation-state alone but instead require a transscalar understanding of the sort offered in "A World Search for Democracy."

In the remainder of this chapter, the first two sections clarify what I mean by a transnational political imaginary. I then illustrate the multiple dimensions of Du Boisian democracy through close reading of his most elaborate expressions of democratic theory—"Of the Ruling of Men" and "A World Search for Democracy." The ending section provides a chapter outline.

Where Is Democracy? Where Is Du Bois?

To get a handle on what I mean by characterizing world democracy as a *transnational political imaginary*, it is helpful to break the term down to its constituent parts. To start, one can conceptualize the transnational in terms of its specific understanding of political order and the spatiality of politics beyond the nation-state, the primary actors in this political order, and how they interact with one another. From this perspective, the transnational stands in contrast to the international and the cosmopolitan as a specific way of imagining "the world" as a political space. One the one hand, we might conceive of "the world" in terms of the *cosmos* of cosmopolitanism, which "typically speaks to us as individuals, stressing our rights and obligations as human beings rather than as members of a community or citizens of a nation."[19] In this view of the world as *cosmos*, individuals disclose themselves to each other as members of a world community whose primary loyalties are to humanity rather than their particular communities. On the other hand, "the world" often appears to us as an international political space that centers on the relations and interactions between nation-states conceived as sovereign entities. In this representation, the driving forces of global politics are the conventional stuff of international relations—diplomacy, war, trade, and so on—where states are the primary actors of concern.[20] While states are undeniably central actors, such a rendering casts "the

---

19. Anne Philips, "Global Justice: Just Another Modernisation Theory?," in *Empire, Race, and Global Justice*, ed. Duncan Bell (Cambridge University Press, 2019), 146.

20. Or Rosenboim, *The Emergence of Globalism: Visions of World Order in Britain and the United States, 1939–1950* (Princeton University Press, 2019), 3–4.

world" as a distinct political sphere confined to relations within the interstate system, which then appears separate from "domestic" politics within nation-states.

My purpose in drawing these distinctions is not to reify them as ontological facts but to suggest that they imply different "conceptualization[s] of the world as well as . . . grammar[s] of political practice."[21] Distinct from the international and cosmopolitanism, the transnational conceives of "the world" in terms of interconnections and relations between peoples, communities, social movements, and other nonstate actors that move across and through the borders of race, nation, empire, and colony without neglecting the significance of nations and states.[22] More precisely, I conceive of the transnational in terms of the politics that occur in the interstices between the domestic and the international and other scalar sites. To attend to this is to simultaneously acknowledge that these realms of political action are not ontological realities so much as they are political constructions, "the contested outcomes of social, political, and economic processes."[23] The prefix *trans*—meaning "to bear across" and "to change"—"denotes both moving through space and across lines, as well as changing the nature of something."[24] In this regard, the concept of transnational democracy does not point to an "alternative political realm" distinct from international (interstate) and domestic (state) politics nor simply to a regional locus of exchange (e.g., Pan-African or Afro-Asian solidarity).[25] Rather, it highlights the ways that democracy within the nation can be transformed and reconstituted through the cross-national circulation of political ideas

---

21. Samera Esmeir, "On Becoming Less of the World," *History of the Present* 8, no. 1 (Spring 2018): 98.

22. Julian Go and George Lawson, "Introduction: For a Global Historical Sociology," in *Global Historical Sociology*, ed. Julian Go and George Lawson (Cambridge University Press, 2017), 8–9.

23. Stuart Schrader, *Badges Without Borders: How Global Counterinsurgency Transformed American Policing* (University of California Press, 2019), 15; Go and Lawson, "For a Global Historical Sociology," 26.

24. Aihwa Ong, *Flexible Citizenship: The Cultural Logics of Transnationality* (Duke University Press, 1999), 4.

25. Valdez, *Transnational Cosmopolitanism*, 110. Angela Zimmerman notes that at its best, transnational historical research does not focus on regions so much as border crossers, whether they be people, groups, or commodities, following them wherever they may go; see Angela Zimmerman, "Reconstruction Along the Global Color Line: Slavery, International Class Conflict, and Empire," in *Interpreting American History: The New South*, ed. James Humphreys (Kent State University Press, 2018), 54.

and practices that move across boundaries between nations, colony and metropole, and the international and domestic.

The transnational marks off not so much a separate domain of politics as it does delineate a "different perceptual field" that attends to the interstices between the national and international. "A World Search for Democracy," with its focus on the movement across multiple political sites and scales, prompts the question, "Where is Du Bois?" That is, from what scalar location does he theorize democracy—for example, the local, national, or international—and how does this spatial dimension of his political thought generate new insights about how to conceive of democratic politics in a globalized world?[26] My preliminary answer to these questions, which this book elaborates, is that Du Bois is a transnational democratic thinker who is perpetually in transit between the bounded space of national politics and the globally interconnected yet colonially stratified world of inter-imperial politics in the twentieth century. My intention is not to fix the location of Du Bois's democratic thought on a single scale of analysis but rather to focus on the movement across these scales and the interconnections between them. Conceiving of the transnational in this way points to a different kind of politics wherein the object of contestation is not solely *first-order questions* concerning the nature of *kratos* (power) that is held by the *demos* (people) or *second-order questions* concerning the boundaries of the *demos* (i.e., the boundary problem), but more prominently *third-order questions* concerning the spatiotemporal dimensions of democratic politics. For Du Bois, the background conditions of space, scale, and temporality both limit and enable various responses to these first- and second-order questions.

By *transnational democracy*, I do not simply mean institutions of political decision-making at either the global or the regional level. Rather, I turn attention to the way democratic struggles for self-rule move across and through the boundaries of the nation-state in three distinct ways. First, transnational democracy captures the *cross-national exchange of democratic thought and practice* across national/imperial contexts. For instance, throughout his career, Du Bois linked the denial of black suffrage in the United States to the denial of self-government in European colonial possessions. In this way, mechanisms of colonial rule condition the character of democratic politics

---

26. These questions build on Mary Dietz's analysis of Aristotle as a "dualizer" politically positioned "between subject and citizen" and as a "transpoleis" thinker that stands "between polis and empire"; Mary Dietz, "Between Polis and Empire: Aristotle's Politics," *American Political Science Review* 106, no. 2 (May 2012): 276–78, 289.

in the metropole such that forms of colonial exploitation and domination abroad lead to the consolidation of liberal democracy at home. But, as chapter 3 shows, it is also the case that economic exploitation in the colonies delimited democracy within the metropole by confining popular struggles to the formal realm of political government, impeding popular control over the economic realm of production and distribution. As a result, efforts to uplift European labor are limited by the refusal to integrate colonial peoples into the worldwide labor movement. It is in this way that economic democracy in America is "nullified by the dominance of the colonial idea among the great nations of Europe."[27]

Second, transnational democracy entails a *transscalar conception of popular rule* that points to connections between democratic practice at the level of local, national, and international politics. In his involvement with the League of Nations and the UN following the two world wars, Du Bois keenly understood that democracy within the nation-state also required international democracy. Chapter 5 shows how in his argument for an anticolonial conception of democratic peace, Du Bois moved across and against multiple scales of political power from the boardrooms and committee meetings of the NAACP to the regional solidarities of the Pan-African Congress up to the global politics of the UN and the anti–nuclear proliferation movement. For Du Bois, the abolition of racism and colonialism within discrete imperial orders and international peace were mutually reinforcing, interdependent dynamics. This view required a conception of democracy that stood against the entwined processes of war, colonialism, and global capital accumulation and that simultaneously moved across the multiple scales of power that enabled these processes. If interimperial competition for the spoils of colonialism was a primary cause of world war, then a cooperative international order necessarily rested on the proliferation of democratic institutions and habits throughout the colonies. Yet, the proliferation of such habits could not take place in the abstract. Such a demand was tied to a vision of political economy oriented toward securing the diffusion of democracy as a way of life in the material basis of global economic equality.

The objective here is not just to emphasize that Du Bois operates in multiple scalar locations of democratic politics. Rather, it is to foreground the *trans*-scalar movement *across* these locations. This complicates a conventional portrait of Du Bois's intellectual biography wherein he gradually

---

27. W. E. B. Du Bois, "Is It Democracy for Whites to Rule Dark Majorities?," in *Writings by W. E. B. Du Bois in Periodicals Edited by Others*, vol. 4, *1945–1961*, ed. Herbert Aptheker (Kraus-Thomson, 1982), 5.

extends his domestic preoccupation with the color line beyond the borders of the nation-state to the international. In this kind of narrative, Du Bois's transnational orientation appears as an artifact of his later political thinking as he becomes increasingly discontent with the limits of pursuing civic enfranchisement from within the constitutional nation-state.[28] In such accounts, to the extent that he becomes a transnational thinker, he moves from the *inside out* by scaling up his critique of US white supremacy, from the small scale of New England town politics, to antidiscrimination campaigns in national politics, to shaming the United States for discrimination in international forums. Yet, as Adom Getachew and Jennifer Pitts have noted, Du Bois also spoke to national audiences from a world stage, moving from the *outside in* to show how the global forces of war, peace, and colonial capitalism structured the politics of the domestic color line.[29] A transscalar perspective on transnational democracy is thus attuned to the multidirectional and intersecting forms of movement across multiple spatial scales of democratic struggle.[30]

In the third and most important instance, transnational democracy names a *spatial strategy of contesting the borders and boundaries of democracy*, specifically the boundaries between domestic and international politics. Contesting this distinction was a persistent feature of Du Bois's democratic thought and politics throughout his career. As I show in chapter 4, the United Nations founding charter relegated questions of discrimination and colonial disenfranchisement to the "domestic jurisdiction" of imperial nation-states and thus outside the purview of international authority.[31] The result was to reinforce the separation of domestic and

---

28. See Elvira Basevich, *W. E. B. Du Bois: The Lost and the Found* (Polity, 2021), 217–19.

29. Adom Getachew and Jennifer Pitts, "Democracy and Empire: An Introduction to the International Thought of W. E. B. Du Bois," in *W. E. B. Du Bois: International Thought*, by W. E. B. Du Bois, ed. Getachew and Pitts (Cambridge University Press, 2022). On this point, Charise Burden-Stelly and Gerald Horne similarly write of Du Bois's peace activism in the 1950s: "From standing on a civil rights platform and reaching out to the world, he was now standing on a world platform and reaching back to his homeland"; Charise Burden-Stelly and Gerald Horne *W. E. B. Du Bois: A Life in American History* (ABC-CLIO, 2019), 162.

30. Here I am indebted to Begum Adalet, who cues attention to political practices of "scaling," understood not just as movement between political units but as the contestation and recalibration of relations and hierarchies among them; Begum Adalet, "Infrastructures of Decolonization: Scales of Worldmaking in the Writings of Frantz Fanon," *Political Theory* 50, no. 1 (2022): 8.

31. W. E. B. Du Bois, "Colonies and Peace" (1945), Du Bois Papers, box 229, pp. 2–3.

international politics embedded in Westphalian conceptions of sovereignty. In his claims for "human rights" of African Americans, Du Bois contested this division of international law and internal state sovereignty by linking the exclusion of African Americans as second-class citizens with the domination of "colonial peoples" abroad.[32] Linking this third sense of transnational democracy to the first two, it is precisely dominant frameworks of international law that enshrine Westphalian sovereignty that prevent such transscalar and cross-national movements of democratic practice. Insofar as they mutually rely on one another, these three senses of transnational democracy represent integrated features of a single framework.

Within this framework, I cast transnational democracy less as a discrete level of democratic decision-making or even as a way of institutionalizing popular sovereignty beyond the nation-state.[33] Rather, I see it as a metademocratic mode of contestation by which its progenitors and practitioners challenge the spatiotemporal imaginary that undergirds arrangements of shared political power.[34] That is, transnational democratic thought and practice seek to reconfigure the background conditions of political institutions that affirm the analytic and institutional bifurcation of domestic and international politics.[35] As we saw in the beginning of "A World Search for Democracy," Du Bois shifts the parameters of democratic theory from "what" (i.e., what is popular rule?) and "who" (i.e., who are the people?) to "where" (i.e., where is the space and scale of democracy?). In posing these questions, he challenges what Nancy Fraser calls the "Keynesian-Westphalian frame" wherein answers to first-order (what) and second-order (who) questions proceed from within the fixed scale of "modern territorial states" and address "relations among fellow citizens, to be subject to debate

---

32. W. E. B. Du Bois, "Human Rights for All Minorities," in *W. E. B. Du Bois Speaks: Speeches and Addresses, 1920–1963*, ed. Philip Foner (Pathfinder Press, 1970).

33. See, e.g., David Held, *Democracy and the Global Order: From the Modern State to Cosmopolitan Governance* (Stanford University Press, 1995); Jurgen Habermas, *The Postnational Constellation: Political Essays* (MIT Press, 2001).

34. By *metademocratic*, I mean that the background assumptions, terms, conditions and imaginaries of democratic decision-making are themselves subject to critique, negotiation, and modification. See Nancy Fraser, *Scales of Justice: Reimagining Political Space in a Globalizing World* (Columbia University Press, 2009); James Tully, *Public Philosophy in a New Key*, vol. 2, *Imperialism and Civic Freedom* (Cambridge University Press, 2008).

35. I adapt the language of institutional bifurcation from Julian Go's notion of "analytic bifurcation" to characterize the methodological nationalism of sociology; Julian Go, *Postcolonial Thought and Social Theory* (Oxford University Press, 2016), chap. 3.

within national publics, and to contemplate redress by national states."[36] In this framing, social movements orient claims for redistribution directed at economic inequalities and claims for recognition directed at status inequalities toward the territorial nation-state and seek redress from within its borders. In contesting this Keynesian-Westphalian frame virtually at its inception in the twentieth century, Du Bois issues a set of metademocratic claims that redirect the grammars, narratives, and spatial imaginaries underlying democratic ideals toward a polyspatial and transscalar orientation.

In doing so, he conjures a transnational imaginary that contests the confinement of democratic claims for redistribution and recognition to the domestic political arena of imperial nation-states. Understood in this way, transnational democracy is at root a mode of unsettling the institutionalized boundaries between international law and nation-state sovereignty. For Du Bois, the spatial boundaries governing struggles against racial domination and for democracy are not pregiven or prestructured. Rather, they are objects of conflict and contestation as well as products of political processes.[37] Put another way, assertions about the proper scale and space of democratic politics are elements of political strategy rather than background conditions of normative principles dictating the legitimacy of decision-making procedures. Indeed, the fact that Du Bois ends his epistolary novel without definitively answering the question—"Where is democracy?"—suggests that the question is inherently undecidable and irreducible to normative principles of democratic legitimacy. A central component of a transscalar conception of democracy is the refusal to fix the normativity of democratic possibilities to a singular scale, whether it is the city-state, the nation-state, or the cosmopolis, or something else altogether.

One of the central claims of the manuscript is that a key component of Du Bois's radical democratic politics resides in his attempt to challenge the hard separation of foreign and domestic politics.[38] Rejecting schematic binaries that cast him as either liberal *or* Marxist or as an accommodationist *or* separatist, I view Du Bois as a radical democrat (though, as I will argue later, of a peculiar kind) who embraced a strategic vision of trans-

36. Fraser, *Scales of Justice*, 12.

37. As Carlo Galli has theorized at length, space is both constructed in and through as well as presupposed by struggles for political power; see Carlo Galli, *Political Spaces and Global War* (University of Minnesota Press, 2010).

38. On the persistence of such distinctions in US radical internationalisms, see Aziz Rana, "Renewing Working-Class Internationalism," *New Labor Forum* 28, no. 1 (2019): 30–38.

formative, multiracial democracy. In seeking to abolish systems of power, privilege, and property rooted in racial oppression, his vision of radical democracy was grounded in an anti-imperialist orientation that views colonialism abroad and capitalism at home as inextricably linked.[39] A key part of this radical democratic vision, I argue, was a transnational orientation that involved contesting conventional designations between domestic and international politics in the aforementioned three ways. In styling Du Bois's practical political engagements and theoretical reflections as a "search," I explore how he was continually grasping for and experimenting with various spatial grammars through which to capture the embeddedness of democratic practice in the context of global forces of class exploitation, white supremacy, world war, and colonial rule. For Du Bois, radically transforming the United States into a multiracial polity required a transscalar understanding of democracy equally attuned to the transformation of the imperial world order.

Interpreting Spatial Imaginaries

With these pieces in place, I can now clarify what I mean by transnational democracy as a "political imaginary." For the purposes of this book, I define a *political imaginary* as the deeply rooted background conditions of social and political thought that constitute "the macromappings of social and political space through which we perceive, judge, and act in the world" and that provide "the most general parameters within which people imagine their communal existence."[40] Charles Taylor helpfully distinguishes a social imaginary from social theory. For Taylor, "ordinary people 'imagine' their social surroundings." These imaginings are not expressed in "theoretical terms" but are carried on in "images, stories, and legends."[41]

Similarly, we might posit, only for heuristic purposes, a distinction between democratic theory and imaginary to highlight how political actors and thinkers envision democracy not simply as an internally coherent set of theoretical norms and principles but as a collection of images, historical

---

39. Manning Marable and Leith Mullings, "The Divided Mind of Black America: Race, Ideology, and Politics in the Post–Civil Rights Era," *Race & Class* 36, no. 1 (1994): 69–70.

40. Manfred Steger, *The Rise of the Global Imaginary: Political Ideologies from the French Revolution to the Global War on Terror* (Oxford University Press, 2008), 6.

41. Charles Taylor, *Modern Social Imaginaries* (Duke University Press, 2004), 23.

narratives, utopian longings, founding mythologies, and spatial mappings. If theories are "systematic articulated bodies of argumentation," then they are distinct from imaginaries that draw not from the rules of theoretical analysis but from the fictive elements of speculative fantasies and collective mythologies through which people envision shared political space and the temporal emplotment of political community.[42] The point here is not to posit a stark separation between the two. It is, rather, to pay attention to the tacit spatial imaginaries that often underpin democratic theory as taken-for-granted pregivens and background conditions. What I seek to show in the next section and throughout this book is how Du Bois's democratic theory is couched within a broader transnational imaginary that reimagines the spatiotemporal scope of modern democratic politics. Such imaginaries institute social and political order by allowing people to envision themselves as a governed whole in time and space. At the same time, social and political imaginaries are subject to contingency and contestation. Political thought, as such, is not simply a theoretical activity. It is itself a political activity through which society makes and remakes itself by contesting the "imaginary institution of society," the taken-for-granted background assumptions and narratives that underpin political order and structure the limits around which that order can be reimagined.[43]

By evoking world democracy as an "imaginary," I also intend to highlight what Sheldon Wolin considers the visionary qualities of political theory. Comporting with the etymological connotations of *theoria* as sight, political theory offers a cartographic perspective—what Wolin refers to as an "architectonic vision"—wherein political imagination is deployed to map relations of power and authority that make up "the total ordering political phenomena."[44] Such a vision is imaginative in two ways: (1) in the sense that any representation of political order is necessarily an aesthetic representation rather than a literal depiction, and (2) in the sense that the political theorist seeks to conjure aesthetic representations of alternative visions of political order. For Wolin, the notion of "political space" is constitutive of these visionary qualities of political theory and the languages used to represent political order. In its visionary qualities, any form of political theory

---

42. Duncan Bell, *Reordering the World: Essays on Liberalism and Empire* (Princeton University Press, 2016), 93.

43. Cornelius Castoriadis, *The Imaginary Institution of Society* (MIT Press, 1998); Cornelius Castoriadis, *Figures of the Thinkable* (Stanford University Press, 2007).

44. Sheldon Wolin, *Politics and Vision: Continuity and Innovation in Western Political Thought* (Princeton University Press, 2004), 19.

combines a variety of ordinary linguistic structures and specialized concepts as well as a "concealed or latent metaphysic" that deals in underlying assumptions about space and time. Whereas political theorists might not refer to these underlying metaphysical frameworks in the language of "political space," they do speak in synonymous terms such as *city, state, nation*, or even *world* or *globe*. Such categories conceal an underlying "political metaphysic" that animates the imaginative aims of political theory.[45] What interests me here is the way political space is represented by Wolin as concealed or latent in political theory, a background condition rather than an explicit concern in its own right.

As I will show throughout, Du Bois brings languages of political space and scale to the forefront as an overt grammar of politics rather than a concealed metaphysics. From this perspective, linguistic and figurative representations of "political space" are not so much of ontological realities as they are contested constructions that invite attention to how questions of space and scale can become political matters in their own right. This view requires further attention to the imaginative modes of spatial and temporal representation—the geographic mappings, narratives, tropes, metaphors, mythologies, and utopian dreams—that political actors use to envision new political possibilities. The political theorist Carlo Galli has provocatively called for placing the study of political space at the center of the history of political thought, by which he means "implicit spatial representations" that are often tacitly embedded in political concepts.[46] If political concepts are organized and structured around implicit spatial dimensions, then my interpretive goal is to render explicit the "spatial grammars" that underlie Du Bois's democratic thought and that give substance to his vision of world democracy. Less a priori terms of political action, I treat these spatial representations as imaginative renderings that participate in a play of competing forces, interests, and perspectives in a battle for ideological hegemony. Political space is not simply a pregiven and neutral container that structures political action and theoretical reflection. It is, as critical geographers have long noted, produced through political practice and social relations.[47]

The point is not simply to uncover the perceptions of space-time that influence political thinking. It is to attend to the speech acts being performed

---

45. Wolin, *Politics and Vision*, 16.

46. Galli, *Political Spaces*, 4.

47. Gearoid O'Tuathail, *Critical Geopolitics: The Politics of Writing Global Space* (Routledge, 1996).

in the deployment of these grammars and tropes.[48] Put another way, my argument is that Du Bois is not being passively shaped by various spatial contexts but that he is actively searching for spatial grammars to convey new connections. Grasping how this is so requires a shift in inquiry from how perceptions of political space shape political theory to how political actors engage in a "politics of space" and a critical analysis of "spatial politics" that involves transforming the underlying parameters of democratic struggle.[49] These shifting spatial scales and the perceptions of space and scale they engender do not just influence political thought. Subjecting the boundaries between distinct scales of political action to contestation and disagreement is itself a radical democratic strategy. Much more than a descriptive statement or an abstract utopian longing, the "world" in world democracy is a "constitutive frame," a performative act of democratic world making that seeks to constitute its own object.[50] This task of democratic world making is not simply one of conjuring new theoretical visions of democratic possibility. It is an imaginative task of rethinking the space and time of democracy that draws as much on fictive, rhetorical, and mythic elements as it does theoretical discourse.

Dimensions of Democracy

To elaborate world democracy as a transnational political imaginary, it is necessary to clarify the relationship between democratic theory and democratic imaginary as well as Du Bois's conception of democracy. Democracy, arguably, is the central ideal of Du Bois's political thought. Reflecting on his own education in Great Barrington, Cambridge, Nashville, and Berlin,

---

48. I take the term "spatial grammar" from Clive Barnett, whom I follow in using it as a "way of reading spatial and temporal figures in political thought with an eye to what is really at stake in their expression" and to "establish what spatial and temporal vocabularies do in the course of developing arguments"; Clive Barnett, *The Priority of Injustice: Locating Democracy in Critical Theory* (University of Georgia Press, 2017), 6.

49. Henri Lefebvre, *The Production of Space*, trans. Donald Nicholson-Smith (Wiley-Blackwell, 1991), 60.

50. Sebastian Conrad, *What Is Global History?* (Princeton University Press, 2016), 185. Also see Adom Getachew, *Worldmaking After Empire: The Rise and Fall of Self-Determination* (Princeton University Press, 2019); Duncan Bell, "Making and Taking Worlds," in *Global Intellectual History*, ed. Samuel Moyn and Andrew Sartori (Columbia University Press, 2013), 254–79.

Du Bois admitted, "My attention from the first was focused on democracy and democratic development and upon the problem of the admission of my people into the freedom of democracy."[51] Nevertheless, his conception of democracy is multifaceted, comprising a constellation of interconnected and at times discordant elements. For instance, as will become clear, Du Bois draws on a range of contradictory ideological currents in formulating his world democratic imaginary, such as Fabian socialism, Wilsonian liberal internationalism, Leninist and Marxist internationalisms, and most importantly, Pan-Africanism. Such a diverse array of ideological currents constitute the central elements of Du Bois's transnational imaginary. Yet although these currents are couched within a broader vision of world democracy, none of them exhaustively define it alone, which suggests that world democracy does not contain a single ideological orientation. It is riddled with tensions, paradoxes, and contradictions.

In the rest of what follows, I outline what I see as the three central dimensions of Du Bois's democratic theory: the economic, political, and epistemic.[52] I further elaborate each of these three dimensions in order to show how they are nested within a broader political imaginary that reenvisions spatial parameters by embracing the transscalar movement across and contestation of the various scalar sites of world politics. To the extent that they comprise durable features of his democratic theory, each of these dimensions and the relations between them point outward beyond the nation-state toward a worldly perspective that centers the transnational interconnections among democratic struggles against race, empire, and global capitalism. In this elaboration, I focus on "Of the Ruling of Men" and "A World Search for Democracy," while also connecting these writings to other works and archival sources.

THE ECONOMIC DIMENSION

One of the key dimensions of Du Boisian democracy regards his persistent concern with expanding norms of popular control beyond the formal realm of politics to the economic domain of income, labor, distribution, and pro-

---

51. W. E. B. Du Bois, *Dusk of Dawn* (Oxford University Press, 2007), 14.

52. For a similar dimensional reading of "A World Search for Democracy," see Anthony Obst, "'Revolution of Thought and Action': W. E. B. Du Bois's World Search for Abolition Democracy," *Lateral: Journal of the Cultural Studies Association* 11, no. 2 (Fall 2022), https://csalateral.org/issue/11-2/revolution-thought-action-du-bois-world-search-abolition-democracy-obst/.

duction. "In many of the most important matters of modern life," Du Bois wrote, "there is little democratic control; for instance, in the determination of the kind of work which men do; in the decisions as to the sort and quantity of goods produced and the way in which goods and services are distributed among consumers; in the ownership and division of power based on income." For Du Bois, the quest for "democratic control over industry and income" in both colony and metropole is central to "the future of world democracy."[53] This idea of democratic control over industry led to a consistent distinction between "political democracy" (i.e., popular control over government) and "industrial democracy" (i.e., popular control over the economy).[54] The primary limitation of democratic theory regards its exclusive concern with methods of electing officials and its refusal to "admit that the production and distribution of wealth is within its domain."[55] In "A World Search for Democracy," Jane explicitly professes her conviction that the failure to extend norms of democratic control to industry is the source of present democratic frustrations. In planning Jones's search, she implores her friend, "You are my ambassador to prove this. Do not fail me."[56] If democracy means that the people have the power to control government, then this power is inseparable from the power to control the means of production and distribution of wealth and income.

In a certain sense, Du Bois's distinction between political and industrial democracy reflects Marx's distinction between political and human emancipation. If political emancipation is tied to the extension of the franchise to previously excluded groups, human emancipation involves overcoming modern alienation generated by the splitting of the self into two separate spatial domains, the political and the economic. Tied to liberal norms that posit the strict separation between politics and economics, modern democratic theory provides few means of assessing and challenging this spatial limitation of democratic control to the political realm of voting, elections, and government. As Jane puts it, the power to decide "what and when democracy ... shall rule" and the extent to which norms of democratic control should prevail "lies outside democracy entirely, and in the hands of a powerful oligarchy."[57] In England, for instance, democracy is confined within

---

53. W. E. B. Du Bois, *Black Folk Then and Now* (Oxford University Press, 2007), 266–67.

54. Du Bois, *Black Folk*, 272; Du Bois, *Color and Democracy*, 300–301.

55. Du Bois, "World Search," fragment, Du Bois Papers, box 225, p. 18.

56. Du Bois, "World Search," Du Bois Papers, box 225, p. 6.

57. Du Bois, "World Search," Du Bois Papers, box 225, p. 10.

predetermined and set limits by permitting indirect influence of the demos over state action. Liberalism, in its call for a "limited democracy" that places economic inequality and poverty outside the domain of democratic conflict, is another name for "oligarchy, or the rule of a group or class."[58]

Where Du Bois moves beyond Marx is in viewing this separation of political and industrial democracy as premised on imperialism and the exploitation of the colonized world by Europe and the United States. To break democratic control over industry, industrial oligarchs use colonialism to divide the global working class based on race. With its limitation of democratic control to the political dimension, liberal democracy provides the support for industrial oligarchy. Du Bois explains, "Industrial oligarchy needs wealth, great wealth. Its path is a path of gold, its expenditure the greatest on earth. It cannot brook democratic interference—leveling of income."[59] The working classes of the imperial metropole sharing in the spoils of colonial exploitation limits democratic control from moving into the economic and industrial dimension. Through imperial control over colonies and "spheres of influence, cheap labor and cheap materials could be gathered from the ends of the earth, not only displacing home labor again, but accumulating in the hands of the owners of capital a new mass of wealth and new power base upon it."[60] The effect of this arrangement of democratic imperialism is an extension of the franchise for the white working classes and a simultaneous limitation of democratic control to the political realm. By granting the masses of working men and women financial, political, and psychological shares reaped from colonial pillage, industrial oligarchy becomes a mode of class rule premised on the limitation of democratic control to a confined and tightly regulated sphere of activity. The close connection between liberal democracy and colonial exploitation becomes a mode of reinforcing the class rule of the bourgeoisie. Liberal democracy is the response of industrial oligarchs to the demand of the masses for entrance into the new democracy enabled by the exploitation of slavery and imperialism.

This dependence of liberal democracy and industrial oligarchy on colonial imperialism poses a challenge to Marxian notions of economic democracy. Du Bois writes:

> Singular is the light which all this throws on the Marxian philosophy—on surplus value and class consciousness. Marx assumed logically that when

58. Du Bois, "World Search," Du Bois Papers, box 225, p. 16.
59. Du Bois, "World Search," Du Bois Papers, box 225, p. 15.
60. Du Bois, "World Search," Du Bois Papers, box 225, p. 24.

a labor class had been reduced to a nadir it had nothing to lose but its economic chains. It had no effective motive except that of increasing its income and it would cling together into one gigantic fist to hammer its way to economic freedom. But across this idea in a way that Marx did not realize was race prejudice and race antagonism, an inculcation of human hate and the despising of men, and particularly black men, born into the world simultaneously with capitalism.... The great profit of modern Europe and America comes from the exploitation of colored human labor in Asia, Africa, and America.[61]

For Marx, capitalism erased national distinctions, tying together international laboring classes in a single movement opposed to global capital. Du Bois, however, understood that the white working classes did indeed have something more to lose than their chains. The union of imperialism and industrial capitalism generates a "profit in caste," a distinct form of racial value production that positions European working classes above colonial laboring classes. The "income-bearing value of race prejudice" allowed the European and US working classes to augment their income and status position through the construction of imperial systems of racial inferiority.[62] As a result, the international socialist movement split into two, a white labor movement in the imperial metropoles and a nonwhite labor movement in the colonies. Through this division of the international working class, white laborers turned their backs on "industrial democracy" by joining capital in "sharing the loot from exploited colored labor."[63] By failing to develop anticolonial and transnational solidarities, the white labor movement exchanged democratic control over industry for a narrow form of minimalist, electoral democracy.

In this revision of the international dimensions of Marxist thought, colonial imperialism posed the primary obstacle to the consolidation of industrial democracy on a world scale. Du Bois writes, "In the first place, it ought by this time to be realized by the labor movement throughout the world that no industrial democracy can be built on industrial despotism, whether the two systems are in the same country or in different countries, since the world today so nearly approaches a common industrial unity."[64] In other words, there can be no uplift of white labor without the uplift of labor

---

61. Du Bois, "World Search," Du Bois Papers, box 225, p. 27.
62. Du Bois, *Black Folk*, xxxii; Du Bois, *Dusk of Dawn*, 65.
63. Du Bois, "World Search," Du Bois Papers, box 225, p. 82.
64. W. E. B. Du Bois, *Darkwater: Voices from Within the Veil* (Verso, 2016), 39.

in Africa, Asia, and Latin America. Because of the global interdependence of national industry, attempts to achieve industrial democracy within the nation-state without embracing global class struggle for greater democratic control of industrial production will inevitably devolve into despotism. Du Bois refers to the outcome of these dynamics as "industrial imperialism"—a specific power-sharing arrangement between labor and capital that depends on the fracturing of the working class between a white and a colonized labor force and that in turn puts a greater amount of power and wealth in "the hands of the great European captains of industry."[65] In response, he envisioned industrial democracy as a multiracial form of democratic socialism that can only take root through a transnational imaginary that is attentive to the global challenges deriving from the intertwined legacies of capitalism, war, and empire. This vision of industrial democracy is closely bound to utopian visions of world peace. If the primary drive toward world war is imperial competition for economic control of the colonies, then a shared struggle of expanding democratic control to industry in both colony and metropole is at once a struggle against war and militarism.

THE POLITICAL DIMENSION

Despite shifting political contexts and predicaments, throughout his life Du Bois adhered to a remarkably stable conceptualization of the political dimension of democracy:

> The real argument for democracy is . . . that in the people we have the source of that endless life and unbounded wisdom which the rulers of men must have. . . . Democracy alone is the method of showing the whole experience of the race for the benefit of the future and if democracy tries to exclude women or Negroes or the poor or any class because of innate characteristics which do not interfere with intelligence, then that democracy cripples itself and belies its name.[66]

In the last decade of his life, he would strike a similar chord in writing, "Democracy is not perfect. It only promises that by continuous appeal to the experience and commonsense of the mass of people in any case, but particularly if these people be increasingly educated, you get the closest approach

---

65. Du Bois, *Darkwater*, 80.
66. Du Bois, *Darkwater*, 84.

to universal wisdom that human beings can hope for."[67] As these passages reveal, the value of democracy lies in its ability to generate an unbounded and universal wisdom on which "the rulers of men" can base systems of popular rule. It is only by widening participation through expanded suffrage and into domains of life deemed private and apolitical that rulers can mobilize this knowledge and wisdom.

The widening of the franchise was not the logical product of natural rights doctrine but rather rested on a theory of democracy as the source of unbounded wisdom. The purpose of this expanded franchise was not to secure individual rights or elicit the consent of the ruled so as to maintain state legitimacy. It was, rather, to pool a wider reservoir of knowledge on which political rule rests.[68] From this perspective, exclusion from the franchise is not a problem of justice that violates the rights of citizens to equality before the law. Exclusion is a problem for democratic governance because it prevents rulers from utilizing the unbounded knowledge, experience, and wisdom of the masses. Du Bois writes, "With the best will and knowledge, no man can know women's wants as well as women themselves. To disfranchise women is deliberately to turn from knowledge and grope in ignorance."[69] Central to the political dimension of democracy is an argument for the incorporation of the "excluded wisdom" of women, racialized and colonized minorities, and the working classes.[70] The problem of political rule is determining methods for acquiring and pooling the knowledge necessary for good government. Drawing on Aristotelian categories of political science, Du Bois classifies different forms of government in terms of different methods for cultivating and implementing this knowledge. If monarchy is "the method of the benevolent tyrant" and oligarchy is "the method of the select few," then democracy is "the method of the excluded groups."[71]

---

67. W. E. B. Du Bois, "Democracy Fails in America" (June 1954), Du Bois Papers, box 205, p. 1.

68. Cedric de Leon and Michael Rodríguez-Muniz, "The Political Sociology of W. E. B. Du Bois," in Morris et al., *Oxford Handbook of W. E. B. Du Bois*, 7. Globally, Kevin Duong argues that this program of universal suffrage translates into a vision of decolonization that ensures self-rule and self-determination to all peoples of the world, especially colonized groups under the political and economic control of European imperial powers; see Kevin Duong, "Universal Suffrage as Decolonization," *American Political Science Review* 115, no. 2 (May 2021): 412–28.

69. Du Bois, *Darkwater*, 84.

70. Du Bois, *Darkwater*, 83.

71. Du Bois, *Darkwater*, 82.

Theories of racial and gender inferiority are not simply violations of justice or natural right. They impede the ability of unbounded wisdom to influence political rule.

Such a definition leads Du Bois to a transscalar reflection on democratic ideals and forms that attend to the interconnection of multiple sites of democratic decision-making from the microlevel of committees and boards of directors to the macrolevel of world politics. Du Bois's concern with democracy at the small scale of boards and committees was clearly a symptom of his ongoing conflict with the undemocratic organization of the NAACP. In 1946, immediately following his participation in the UN Conference on International Organization, Du Bois lamented that the NAACP was run from the top down through the "concentration of power and authority in the hands of a small tight group which issues directives to the mass of members who are expected to be glad to obey." He went on to suggest that such an oligarchic theory of the select few is as old as the history of government itself and will persist until organizations like the NAACP realize that "the source of wisdom lies down among the masses because there alone is the endless experience which is complete Wisdom." The difficulty was in finding a method to "tap this reservoir of wisdom and then find leadership to implement it."[72] Such statements reflect not only the conviction that the NAACP must have a foundation in mass movements but also ongoing frustrations with its power structure. NAACP leaders continually muzzled and sought to silence Du Bois for his heterodox political views, so much so that he was fired from the NAACP a second time for publicly expressing his approval of Henry Wallace as a 1948 presidential candidate.

Telescoping his perspective out from committees and boards, this understanding of democracy as a method of generating unbounded wisdom deeply influenced what Du Bois calls a "new conception of democracy—a democracy of minorities which becomes a reservoir of openly expressed opinion and desires."[73] Nick Bromell writes that, for Du Bois, democracy "continually tries to make room for the differences it encounters by habitually seeking an enlargement of the whole."[74] New differences, opinions,

---

72. W. E. B. Du Bois, "Memorandum to the Secretary for the NAACP Staff Conference" (October 10, 1946), in *Against Racism*, 258–59.

73. W. E. B. Du Bois, "A Pragmatic Program for a Dark Minority," unpublished manuscript (1935), Du Bois Papers, box 213, p. 8.

74. Nick Bromell, "Honest and Earnest Criticism as the 'Soul of Democracy:' Du Bois's Style of Democratic Reasoning," in Bromell, *Political Companion to W. E. B. Du Bois*, 166.

and desires are not a problem that democracy must overcome; they are vital resources in their own right. Enlarging the whole brings to the polity distinctive experience and knowledge.[75] As I will further explore, however, Du Bois refuses to confine this conception of democracy within national borders. The enlargement of the whole and the turn to excluded wisdom requires constantly contesting the spatial coordinates of democracy. Heeding excluded wisdom and enlarging the polity entails cultivating a transnational constituency composed of colonized minorities: "No federation of the world, no true inter-nation—can exclude the black and brown and yellow races from its counsels. They must equally and according to number act and be heard at the world's council."[76] Stretching from his involvement with the League of Nations to his work at the UN, Du Bois coupled this striving for a "true inter-nation" with a demand that the excluded wisdom of colonial peoples have democratic representation before the institutions of global governance.

The language of a "true inter-nation" is a fascinating yet neglected feature of Du Bois's broader transnational thought. Whereas this 1920 use of the term appears sui generis, it was similarly used by the French anthropologist Marcel Mauss in the context of the establishment of the League of Nations and his skepticism of European socialists who would dissolve the nation into the ether of proletarian internationalism. Mauss wrote, "An internationalism worthy of the name . . . is not a denial of the nation. It situates it. The internation would be the opposite of such a-nationism. It is also, therefore, the opposite of nationalism, which isolates the nation."[77] On the one hand, the idea of an inter-nation stood in contrast to notions of a supranational world state and abstract cosmopolitanism that transcended the nation and dissolved national specificities (i.e., the a-nation). On the other hand, it was also opposed to forms of nationalism that isolated the nation as a social fact. Without suppressing national and local differences, the idea of an inter-nation would seek to bring nations into cooperation with one another so that they were in a sense coproductive of one another.[78] Du Bois appears to affirm much of this meaning of the term, but in calling

75. Du Bois, *Darkwater*, 83.

76. Du Bois, *Darkwater*, 85.

77. Mauss quoted in Bernard Stiegler, *States of Shock: Stupidity and Knowledge in the 21st Century* (Polity, 2015), 179.

78. Anne Alombert, "Towards a Bifurcation: Internation and Interscience in the Twenty-First Century," in *Bernard Stiegler: Memories of the Future*, ed. Bart Buseyne et al. (Bloomsbury, 2024), 175.

for the inclusion of colonized and racialized populations into the councils of a world federation, he adds another layer. The question here concerns the constituency of such an inter-nation: would it be states, individuals, or peoples who exceeded the boundaries of states? Rather than simply a union of states and nations, a "true inter-nation" comprised a global, majoritarian alliance that came to the world council to challenge the state's monopoly on the representation of rights within the international order.[79]

Creating a "true inter-nation" thus required constructing a transnational, anticolonial constituency through a politics of global majoritarianism. In this task, Du Bois carved out a central place for the power of popular majorities within his democratic theory. Democracy does not demand complete equality in education and income but simply "the widest possible consultation with the mass of citizens on the theory that only in this way can you consult the ultimate authority and ultimate sovereignty."[80] Nevertheless, this notion of "ultimate sovereignty" is a contingent construction. While a steadfast proponent of majority rule, Du Bois also recognized that the boundaries composing the majority that represent ultimate sovereignty are constantly shifting and subject to political contestation. As new perspectives, wisdom, and interests color the ultimate sovereignty of the people, new sources of confusion, conflict, and contestation arise. In this regard, democracy does not simply mean extending the franchise within a predefined political sphere through the inclusion of the excluded. Rather, new perspectives redefine and reshape the social whole through "disarrangement and confusion to the older equilibrium."[81] Democracy entails the destabilization and contestation of the boundaries of the political initiated by the addition of new perspectives and outlooks.

This dynamic gives rise to a central yet underappreciated feature of Du Bois's transnational political imaginary, what I call a theory of *constructed and contingent majoritarianism*. In "Of the Ruling of Men," Du Bois references an obscure civics textbook written by the journalist Charles Nordhoff called *Politics for Young Americans*, quoting an adage from a short chapter on the "The Importance and Duty of the Minority." Countering the common belief that the primary duty of the minority is to succumb to the will

---

79. Homi Bhabha, "Global Minoritarian Culture," in *Shades of the Planet: American Literature as World Literature*, ed. Wai Chee Dimock and Lawrence Buell (Princeton University Press, 2007), 192–93.

80. W. E. B. Du Bois, "The Possibility of Democracy in America" (March 1928), Du Bois Papers, box 211, p. 2.

81. Du Bois, *Darkwater*, 84.

of the majority, Du Bois quoted Nordhoff, "The first duty of a minority is to become a majority."[82] As an example of this, Nordhoff upheld the abolitionist movement in the United States, which comprised a determined minority that advertised their cause and seized the opportunity to become a popular, mass-based movement. In Du Bois's mind, Nordhoff's insight and example "has its underlying truth, but it also has its dangerous falsehood; viz., any minority which cannot become a majority is not worthy of consideration."[83] The best political strategy for oppressed minorities is not simply to seek protection from the tyranny of the majority through counter-majoritarian and antidemocratic measures. It is to build a majoritarian coalition and become a popular democratic force. Du Bois goes on, "We have attempted to enthrone any chance majority and make it rule by divine right. We have kicked and cursed minorities as upstarts and usurpers when their sole offense lay in not having ideas or hair like ours."[84] The notion of "chance majorities" suggests that the problem with modern democratic theory is not the doctrine of majority rule per se but an understanding of majorities and minorities as naturalized, prepolitical groups rather than as contested creations that are themselves the product of political processes.[85]

If majorities do not have an inherent and divine authority but are contingent constructions, then any authority they do embody is a provisional achievement subject to reordering and transformation. By warning "against the politically deadening effects of uncritical adherence to the views of the majority," in Lawrie Balfour's words, Du Bois further shows how the ossification of majority rule undercuts the unbounded wisdom generated by democracy.[86] Yet he counters this "doctrine of the divine right of majorities" not with blanket condemnation of majority rule but with the idea that political majorities are themselves political constructions that can be unmade and remade. The remedy for democratic absolutism is not the permanent fixation of minority rights or the pernicious condemnation of "mob rule." The remedy lies "in calling these same minorities to council."[87] In doing so,

---

82. Charles Nordhoff, *Politics for Young Americans* (Harper, 1875), 136.

83. Du Bois, *Darkwater*, 87.

84. Du Bois, *Darkwater*, 88.

85. For a fascinating exploration of these dynamics in Indian political thought, see Vatsal Naresh, "Problems of an Other's Making: Ambedkar, Caste, and Majoritarian Domination," preprint, *American Political Science Review*, December 17, 2024, https://doi.org/10.1017/S0003055424001126.

86. Balfour, "*Darkwater*'s Democratic Vision," 551.

87. Du Bois, *Darkwater*, 88–89.

the boundaries between majority and minority become subject to critical scrutiny. Contingent majoritarianism thus conjoins faith in the capacity of popular majorities to rule with wisdom to a critical analysis of how those very same majorities ossify by developing means of protecting their power through mechanisms of political exclusion. Put otherwise, Du Bois rejects the view that majorities and minorities are prepolitical groups corresponding to races, nations, or religion. Rather than a priori constraints on the democratic process, popular majorities are the contingent and constructed outcome of that process itself.

THE EPISTEMIC DIMENSION

In the epistemic dimension of his democratic theory, Du Bois counteracted a prevailing tendency in the twentieth century that cast doubt on classical notions of popular control in favor of an elitist conception of democracy as a method of selecting leaders. Exemplified by Walter Lippmann and Joseph Schumpeter, the elitist (or minimalist) conception of democracy held that modern citizens were rationally unfit for the demands of classical theories of democracy. Indeed, Schumpeter and Lippmann did much to establish the contours of Cold War democratic theory, which incorporated a negative image of the demos as masses most forcefully developed by antidemocratic theorists such as Plato and James Madison into democratic theory itself. The result was a blurred line "between the demos as the foundation of democracy and the masses as a fatal threat to it."[88] Postwar democratic theorists addressed these fears of the demos as mass not by stepping outside of democratic theory but by reimagining its basic terms and logics. Instead of an image of government as the pursuit of the general will or the enshrinement of popular sovereignty, they reconceived democracy in instrumental terms as a method of pursuing individual interests and selecting political leaders. As a result, the antidemocratic tendency to cast the people as a mob that marks the origins of Western political thought became integrated into mainstream democratic theory.[89]

Du Bois lived through a time when these contours of contemporary democratic theory took shape and ultimately became ascendant during the

---

88. Kyong-Min Son, *The Eclipse of the Demos: The Cold War and the Crisis of Democracy Before Neoliberalism* (University Press of Kansas, 2020), 39.

89. J. S. McClelland, *The Crowd and the Mob: From Plato to Canetti* (Routledge, 1989), 1; Joseph Femia, *Against the Masses: Varieties of Anti-Democratic Thought Since the French Revolution* (Oxford University Press, 2001).

last decades of his life. In 1956, he outright rejected Lippmann's depiction of the masses as an irrational mob incapable of self-rule. Du Bois quoted Lippmann: "Where mass opinion dominates the government, there is a morbid derangement of the true functions of power. The derangement brings about the enfeeblement, verging on paralysis, of the capacity to govern."[90] Du Bois then went on to connect this conception of the demos as mob to the denial of black suffrage following the collapse of Reconstruction and the denial of self-government to the colonies. The prevailing view of modern citizens as incapable of public deliberation and concerted collective action was thus closely connected to colonial and racial justifications of *herrenvolk* (master race) democracy.

Foregrounding this context is necessary to correct the limits of elitist interpretations of Du Bois's democratic thought. Robert Gooding-Williams Jr. is largely right to suggest that Du Bois's political sensibilities revolve around a Weberian conception of politics as leadership and rule rather than an Arendtian conception of politics as collective deliberation and action.[91] Yet this suggestion should not blind us to some of the radically democratic features of Du Bois's conception of politics as ruling, specifically his faith in popular judgment and the validity of what he called "excluded wisdom." For all the attention that has been paid to the notion of "the talented tenth," less concern has been given to his notion of "the submerged tenth," the exclusion of which from political rule would result in the loss of "untold value."[92] Despite his custodial vision of black politics, Du Bois never succumbed to the pernicious image of the demos as mob at the center of prevailing streams of twentieth-century democratic theory. It is in this regard that I consider Du Bois a peculiar kind of radical democrat: one who combined a custodial view of politics as leadership with a romantic faith in popular judgment.

In "Of the Ruling of Men," Du Bois reiterates his point that the greatest challenge to democratic self-rule is "widespread ignorance" in both the political and economic realms.[93] Yet he refuses to place the problem of ignorance on the individual or in the realm of human nature and mass psychology. Du Bois writes, "We say easily, for instance, 'The ignorant ought

---

90. Du Bois, "Democracy in America" (February 13, 1956), Du Bois Papers, box 216, p. 2.

91. Robert Gooding-Williams Jr., *In the Shadow of Du Bois: Afro-Modern Political Thought in America* (Harvard University Press, 2009). See also Wilson Moses, *Creative Conflict in African American Thought* (Cambridge University Press, 2004), chapter 11.

92. Du Bois, *Darkwater*, 83.

93. Du Bois, *Darkwater*, 78.

not to vote.' We would say, 'No civilized state should have citizens too ignorant to participate in government,' and this statement is but a step to the fact: that no state is civilized which has citizens too ignorant to help rule it." Here Du Bois reverses the valence of elite theory by treating ignorance as a problem not of individual psychology but of social organization. In this view, the education of democratic citizens is endogenous rather than exogenous to political participation. As Du Bois puts it, "education is not a prerequisite to political control—political control is the cause of popular education." The education of citizens and the overcoming of ignorance is a product rather than prerequisite of popular control. Claims about the inexperience and ignorance of the masses are at once claims to rule that exclude women, the working classes, and the colonized by relegating them to a regime of "benevolent guardianship."[94]

In "A World Search for Democracy," Du Bois similarly confronted "the problem of the mob" driving elite democratic theory.[95] To the extent that the demos came to behave like a mob, it was because of the ignorance generated by the underlying system of education. "Indeed democracy's most ghastly failure is in education and that primarily because we have never believed that the mass of men can really become intelligent."[96] If modern citizens are incapable of collective action and unfit for self-rule, as elite theories held, the blame was to be placed not on the citizens themselves but on the economic and educational system that produces conditions of ignorance in the masses. Echoing John Dewey's famous rejoinder to Lippmann, Du Bois held that "the problem of the mob" is not one of human nature or mass psychology but is a problem of education and social organization. Du Bois agreed with Lippmann that democracy throughout the world was in a period of crisis following World War I because "voters were asked to make decisions on which they had neither sufficient intelligence nor experience to decide." Lippmann, however, failed to consider that the epistemic problem of civic ignorance rested atop the more fundamental problem of poverty. Elite theories of democracy as a method of electing leaders neglected "the fact that most voters were so near starvation that they could not cast an unfettered vote even were they intelligent enough to know how to vote." Poverty thus nullified the basic democratic assumption that wisdom and experience would come through political participation itself. In claiming

---

94. Du Bois, *Darkwater*, 81.

95. Du Bois, "World Search," fragment, 6.

96. Du Bois, "World Search," 3.

that "economic slavery brought mob-law," Du Bois points to the underlying material and economic conditions that produce the masses as mob.[97]

The economic and epistemic dimensions of democracy are thus intricately linked. Jane closes "A World Search for Democracy" by proclaiming, "The end of our search is this: the world cannot escape the logic of democracy. It is hindered by ignorance, illness, dishonesty, and poverty; these four but the greatest of these is poverty. Men are ignorant mainly because they are poor. They are sick because they are poor and ignorant. They are criminal because they are poor, ignorant, and sick. And they are poor, not because they are lazy but because we regard poverty as inevitable for the mass of men."[98] As Jane makes clear, the epistemic problem of ignorance has its roots in the economic problem of poverty. In these points, Jane echoes the opinion of another of Du Bois's fictional characters: Matthew Townes, who in countering the aristocratic tendencies of the world committee of the darker races led by Princess Kautilya, proclaimed, the "masses of men of all races might be the best of men simply imprisoned by poverty and ignorance."[99] Poverty erodes the capacities of citizens to rule themselves, and poverty itself is rooted in a global political economy marked by the colonial exploitation of labor. Developing the capacities of citizens for self-rule requires a worldly imagination. That is, the educational prerequisites of democracy at the domestic level cannot be adequately developed in a global capitalist economy.

Within a worldly perspective, the mutually reinforcing dynamics of economic poverty and ignorance pose significant obstacles to the realization of world democracy and self-rule in the colonies. In his critique of the UN, Du Bois posited that the real problem of world war was a "problem of democracy," a question of whether the "logic of democracy" will be extended to colonial peoples so that they may have "effective voice in their government." In addressing this question, Du Bois made clear that the interrelated problems of decolonization, international cooperation, and world peace were again determined through the epistemic and economic dimensions of democracy. The spread of democracy to the colonies and throughout the world has proceeded slowly "because the mass of people do not have the intelligence, the knowledge, or the experience to enable them to bear the responsibility of rule." Yet the problem of limited intelligence does not

---

97. Du Bois, "World Search," 14.
98. Du Bois, "World Search," 122.
99. W. E. B. Du Bois, *Dark Princess* (Oxford University Press, 2007), 179.

arise because of racial inferiority or natural inequality. It is the product of the social organization of global capitalism where the wealth, power, and income of the imperial metropole rests on the exploitation and impoverishment of the colonial world. Du Bois proclaimed, "The real reason for lack of intelligence and experience among the mass of people is poverty."[100] The global stratification engendered by colonial capitalism is therefore a democratic problem because it erodes the collective intelligence of colonial peoples.

In this regard, colonial theories of racial inferiority that cast colonial peoples as unfit for democratic self-rule are a global variant on the underlying theme of the mob in democratic theory. Just as elite democratic theorists cast the figure of "the mob" as an expression of the anarchical impulses of mass desires for economic leveling, imperial ideologies of racial inferiority cast a democratically organized colonial people as a threat to global capitalist interests. In its epistemic dimension, Du Bois conceived of democracy as a "way of life," a collection of habits, practices, customs, and wisdom that provide the cultural support for democratic institutions. In 1945, he wrote, "The 19th century idea of race inferiority is no longer tenable. If now instead of that idea we are willing to admit that democracy is a way of life for all peoples, there comes a question as to when and how it is to be applied to the mass of peoples living in colonies."[101] Colonialism not only negated the right of self-government to colonial peoples; it eroded the political habits and epistemic capacities of colonial peoples.

Du Bois struck a similar chord in writing the 1921 Pan-African Manifesto, where he proclaimed, "The beginning of wisdom in interracial contact is the establishment of political institutions among suppressed peoples. The habit of democracy must be made to encircle the earth. Despite the attempt to prove that its practice is the secret and divine gift of the few, no habit is more natural or more widely spread among primitive people, or more easily capable of development among masses."[102] The search for world democracy must begin with affirming the epistemic capacities for the development of democratic habits among the colonized masses. Du Bois, like other anticolonial thinkers, rejected the conception of ruler as a trustee holding a central place in Western political thought. John Locke, for instance, held that legislatures do not possess arbitrary power but act as a trust to the

---

100. Du Bois, *Color and Democracy*, 287.

101. Du Bois, "Is It Democracy," 4.

102. W. E. B. Du Bois, "To the World: Manifesto of the Second Pan-African Congress," *Crisis* 23, no. 1 (November 1921): 6.

people. In his speech on Charles James Fox's India Bill, Edmund Burke held that the British people ruled over India as a trust. In the twentieth century, the League of Nations affirmed this more humane version of empire whose apotheosis was the permanent mandates commission, which converged imperial economics and welfare economics into a vision of empire that held the development of colonized peoples as its stated good.[103]

In Du Bois's transnational imaginary, the problem with the conception of ruler as trustee and elite democratic theory that casts colonized peoples as unfit for self-rule is not simply the denial of democratic freedom. More pointedly, it is that the denial of the epistemic capacities and democratic habits of colonial peoples is a prime cause of world war.[104] For this reason, the Pan-African Manifesto affirms, "The absolute equality of races—physical, political, and social—is the founding stone of world peace and human advancement."[105] Global peace thus requires a systematic vision of decolonization that extends self-determination to the colonies while also undoing the poverty and underdevelopment wrought by global capitalism.

Putting these epistemic issues in the broader global contexts of empire and colonialism allows democratic theorists to see the way in which what rhetoricians call *demophobia*—the fear and hatred of the masses—lays the foundations for empire, militarism, and global war.[106] As Du Bois wrote in 1945, "Democracy has failed because so many fear it. They believe that wealth and happiness are so limited that a world full of intelligent, healthy, and free people is impossible, if not undesirable."[107] Reflecting the epistemic vision of democratic habits encircling the earth, he asserted that "the experiment of democracy" proceeds slowly only because "the mass of people do not have the intelligence, the knowledge, or the experience to enable them to bear the responsibility of rule." The real reason for the stalled extension of this lack of intelligence, however, is not because of "congenital

---

103. Leonard Barnes, *Empire or Democracy? A Study of the Colonial Question* (V. Gollancz, 1939), 191–92; C. L. R. James, *The Life of Captain Cipriani: An Account of British Government in the West Indies* (Duke University Press, 2014); Getachew, *Worldmaking After Empire*, 81.

104. In this regard, Du Bois importantly globalizes epistemic arguments for democracy. See Hélène Landemore, "An Epistemic Argument for Democracy," in *Routledge Handbook of Political Epistemology*, ed. Michael Hannon and Jeroen de Ridder (Routledge, 2021).

105. Du Bois, "To the World," 5.

106. Robert Ivie, *Democracy and America's War on Terror* (University of Alabama Press, 2005), 10–49.

107. Du Bois, *Color and Democracy*, 302.

stupidity" or "biological race" but because of poverty, which erodes the capacities of the people for collective intelligence.[108] One of the obstacles to the worldwide spread of democratic habits is the persistence of US imperial power and "a peculiar extension of provincialism" rooted in colonial American culture and that exhibits itself in the countermajoritarian composition of Congress, what Du Bois called "American Tory hatred and fear of democracy."[109] Rather than a parochial problem and peculiarity of the US political system, however, this fear of democracy fostered the problems of war, empire, and the global disenfranchisement of colonial peoples.

⁂

Across these three dimensions, we see how Du Bois continually moved across multiple scales of political engagement and in doing so contested the boundaries imposed around discrete democratic dilemmas in order to grasp how they formed an interlocking, structural whole. The chapters that follow dive more deeply into each of these three dimensions. Focusing on the economic dimension, chapter 3 explores how Du Bois confronted the entanglement of democracy within European metropoles with the deferral of democratic rule in the colonies. Specifically, it explores a largely neglected global analogue to the wages of whiteness on the domestic level that I call "the dividends of empire." While the wages of whiteness are typically thought to operate as an exclusive feature of the US capitalist order, I explore how Du Bois also turned economic metaphors such as "wages," "dividends," and "shares" to capture the nature of transnational whiteness. The language of "dividends" and "shares"—derived from the logics of financial capitalism—points to the corporate structure of transnational whiteness wherein international socialist movements trade economic control over industrial democracy for different forms of political and psychological compensation. Distinct from a wage, which implies an exchange for services performed, the discourse of financial capitalism captures a slightly different logic of white imperial compensation. Du Bois's transnational vision pushed democracy beyond its political boundaries to encapsulate the economic realm. The boundaries between the political and economic, however, were intricately connected to the perceived boundaries of "the international" in socialist movements, which at times excluded the colonies from their purview. His understanding of global capitalism brought him to

---

108. Du Bois, *Color and Democracy*, 287.

109. Du Bois, *Color and Democracy*, 293–95.

place economic democracy at the global level, as a set of interconnected forms of industrial democracy where democratic control over the economy requires transnational modes of solidarity.

Echoing the effort outlined in this chapter to build a democratic internation through the construction of a global anticolonial majority, chapter 4 shows how Du Bois applied the theory of contingent majoritarianism in contesting the dominant founding imaginary of the United Nations in the 1940s as an international democracy of sovereign states each with authority over their own domestic jurisdiction. This attachment to state sovereignty rendered colonial peoples as minorities within discrete nation-states or imperial systems by disconnecting their shared political struggles for self-determination. For Du Bois, excluding colonial peoples from global democratic representation was a constitutional problem central to the mission of the UN. By relegating the colonial problem to the jurisdiction of sovereign states, the UN Charter failed to address the primary cause of world war: interimperial competition for economic control of colonies. To overcome these problems, Du Bois used of the language of "colonial peoples" as what constructivist democratic theorists call a "representative claim"—that is, a performative claim that calls into being the very constituency it purports to represent.[110] In his engagements with the UN in the 1940s, he exploited the conceptual elasticity of such terms as "colonial status" and "colonial peoples" to build a transnational majority on a world scale. The conceptual capaciousness of the term "colony" and its cognates connected disparate forms of domination and dependence across boundaries of race, nation, and empire, thus binding colonial and semicolonial peoples together in a common program of international action. In this way, Du Bois called the excluded wisdom of colonial peoples to the world council so as to constitute a true inter-nation based on the will of the colonized global majority.

Drawing on neglected correspondence and archival episodes such as his indebtedness to British socialists like H. G. Wells, chapter 5 revolves around a reinterpretation of Du Bois's 1947 book *The World and Africa* and his broader Pan-African activism. *The World and Africa* is most typically interpreted as the logical culmination of a long series of books on Africa, including *The Negro* (1915), *Africa: Its Place in Modern History* (1930), and *Black Folk Then and Now* (1939). Extant accounts read these works primarily as historical narratives vindicating the "spiritual gift" of African peoples to modern civilization. Against these accounts, I argue that *The World and*

---

110. Michael Saward, "The Representative Claim," *Contemporary Political Theory* 15, no. 3 (2006): 314.

Africa intervenes in a different problem-space than the earlier books of the series. Specifically, I suggest that it was less a means of vindicating the gift of African peoples to world civilization than it was an attempt to vindicate the capacities of African peoples for self-government. From this perspective, Du Bois's reclamation of precolonial African forms of democracy and communal ownership constituted an attempt to historically narrate a vision of democratic peace in which the conditions for world war would cease only by affirming the epistemic capacities and political habits of colonized peoples to govern themselves. Focusing on Du Bois's critique of what he called "racial provincialism" and his enlistment of the Greek myth of Andromeda as a symbolic constellation of world democracy, I trace the intersections of democracy, race, and war throughout his peace activism from World War I to the 1950s. In doing so, I foreground the centrality of Du Bois's Pan-Africanism to his transnational politics, which rather than an attempt to vindicate the contributions of Africa to world civilization was part of a broader utopian vision of world democracy wherein a kind of democratic peace was attained through the affirmation of the habits of colonial peoples for popular self-rule.

Like the three dimensions of space, these three dimensions provide the coordinates within which to conceptually map Du Bois's vision of world democracy. Yet in addition to these, there is a fourth dimension of world democracy that encapsulates all the others that is necessary to first explore, what Du Bois calls "the fourth dimension of color." Focusing on his pre-1914 writings and speeches, chapter 2 traces the evolving spatial and temporal conceptions embedded in W. E. B. Du Bois's notion of the global color line and explores how they underpinned his early vision of world democracy. Utilizing the work of Mikhail Bakhtin and Reinhart Koselleck, I reinterpret the global color line as a series of "chronotopes"—that is, tropes of time-space that capture temporal and spatial relationships expressed in literary and political discourse. Shifting focus from representations of the color line as a "veil" to technoscientific tropes such as "the fourth dimension," "evolution," and the "annihilation of distance," I argue that Du Bois's early transnational thought offered a vision of "interracial utopianism" wherein the interconnection of human groups across boundaries of race and nation would usher in a new global order marked by world peace and international cooperation. In this vision, Du Bois prophesized that increased global intercourse enabled by the imperial spread of Western communication and transportation technologies would allow for the transcendence of the global color line and the cessation of war between states. The culmination of this vision was the 1911 Universal Races Congress, which portended a futuristic vision of international democracy, a "real democracy of the nations."

The chapter then shows how the experience of World War I upended Du Bois's utopian vision of interracial cooperation, which became sedimented underneath more cataclysmic horizons of expectation regarding the possibility for the transcendence of the color line in the modern world. As a result, "world democracy" became the name for a new spatial imaginary defined by the simultaneous struggle against global class exploitation, colonial rule, and war and militarism.

At the end of chapters 2 through 5, the concluding section will assess both the limits and the pervasive appeal of the language of "world democracy" to Du Bois and adjacent anticolonial and anti-imperial intellectuals against the backdrop of the ideological exhaustion of the US-led liberal international order and the rise of a pluralistic, multipolar world order in the present. Ultimately, my purpose is not necessarily to call for recovery of this vision of world democracy. Rather, in paying attention to the spatial grammars that comprise this political imaginary, my interest is in the language of world democracy as a mode of problematization that is attentive to contesting and renegotiating the spatial and temporal conditions of democratic politics.

[CHAPTER TWO]

"The Fourth Dimension of Color"

Interracial Utopianism in the Age of Empire

> The great problem facing the World, is to achieve such wide contact of human cultures and mutually beneficent intercourse of human beings as will gradually by inspiration, comparison, and wise selection, evolve the best civilization for the largest number of human beings.
>
> W. E. B. Du Bois, "The Future of Europe in Africa"

> Morally speaking, then, the crucial issue is whether our vision of democracy can clear-sightedly cross the color line, and whether we can break through the barriers of color and cultural racialism and reach the necessary goal of world democracy.
>
> Alain Locke, "Color: Unfinished Business of Democracy"

This chapter examines the relationship between the global color line and Du Bois's incipient vision of world democracy in the first decades of the twentieth century. Although it has been discussed exhaustively by scholars, extant interpretations have neglected a crucial component of Du Bois's initial formulations of the global color line and how his understanding profoundly shifted over the course of the twentieth century. Utilizing the work of Russian literary theorist Mikhail Bakhtin, I reinterpret the global color line as a "chronotope" (literally, time-space), a trope that captures "the intrinsic connectedness of temporal and spatial relationships that are artistically expressed in literature."[1] Drawing on non-Euclidean geometry and Einstein-

---

Epigraphs: Du Bois, "Future of Europe in Africa," 196; Alain Locke, "Color: Unfinished Business of Democracy," in *The Works of Alain Locke*, ed. Charles Molesworth (Oxford University Press, 2012), 535.

1. Mikhail Bakhtin, "Forms of Time and of the Chronotope in the Novel," in *The Dialogic Imagination* (University of Texas Press, 1981), 84. I take the idea of the color line as chronotope from David Luis Brown, *Waves of Decolonization: Discourses of Hemispheric Citizenship in Cuba, Mexico, and the United States* (Duke University Press, 2008).

ian relativity, Bakhtin characterized time as the fourth dimension of space. Chronotopes thus comprise tropes and metaphors that linguistically capture this inherent inseparability of time and space in figurative representation. In chronotopic representations, as Bakhtin puts it, "time, as it were, thickens, takes on flesh, becomes artistically visible; likewise, space becomes charged and responsive to the movements of time, plot and history."[2] For my purposes, a chronotope captures the way that geographic mappings of political space relate to and shape narratives of historical time (e.g., narratives of utopia, progress, evolution, race struggle, perpetual peace).

Understood as a chronotope, as a specific representation of the compression of space-time characteristic of the early twentieth century, the conceptual structure of the global color line derives its meaning from the geohistorical imaginaries that underpin Du Bois's transnational democratic thought. My objective in this chapter is to trace these evolving spatiotemporal conceptions embedded in the global color line and explore how they give substance to the transnational imaginary of world democracy. In doing so, I begin to elaborate my claim that world democracy is not so much a theory of a world state or a model of global governance as it is a political imaginary, a complex assemblage of tropes, metaphors, narratives, utopian desires, and space-time imaginings. Accordingly, grasping this vision of world democracy requires more than a theoretical analysis of its implicit normative principles and proposals. It requires attention to the figurative constructions of space and time that make an abstraction such as world democracy thicken and take on flesh, as Bakhtin would put it. I am thus interested in the spatiotemporal grammars within which Du Bois envisions new democratic and explicitly utopian possibilities, which both draw on and reconfigure a range of internationalist, imperial, and global visions circulating in the transatlantic political culture of the early twentieth century.

Within this interpretive framework, the central argument of this chapter is that Du Bois's early renditions of the global color line engendered a vision of "interracial utopianism," a utopian view in which the interconnection of human groups across boundaries of race and nation would inaugurate a new global order marked by world peace and international

---

2. Bakhtin, "Forms of Time and of the Chronotope in the Novel," 84. Reinhart Koselleck similarly uses the German term *Zeitraum* (space-time) to examine how "the mutual relationality of space and time in their respective articulations" underpin conceptual meaning. See Reinhart Koselleck, *Sediments of Time: On Possible Histories* (Stanford University Press, 2018), 34.

cooperation.³ The shifting meaning of the global color line, therefore, structures temporal expectations for the future precisely through its depictions of space. In this vision, increased interconnection enabled by the spread of Western communication and transportation technologies would allow for greater international cooperation, leading to the transcendence of the global color line. The culmination of this vision of interracial utopianism was the Universal Races Congress (URC), held in London in 1911 and which portended a futuristic vision of international democracy, a "real democracy of the nations."⁴ The URC showed not only how the "problem of race is a world problem" but also how it could be transcended through new global imaginaries in which the annihilation of distance between races and nations would enhance interracial contact, inaugurating a new world order of peace and international cooperation. Within this utopian worldview, the problem of interracial contact was a problem of planetary segregation created by the interimperial European order. However, "the physical shrinking of the world in our day" caused by this same imperial order also harbored the immanent potential to resolve this problem.⁵ Implicit in interracial utopianism, I will suggest, was that the primary cause of war was a clash between the white and nonwhite worlds in which the color line threatened world peace through the specter of race war.

As I show later, the experience of World War I transformed the techno-utopianism implicit in these conceptions of space-time and, along with it, generated a different and more complex conception of the global color line. Before World War I, Du Bois believed that greater interracial contact enabled by technologies of global interconnection brought with it new hopes and dreams of democratic possibility. "In this widespread contact of men,"

---

3. I follow Duncan Bell in defining a utopian claim as one that "invokes or prescribes the radical transformation or elimination of at least one of the pervasive practices or ordering principles that shape human life. These include poverty, socio-economic inequality, war, the biochemical composition of the environment and the ontological constitution of human beings, including death itself." To this list I would add racism. See Duncan Bell, "Before the Democratic Peace: Racial Utopianism, Empire, and the Abolition of War," *European Journal of International Relations* 20, no. 3 (September 2014): 658. My focus is on the utopian impulses and desires within Du Bois's thought rather than on utopia as a literary form or political program. See Frederic Jameson, *Archaeologies of the Future: The Desire Called Utopia and Other Science Fictions* (Verso, 2005), 1–9.

4. W. E. B. Du Bois, "Coming of the Lesser Folk" (1911), in *Writings by W. E. B. Du Bois in Periodicals Edited by Others*, vol. 2, *1910–1934*, ed. Herbert Aptheker (Kraus-Thomson, 1982), 46.

5. Du Bois, "Coming of the Lesser Folk," 45.

Du Bois wrote, "the problem of humanity is taking new forms and *democracy is getting new meanings*."⁶ These new meanings of democracy emerged from changing perceptions of time and space. Yet the experience of World War I complicated Du Bois's utopian vision of interracial cooperation, thus subtly altering the horizon of expectations derived from his interracial utopianism. Rather than a race war fought between the white and nonwhite worlds, World War I assumed the form of an intra-European conflict ignited by economic jealousies in the contest for domination of the nonwhite world. To grasp this reality, Du Bois began to articulate a more complex vision of world democracy that moved beyond interracial utopianism, most profoundly expressed in his 1925 essays "Worlds of Color" and "The Negro Mind Reaches Out." To account for the causes of the war, he foregrounded the global entanglement of the labor question and the color line. As a result, "world democracy" became the name for a new spatial imaginary defined by the simultaneous struggle against global class exploitation, colonial rule, and war and militarism. Understood in this context, Du Bois's initial figuration of the global color line in terms of interracial utopianism represents a superseded future, or what the conceptual historian Reinhart Koselleck calls a "future past," a utopian image of the future that becomes sedimented in the archival and linguistic traces of the past.⁷

Paying attention to the color line as a chronotope reveals how Du Bois incorporated into his political vocabulary temporal experiences and spatial perceptions associated with the compression of space-time in "the age of empire" (1875–1914).⁸ The concept of the color line is not just a descriptive depiction of the reality of racial segregation and imperial aggression. It is also what Koselleck calls a "hypothetical projection" that anticipates new horizons of expectation for the future.⁹ For Koselleck, concepts have temporal structures that govern their use but that also reflect, reinforce,

---

6. W. E. B. Du Bois, "The World Problem of the Color Line," in *W. E. B. Du Bois on Asia: Crossing the World Color Line*, ed. Bill Mullen and Cathryn Watson (University Press of Mississippi, 2005), 35. Emphasis added.

7. Reinhart Koselleck, *Futures Past: On the Semantics of Historical Time*, trans. Keith Tribe (Columbia University Press, 2004).

8. Eric Hobsbawm, *The Age of Empire, 1875–1914* (Pantheon, 1987).

9. Reinhart Koselleck, "Introduction and Prefaces to *Geschichtliche Grundbegriffe*," *Contributions to the History of Concepts* 6, no. 1 (Summer 2011): 31. I draw on Koselleck's "conceptual history" both as a means of examining the morphology of concepts over time and as a method of textual analysis. See Kari Palonen, "An Application of Conceptual History to Itself," *Redescriptions: Political Thought, Conceptual History and Feminist Theory* 1, no. 1 (1997): 39–69.

and alter the realities they represent. The temporal structure of any concept is defined by the interrelation of *experience* (the lived experience of "the present-past" that is recorded and remembered in the present) and *expectation* (the horizon of temporal anticipation that is derived from experience). The characteristic of modern temporality, and thus modern political concepts, is that the gap between experience and expectation widens as the tempo of modern life accelerates.[10] Koselleck writes, "The more a particular time is experienced as a new temporality, as 'modernity,' the more that demands made of the future increase." As increased rates of change come to characterize new conceptions of temporality, new possibilities and utopian longings arise as the experience of fixed and frozen time recedes. Yet with increased temporal acceleration comes a different experience of the future in which any "given present" is more likely to rapidly become a "superseded former future," giving rise not only to new experiences of time but also to new expectations for the future.[11] That Du Bois was deeply engaged in such "future thinking" is evident in his proclamation that the relation between the global color line and democracy is "the problem of the future world."[12]

In what follows, I show how Du Bois's shifting understanding of the spatial and temporal dimensions of the global color line shaped his evolving vision of world democracy. The first section examines representations of time and space in Du Bois's initial formulation of the global color line in two chronotopes—"the fourth dimension" and "the belt"—which foregrounds how utopian longings emerge out of new spatial perceptions. For Du Bois, the color line was produced by global histories of empire, slavery, and colonialism, early forms of globalization that produced new perceptions of space-time by bringing the world into increased economic and political contact. Yet the global color line was not simply a name for racial and colonial division. European imperialism constituted the world as an interconnected whole. By increasing interracial contact, the global color line also connected disparate populations in a single web of shared destiny, providing the very conditions for its transcendence. The second section contextualizes

---

10. David Scott helpfully elucidates this central feature of Koselleck's conceptual history; Scott, *Conscripts of Modernity*, 42–43. Also, on the "time-structures" implicit in "linguistic-structures," see J. G. A. Pocock, *Politics, Language, and Time* (University of Chicago Press, 1989), 40.

11. Koselleck, *Futures Past*, 3.

12. Du Bois, *Dusk of Dawn*, xxxiii; Mark Mazower, *Governing the World: The History of an Idea, 1815 to the Present* (Penguin, 2013), 25. For an excellent elaboration of these themes, see Eric Porter, *The Problem of the Future World: W. E. B. Du Bois and the Race Concept at Midcentury* (Duke University Press, 2010).

how out of this dialectical view of the global color line, Du Bois articulated his emergent vision of world democracy as a form of interracial utopianism that counteracted transnational and white supremacist visions of racial utopianism in the early twentieth century. Drawing on social Darwinism, Du Bois inverted the racial tenor of evolutionary tropes by showing how greater interracial contact enhanced rather than diminished civilizational development. The triumph of this utopian vision was the 1911 Universal Races Congress, which is the focus of the third section. The fourth and final substantive section illustrates how World War I transformed Du Bois's understanding and with it reshaped the spatial and temporal dimensions of his vision of world democracy. I close by exploring how, despite the eclipse of interracial utopianism, utopian elements persisted in Du Bois's transnational thought.

The Color Line as Chronotope

The concept of the color line is a complex metaphoric assemblage, its central logics and meanings represented not solely through sociological description but also through literary allusion. Perhaps the central metaphor representing the color line is the veil, which is itself a complex chronotope that has its own unique spatial and temporal structures. In this section, I reinterpret the color line through another set of metaphors that better capture its global aspects as well as its functioning as a chronotope in Du Bois's transnational thought. Specifically, I show how the scientific idea of "the fourth dimension" structures one of Du Bois's first formulations of the color line in his 1889 science fiction short story written at Harvard College, "A Vacation Unique." As previously suggested, Bakhtin drew on Einsteinian theories of relativity to characterize a chronotope in terms of its ability to represent the fourth dimension, a figurative representation that captures the interrelation and reciprocal functioning of spatial and temporal structures in literature. In one of his first literary explorations of the color line, Du Bois invoked the language of "the fourth dimension of color," which reflected the influence of a transatlantic literary and scientific culture most popularly associated with Einsteinian theories of relativity and that transformed underlying conceptions of temporality and spatiality in the fin de siècle period.[13] The other central metaphor I explore to delineate the color line as chronotope is its representation as a "belt" that spans the world.

---

13. Du Bois and Einstein had a correspondence that spanned almost two decades from the 1930s to the 1950s. See Fred Jerome and Rodger Taylor, *Einstein on Race and*

THE FOURTH DIMENSION OF COLOR

When W. E. B. Du Bois first claimed that "the problem of the twentieth century is the problem of the color line" at the first Pan-African Congress in July 1900, it was clear that a broader worldview was central to his meaning. The destiny of "the darker races of mankind" was closely bound to the question of how far phenotypical differences would "be made the basis for denying to over half the world the right of sharing to utmost ability the opportunities and privileges of modern civilization."[14] By the time he repeated this language in *The Souls of Black Folk* (1903), the language of the color line would become a staple in Du Bois's rhetorical repertoire. One decade earlier, in arguably his first piece of written work where the recognizable features of the color line were discernable, Du Bois turned to a different metaphor to capture the spatial and temporal structures of the race concept. Du Bois likely wrote his fragmented story, "A Vacation Unique," in 1899 while taking a philosophy course with William James at Harvard. Reading as a science fiction short story, the narrative is, in Shamoon Zamir's words, a "biting satire on American racism and Teutonic nationalist self-fashioning."[15]

The narrative tells the tale of a white and a black student who together plan a cross-country tour over summer break. In planning for the vacation,

---

Racism (Rutgers University Press, 2006). I build here on a range of scholars who have examined Du Bois's use of the trope of the fourth dimension. Nancy Bentley focuses on the trope as a means of representing "novelistic space"; see Nancy Bentley, "The Fourth Dimension: Kinlessness and African American Narrative," *Critical Inquiry* 35, no. 2 (Winter 2009): 270–92. Christopher White and Matthew Hughey see in the trope a means by which Du Bois spoke of spiritual and otherworldly concerns rooted in the occult; see Christopher White and Matthew Hughey, "Above the Color Line: W. E. B. Du Bois's Otherworldly Perspective and a New Racial Order," *Journal of the Academy of American Religion* 91, no. 3 (September 2023): 605–20. My analysis most heavily dovetails with that of Nicole Waligora-Davis, who explores this language as "a geopolitics radically refashioned within an ambitious vision of democratic possibility"; Nicole Waligora-Davis, "W. E. B. Du Bois and the Fourth World," *New Centennial Review* 6, no. 3 (Winter 2006): 60.

14. W. E. B. Du Bois, "Address to the Nations of the World," in *W. E. B. Du Bois Speaks, 1890–1919*, ed. Philip Foner (Pathfinder Press, 1970), 125.

15. The story survives in two forms: (1) as a handwritten fragment in the Du Bois Collection, Franklin Library Special Collections and Archives, John Hope and Aurelia E. Franklin Library, at Fisk University, and (2) as a transcription by Francis Broderick, who wrote a thesis on Du Bois in the 1950s. In what follows, I will quote from both versions, which are presented in Shamoon Zamir, *Dark Voices: W. E. B. Du Bois and American Thought, 1888–1903* (University of Chicago Press, 1995). The Zamir quotation in the text is from pp. 46–47.

the black student suggests to his classmate that he consent to an operation that would make him black for the duration of the summer, after which the student would regain his whiteness and return to Harvard. The theme of human body modification was fast becoming a staple of Victorian-era science fiction, most famously portrayed in novels by H. G. Wells such as *The Island of Dr. Moreau* (1896) and *The Invisible Man* (1897). Much as double consciousness affords a kind of second sight, the biological manipulation of the white student granted him a new social perspective inaccessible to the white gaze. In crossing the color line, the white student entered a higher state of being. The black student warns his white classmate, "by becoming a N**ger you step into a new and, to most people, entirely unknown region of the universe—you break the bounds of humanity and become a . . . colored man."[16] In assuming a new spatial and temporal existence, the perception the white student gains allows him to transcend the limits of ordinary consciousness. The black student calls this unknown domain of the universe "the fourth dimension of color." He counsels his white companion, "Spend summer in that portion of space, viewing [the] world's intestines from [a] new point of view. Not impossible: merely disguise the self as [a] Negro and travel around and see the world from the Negro point of view."[17] Implicit in this narrative is the idea that the new experiences afforded by this spatial exploration of unknown regions will instill new bonds of sympathy and understanding in the white student.

Through these spatial and temporal tropes, Du Bois issues a satirical critique of hegemonic ideologies of Anglo-Saxonism and Teutonism circulating in transatlantic political culture. He closed the story by saying, "I don't deny Anglo-Saxon civilization has done much; I just deny it has done all. Only the . . . Quakers still remember God. Among [the] rest, 'not that I is above Thee but that I despises thee'—there is the death warrant of Teutonic civilization."[18] The language here clearly echoes Du Bois's Harvard baccalaureate address, "Jefferson Davis as a Representative of Civilization" (1890). In this speech, he mocks not Jefferson Davis the man but the type of civilization he represents, one that glorifies "individualism coupled with might" and "the cool logic of the club." In this type of civilization, freedom rests on enslavement and domination. Davis was the "the peculiar champion of a people fighting to be free in order that another people should not be free." Such a civilization embraced a peculiar view of historical progress

---

16. Du Bois, "Vacation Unique," in Zamir, *Dark Voices*, 221.

17. Du Bois, "Vacation Unique," in Zamir, *Dark Voices*, 222–23.

18. Du Bois, "Vacation Unique," in Zamir, *Dark Voices*, 224–25.

that logically meant "the advance of a part of the world at the expense of the whole; the overweening sense of the I, and the consequent forgetting of the Thou."[19] Echoing this language in "A Vacation Unique," Du Bois suggests that rejecting the relational interdependence of I and Thou, a spatial realm akin to the fourth dimension, will inevitably lead to the decline of Teutonic ascendancy.

To advance to a higher state of social being, the conception of freedom for some premised on the enslavement of others must be rejected, and along with it the notion of progress for a part of the world through the exploitation of the whole. By crossing the color line, the racial modification of the white student represents the transcendence of Teutonic individualism, culminating in a pluralistic and relational conception of freedom where I and Thou are intertwined and mutually contribute to the advance of civilization. To convey this point, Du Bois drew on a series of tropes circulating in "scientific romances" of the period. One of these was Edward Abbott's 1884 satire *Flatland: A Romance of Many Dimensions*. In it, Abbott personifies a square, Mr. Field, who is confined to life in the two-dimensional world of Flatland where space moves only bidirectionally. In his adventures, he travels to the one-dimensional world of Lineland where space moves in only one direction, and where he is mocked and persecuted when he tries to tell the residents of a higher, two-dimensional state of being. Mr. Field also travels to the three-dimensional world of Spaceland. When he returns to his home world of Flatland, he is again persecuted and imprisoned for telling his cocitizens of a higher dimension. As Elizabeth Throesch observes, Abbott's *Flatland* relies on a dimensional analogy, a thought experiment "where the writer asks the reader to imagine a flat or two-dimensional world complete with living, intelligent, two-dimensional beings, in order to then imagine the relationship between our world and a four-dimensional one."[20]

In a similar manner, Du Bois's narrative of a white student crossing the color line serves as a thought experiment that allows the reader to imagine a world that transcended the color line. Doing so, he suggests, is as difficult to comprehend as a two-dimensional being imagining three-dimensional space. Yet, the purpose was not simply to say that perceiving the fourth dimension was impossible. Rather, Du Bois conjoins utopian desire with satirical wit. Just as a three-dimensional being would face persecution in

---

19. W. E. B. Du Bois, "Jefferson Davis as a Representative of Civilization" (June 1890), Du Bois Papers, box 196, pp. 2–3.

20. Elizabeth Throesch, *Before Einstein: The Fourth Dimension in Fin-de-Siècle Literature and Culture* (Anthem Press, 2017), 24.

a two-dimensional world, those calling for the transcendence of the color line through new visions of human unification would also face fear and anger in a world bound by lower states of perception. As I will show in the next section, Du Bois hoped that a higher state of perception would arise through technological and scientific advancement. As Zamir tells it, "Abbott's aim is to satirize strategies of enforced conformity, fears of difference, and anxieties about social revolution."[21] Du Bois deliberately likens the white student undergoing racial modification to Mr. Field, who, experiencing a higher spatial dimension through travels to unknown regions of the universe, must try to convince his fellow residents of Flatland to adopt a higher mode of three-dimensional consciousness. The language of the fourth dimension thus provided the means of speculating about the evolution of higher forms of interconnected consciousness beyond the limitations imposed by the color line.

Abbott did not go this far, but one can take his story further and imagine how a three-dimensional being would respond to the experience of four-dimensional space. In his invocation of "the fourth dimension of color," Du Bois imagined such a possibility. The idea of the fourth dimension arose out of the emergence of non-Euclidean geometry in the nineteenth century. An eccentric mathematician and philosopher, Charles Howard Hinton, penned one of the most popular explorations of the idea in "What Is the Fourth Dimension?" (1884).[22] In it, Hinton provided an inquiry into the representation of higher states of being. Suspending the ontological question of whether there are in fact higher dimensions of human perception, Hinton's task was to ascertain how they might be represented through mathematical systems bound to Euclidean representations of geometric space. Likening his inquiry to Plato's allegory of the cave, Hinton wrote, "As our world is in three dimensions is to a shadow or plane world, so is the higher world to our three-dimensional world. That is, the higher world is four-dimensional; the higher being is, so far as its existence is concerned apart from its qualities, to be sought through the conception of an actual existence spatially higher than that which we realize with our senses."[23]

---

21. Zamir, *Dark Voices*, 51.

22. This essay was reprinted as Charles Hinton, "What Is the Fourth Dimension?," in *Speculations on the Fourth Dimension: Selected Writings of Charles H. Hinton* (Dover, 1980), 1–22. Du Bois was exposed to Hinton through William James's philosophy class and had notes on the text. It is also worth noting that James had brief correspondence with Hinton. See Zamir, *Dark Voices*, 50–51; Throesch, *Before Einstein*, 107–31.

23. Charles Howard Hinton, *The Fourth Dimension* (Swan Sonnenschein, 1906), 2–3.

Through equal parts literary speculation, mathematical formulation, and logical induction, Hinton showed that "by supposing away certain limitations of the fundamental conditions of existence was we know it, a state of being can be conceived with powers far transcending our own."[24] From this perspective, one could speculate about higher states of existence. The problem for Hinton was that there was no image to make the fourth dimension intelligible to three-dimensional perception. To overcome this, he invented the *tesseract*, a four-dimensional cube composed of a smaller cube nested inside a larger cube.

In raising the possibility of new spatial perceptions beyond three-dimensional space, the idea of the fourth dimension in the hands of such authors as Henry James and William James was much less a mathematical concept than a philosophical trope that pointed to higher states of being. It is important to mention, however, that for these figures as well as for Du Bois, Abbott, and Hinton, the fourth dimension was primarily spatial. It was H. G. Wells who, in his 1895 novella *The Time Machine*, first cast the fourth dimension as what Bakhtin called a "chronotope," a figurative representation of space-time. In the opening scene of the Wells story, the protagonist named the Time Traveler explains the power of his invented device to his houseguests by evoking the fourth dimension as the temporal aspect of space: "There is no difference between Time and any of the three dimensions of Space except that our consciousness moves along it."[25] In this way, time is merely the fourth dimension of space. If objects can move through space according to three dimensions (length, width, and height) and if time is merely a form of space, the Time Traveler wagers, then they can hypothetically move through time. In the first decade of the twentieth century, physicists such as Hermann Minkowski and Albert Einstein would give these literary representations scientific substance through the notion of four-dimensional space-time at the center of the special theory of relativity.[26]

Nevertheless, insofar as it harbors an embrace of the transcendence

24. Hinton quoted in Zamir, *Dark Voices*, 50.

25. H. G. Wells, *The Time Machine*, in *Three Prophetic Science Fiction Novels of H. G. Wells* (Dover, 1960), 267.

26. None of this is to suggest that Du Bois was influenced by Einsteinian relativity, which as Throesch notes did not reach a popular audience until the 1920s (Throesch, *Before Einstein*, 1–2). See Linda Henderson, *The Fourth Dimension and Non-Euclidean Geometry in Modern Art*, rev. ed. (MIT Press, 2018); Florian Cajori, "Origins of Fourth Dimension Concepts," *American Mathematical Monthly* 33, no. 8 (October 1926): 404–6.

of racial history through movement across racially structured spaces, Du Bois's spatial invocation of the fourth dimension is resolutely temporal and thus constitutes a chronotope in Bakhtin's sense. Drawing together Hinton's idea of the fourth dimension with Abbott's Flatland, Du Bois provided a social and political counterpart to literary explorations of four-dimensional space, which stands in relation to three-dimensional space just as three-dimensional space is to two-dimensional space, and so on. As I show in the next section, the fourth dimension reflected the emergence of new global imaginaries of the fin de siècle period marked by higher states of political existence and spatially expansive understandings of political belonging. The idea of the fourth dimension and its relation to modern physics is complex, but what is important is its postulation of a higher mode of existence acquired through new experiences of space-time and thus new expectations for the future. Du Bois saw in the concept a way to represent not only the spatial limitations of social and political existence but also their utopian transcendence.

"THE COLOR LINE BELTS THE WORLD"

The trope of the fourth dimension invoked a reconceptualization of space-time that would allow the transcendence of the color line through a utopian program of interracial sympathy and understanding. While Du Bois left the language behind, it clearly left a deep imprint concerning the vexed question of how to represent the spatiotemporal dimensions of the color line. In one of his first proclamations of the global color line, Du Bois explicitly invoked themes of spatial and temporal perception. In "The Present Outlook for the Dark Races of Mankind" (1900), which was first presented to the third annual meeting of the American Negro Academy, Du Bois discussed "the problem of the color line not simply as a national and personal question but rather in its larger world aspect in time and space." Eschewing national historiography, he saw the global color line as a matter of both world history and social philosophy, to which representations of space and time through the adoption of a "larger point of view" are central. Viewed philosophically and historically, the color line provides "the secret of social progress" and symbolically represents "the social forces which move and modify" the present age.[27] In offering a global view of the color line as a

---

27. W. E. B. Du Bois, "The Present Outlook for the Dark Races of Mankind," in *The Problem of the Color Line at the Turn of the Twentieth Century: The Essential Early Essays*, ed. Nahum Chandler (Fordham University Press, 2014), 111.

world problem, Du Bois targeted provincial views of the race question as a problem confined to singular scales of analysis.

In this speech and in subsequent works on the global color line, the central chronotope is not the veil but rather the belt. Du Bois proclaims, "the color line belts the world . . . the social problem of the twentieth century is to be the relation of the civilized world to the dark races of mankind."[28] In this figuration of the color line belts, Du Bois registers its metaphorical meaning not as a noun but as a verb, thus effectively turning attention away from what the color line *is* to what it *does*. As a world-spanning belt, the color line not only divides the world. More profoundly, it draws the world together and binds oppressed populations into a unified whole, laying the dialectical foundations for its own transcendence and the creation of an international order marked by the unification of humankind. One can discern three related meanings of the color line belt. The first is that the color line spans and divides the planet across racial lines, separating the white world and the nonwhite world in a system of global segregation. Second, the color line connects racialized and colonized populations across the borders of empire, nation, language, and colony. Through such language, Du Bois tied together vastly different systems of power in a single archipelago of racial domination.[29] Third, the color line constricts the progressive force of the world movement. Yet in binding the world together in a network of economic and political exchange, the color line will lead to its own overcoming.

The formal structure of the speech itself illustrates this notion of the belt as a chronotope. The first half of the speech explores the spatial aspect of the global color line, placing the problem in the broader context of European imperialism that defined fin de siècle international order.[30] Du Bois begins by discussing various imperial formations and the rule of colonial populations in the Portuguese, French, Belgian, Spanish, and British Empires, offering a geographic survey that connects disparate sites of domina-

---

28. Du Bois, "Present Outlook," 112.

29. On these first two points, Vilashini Coopan similarly writes that the color line "performs its work precisely as the agent of double meanings: divisions *and* connection, differentiation *and* affiliation, historical sin *and* future salvation, spatial marker *and* temporal measure"; Vilashini Coopan, "Move on Down the Line: Domestic Science, Transnational Politics, and Gendered Allegory in Du Bois," in *Next to the Color Line: Gender, Sexuality, and W. E. B. Du Bois*, ed. Susan Gillman and Alys Eve Weinbaum (University of Minnesota Press, 2007), 36.

30. Cf. Nahum Chandler, *Beyond this Narrow Now: Or, Delimitations, of W. E. B. Du Bois* (Duke University Press, 2022), 171–72.

tion into an interconnected network of colonial exploitation. Historically, these patterns of European imperial dominance leave the colonial world impoverished. "The history of Asia," Du Bois states, "is but the history of the moral and physical degeneration which follows the unbridled injustice of conquerors toward the conquered." The optical arc of the speech then crosses the Pacific and comes to South America "where the dark blood of the Indian and Negro has mingled with that of the Spaniard." Although the color line is less pronounced and more amorphous there, it nevertheless produces similar results of poverty and ignorance.[31]

Finally, Du Bois moves north to the race problem in the United States, connecting the exclusion of African Americans to "the new imperial policy" exemplified in the conquest of Puerto Rico, Cuba, and the Philippines. Calling for "an attitude of deepest sympathy and strongest alliance" with these colonized populations, Du Bois proclaims that "all must stand united under the stars and stripes for an America that knows no color line in the freedom of its opportunities."[32] In this geographic survey, Du Bois not only shows the entanglement of diverse sites of democratic struggle against racism and colonialism. He also links the race question in the US to the broader history of European imperialism. In these passages, Amy Kaplan notes, "Du Bois imagined the utopian potential in imperial expansion for unraveling the boundaries of nations and colonies."[33] That is, Du Bois depicts the color line and empire in a dialectical relationship by enlisting imperial arguments against racism and empire. While entrenching the color line, imperial expansion also breaks down national borders, connects the world in a deeper web of shared destiny, and cultivates transnational solidarities. In this way, the kind of racial intermingling within the United States foreshadows new global futures.

In a 1906 essay called "The Color Line Belts the World," he similarly elaborated the dialectical relationship between empire and the color line through the chronotope of the belt:

> The tendency of the great nations of the day is territorial, political, and economic expansion, but in every case this has brought them in contact with darker peoples, so that we have to-day England, France, Holland, Belgium, Italy, Portugal, and the United States in close contact with

---

31. Du Bois, "Present Outlook," 113–14.

32. Du Bois, "Present Outlook," 118.

33. Amy Kaplan, *The Anarchy of Empire in the Making of U.S. Culture* (Harvard University Press, 2020), 177–78.

brown and black peoples, and Russia and Austria in contact with the yellow. The older idea was that the whites would eventually displace the native races and inherit their lands, but this idea has been rudely shaken in the increase of American Negroes, the experience of the English in Africa, India, and the West Indies, and the development of South America. The Policy of Expansion, then, simply means world problems of the Color Line. The question enters into European imperial politics and floods our continents from Alaska to Patagonia.[34]

While imperialism displaces native peoples and subjects them to ruthless forms of exploitation and dispossession, it also puts Europeans and the "darker peoples" into contact with each other. That is, empire entrenches the color line at the same time that, in being the agent of interracial contact, it also allows for the dialectical transcendence of the global color line. As I will explore in more detail later in this chapter, the utopian strand of thinking embedded in this view of empire was a persistent feature of Du Bois's earlier transnational thought in which he repurposes imperial arguments in his quest to abolish the global color line by means of utopian transcendence. In this way, his incipient vision of world democracy does not simply arise in opposition to empire. It arises out of the transnational imaginaries and the globalized world that empire has created.

In the second half of "Present Outlook," Du Bois moves from a "view of the race problem in space" to considerations of its temporal dimension.[35] He begins this section of the speech by proclaiming: "We stand to-night on the edge of the year 1900. Suppose in fancy we turn back 100 years and stand at the threshold of the year 1800. What then could be called the Problem of the Century?"[36] If the global color line is the problem of the twentieth century, it is layered like a palimpsest on the problems of previous centuries. The problem of the nineteenth century was the relation of the political rights of the masses and laboring classes to the modern state. The solution to this problem, Du Bois announces, was universal suffrage, a conception of democracy based on the consent of the governed. In the nineteenth century, the primary obstacle to the expansion of the suffrage to the masses was fear that the "brutish mob" would level the intelligence of the nation by proclaiming the universal rights of man.[37] Implicit in this elite view was

34. Du Bois, "Color Line Belts the World."
35. Du Bois, "Present Outlook," 119.
36. Du Bois, "Present Outlook," 120.
37. Du Bois, "Present Outlook," 120.

the belief that advanced civilization required a laboring mudsill, a lower stratum to prop up the economic base of civilization. As the white masses acquired political rights, they shifted this hierarchy onto racialized populations under systems of slavery and colonialism. In this way, the problems of the twentieth century—race and colonialism—provided a resolution to the problem of the nineteenth century. Racial exploitation was layered on top of and provided solutions to the contradictions posed by democratization in the nineteenth century.

Du Bois also registers the utopian impulse resonant with his account of the fourth dimension in the temporal aspects of the color line. Proclaiming that the world has grown to encapsulate a "brotherhood of men," he prognosticates that the next century would expand "the boundaries of humanity so wide that they will include all men in spite of the color of their skins." Such an age would be defined by a universal vision of perpetual peace and a rejection of "the undoubted decadence of war." Du Bois continues, "The 20th century is destined to see national wars, not disappear to be sure, but sink to the same ostracism in popular opinion as the street fight and the brawl among individuals." The driving force of this vision of peace would be greater interracial contact and development among racialized and colonized groups. As "groups of undeveloped peoples" come "in contact with advanced races under the same government," the impulses for war and national plunder would recede.[38] In structuring the speech in this way, Du Bois makes clear that the phenomenological experience of shifting perceptions of space and time is central to a global understanding of the color line.

Interracial Utopianism and the Annihilation of Distance

When Du Bois first proclaimed that the problem of the color line was the problem of the twentieth century in 1900, it was a brave new world indeed. The late nineteenth century was a period of accelerated migration and global interconnection that produced new cultural images and political dreams of the world as an integrated unity. Increasing consciousness of global interconnection was inseparable from the spread of new communication and transportation technologies such as the steamship, the railway, the telegraph, and the airplane. This pervasive sense of living through a new epoch marked by previously unimaginable technological advance had

---

38. Du Bois, "Present Outlook," 121–22.

a profound effect on spatial and temporal consciousness.[39] Such technological progression signaled the increasing potential for science to transform social and political order and overcome the fundamental afflictions of the human condition. As new technologies annihilated distance, utopian thinkers imagined new forms of postnational federation and spatially extended forms of transnational citizenship that spanned the borders of nation-states. Through these new spatial and temporal imaginaries, it was possible to imagine a future where increased global interconnection brought not war and conflict but unity and cooperation. In providing new possibilities for expansive spatial perception, these imaginaries enabled the cultivation of transnational connections that spanned the boundaries of race, nation, and empire.

Evident in his participation in organizing the first Pan-African Congress in London in 1900, one of the first meetings of racially and colonially subjugated peoples focused on building transnational political alliances, Du Bois clearly understood that this enhanced connectivity provided the opportunity to imagine new political possibilities for an increasingly globalized world.[40] The influence of shifting spatial and temporal conceptions on the congress was clearly visible in "Address to the Nations of the World," the primary manifesto issued by the organization and largely penned by Du Bois. Through the technological processes of space-time compression, the world appeared to the congress as one composed of connections and experiences that stretched beyond those of one's nation or region.[41] The "Address" directly noted how changing perceptions of time and space could transform race relations. In the modern age when "the ends of the world are being brought so near together," the millions of black, brown, and yellow peoples through the world "are bound to have a great influence upon the world in the future, by reason of sheer numbers and physical contact."[42] Granting these excluded populations greater opportunity for education and self-development would hasten a beneficial effect on world development. In this progressive vision, greater interracial contact across the color line would allow an untapped source of knowledge to influence problems of

---

39. Mazower, *Governing the World*, 25–26.

40. Hakim Adi, *Pan-Africanism: A History* (Bloomsbury, 2018), 19–23. The first Pan-African Congress was organized by the Trinidadian barrister Henry Sylvester Williams. For an excellent account, see Thomas Smith, *Emancipation Without Equality: Pan-African Activism and the Global Color Line* (University of Massachusetts Press, 2018).

41. Smith, *Emancipation Without Equality*, 1–2.

42. Du Bois, "Address to the Nations of the World," 125.

democratic government. By bringing segregated races into contact, technological forces of globalization would transform human consciousness and the course of human civilization.

Embedded in Du Bois's vision of the transcendence of the color line through globalization were common tropes associated with the popular phrase heralding "the annihilation of distance." The phrase stretched back to the 1840s and 1850s when the spread of railways began to alter the spatial imagination of Europe and the US by abolishing distance and accelerating rates of continental interconnectivity. Reflecting on the expansion of commercial relations through technological innovation, Ralph Waldo Emerson declared "distance annihilated" while Karl Marx foresaw "the annihilation of space by time." By the end of the century, the introduction of infrastructural technologies such as the electric telegraph accelerated these transformations in the way individuals experienced time and space, uprooting previous experiences of Newtonian time as universal and absolute.[43] The increased technological capacity for both physical and social interaction across state boundaries abolished previous constraints that defined international order in the early modern period.[44] As spatial distance diminished, the expanded scale and accelerated tempo of political life engendered new horizons of expectation for the future. By the turn of the twentieth century, these forms of spatial and temporal consciousness spawned new utopian dreams heralding the dawn of a globalized and interconnected age through the elimination of physical distance. Novel forms of political association that stretched beyond the nation-state appeared not just possible but inevitable.[45]

It is in the context of these new spatial imaginaries marked by techno-optimism that we should view Du Bois's initial declarations of the global color line and his visions of global interracial solidarity. At the turn of the

---

43. David Harvey, *Justice, Nature, and the Geography of Distance* (Blackwell, 1996), 241–42; Ralph Waldo Emerson, "The Young American," in *Complete Works of Ralph Waldo Emerson*, vol. 1 (Houghton Mifflin, 1904), 452; Karl Marx, *Grundrisse* (Penguin, 1973), 524. Daniel Deudney notes that although these kinds of sentiments are now obvious and commonplace, in the fin de siècle period "these phenomena were novel and portentous, making this era's platitude that era's revelation"; Daniel Deudney, *Bounding Power: Republican Security Theory from the Polis to the Global Village* (Princeton University Press, 2007), 218–20.

44. Barry Buzan and George Lawson, *The Global Transformation: History, Modernity, and the Making of International Relations* (Cambridge University Press, 2015), 67–95.

45. Bell, "Making and Taking Worlds," 263–64.

century, Du Bois reflected in his *Autobiography* (1962), "The triumphs of the scientific world thrilled me: the X-ray and radium . . . the airplane and the wireless. The machine increased technical efficiency, and the North and South Poles were invaded."[46] Such technologies represented the triumph of a new global consciousness that emerged through proliferating networks of commerce and communication. The condensation of space-time afforded by new communicative infrastructures also generated tendencies for global forms of "race contact." Historically and socially, this meant a form of world movement that was a "continuing growth" rather than a "finished product." As races came in increasing contact with one another, racial groups constantly underwent change in composition. This conception of race corresponded to new ideas of society defined by ever-changing rather than "fixed social structures."[47] Technologies of globalization thus profoundly transformed and unsettled rigid notions of race. By 1911, Du Bois had clearly extended this spatial imaginary in declaring that "the question of contact between differing masses and groups of men is being daily made critical by the physical shrinking of the world today."[48]

These advances in communication and transportation further led to the proliferation of transnational affinities in both colony and metropole at the dawn of the twentieth century. During this period, increased capacity for transnational interaction generated a spate of new political movements that imagined forms of political belonging across the formal boundaries of nation and empire in Great Britain and its dominions ("Greater Britain"), Latin America (Pan-Hispanism), German-speaking Europe (Pan-Germanism), Slavic communities (Pan-Slavism), the Americas (Pan-Americanism), and Afro-descendant peoples (Pan-Africanism). If the printing press in the early modern period allowed the nation to emerge as, in Benedict Anderson's famous phrase, an "imagined community," technologies such as the steamship and the telegraph similarly allowed participants in these movements to envision the inter-nation as an imagined form of political association.[49] As Musab Younis observes, "The same technological advances in the

---

46. Du Bois, *Autobiography*, 130.

47. Du Bois, *Autobiography*, 131.

48. Du Bois, "Coming of the Lesser Folk," 45.

49. Benedict Anderson, *Imagined Communities: Reflections on the Origin and Spread of Nationalism* (Verso, 1983). See also Musab Younis, "United by Blood: Race and Transnationalism During the Belle Époque," *Nations and Nationalism* 23, no. 3 (2017): 484–86; Cemil Aydin, *The Politics of Anti-Westernism in Asia: Vision of World Order in Pan-Islamic and Pan-Asian Thought* (Columbia University Press, 2007), 31–37.

fields of communication and travel that opened the door for new imaginative possibilities for white Europeans also enabled disparate communities in the colonized world to imagine themselves, often for the first time, as collectively racialized subjects of a European world order."[50]

The utopian visions enabled by these transnational imaginaries cut both ways, as solidarities invested in reinforcing racialized visions of global order and transnational white domination, on the one hand, and as those invested in reimagining and transforming global order as an institutionalized realization of international racial emancipation, on the other. Regarding the former, Duncan Bell has explored how transnational efforts to ensure Anglo-Saxon global supremacy fostered institutional visions of "racial utopianism" that imagined a renewed Anglo-American union as a model for global governance. Exemplified in the work of such figures as Cecil Rhodes, H. G. Wells, and Andrew Carnegie, racial utopianism revolved around a shared (even if internally contested) dream that the unification of the Anglo-Saxon race in a transnational federation could eliminate the drive for war and ensure world peace. Racial utopians envisioned more than just security agreements that stalled the forces of war and aggression between Great Britain and the United States. They also offered an expansive dream of "universal racial peace: interstate war itself could be abolished through Anglo-world unity."[51] In other words, Anglo-Saxon unity and global dominance not only brought peace within the race but also ensured a perpetual peace between races and nations. Carnegie proclaimed that "the new nation" to arise from Anglo-American reunification would "dominate the world and banish from the earth its greatest stain—the murder of men by men."[52] The institutional architecture of these visions took varied forms, ranging from loose networks of economic integration to full-blown imperial federations defined by shared citizenship in the constituent states. Yet at the center of these visions was a shared conception of race as a "biocultural assemblage," an understanding of the Anglo-Saxon race as bound by shared language, religion, culture, and law.[53]

The mechanisms whereby a racialized vision of international order

---

50. Younis, "United by Blood," 500.

51. Bell, "Before the Democratic Peace," 657. See also Anthony Pagden, *Peoples and Empires: A Short History of European Migration, Exploration, and Conquest, from Greece to the Present* (Random House, 2007), 143–52.

52. Carnegie quoted in Bell, "Before the Democratic Peace," 659.

53. Duncan Bell, "Beyond the Sovereign State: Isopolitan Citizenship, Race and Anglo-American Union," *Political Studies* 62, no. 2 (2014): 418–34.

brought about the desired effects of world peace and international cooperation were twofold. On the one hand, shared military might and economic resources of the Anglo-American alliance would ensure peace by deterring the incentives for war through the threat of military dominance. On the other hand, race itself became a claim for moral legitimacy that emphasized the special destiny and unique capacity of the Anglo-Saxon race to rule and civilize the world.[54] For figures like Wells and Carnegie, Anglo-Saxon union was merely a stepping stone for the creation of a global federation if not a world state. For Wells, the creation of a "great federation of white English-speaking peoples" would bring the final stage of human evolution by altogether abolishing war and ensuring a "final peace of the world."[55] Claiming that "oceans no longer constitute barriers between nations," Carnegie argued that "the federal system of government has proved that immense areas can be successfully governed under one head, and can exist as one power." Because of the increased tempo of international communication, federal systems can effectively rule over disparate parts of the globe. By allowing virtually synchronous debate, technologies like the telegraph render time and distance obsolete. Confessing that his vision is indeed utopian, Carnegie foresaw that Anglo-American union would lay the foundation for "the Parliament of Man and the Federation of the World."[56]

In this context, one can read efforts at instilling transnational affinities through the Pan-African Congress and the Universal Races Congress of 1911 as a counterhegemonic utopian desire that both reflects and stands in opposition to these visions of racial utopianism.[57] Through critiques of racism, transnational whiteness, economic exploitation, and nation-state sovereignty, participants in these programs offered countervisions of *interracial utopianism*. If racial utopianism rests on "white supremacist visions" calling for "the racial pacification of the globe," interracial utopianism linked world

---

54. Bell, "Before the Democratic Peace," 660.

55. H. G. Wells, *Anticipations of the Reaction of Mechanical and Scientific Progress upon Human Life and Thought* (Harper, 1901), 282–83. See also Duncan Bell, "Founding the World State: H. G. Wells on Empire and the English-Speaking Peoples," *International Studies Quarterly* 62, no. 4 (December 2018): 867–79.

56. Andrew Carnegie, *The Reunion of Britain and America: A Look Ahead* (Andrew Elliot, 1898), 10, 30.

57. Younis, "United by Blood," 494–99; Barbara Bair, "Pan-Africanism as Process: Adelaide Casely Hayford, Garveyism, and the Cultural Roots of Nationalism," in *Imagining Home: Class, Culture and Nationalism in the African Diaspora*, ed. Robin Kelley and Sidney Lemelle (Verso, 1994).

peace to the abolition of the global color line and the increased interaction of races and nations across the color bar.[58] In his interracial utopianism, Du Bois offered a vision that was the direct inverse of the racial utopians. Where the racial utopian vision rested on a racialized vision of universal peace that required the displacement and segregation of nonwhite populations and that justified Anglo-Saxon superiority, interracial utopianism tied visions of world peace to race contact on a global scale and the demand for self-government of colonized and racialized populations.[59]

In a 1910 editorial, Du Bois wrote in his new capacity as editor of *The Crisis*, "Human contact, human acquaintanceship, human sympathy are the great solvents of human problems. Separate school children by wealth the result is class misunderstanding and hatred. Separate them by race and the result is war."[60] War was a problem, therefore, spawned by racial segregation. Through increased global communication among racialized and colonized populations and with imperial citizens in the metropole, Du Bois held to a vision of peace where deeper bonds of sympathy would divert the drive for war and expansion. Like racial utopians, he championed new transportation and communication technologies for their ability to connect distant populations in both metropole and colony. For perhaps the first time, citizens in the metropole could almost instantaneously read about dynamics of colonial government, bearing witness to its horrors and violence. The result, Du Bois hoped, would be a "union of intelligence and sympathy" that would overcome the spatial segregation of the Jim Crow order in the United States and the imperial order composed of European colonial possessions.[61]

Yet these possibilities were obstructed by social Darwinist views equating the "competition of races" and "survival of the fittest" with "the triumph of the good, the beautiful and the true."[62] In response, Du Bois engaged

58. Bell, "Before the Democratic Peace," 647.

59. My account resonates with Juliet Hooker's argument that Du Bois's writings on racial intermixture points towards an Afro-futurist vision of "racial utopias that dare to imagine a world not dominated or defined by whiteness"; Juliet Hooker, *Theorizing Race in the Americas: Douglass, Sarmiento, Du Bois, and Vasconcelos* (Oxford University Press, 2017), 118. My concern in this chapter is less with issues of interracial intimacy and intermixing than with how the shrinkage and acceleration of space-time produced new democratic possibilities.

60. W. E. B. Du Bois, "Editorial," *Crisis* 1, no. 1 (November 1910): 10.

61. W. E. B. Du Bois, "The Relations of the Negroes to the Whites in the South," *Annals of the American Academy of Political and Social Science* 18 (July 1901): 140. On the role of sympathy in Du Bois's early thought, see Rogers, "People, Rhetoric, and Affect.".

62. Du Bois, "Relations of the Negroes to the Whites," 122.

in a peculiar and underappreciated intellectual move by appropriating and revising rather than rejecting social Darwinism and the chronotope of evolution.[63] In a paper delivered to the National Negro Conference in 1909 on "The Evolution of the Race Problem," he revised the language of race struggle to mean not competition between inferior and superior races but instead a struggle against the color line and white hegemony. He largely accepted the social Darwinist view that "civilization is a struggle for existence." He went on to claim, however, that Darwinism has been given a faulty interpretation in which "yellow and black peoples are the ones rightly doomed to eventual extinction." Rather, the imperial hegemony of the white race threatens the survival of "some of the worst stocks of mankind" through sheer force and coercion, leading to the inversion of Darwinian laws of nature.[64]

It is in the white settler colonies of Australia, South Africa, and the United States where this inversion is most evident. By upholding racial segregation, white settler populations quarantine themselves from the progressive movement of history that arises from social intercourse among diverse peoples. In their insistence on separating races through colonialism, apartheid, and Jim Crow, white settlers succumb to an "outrageous programme of wholesale human degeneration" and are exhibiting "many signs of degeneracy" such as falling birth rates. Faced with such evolutionary degeneration, the efforts of white settlers in the Americas, Australia, and South Africa to fence in land and segregate the darker races is not a sign of their power but of their physical inability to "take possession of the world."[65]

In this surprising revision, Du Bois reverses the spatial and temporal valence of social Darwinist vocabularies of race struggle, survival of the fittest, and superior and inferior peoples. Rather than a sign of degeneracy, race contact across vast spaces on a planetary scale becomes a necessary force for advancing human civilization to a higher stage. Far from a call for the

---

63. In making these arguments, I draw on Inder Marwah's account of how Indian nationalists appropriated Darwinian theories of evolution for anticolonial purposes: Inder Marwah, "Darwin in India: Anticolonial Evolutionism at the Dawn of the Twentieth Century," *Perspectives on Politics* 21, no. 3 (September 2023): 880–95.

64. W. E. B. Du Bois, "The Evolution of the Race Problem," in *W. E. B. Du Bois Speaks, 1890–1919*, 202–3. Robert Bernasconi notes, "Instead of attacking social Darwinism, Du Bois, who was not beyond appealing to the idea of the survival of the fittest himself, argued that its true meaning had been misunderstood in the popular imagination"; Robert Bernasconi, "Our Duty to Conserve: W. E. B. Du Bois's Philosophy of History in Context," *South Atlantic Quarterly* 108, no. 3 (2009): 534.

65. Du Bois, "Evolution of the Race Problem," 205–6.

dominance of superior over inferior peoples, the survival of the fittest harbors a demand to live in peaceful cooperation in a world of inevitable social interaction across divisions of race and nation. Reflecting the annihilation-of-distance theme, Du Bois argued, "The earth is growing smaller and more accessible. Race contact will become in the future increasingly inevitable, not only in America, Asia and Africa, but even in Europe." In the face of these evolutionary dynamics, the price of continued colonial repression was "moral retrogression and economic waste unparalleled since the age of the African slave trade," resulting in the evolutionary stalling of civilizational development.[66] In this geohistorical imagination, the cultivation of sympathy across the color line through the technological transformation of spatial consciousness generated a new philosophy of history in which greater race contact prompted the advance of civilization.

It is widely noted that the anthropologist Franz Boas undoubtedly influenced Du Bois's revision of Darwin. In Du Bois's own recollection, it was Boas's commencement address at Atlanta University in 1906 that awakened him from the historiographical prejudice that Africa was outside history altogether.[67] In contrast to social Darwinism's conventional emphasis on laws of history, competition, and racial separation, Boas's interpretation emphasized historical contingency, cultural particularity, and interracial contact. In this evolutionary view, history advances through the contingent interactions of civilizations over time rather than through the preservation of innate biological characteristics.[68] But it should also be noted that this alternative view of Darwinian evolution was a staple of transatlantic progressive thought, evident in a range of figures from Peter Kropotkin to John Dewey to Leonard Hobhouse. It is not coincidental that many of these thinkers who shared this Darwinian view of evolution as a cooperative rather than a competitive endeavor also spoke at the 1911 Universal Races Congress in London. Such revisionist Darwinism clearly underpinned the utopian aspirations of the URC, which held that the prime cause of race conflict is "the tacit assumption that the present characteristics of a people

---

66. Du Bois, "Evolution of the Race Problem," 207–8; Alexander Livingston, "The Cost of Liberty: Sacrifice and Survival in Du Bois's *John Brown*," in Bromell, *Political Companion to W. E. B. Du Bois*, 230–32.

67. Du Bois, *Black Folk*, xxxi.

68. Julia Liss, "Diasporic Identities: The Science and Politics of Race in the Work of Franz Boas and W. E. B. Du Bois, 1894–1919," *Cultural Anthropology* 13, no. 2 (May 1998): 127–66; Charles Briggs, "Genealogies of Race and Culture and the Failure of Vernacular Cosmopolitanisms: Rereading Franz Boas and W. E. B. Du Bois," *Public Culture* 75, no. 1 (January 2005): 75–100.

are the expression of permanent qualities."[69] The assumption of fixed biological types violates evolutionary laws demanding civilizational progress as a function of interracial contact.

The World in Council and the Races in Conference

At the turn of the twentieth century, Du Bois was constantly searching for spatiotemporal grammars (i.e., chronotopes) through which to articulate his incipient vision of interracial utopianism. In the vocabulary of the fourth dimension, the color line belts, the annihilation of distance, and evolution, he tied his conception of the color line to a spatiotemporal imaginary in which greater interracial contact enabled by technologies of globalization would usher in a new utopian age and lead to the abolition of the color line. In this section, I outline the pinnacle and partial eclipse of this vision of interracial utopianism. Together, this and the final section show how World War I led to a revision of the color line and consequently his vision of world democracy.

Before the Universal Races Congress was held in London in July 1911, Du Bois had participated in organizing and promoting the event. In the pages of *The Crisis*, for instance, he issued editorials heralding the possibilities the conference would generate. Reflecting his sense that interracial contact and sympathy across the color line would lay the foundation for global peace, Du Bois proclaimed that it is only through "world-wide contact of men in which the voices of all races are heard shall we begin that contact and sympathy which in God's good time will bring out of war and hatred and prejudice a real democracy of races and nations."[70] In this vision, world democracy implied less a program of decolonization and self-determination for colonial peoples than the inclusion of racialized and colonized populations within the constitutional structures of imperial nation-states. The URC would lay the foundation for the global spread of democracy to racial and colonial subjects by breaking down the barriers that impeded interracial contact. The idea of a world congress where representatives of all races and nations would meet on a plane of equality was a centerpiece of utopian thought in the nineteenth century. Felix Bodin's 1834 *Le roman de l'avenir* (The novel of the future), for instance, imagined a meeting of the Universal Congress in the Central American republic of Benthamia (named

---

69. W. E. B. Du Bois, "Races," *Crisis* 2, no. 4 (August 1911): 157.

70. W. E. B. Du Bois, "The Races in Conference," *Crisis* 1, no. 2 (December 1910): 17.

after Jeremy Bentham, who coined the term "international" to designate a distinct realm of law and politics). Such depictions of a world parliament that unites races and nations envisioned an international order that would reconcile the world's diversity into a single political body.[71]

Organized by the Hungarian ethicist Gustave Spiller, the URC convened representatives from European parliaments, social scientists, practitioners and professors of international law, and a range of representatives from various racial groups. The primary objective of the Congress was scientific—to discuss and bring into modern consciousness novel scientific understandings of race relations between the peoples of the East and West. Yet participants also sought to connect the cause of interracial cooperation and understanding to that of world peace: "To those who regard the furtherance of international good will and peace as the highest of all human interests, the occasion of the First Universal Races Congress opens a vista of almost boundless promise." In this vision of global peace, the primary cause of war has been "the existence of race antipathies." While modern wars are inflamed in the last instance by ambitions for power, border conflicts, and economic rivalries, "it will be found, in almost every instance, that the pre-existence of social and racial enmity has in reality determined the breach which particular incidents had merely precipitated."[72] Universal racial equality in international politics served the purpose of world peace by providing a countervailing force to Western imperial power. Only when the democratic institutions of the West are counterbalanced by the spread of democracy among racialized and colonized populations will the mental outlook and social aims of the races and nations become identical.

By eliminating the causes of war in racial antipathy, "interracial contact" would establish the conditions for world peace.[73] Like racial utopians such as Wells and Carnegie who saw Anglo-Saxon union as the foundation for a global federation, the interracial utopians at the URC also conjured hopes that the congress might "form the nucleus of a vast international federation" premised on a "new conception of humanity."[74] Accordingly, the scientific mission of the URC was to bring about new racial understandings that would further its goals of human unification. One of the main conclusions

71. Mazower, *Governing the World*, 23–24.

72. W. E. B. Du Bois, "The Races Congress," *Crisis* 2, no. 5 (September 1911): 200–201. For a record of the meeting, see Gustav Spiller, ed., *Papers on Inter-Racial Problems: Communicated to the First Universal Races Congress* (P. S. King & Son, 1911).

73. Du Bois, "Races Congress," 201.

74. Du Bois, "Races Congress," 206–7.

of the congress was that "the establishing of harmonious relations between the various divisions of mankind is an essential condition precedent to any serious attempt to diminish warfare."[75] This conception of peace and democracy achieved through interracial contact is powerfully visualized in the aesthetic archive of the URC.

A visual rendering of the Universal Races Congress published in *The Crisis* (figure 1) portrays representatives of the five races of the world all staring into a terrestrial globe under the heading "The World in Council." The image distills key themes of Du Bois's transnational imaginary. As we saw in chapter 1, Du Bois viewed democracy in epistemic terms as a method of cultivating the "excluded wisdom" of marginalized groups as the basis for democratic government. The image powerfully illuminates the perspectivism implicit in this epistemic view of democracy. The purpose of approximating the unbounded wisdom of the excluded is not simply to have a stable epistemic foundation for democratic decision-making. In viewing the world from distinct vantage points, the image illustrates how world democracy is less an attempt to find a defined set of viewpoints that can be translated into policy than it is a play of conflicting perspectives. Reflecting transformations in spatial and temporal consciousness away from Newtonian absolutism (i.e., the experience of space and time as fixed), the multiplication of perspectives in the image illustrates the relativistic proliferation of spatial experiences.[76] In multiplying the perspectives of the world in council, the image rejects the modern ideal of disembodied reason that views the world from an Archimedean point of stable objectivity. Instead of a teleological end point, this play of perspectives results in a contingent historicism that revels in "the possibility of infinite development." The image thus portrays a visual illustration of Du Bois's call for a "true inter-nation" achieved through the equal and cooperative engagement of races acting together at "the world's council."[77]

The seal of the URC (figure 2) similarly pictures Columbia as the feminine personification of the Americas linking hands with her African counterpart. In the background is a picture of the globe adorned with a banner proclaiming in Latin, "Harmony between nations and peoples." By calling for peace not just between nations but also between peoples, the seal

75. Du Bois, "Races Congress," 209.

76. On Newtonian absolutism, see Stephen Kern, *The Culture of Time and Space, 1880–1918* (Harvard University Press, 2003).

77. Du Bois, *Darkwater*, 85.

THE WORLD IN COUNCIL, LONDON, JULY 26-29

"*I believe that all men, black and brown and white, are brothers, varying through time and opportunity, in form and gift and feature, but differing in no essential particular, and alike in soul and in the possibility of infinite development.*"

FIGURE 1. "The World in Council, London, July 26–29." Artistic rendering of the Universal Races Congress in *The Crisis*, August 1911, 156. Image courtesy of Modernist Journals Project, Brown and Tulsa Universities, https://modjourn.org/issue/bdr522262/#.

FIGURE 2. Seal of the Universal Races Congress depicted on the cover of *The Crisis*, September 1911. Image courtesy of Modernist Journals Project, Brown and Tulsa Universities, https://modjourn.org/issue/bdr522307/.

conveys the idea that in an imperial world order, racial divisions do not neatly map onto national distinctions. In such a situation, racialized and colonized peoples seeking democratic inclusion within national formations must cultivate transnational affinities with each other across the color line belts of the world. Transcending the color line requires an increase in communication and interaction among oppressed populations, exemplified in the organization of the URC itself. The seal was virtually omnipresent at the congress. It appeared on all official business of the proceedings, and participants were encouraged to continue using the seal when they departed for home. It also appeared on the cover of the September 1911 issue of *The Crisis*, which contained Du Bois's most extensive reporting on the event, in some cases providing lengthy excerpts and commentary on the presentations and scientific discussions that transpired.

At the end of his reporting, Du Bois appended a single stanza of a poem he read before the congress titled "A Hymn to the Peoples":

> Save us, World Spirit, from our lesser selves!
> Grant us that war and hatred cease,
> Reveal our souls in every race and hue!
> Help us, O Human God, in this Thy Truce
> To make Humanity divine!

The poem clearly strikes utopian chords whereby overcoming the divisions of the color line ushers in a new age of divinely ordained peace. In directing the hymn to "the peoples" rather than just nations, Du Bois called into existence a pluralized vision of a global demos that overcomes the rigidity of national divisions and loyalties. Almost a decade later, he republished a full version of the poem as the final entry in *Darkwater* (1920), extending many of the same themes of utopian transcendence. Echoing his praise of the URC, the full version speaks of "the primal meeting of the Sons of Man, / Foreshadowing the union of the World!" Coming on the heels of World War I, however, the reference here was likely to the Paris Peace Conference rather than the URC. With the tragedy of the war clearly in mind, the poem goes on to strike a darker tone: "We are but weak and wayward men, / Distraught alike with hatred and vainglory; / Prone to despise the Soul that breathes within." It then ends with the single stanza of the original poem calling on the world spirit to save us "from our lesser selves."[78] While the full version retains the optimistic tenor of the single stanza first published in *The Crisis*, the juxtaposition of this with the bleakness of the middle stanzas is striking.

These tensions between utopia and despair heighten when considering that as published in *Darkwater*, the poem directly follows the science fiction short story, "The Comet."[79] Political theorist Lawrie Balfour shows how the argumentative force of *Darkwater* revolves around the "creative juxtaposition of different modes of writing." The text proceeds through a pairing of essays bookended by various forms of literary experimentation, most often poetry. This pairing of argument and poetry invokes what Balfour calls

---

78. Du Bois, *Darkwater*, 161–62.

79. I follow Paul Kincaid in defining science fiction not in terms of consistent and patterned genre conventions but in terms of "family resemblances" and polyvalent elements that can be braided together in infinite combinations and permutations; see Paul Kincaid, "On the Origins of Genre," *Extrapolations* 44, no. 4 (Winter 2003): 409–19. On the role of race and colonialism in science fiction, see John Rieder, *Colonialism and the Emergence of Science Fiction* (Wesleyan University Press, 2008); Isiah Lavender, *Race in American Science Fiction* (Indiana University Press, 2011).

a "kind of self-disclosure, calling attention to the distinctive, and limited, perspective of the author, and suggesting that the ideas he presents are entangled with the narrative choices through which they are expressed."[80] As Balfour notes, utopian themes of peace and racial transcendence are replete throughout the text. The final pairing, however, vividly displays a recurring tension between cataclysmic and utopian perspectives. Through this juxtaposition, *Darkwater* ends "in a swirl of romantic longing and tragic reversal" that reveals the entwinement of new democratic possibilities with the persistent threat of their foreclosure.[81] Extending Balfour's point, I argue that this pairing of perspectives illustrates the submersion of interracial utopianism underneath more cataclysmic visions of the future in the wake of World War I. "The Comet" dramatizes new spatial and temporal experiences defined not by the surging inevitability of peace through interracial contact but by the endurance of the color line through cataclysmic global transformation and enhanced transnational connection. By 1920, interracial utopianism became a future past, a superseded expectation for the future layered under new space-time imaginings that remains in view yet never within grasp.

In broad strokes, "The Comet" tells the story of interracial romance at the end of the world. The protagonist, a poor black man named Jim, works organizing records in the basement vaults of a bank on Wall Street, a job deemed too dangerous and unpleasant for white employees. When he finishes the job and ascends to the upper level, Jim finds nothing but the stillness of death permeating the lobby. Outside on Wall Street, he finds everyone dead and realizes that a comet has passed close by earth, spilling poisonous gas into the atmosphere. Searching the city to see if anyone else is alive, Jim eventually finds a rich white woman named Julia, and they begin to speculate that they are the last living people on earth. The progression of the narrative builds toward racial transcendence, suggesting that only a cataclysmic natural disaster will be powerful enough to abolish the

---

80. Balfour, "*Darkwater*'s Democratic Vision," 537, 539–40.

81. Balfour calls "Hymn" an "extravagant paean to the possibility of reconciliation across racial, national, and religious lines" ("*Darkwater*'s Democratic Vision," 554–55). For a similar reading of "The Comet," see Saidiya Hartman, who calls it a "speculative fiction and satire of failed democracy"; Saidiya Hartman, "The End of White Supremacy, an American Romance," *Bomb*, June 15, 2020, https://bombmagazine.org/articles/the-end-of-white-supremacy-an-american-romance/. Juliet Hooker similarly reads "The Comet" as a tragedy against and in relation to the romantic and utopian tenor of Du Bois's 1928 novel *Dark Princess*; see Hooker, *Theorizing Race in the Americas*, 134–35.

color line. As they search the city for survivors yet find nothing but death and silence, Julia struggles to overcome her prejudice and feelings of loneliness: "For the first time she seemed to realize that she was alone in the world with a stranger, with something more than a stranger—with a man alien in blood and culture, unknown, perhaps unknowable."[82] By emphasizing themes of disconnection and unknowability, Du Bois builds a degree of suspense into the plot, leaving the reader to wonder about the unification of Jim and Julia. Eventually a new vision of the world arises before Julia as she realizes she is "primal woman; mighty mother of all men to come and Bride of Life," an Eve-like figure who looks upon Jim "no longer as a thing apart" but as the "All-father" of a new race to be.[83] This vision of a new postracial world, however, recedes with the honk of a car horn as Julia reunites with her father and a group of white men who threaten to lynch Jim.

The setting of the story in New York foregrounds the centrality of Du Bois's ever-present worldview. In the story, New York serves as a microcosm for the world in two ways. First, New York epitomized a new cosmopolitan culture taking root at the time. Philosophers of transnationalism and cultural pluralism such as Randolph Bourne and Horace Kallen modeled their new notions of a pluralistic national identity partially on their experiences in New York. America, Bourne wrote in 1916, is "not a nationality but a trans-nationality, a weaving back and forth, with the other lands, of many threads of all sizes and colors."[84] Du Bois, in contrast, exposed how this transnational vision of American identity foundered on the color line. Second, the setting of Wall Street focuses the reader's attention on the center of an increasingly globalized and powerful system of financial capitalism. The cataclysms produced by the color line were synonymous with those of a globalized system of finance capital whereby the profit of financial speculation rests on the colonization of racialized labor in imperial outposts.

---

82. Du Bois, *Darkwater*, 155.

83. Du Bois, *Darkwater*, 158. Reiland Rabaka interprets Jim and Julia as a "post-apocalyptic Adam and Eve" inhabiting an inverted Garden of Eden. Rather than a plush and fertile field of possibilities, Jim and Julia are in a desolated wasteland ripe with potential for new forms of social relation; Reiland Rabaka, *W. E. B. Du Bois and the Problems of the Twenty-First Century: An Essay on Africana Critical Theory* (Lexington, 2007), 67. For Afrofuturist readings of the story, see Adriano Elia, "W. E. B. Du Bois's Proto-Afrofuturist Short Fiction: 'The Comet,'" *Il Tolomeo* 18 (December 2016): 173–86; Lisa Yaszek, "Afrofuturism, Science Fiction, and the History of the Future," *Socialism and Democracy* 20, no. 3 (2006): 41–60.

84. Randolph Bourne, "Trans-National America," in *War and the Intellectuals: Collected Essays, 1915–1919* (Hackett, 1999), 121.

Jim's position working in the lower vaults of Wall Street, where he "groped in the bowels of the earth, under the world," tacitly symbolizes the foundations of modern financial capitalism in the speculative potential garnered by the trade in human flesh and the subjugation of black labor.[85]

The cataclysmic tenor of the narrative is astounding considering the fact that Du Bois clearly drew inspiration from H. G. Wells's 1906 novel *In the Days of the Comet*. Wells's was a deliberately utopian tale. Rather than bringing the death and desolation of humanity, the comet strikes the earth with a chemical substance that alters that atmospheric composition of the planet and changes human nature itself, resulting in the abolition of war. That Du Bois would appropriate and shift the narrative structure of the story from one of utopia to cataclysm is telling. "The Comet" is a parable of the entrenchment of race in unconscious forces and drives, thus representing a submersion of his earlier vision of interracial utopianism marked by greater interracial contact and growing sympathy with racial others across the global color line. The story illustrates a shift in Du Bois's thought from romantic narratives of transcendence and progress to cataclysmic narratives of the decline, fall, and collapse of civilization.[86] In this regard, it dramatizes how interracial utopianism persists as a future past, a structure of expectations superseded by new experiences and anticipations. In preceding "Hymn to the Peoples," the story tempers the utopian longings invoked in depictions of the URC. The failed connection between Jim and Julia further indexes Du Bois questioning his faith in the ability of technologies of globalization and interracial contact to transcend the color line, presenting new problems for his vision of world democracy.[87]

Race, War, and the Democratic Imaginary

In this final substantive section, I argue that Du Bois's evolving understanding of the relationship between race and war prompted a shift away from

---

85. Du Bois, *Darkwater*, 150. See also H. G. Wells, *In the Days of the Comet* (Century, 1906).

86. On temporal tropes of decline and cataclysm in Du Bois, see Arthur Herman, *The Idea of Decline in Western History* (Free Press, 1997), 187–220.

87. Hee-Jung Serenity Joo similarly reads "The Comet" as a failed utopia that points to a "more radical desire to rethink capitalist time and space altogether"; Hee-Jung Serenity Joo, "Racial Impossibility and Critical Failure in W. E. B. Du Bois's *Darkwater*," *Science Fiction Studies* 46, no. 1 (March 2019): 107.

interracial utopianism. As utopian elements receded from his transnational democratic imaginary after the URC, the experience of World War I also led to a deeper skepticism of utopian visions and forced him to revise his appropriation of the race struggle thesis by bringing class more directly into the analysis. As a result, he drew on a different repertoire of spatial and temporal grammars to articulate the interconnected problems of global capitalism, world democracy, and the color line.

With the start of World War I, Du Bois immediately began to revise his view of the color line. While he admitted that it would be easy to assume that the problem of the war was separate from that of race, such a view would be a mistake, he argued: "The present war in Europe is one of the great disasters due to race and color prejudice and it but foreshadows greater disasters in the future." The cause of the war was not simply "national jealousy" or race rivalry. Rather, it was "the wild quest for Imperial expansion" among European powers.[88] Thwarted by the superior power of France and Britain in Africa and South Asia and by the Monroe Doctrine in South America, Germany was increasingly shut out from the acquisition of colonial territory. The coveting of French and British colonies by Germany in the tropical areas inhabited by black, yellow, and brown peoples drove the European nations to war. In this way, the theory of racial inferiority, the exploitation of colonized labor, and the denial of democratic aspirations to colonized peoples constituted the central forces leading to world war.

This analysis by Du Bois ushered in a new understanding of the relationship between race and war that profoundly shifted away from the imaginary of interracial utopianism. As we saw earlier in this chapter, interracial utopianism revolved around a global imaginary of race war that shaped not only the thought of those seeking to uphold international racial order but also those seeking to contest it.[89] The underlying assumption of the Universal Races Congress, for instance, was that racial animosity proved to be the most durable source of national aggression. If war engulfed the world, for the interracial utopians, the primary culprit would be a race war between the white world and the darker races. In "The Present Outlook for the Dark

---

88. W. E. B. Du Bois, "World War and the Color Line," *Crisis* 9, no. 1 (November 1914): 28.

89. Alexander Barder, *Global Race War: International Politics and Racial Hierarchy* (Oxford University Press, 2021); Jacob Kripp, "The Creative Advance Must Be Defended: Miscegenation, Metaphysics, and Race War in Jan Smuts's Vision of the League of Nations," *American Political Science Review* 116, no. 3 (September 2022): 940–53.

Races of Mankind" (1900), Du Bois saw the transcendence of the color line as closely connected to a global conception of race struggle. Prophesizing a Russo-Japanese war in the "near future," he held that advancing beyond race may require "gigantic strife across the color line."[90] Du Bois later championed the Russo-Japanese War (1904–5), the first moment in the twentieth century when a nonwhite army defeated a white imperial power, as an awakening of nonwhite races on a global scale. Du Bois traces the color line not to 1492 but much farther back, to the Battle of Tours in 732, when Charles Martel led the Franks to victory over the Saracens. Ever since, the white race has claimed "the hegemony of civilization" by linking "white" and "civilized" as synonymous terms. The Japanese victory over Russia broke the spell, inaugurating a new horizon of expectation in which European imperialism and its civilizing mission could no longer proceed unimpeached and unchallenged. Du Bois declared, "For the first time in a thousand years a great white nation has measured arms with a colored nation and has been found wanting. . . . The magic of the word 'white' is already broken and the Color Line in civilization has been crossed in modern times as it were in the great past."[91]

In its victory over Russia, Japan acquired entry into international society and recognition as a "civilized" power by adhering to "the standard of civilization" in international law. As the first non-European country to gain international status and recognition as a civilized state, Japan began to demand the regularization of the standard and its articulation if not codification in specified legal terms.[92] For Du Bois, the awakening of the black and brown races would follow the awakening of the yellow races in due course. For most international thinkers of the time, however, this was not a welcome development. The English political scientist Alfred Zimmern lamented that the Japanese victory weakened "the white man's prestige in the old sense of the word."[93] For such figures as the white supremacist and nativist Lothrop Stoddard, Japanese victory portended fears of "the rising tide of color" and "the yellow peril" where the rising power of "the colored world" over "the

---

90. Du Bois, "Present Outlook," 119.

91. Du Bois, "Color Line Belts the World." See also Aydin, *Politics of Anti-Westernism in Asia*, 71–92.

92. Gerritt Gong, *The Standard of "Civilization" in International Society* (Clarendon Press, 1984), 29.

93. Zimmern quoted in Robert Vitalis, "The Graceful and Generous Liberal Gesture: Making Racism Invisible in American International Relations," *Millennium* 29, no. 2 (2000): 331.

white world" threatened the decline of Anglo-Saxon supremacy. In these views, white supremacy was a global norm that constituted world order.[94]

For Stoddard, white global dominance began to crack in the closing decades of the nineteenth century as the globalized spread of Western ideas gave the "colored world" the ammunition to challenge imperial domination. Stirred by the circulation of Western ideas, the non-Europeans began to view "the white man with a more critical eye and commenced to wonder whether his superiority was due to anything more than a fortuitous combination of circumstances which might be altered by efforts of their own." Adding to this, World War I broke the image of white domination as a "united front." White Europe appeared as being "locked in an internecine death-grapple of unparalleled ferocity."[95] This fracture within the white world generated new dreams of unity among non-European populations. In his condemnation of interracial solidarity, Stoddard argued that the same technological innovations celebrated by Du Bois as harbingers of race contact hastened the decline of global white supremacy: "The white man's very triumphs have evoked this danger. His virtual abolition of distance has destroyed the protection which nature once conferred.... With the development of cheap and rapid transportation, nature's barriers are down."[96] The only solution was to construct artificial barriers in the form of restrictive immigration control that would also restrict communication and cooperation within the "colored world." As evidence of the threat of interracial solidarity to white world order, Stoddard quoted Du Bois's "African Roots of War" (1915), "These races and nations composing as they do a vast majority of humanity, are going to endure this treatment just as long as they must and not a moment longer. Then they are going to fight, and the War of the Color Line will outdo in savage inhumanity any war this world has yet seen."[97]

---

94. Lothrop Stoddard, *The Rising Tide of Color Against White-World Supremacy* (Scribner, 1920), 6–8, 221, 237. The interpretive gloss I draw from is Vitalis, "Graceful and Generous Liberal Gesture," 332–35.

95. Stoddard, *Rising Tide of Color*, 12–13. On Stoddard's anti-imperialism, see John Hobson, *The Eurocentric Conception of World Politics: Western International Theory, 1760–2010* (Cambridge University Press, 2012), 142–49.

96. Stoddard, *Rising Tide of Color*, 301–2. See also Roderick Bush, *The End of White World Supremacy: Black Internationalism and the Problem of the Color Line* (Temple University Press, 2009), 10–11.

97. Du Bois quoted in Stoddard, *Rising Tide of Color*, 14. Du Bois would go on to engage and humiliate Stoddard in a public debate in 1929; see Lewis, *W. E. B. Du Bois: A Biography*, 235–37.

The reality, however, was that Du Bois was much less interested in igniting a race war than he was in understanding the connection between the war and the color line and the threats they posed to world peace. His prognostication of future race war was less a threat of violence than a call to understand the true causes of military conflict so as to forestall a future "world war of races."[98] In "African Roots," he offered a bold and groundbreaking account of the meaning and causes of the war through a radical reinterpretation of J. G. A. Hobson's thesis about "the new imperialism." Hobson, in his 1902 study *Imperialism*, located the origins of imperialism in the need for export outlets of finance capital to deal with problems of overaccumulation in the metropole.[99] Du Bois was undoubtedly influenced by these ideas and was first exposed to them at the URC in 1911, where he saw and reported on Hobson's presentation, which he considered to be among the most forceful at the meeting. In his encapsulation of Hobson's thesis, Du Bois reported that the struggle between imperial nation-states for colonial control was driven by the need to siphon off surplus finance and manufactures. In this account, the "forces that separate and disintegrate the natural unity of men" are primarily economic. For Du Bois, Hobson correctly foregrounded economic considerations by demonstrating that the policy of "modern imperialism was dangerously unsound, and that the ruthless exploitation of the weaker groups was the most dangerous thing in modern life."[100] Despite this focus on economic factors, however, Du Bois noted that broader discussions at the URC largely neglected the labor question.

Chapter 3 explores in more detail how Du Bois diverged from Hobson. For now, I simply underscore the ways in which Hobson's account of the new imperialism prompted Du Bois to foreground the economic question of labor in his new understanding of the global color line. One of Du Bois's objectives in "African Roots" was to clarify the central role that the colonial exploitation of Africa and other colonized peoples played in the democratization of Europe and the United States. Like Hobson, Du Bois held that the overexploitation of industrial workers within the metropole led imperialists to seek new sources of exploitation abroad. Yet where Hobson saw imperialism as parasitic on the nation, benefiting only a subsector of the national economy at the expense of labor, Du Bois argued that the laboring classes were beginning to demand a share of the profits of colonial exploitation. "The white workingman," Du Bois notes, "has been asked to share the

---

98. Du Bois, "World War and the Color Line," 30.

99. J. G. A. Hobson, *Imperialism* (James Nisbet, 1902), 91.

100. Du Bois, "Coming of the Lesser Folk," 46; Du Bois, "Races Congress," 204.

spoil of exploiting 'ch*nks and n**gers.'" The result was "a new democratic nation composed of united capital and labor."[101] By providing economic, political, and psychological benefits to the laboring classes, imperialism enabled accord between labor and capital through a common investment in colonial expansion. The "real causes of war" consist in a conception of "democratic despotism" wherein shared power between labor and capital domestically depends on the profits garnered from imperial expansion and exploitation of colonized labor. Put another way, world war arises through the confinement of democracy within the imperial nation-state and the failure to extend democratic ideals to colonized peoples. Accordingly, ideals of world peace require the treatment of colonial peoples as "free and equal citizens in a world-democracy of all races and nations."[102]

Such an analysis enacts a dramatic shift away from interracial utopianism. In this new spatiotemporal imaginary, competition among imperial powers rather than the specter of race war represents the primary threat to world peace. Moreover, visions of peace materialize not through interracial contact on a global scale but through global class solidarity whereby the laboring classes of the metropole join arms with colonized labor rather than the captains of industry, enabling a kind of industrial democracy on a world scale. The spatial and temporal imaginaries underlying this more sophisticated concept of the color line most forcefully surface in a pair of essays from 1925—"The Negro Mind Reaches Out" and "Worlds of Color."[103] Referencing his earliest proclamation of the color line in 1900, Du Bois reflected in these essays that in its initial formulation it was a "pert and singing phrase." In proposing to reexamine the global color line, he signals a shift in temporal consciousness away from an optimistic faith in progress. Instead, he reexamines the problem of the color line in light of the "roots of the catastrophe" of world war in "the bitter rivalries of economic imperialism" and the colonial exploitation of Africa. Rather than an image of transcendence through global race contact, the color line captures a new set of temporal expectations attentive to how the roots of "world dissension and catastrophe" remain in the unresolved problems of race.[104]

---

101. Du Bois, "African Roots," 709.

102. Du Bois, "African Roots," 711–12.

103. Aside from a few important passages, the essays are virtually identical. I cite from W. E. B. Du Bois, "Worlds of Color," *Foreign Affairs* 3, no. 3 (April 1925): 423–44; and W. E. B. Du Bois, "The Negro Mind Reaches Out," in *The New Negro*, ed. Alain Locke (Simon & Schuster, 1997), 407–8.

104. Du Bois, "Negro Mind Reaches Out," 407–8.

Du Bois then asks a simple question: "What then is the worldview that the consideration of this question offers?" One way to read this question is to ask: what is the worldview that is required to understand the color line? But notice that the worldview is the direct object rather than the acting subject, a perspective offered by consideration of the problem of the color line. The question thus prompts consideration of the relation of the color line to the modern worldview. In posing the question in his way, Du Bois's invocation of the color line "evolves from a focus on finding a common frame through which to make sense of racial injustice among disparate populations of color, to an approach that relates a grasp of that injustice to a more general social and political outlook."[105] In other words, the color line is not simply a central aspect of world politics; it is constitutive of the very notion of a modern worldview.[106] Martin Heidegger famously declared that modernity was "the age of the worldview." Rejecting the idea that every historical age had its own worldview, Heidegger argued that the possibility of having a worldview, of having a picture of the world as an existential whole, was a unique feature of modernity.[107] For Du Bois as well, the color line is not just a feature of international order. It is constitutive of worldliness as such insofar as it grounds any representation of the world as a normative and binding totality. The color line does not simply transform the modern worldview. It structures the process by which the world becomes a view.

One sees how the color line constitutes the very possibility of a worldview through Du Bois's repeated invocation of "worlds of color"—the division of the world into a "white world" and a "colored world."[108] This language of worlds of color was a persistent feature of international racial discourse at the time, with writers like Stoddard invoking the specter of the rise of "the yellow world" as a source of decline for "the white world." Terms such as "the white world" or "the colored world" were not simply shorthand for biological conceptions of racial kind but were framings of worldly political space through logics of race. The world perspective conveyed in this language derives its coherence from a set of expectations and antici-

---

105. Navid Hassanzadeh, "Race, Internationalism, and Comparative Political Theory," *Polity* 50, no. 4 (October 2018): 534.

106. Nahum Chandler writes that "the problem of the color line" is "constitutive of global modernity as . . . a form of problematization"; Nahum Chandler, *X—The Problem of the Negro as a Problem for Thought* (Fordham University Press, 2013), 133.

107. Martin Heidegger, "The Age of the World View," trans. Marjorie Green, *boundary 2* 4, no. 2 (Winter 1976): 350.

108. Du Bois, "Worlds of Color," 431, 443.

pations concerning the relationship between these organizing principles of world politics. Race was no mere modifier of the world perspective. Particular figurations of relations between the races, whether represented through tropes of war and conflict or cooperation, were the primary means by which the world was cognized as such. Racial designations constitute the world perspective not simply in the classification of peoples but more pointedly in "reordering the spatio-temporal coordinates through which to grasp the world." One cannot "frame the world without instituting racial difference in its composition."[109] Race is embedded in the space-time imaginaries that enable the representation of the world as a picture.

Yet the structuring role of race in composing the possibility of the modern worldview exerts its power through its interaction with dynamics of class and global capitalism. Evoking the annihilation-of-distance theme, Du Bois noted how modern industrial capitalism enabled the "conquest of time and space by goods-production, railway, telephone, telegraph and flying machine." In his increased appreciation for the ways that capitalism fomented the physical shrinkage of spatial distance, he highlighted how the problems of labor, work, and income are implicated "in the tremendous and increasingly intricate world-embracing industrial machine" built by European civilization.[110] Grasping the world as picture thus required residing in the interstices of the color problem and the labor problem.

Although modern capitalism tied the world together through economic interdependence, its intricate connection to European imperialism also led to a fracturing of global struggles for democratic control over industry and economy. Reiterating his analysis in "African Roots," Du Bois noted in "Worlds of Color" that the process of "setting the darker races beyond the pale of democracy" through colonial exploitation diffused the contradictions of industrial capitalism by allowing a wider distribution of material wealth and income, which enabled an "agreement between capital and labor in white democracies."[111] In this agreement, labor becomes "the blind executive of the masters of the white world," investing in imperialism by voting for war and expansion and sending their sons as soldiers. In return, laboring classes receive political, economic, and psychological profits in their alliance with capital, leading to a common investment in imperial ideologies

---

109. Mark Jerng, *Racial Worldmaking: The Power of Popular Fiction* (Fordham University Press, 2018), 31–39. Jerng refers to narratives that "embed race into our knowledge and expectations of the world" as "racial worldmaking."

110. Du Bois, "Negro Mind Reaches Out," 407–8.

111. Du Bois, "Worlds of Color," 438.

of racial inferiority and the colonial belief that "white folk are a peculiar and chosen people whose one great accomplishment is civilization." The economic and psychopolitical returns that European laborers receive on these investments make it less likely that they "will ever demand universal democracy for all men," inhibiting the possibility of "world democracy" on a planetary scale. The only hope "lies in the gradual but inevitable spread of the knowledge that the denial of democracy in Asia and Africa hinders its complete realization in Europe."[112]

For Du Bois, the realization of world democracy requires a transnational understanding where struggles for industrial democracy within the European metropole embrace anti-imperial solidarities against the economic exploitation of colonized labor. What is significant in this understanding, wherein the deferral of democratic self-rule in colonial possessions affects the realization of popular sovereignty in England or America, is the spatial imaginary it implies, one defined by entanglement between otherwise discrete political units. Democratic struggles in colony and metropole thus must be understood as interconnected and implicated in a web of reciprocal causality tied together by the color line belts of the world.

Evident in the more pessimistic proclamations of these two essays, Du Bois remained quite sober about the potential for white laborers to realize that the deferral of democracy in the colonies would hinder the full realization of democracy in the metropole. For this reason, perhaps, he put his interracial utopian vision on the back burner and instead turned his hopes more fully toward what might be called "intraracial utopianism" that was realized not through mutual sympathy between the white and darker races but rather through solidarity of colonial and racialized subjects from within the colored world. Nowhere is this intraracial vision more evident than in his 1928 novel *Dark Princess*, which Alys Eve Weinbaum has argued "elaborates a utopian dream of solidarity among the darker peoples of the world by reappropriating" the figure of the "black All-Mother."[113] In the story, the black protagonist, Matthew Townes, meets the Indian Princess Kautilya and shortly after joins "the Council of the Darker Peoples of the World" that challenges "the present white hegemony of the world."[114] The novel culminates in the union of Matthew and Kautilya as they give birth to a

---

112. Du Bois, "Worlds of Color," 442, 444.

113. Alys Eve Weinbaum, *Wayward Reproductions: Genealogies of Race and Nation in Transatlantic Modern Thought* (Duke University Press, 2004), 201.

114. Du Bois, *Dark Princess*, 18.

child that promises to unite the darker races of the world and usher in a new historical era.

Yet rather than a triumphant celebration of transnational solidarity among colonized peoples, I would tentatively suggest against the backdrop of the themes explored in this chapter that *Dark Princess* is better read as a satirical reflection on the complexities and contradictions of democratic world making. A crucial plot element of the novel revolves around the ways in which the representatives of the darker races of the world adhere to ideas of natural aristocracy in their claims to represent the colonized peoples of the nonwhite world. The world council of darker races, in Matthew's view, is profoundly antidemocratic. For instance, against the claims of "natural aristocracy" made by the council to rule "the great sodden masses of all men," Matthew affirms an Aristotelian ideal of rotational rule, "that the mass of the workers of the world can rule as well as be ruled."[115] Later, Matthew is then chastised by other delegates to the council for talking to Princess Kautilya as his equal, being admonished that her "democratic graciousness" should not be taken as a sign of equality. The representative of the Japanese delegation reprimands Matthew for a similar affront, invoking a romantic commitment to ancient hierarchies: "We Samurai have been lords a thousand years and more; the ancestors of her Royal Highness have ruled for twenty centuries—how can you think to place yourselves beside us as equals?"[116]

That the world council of darker races never fully overcomes its antidemocratic tendencies indicates Du Bois's skepticism that intraracial utopianism alone can ever fully bring about his vision of universal democracy on a world scale. Despite all the shifts in his utopian desires through the early twentieth century, there remains a concrete sense that the realization of utopian desire rests upon solidarity among workers across the white world and the colored world. The point here is not that this turn to intraracial utopianism completely displaced his earlier interracial utopianism. Rather, it is that the latter became sedimented underneath the former, a kind of recessive trait that lay dormant, only to resurface fleetingly under different historical conditions.[117] As argued in chapter 3, despite his sense that

---

115. Du Bois, *Dark Princess*, 18–19.

116. Du Bois, *Dark Princess*, 22.

117. For a contrasting account of temporality in Du Bois that remains focused on domestic social change, see Jennie Ikuta, "A Matter of Long Centuries and Not Years: Du Bois on the Temporality of Social Change," *Political Theory* 52, no. 2 (2024): 289–316.

transnational whiteness became embedded in unconscious drives, desires, and habits, Du Bois never completely gave up hope in the distinct possibility of white working-class solidarity with colonized labor giving rise to an industrial democracy on a global scale.

Sediments of Utopia

This exploration of the space-time imaginaries in Du Bois's early transnational thought makes three central interpretive and contextual contributions. First, I have shown how Du Bois used a series of chronotopes associated with the color line to engage in forms of temporal and spatial contestation. For instance, in appropriating notions of the fourth dimension and the color line belts, he satirized Anglo-Saxon images of superiority and instead offered interracial contact as a trope of historical advance. In a different vein, he appropriated and conceptually revised the trope of evolution, which reversed the historical and geographic valence of social Darwinism. Rather than a source of historical decline that contaminates racial purity, interracial contact across the color line ensured the advance of civilization to higher stages. In casting these dynamics in terms of chronotopes, I have aimed to show how spatial and temporal grammars are embedded in political concepts such as the color line. But even more saliently, I have emphasized how Du Bois sought to reframe the problem of the color line by appropriating technoscientific tropes so as to reconfigure the relationship between time and political space. Put otherwise, spatial representations directly structured utopian horizons and temporal expectations for the future.

Second, such spatial and temporal contestations can be read as critical reactions against forms of racial utopianism in global political discourses at the turn of the twentieth century. In contrast to racial utopian visions wherein Anglo-Saxon unity inaugurates world peace and the suspension of war, interracial utopianism offered a romantic view of racial transcendence through global interaction. Reflecting new forms of spatial consciousness marked by the acceleration of time and the annihilation of distance, Du Bois deployed spatiotemporal grammars to convey his shifting understanding of the global color line.

Third, I have argued that Du Bois's exposure to J. G. A. Hobson and the experience of World War I gave rise to a new transnational imaginary marked by different spatial and temporal grammars. In this new democratic imaginary, the global color line was not simply a feature of global order but was constitutive of what it meant to imagine the world as a world. The language of world democracy then shifted from a vision of the suspension of war and conquest through greater interracial contact and shared self-rule to one that required attention to the simultaneity and entanglement of democratic struggles against colonial domination and class exploitation.

While the more utopian spatial imaginaries associated with the language of the fourth dimension did not completely recede, they did become submerged underneath more cataclysmic anticipations for the future. That is, they persisted as dormant, temporal sediments underneath more cataclysmic notions of time following World War I throughout the interwar years. While interracial utopianism encompasses what I call, taking from Koselleck, a superseded future past, appreciating these dimensions of his early transnational thought is vital to understanding the persistent though fainter pulses of utopian desire in his later anticolonial thought. One can especially see the resurgence of these utopian visions amid Du Bois's engagement in debates over the founding of the United Nations. In 1944, he again invoked the fourth dimension in a short commentary on Rayford Logan's *What the Negro Wants* called "Flashes from Transcaucasia." Signaling the transcendence of whiteness through new spatial imaginaries, Du Bois posited in cryptic language that "Transcaucasia" resides in uncharted space in "the fourth dimension beyond the color line."[118] Inspired by this vision of the utopian transcendence of racialized globality, Logan then called for Du Bois to hold the Harlem Colonial Conference to develop a common program of international action among colonial peoples. As chapter 4 shows, it was out of this meeting in Harlem in 1945 that Du Bois began his project of constructing a notion of "colonial peoples" as a majoritarian, global constituency to be inserted into debates surrounding the founding of the UN. The horizon of expectations for the future that characterized the utopian imaginary was constantly shifting with changing historical circumstances and material conditions most significantly associated with the interrelationship between war, race, and global capitalism.

Despite the sedimentation of interracial utopianism underneath more cataclysmic temporal horizons, Du Bois continued to be propelled by a utopian vision of "planetary reconciliation" in the post–World War II years. He thus retained an immanent orientation toward utopianism that, in Gary Wilder's words, "seeks to identify possibilities for alternative arrangements

---

118. W. E. B. Du Bois, "Flashes from Transcaucasia" (1944), box 3, Hugh and Mabel Smythe Papers (MSS57505), Manuscript Division, Library of Congress.

that may already dwell within, or be emerging from . . . the existing order."[119] Although interracial utopianism envisioned cross-racial harmony emerging out of the world that European empires created, it remained abstractly tied to idealistic visions of technoscientific progress and failed to root the transformative possibilities of world democracy in a concrete examination of the economic structure of world politics. By increasingly couching his examination of the global color line within Hobson's economic analysis of imperialism, Du Bois concretized his utopian vision. He also resisted the seductive lure of pessimistic political realism that would reject any vision of planetary reconciliation altogether. In constituting the world as racially stratified economic unity, European imperialism laid the basis for the immanent transformation of that order, and with it the emergence of a higher state of temporal and spatial perception culminating in cross-racial, transnational class solidarity.

---

119. Gary Wilder, *Concrete Utopianism: The Politics of Temporality and Solidarity* (Fordham University Press, 2022), 7–9.

[CHAPTER THREE]

"Unusual Returns"

Transnational Whiteness and the Dividends of Empire

> And what is true in the South faces the nation in this Second World War. No matter what we may think and say of Germany, by singular paradox the race-religion which Germany has suddenly thrust to the front, is but an interpretation of what America and Europe have practiced against the colored peoples of the world ... The problem of the reconstruction of the United States, 1876, is the problem of the reconstruction of the world in 1943.
>
> W. E. B. Du Bois, "Reconstruction, Seventy-Five Years After"

Nowhere did W. E. B. Du Bois's sobriety about the prospects of cross-racial class solidarity so trenchantly surface than in his deepened turn to Marxism in the 1930s. In the early 1930s, Du Bois began to engage in a deeper study of Marxism in relationship to the color line. In a 1933 editorial for *The Crisis* called "Marxism and the Negro Problem," he presented the initial fruits of his textual engagements with Karl Marx.[1] For Du Bois, the vast majority of African Americans belong to the laboring proletariat yet remain segregated from the white proletariat. While political organizations such as the Socialist Party left the problem of racial prejudice unaddressed and assumed that the uplift of white labor necessarily would lead to the emancipation of nonwhite labor, unions such as the American Federation of Labor (AFL) outright excluded black laborers from their ranks. The black proletariat thus faced dual sources of oppression: exploitation by white capital as well as exclusion from white labor movements. This reality challenged conventional Marxist analyses of capitalist society as driven by class conflict between the bourgeoisie and the proletariat. The class structure of US capitalism, rather

---

Epigraph: W. E. B. Du Bois, "Reconstruction, Seventy-Five Years After," *Phylon* 4, no. 3 (1943): 212.

1. W. E. B. Du Bois, "Marxism and the Negro Problem," in *African American Political Thought, 1890–1930*, ed. Cary Wintz (M. E. Sharpe, 1996).

than binary, was composed of tripartite conflict among industrial capitalists, black laborers, and a white laboring class that borders on a petit bourgeoisie. The black proletariat thus found itself flanked on both sides, forced to direct its energies toward two united fronts at once.

These initial ideas culminated in his magnum opus, *Black Reconstruction in America* (1935), wherein he famously examined the division of the US proletariat after Reconstruction by "the public and psychological wage."[2] These "wages of whiteness," in David Roediger's incisive phrase, generated forms of psychopolitical compensation that positioned white laborers above black laborers yet helped industrial capitalists artificially suppress wages, amplifying the extraction of surplus value from the working classes.[3] As Nikhil Pal Singh puts it, the concept of racial capitalism is not simply an assertion about the racial origins of capitalism but is about the "racial differentiation [that] is intrinsic to productive processes of capitalist value creation and financial speculation."[4] Through the psychological wage, Du Bois captured how the production of racial difference enabled the rise of industrial capitalism in the United States by dividing the white and black working classes, with *capital value production* hinging on *racial value production* (i.e., the production of racial difference). In connecting the production of racial and economic value, Du Bois refused, in Lisa Lowe's words, "the idea of a 'pure' capitalism external to, or extrinsic from, the racial formation of collectivities and populations."[5] Racial differentiation is not a separate process from capital accumulation but a primary mode by which the commodity form of value is produced and ongoing relations of production are reproduced.

Following but also departing from recent calls to move "beyond the psychological wage," this chapter explores how Du Bois used distinctive metaphors of value production derived from discourses of financial capitalism

---

2. W. E. B. Du Bois, Du Bois, *Black Reconstruction in America* (Free Press, 1998), 700.

3. David Roediger, *Wages of Whiteness: Race and the Making of the American Working Class* (Verso, 2007).

4. Nikhil Pal Singh, "On Race, Violence, and So-Called Primitive Accumulation," *Social Text* 34, no. 3 (September 2016): 30–31. See also Cedric Robinson, *Black Marxism: The Making of the Black Radical Tradition* (University of North Carolina Press, 1983); Andrew J. Douglas, *W. E. B. Du Bois and the Critique of Competitive Society* (University of Georgia Press, 2019), 10–12.

5. Lisa Lowe, *The Intimacies of Four Continents* (Duke University Press, 2015), 150. See also Robert Knox, "Valuing Race? Stretched Marxism and the Logic of Imperialism," *London Review of International Law* 4, no. 1 (March 2016): 81–126.

such as dividends, shares, and returns on investment to illustrate the economic, psychological, and political benefits that accrue to white workers from their position in the racialized division of labor marking global capitalism.[6] To capture the homology between racial value production and capital value production, Du Bois referred to the "income-bearing value of prejudice" and to white prestige as a "dividend" paid to white laborers alongside his more famous articulation of the psychological wage.[7] He employs this political economic language to explore how certain forms of capitalist value production structurally mirrored forms of racial value production that enact the "differential ethicopolitical valuation of human subjects."[8] I show how these insights about the income-bearing value of prejudice emerged not solely through consideration of capitalist social relations within the nation-state but in considering the transnational structure of global capitalism. In solidifying capitalist rule within the nation-state through colonial exploitation abroad, industrial imperialism produces forms of transnational whiteness—racial affinities and forms of political identification that span the boundaries of imperial nation-states.[9]

While recent work on Du Bois's critique of racial capitalism has productively attended to the global dimensions of whiteness, there remains a sense in some accounts that compensatory logics associated with the psychological wage are restricted to domestic dynamics of racial capitalism *within* the United States. Most prominently, Ella Myers argues that Du Bois's notion of the public and psychological wage, as a concept capturing the mutual imbrication of capital accumulation and racial value production, is "primarily . . . a mechanism of the U.S. social order." To capture the structure of transnational whiteness, she argues instead for a conception of "white dominion," a white entitlement to the land and property of the world that links domestic racial domination to global forms of colonial domination. For Myers, white dominion is a "thoroughly global phenomenon" more akin

6. Cf. Ella Myers, "Beyond the Psychological Wage: Du Bois on White Dominion," *Political Theory* 47, no. 1 (February 2019): 6–31.

7. Du Bois, *Dusk of Dawn*, 75.

8. Singh, "On Race," 30.

9. Attention to transnational whiteness pushes beyond conventional tendencies of theorists of racial capitalism to treat the intersection of capitalist value production and racial value production as a feature of social formations bound by the nation-state. In accounting for how "racial order reinforces that of capitalism," Michael Dawson confines his focus to "the racialized nature of capitalist society in the United States"; Michael Dawson, "Hidden in Plain Sight: A Note on Legitimation Crises and the Racial Order," *Critical Historical Studies* 3, no. 1 (Spring 2016): 146.

to religious devotion than the economic logic of the wages of whiteness, which pertain to the domestic structure of US racial capitalism.[10] Such distinctions neglect key features of globalized racial capitalism and Du Bois's democratic thought by consigning the compensatory logics of whiteness to domestic social order.

In contrast to these assumptions, I argue that the modes of racial differentiation that upheld capitalist social order in the early twentieth century were not confined to the nation-state or distinct imperial formations. Rather, they produced bonds of white solidarity that moved across the borders of nation and empire, giving rise to a form of transnational whiteness I call "the dividends of empire" that exhibits both continuities with and departures from the wages of whiteness in domestic US contexts. Like the wages of whiteness within the US, the dividends of empire granted white workers extraeconomic forms of psychological and political compensation that reshaped transnational working-class solidarities and obstructed the emergence of global industrial democracy. Psychologically, the dividends of empire constituted a form of white prestige in the sense of superiority derived from European conquest of nonwhite populations and territories. Politically, Du Bois linked the dividends of empire to rights of immigration and hospitality that positioned white workers above nonwhite workers through ease of international mobility. Unlike the wages of whiteness, however, the dividends of empire rendered white workers as passive recipients of imperial compensation akin to corporate shareholders who relinquish power over economic decisions for financial benefit. Du Bois characterized transnational whiteness through the languages of financial capitalism (i.e., shares and dividends) to grapple with the failed dynamics of transnational solidarity between white and colonized labor rather than strictly the racial divisions of the US working class. Alongside his efforts to cultivate transnational solidarities among colonial peoples, he also saw the failed potential of transnational solidarity among laboring classes in metropole and colony as at once a worldly and democratic problem.

My primary concern, however, is not just with Du Bois's critique of racial capitalism but also with illuminating the role the financial logics of the dividends of empire play in his transnational democratic thought. The specific form of racial capitalism Du Bois referred to as "the new industrial imperialism" that "degraded colored labor the world over" did not simply restrict the movement of democratic self-rule to colonial peoples on impe-

---

10. Myers, "Beyond the Psychological Wage," 23.

rial peripheries.¹¹ The production of transnational whiteness also impeded the transnationalization of struggles for "industrial democracy" by disconnecting labor struggles in metropole and colony. The confinement of class solidarity to the white working classes and the exclusion of colonized labor prevented the movement of democratic control from the political to the economic sphere. The insulation of industry from democratic control reacts back on the political sphere by consolidating the power of industrial oligarchs over the formal mechanisms of political power. As Du Bois puts it, "until wider democracy does prevail in industry, democracy in government is seriously curtailed."¹² Wider democracy in industry, however, required expanding the spatial scope of democratic struggles for greater economic control over industry beyond the nation-state. Industrial democracy—that is, popular control over economic production and the economic distribution of wealth and income—rests on the global spread of "inter-class sympathy."¹³ The psychological and economic profits generated by colonial exploitation restricted the movement of democratic control into the economic realm by impeding anticolonial solidarity and confining the aims of the labor movement to domestic politics.¹⁴

I develop these arguments through four phases. First, I contextualize Du Bois's theory of imperialism by outlining his engagements with Fabian anti-imperialists in Britain such as J. G. A. Hobson and Leonard Woolf who emphasized the economic factors driving European imperialism. Du Bois revised these economic theories by centering the racialized division of labor in global capitalism as the driving force of European imperialism. Second, I read the notion of the psychological wage alongside Du Bois's writings on imperialism during World War I, turning specifically to "The African Roots of the War" (1915) and "Of the Culture of White Folk" (1917). In doing so, I elaborate the idea of the dividends of empire as a transnational form of whiteness that fuels European imperial expansionism.

---

11. Du Bois, *Black Reconstruction in America*, 630.

12. W. E. B. Du Bois, "The Negro and Communism" (ca. 1931), Du Bois Papers, box 211, p. 1.

13. W. E. B. Du Bois, "The Class Struggle," *Crisis* 22, no. 4 (August 1921): 152.

14. I thus think alongside Lawrie Balfour, who warns against attempts to "distill the democratic elements" of Du Bois's thinking solely from the US political tradition. Reflecting on "the global reach of Du Bois's political thought," Balfour argues that it demonstrates "the impossibility of constructing a theory of democracy that restricts its concern within U.S. boundaries"; Balfour, *Democracy's Reconstruction*, 21–22, 116, 133.

In the third section, I place *Black Reconstruction* in the context of the rise of "the new imperialism" in the late nineteenth century. Imperial themes figure into Du Bois's argument in two respects: (1) in his notion of the Southern plantocracy as an expansionist force, and (2) in his characterization of the dictatorship of capital after Reconstruction as a form of "industrial imperialism." From these two vantage points, Du Bois provides a revisionist account of imperialism by linking new forms of European expansionism after the Berlin Conference (1884–85) to the collapse of the "abolition-democracy" following Reconstruction. I close by turning to his World War II–era work to foreground the implications of this account for critical democratic theory. Specifically, I argue that the dividends of empire restrict the scale and scope of democracy to the formal realm of the nation-state, impeding the emergence of a transnational form of industrial democracy.

Fabianism and the Global Color Line

It is widely noted that Du Bois's analysis of "the new imperialism" in "The African Roots of War" has a notable resonance with other examinations of imperialism during the period, most notably those of J. G. A. Hobson and V. I. Lenin. Indeed, it is a common and oft-repeated assumption that Du Bois's analysis in 1915 "anticipated" Lenin's arguments in *Imperialism, the Highest Stage of Capitalism* (1917) by two years.[15] Such proleptic reading that focuses on the anticipation of one author's ideas by another, however, obscures the broader historical and intellectual context in which Du Bois was operating. Taking a cue from Adolph Reed Jr., I argue that the more relevant overlaps in Du Bois's initial theorization of imperialism are not with Leninism but rather with Fabian socialism and anti-imperialism. Although he is right to suggest the central role of Fabianism in shaping Du Bois's thought, Reed focuses largely on US discourse and ignores its broader transatlantic orientation as well as questions of empire. Moreover, Reed's intention in

---

15. Lewis, *W. E. B. Du Bois: A Biography*, 327; John Narayan, "The Wages of Whiteness in the Absence of Wages: Racial Capitalism, Reactionary Intercommunalism and the Rise of Trumpism," *Third World Quarterly* 38, no. 11 (2017): 2483; Eric Sundquist, *To Wake the Nations: Race in the Making of American Literature* (Harvard University Press, 1994), 582; Marable, *W. E. B. Du Bois: Black Radical Democrat*, 94; Bill Mullen, *Un-American: W. E. B. Du Bois and the Century of World Revolution* (Temple University Press, 2015), 20.

foregrounding the Fabian elements of Du Bois's thought in his faith in the ability of a meritocratic elite to guide gradualist economic change through bureaucratic rationality is to correct what he sees as a scholarly overemphasis on Du Bois's radical socialism.[16]

My intention here is somewhat the reverse: to illuminate how he steps into a series of transatlantic debates and radically repurposes them to different ends. I explore in this section how the Fabian anti-imperialism of Hobson and others not only influenced Du Bois but also provided occasion for him to break with its central modes of analysis. It requires no original insight to note that Du Bois borrowed insights from Hobson.[17] By better contextualizing Du Bois's analysis of imperialism alongside textual exegesis of Hobson and others, however, we can see how Du Bois revised and repurposed Fabian anti-imperialism, a revision that would become a defining feature of his transnational democratic thought until the end of his life. None of this is to downplay the role of Marxism and Leninism in shaping Du Bois's thought in the 1930s and beyond (as we will see in chapter 4). It is, rather, to suggest that this deepened engagement with Marxism did not represent a radical epistemological break in his political thought so much as it did a refinement of a number of tendencies that were already present.[18]

The word *imperialism* became a part of popular political discourse during the 1890s, when it acquired both its economic and pejorative connotations. The "new imperialism," according to Eric Hobsbawm, was "the natural by-product of an international economy based on the rivalry of several competing industrial economies, intensified by the economic pressures of the 1880s."[19] The term signified an international order marked by competition among national economies to stabilize domestic labor markets in a period of immense market volatility. As such, the new imperialism represented a turn away from laissez-faire competition to competition between financial oligarchs who favored state intervention to acquire access to foreign markets. Hobson's 1902 study, *Imperialism*, further popularized both the term and this familiar interpretation in transatlantic political discourse.

During World War I, Du Bois provided a revisionist account of the new imperialism by breaking with Hobson and broader currents of Fabian

---

16. Adolph Reed Jr., *W. E. B. Du Bois and American Political Thought: Fabianism and the Color Line* (Oxford University Press, 1997), 83–89.

17. Lewis, *W. E. B. Du Bois: A Biography*, 328.

18. Andrew J. Douglas, "Du Bois and Marx's Influence," 1–19.

19. Hobsbawm, *Age of Empire*, 67.

anti-imperialism in two ways.[20] First, whereas Hobson saw imperialism primarily in terms of the export of finance capital and the need to assert dominance over foreign markets, Du Bois viewed the racial exploitation of labor as the driving force of European imperialism. Hobson traced the new imperialism to problems of the overaccumulation of capital in the European metropole, which suppressed industrial wages by creating an imbalance between the productive powers of industry and stalled growth of consumption. Because of the overaccumulation of capital, which drives down wages and in turn prevents the absorption of surplus commodities in domestic markets, imperialists sought outlets for the export of superfluous capital in foreign markets and colonial possessions to compensate for "the maldistribution of consuming power."[21] To correct these imbalances, colonialism provided outlets for the disposal of financial capital. The consequence of this analysis was a kind of economic reductionism wherein the construction of racial status was viewed as at best incidental to the driving forces of imperialism.

Du Bois agreed with Hobson that the engine of the new imperialism was competition among European empires for control of colonial possessions. He added, however, that the "economic taproot" of this expansionist drive, as Hobson called it, was not simply the need to alleviate mounting pressures of overaccumulation through the search for control of foreign markets, which could then serve as outlets for the surplus manufactures and the investment of surplus finance capital. Rather, it was the need for greater exploitation of the colonial labor force, which lessened the exploitative pressures on domestic working classes. By minimizing the rate of labor exploitation within the metropole, imperialism mitigated the sources of class conflict generated by the overaccumulation of capital and the suppression of industrial wages, thus bringing about an "industrial peace" that came at the "mightier cost of war abroad."[22] In other words, imperialism stabilized domestic class relations by exporting the intensification of labor exploitation necessary for capital accumulation abroad. Providing what David Harvey calls a "spatial fix," imperialism displaced class conflict within the

---

20. Gregory Claeys rightly notes that terms such as "Fabian anti-imperialism" should be qualified. Fabian anti-imperialists did not so much reject empire as they did embrace "their own kind of empire" where the world's resources could be more efficiently managed by European imperial powers such as Britain for the benefit of colonized peoples; Gregory Claeys, *Imperial Sceptics: British Critics of Empire, 1850–1920* (Cambridge University Press, 2010), 260–61.

21. Hobson, *Imperialism*, 91.

22. Du Bois, "African Roots," 711.

imperial metropole onto relations of the racial exploitation of labor in the colonies.[23]

The intersection of race and economics was central to Du Bois's analysis of imperialism. By the time Du Bois wrote, economic explanations of World War I were prevalent in transatlantic political discourse. William English Walling, the prominent peace activist and cofounder of the National Association for the Advancement of Colored People, pointed out that emphasizing the economic dimension was so obvious as to be virtually needless: "In the opinion of internationalists, war can be abolished neither by armament [n]or [by] disarmament.... War can be abolished only by abolishing the causes of war, which every practical man admits are economic."[24] The adoption of an economic perspective was by no means original, nor was it restricted to the more radical interpretations of such figures as Lenin or Rosa Luxemburg. The emphasis on labor relations and international economic competition was a staple of socialist anti-imperialism in both Britain and the United States. What made Du Bois's analysis original was not simply his focus on the intersections of class and race as the driving force of imperialism but the nuanced blend of material and status-based factors.

One sees this nuance in contrast to Leonard Woolf, a prominent Fabian anti-imperialist.[25] Following World War I, drawing on Hobson and others, Woolf was one of the first to theorize what he called "economic imperialism." In *Empire and Commerce in Africa* (1920), which Du Bois reviewed, Woolf wrote:

> Under this term I include the international economic policy of the European States, of the U.S.A., and latterly of Japan, in the unexploited and non-Europeanized territories of the world. The policy of Economic Imperialism of the exploitable territory, the policy of spheres of influence, and the policy of obtaining economic control through other means ... I qualify it with the word economic because the motives of this imperial-

---

23. David Harvey, "Globalization and the Spatial Fix," *geographische revue* 2 (2001): 23–30.

24. William English Walling, "Socialists and Imperialism," in *Towards an Enduring Peace: A Symposium of Peace Proposals and Programs, 1914–1916*, ed. Randolph Bourne (American Association for International Conciliation, 1916), 36.

25. Woolf was a widely acknowledged expert on international affairs among Fabian intellectuals and politicians. In 1918, he broke with the Fabian Society. He then joined the Labour Party, where he was commissioned to write *Empire and Commerce in Africa* and went on to become a leading anti-imperialist thinker in Britain. See Peter Wilson, *The International Theory of Leonard Woolf* (Palgrave MacMillan, 2003), 2–3.

ism are not defence or prestige nor conquest nor the "spread of civilization," but the profit of the citizens, or of some citizens, of the European state.[26]

Du Bois largely agreed with this characterization, but his innovation was to expand the meaning of "the profit of the citizens" beyond its economic dimension. For Woolf, the civic profits generated by imperialism did not take the form of racial prestige but were purely economic. As argued subsequently in this chapter, Du Bois's exploration of the dividends of empire captured more complex forms of profit beyond economic value production. Instead, it brought together material and status-based explanations by showing how the production of economic value relied on the production of racial value.[27] Imperialism not only generated economic value enriching the citizens of the metropole. It also engendered a psychological "profit in caste" by "bolstering the *amour-propre* of Europe" through ideologies of the civilizing mission.[28]

The second way in which Du Bois broke with Hobson and Fabian anti-imperialism was that whereas Hobson saw democracy and imperialism as antithetical, Du Bois attended to the ways that liberal democracy within the European metropole rested upon imperial expansion abroad. Central to Hobson's theory of imperialism was the assumption that it benefited solely the interests of the financial sector rather than the metropole as a whole. Hobson noted that imperialism is at once "bad business for the nation" even as it is "good business for certain classes." While ultimately "irrational from the standpoint of the whole nation," it had real effects on the domestic politics of the metropole.[29] If "autocratic government" in the colonies "naturally reacts upon domestic government," then it does so by consolidating the economic and political hegemony of capitalist oligarchs at the expense of the public good.[30] By strengthening capitalist dictatorship, imperialism

---

26. Woolf quoted in Peter Wilson, "Fabian Paternalism and Radical Dissent: Leonard Woolf's Theory of Economic Imperialism," in *Imperialism and Internationalism in the Discipline of International Relations*, ed. David Long and Brian Schmidt (SUNY Press, 2005), 124.

27. In these arguments, Du Bois combines socialist critiques focusing on the economic dimension with sociological theories of imperialism that see it as a drive for status and prestige. On these distinctions, see Wolfgang Mommsen, *Theories of Imperialism*, trans. P. S. Falla (Random House, 1980), 15–19.

28. Du Bois, *Black Folk*, xxxii.

29. J. G. A. Hobson, *Imperialism*, 51–52.

30. J. G. A. Hobson, *Imperialism*, 154.

parasitically feeds on democratic struggles (e.g., suffrage expansion) and social reform movements. In its antagonistic relationship with democracy, it usurps "the authority and voice of the people."[31] The solution to imperialism required attacking the root of the problem: the overaccumulation of capital. Specifically, democratic movements must seek "popular control" of representative institutions and a "sound system of taxation" to redistribute surplus wealth to the working classes or public coffers.[32] By strengthening the power of the working classes, social democracy and trade unionism could drain the surplus capital that provided the initial stimulus for imperialism.

Hobson did not naively believe that popular classes or social reform movements were necessarily opposed to imperialism. In his observations, broad sections of the population did in fact succumb to chauvinistic enthusiasm for expansion even though it contradicted their economic interests. This popular support occurred because of the elite manipulation of public opinion by the ruling classes with interests in direct overseas investment. With control over the popular press, the ruling classes used jingoistic nationalism to induce the masses to support the imperialist project and advance their narrow class interests. To capture this manipulation and allow his theory to hang together coherently, Hobson supplemented his economic theory of imperialism with a "socio-political analysis of mass-behavior," which rested on the presumption of false consciousness whereby mass support for imperialism entailed privileging national prestige over class interests.[33]

For Du Bois, in contrast, liberal democracy within the metropole and imperialism abroad were entangled with each other, resulting in the paradox of "democratic despotism." Du Bois wrote, "It is this paradox which allows in America the most rapid advance of democracy to go hand-in-hand in its very centers with increased aristocracy and hatred toward darker races, and which excuses and defends an inhumanity that does not shrink from the public burning of human beings."[34] The paradox of democratic despotism was not simply that political and economic democratization within the imperial metropole proceeded alongside the political subjugation and economic exploitation of the colonies. Rather, the two were mutually constitutive of each other such that the emergence of liberal, representative

---

31. J. G. A. Hobson, *Imperialism*, 134.
32. J. G. A. Hobson, *Imperialism*, 95, 104.
33. Mommsen, *Theories of Imperialism*, 15.
34. Du Bois, "African Roots," 709.

democracy, marked by political and economic concessions to the European working classes, rested on colonial domination. Democratic despotism thus names a cross-class racial alliance of white labor and white capital wherein the economic, political, and affective bonds uniting the two otherwise contradictory poles derive from shared commitments to colonial expansion.[35] This cross-class alliance, however, was not held together simply by elite control of the popular press and jingoistic nationalism, as it was for Hobson. Rather, its affective glue came from the dividends of empire: the economic, psychological, and political spoils of colonial conquest granted as white compensation.

While white laboring classes did derive concrete psychological and economic benefits from this imperial alliance, this gain was not without cost. Industrial imperialism did grant greater democratic rights (e.g., expanded suffrage and social rights) to the masses, but the liberal version of democracy upheld by this covenant between labor and capital was restricted to the political sphere of government where capital maintained the upper hand. Du Bois wrote, "The greater the international jealousies, the greater the corresponding costs of armament and the more difficult to fulfill the promises of industrial democracy in advanced countries."[36] Du Bois routinely distinguished between *political democracy* (democracy in government) and *industrial democracy* (the economic realm). In tying labor and capital together in a cross-class alliance fixed within the nation-state, imperialism

---

35. Alberto Toscano, "America's Belgium: W. E. B. Du Bois on Race, Class, and the Origins of World War I," in *Cataclysm 1914: The First World War and the Making of Modern World Politics*, ed. Alexander Anievas (Brill, 2016), 248; Inés Valdez, "Empire, Popular Sovereignty, and the Problem of Self-and-Other Determination," *Perspectives on Politics* 21, no. 1 (March 2023): 109–25; Jonathan Hansen, *The Lost Promise of Patriotism* (University of Chicago Press, 2003), 167; Maulana Karenga, "Du Bois and the Question of the Color Line: Race and Class in the Age of Globalization," *Socialism and Democracy* 17, no. 1 (2003): 141–60.

36. Du Bois, "African Roots," 713. The language of industrial democracy itself reflects the longer genealogy of colonial racialism. Fabian socialists Sidney and Beatrice Webb, who coined the term *industrial democracy*, stated that the study of the structure of the trade union movement in Britain "lays bare, more completely than any other records known to us, the real nature and action of democratic organization in the Anglo-Saxon race"; Sidney Webb and Beatrice Webb, *Industrial Democracy* (Longmans, Green, 1897), 149. Tropes of both industry and democracy were linked to a stadial view of race development and were seen as products of Anglo-Saxon racial qualities. In this regard, Du Bois was both appropriating and transforming the language of industrial democracy.

domesticated democracy by restricting its spatial movement vertically to a wider world scale and horizontally into the economic realm of popular control over industry.[37] The dividends of empire drove white labor to remain in union with capital within the nation-state and refuse a transnational class alliance with colonized labor, thus impeding the formation of industrial democracy beyond the nation-state.

As commentators have noted, Du Bois's notion of "democratic despotism" clearly and perhaps self-consciously borrows from Alexis de Tocqueville, who used the term to capture new, milder forms of despotism oriented around the majoritarian imposition of social uniformity that emerge in egalitarian societies.[38] Although this derivation is certainly plausible, the more likely reference was the sociologist Franklin Giddings's notion of "democratic empire." Hobson himself had targeted Giddings and other "Fabian Imperialists" such as Benjamin Kidd for their claims that the exploitation of the tropics was a "material necessity" to sustain the standard of European civilization.[39] In his 1900 book *Democracy and Empire*, Giddings argued not only that democracy and empire could be made consistent with each other but also that imperial expansion provided the necessary foundation for democratization. Further engaging with Leo Tolstoy's doctrine of nonresistance against evil, Giddings argued that the Darwinian struggle for existence itself is necessary to "bring about a human brotherhood in which the non-resistance of evil would be a successful working rule." For Giddings, the "gospel of non-resistance"—the idea that the strong should carry the burden of the weak—ignores the Darwinian law that "all progress comes from the remorseless struggle for existence."[40]

In Giddings's view, it is democracy asserting itself through imperial expansion and autocratic rule in the colonies that leads to nonaggression both domestically and internationally. Domestically, Giddings argued that the United States provides proof that democratic empires make class warfare virtually unknown. Internationally, there will be no cessation of war until democratic empire is made to "embrace all nations." He continues,

37. Kaplan, *Anarchy of Empire*, 171–212.

38. De Leon and Rodríguez-Muniz, "Political Sociology of W. E. B. Du Bois"; Adom Getachew and Jennifer Pitts, "Disclosing the Problem of Empire in Du Bois's International Thought," in Morris et al., *Oxford Handbook of W. E. B. Du Bois*, 3.

39. J. G. A. Hobson, *Imperialism*, 236.

40. Franklin Giddings, *Democracy and Empire: With Studies of their Psychological, Economic, and Moral Foundations* (MacMillan, 1900), 344.

"Only when the democratic empire has compassed the uttermost parts of the world will there be that perfect understanding among men which is necessary for the growth of moral kinship."[41] Under democratic empire, what Du Bois called "industrial peace" between social classes within the imperial metropole is closely bound to the progress obtained through democratic expansionism. What is notable in this argument, which stands in contrast to Hobson's suggestion that democratization and social reform are antithetical to the new imperialism, is that Du Bois critically inverts Giddings's notion of democratic empire. Rather than providing international peace, the combination of democracy at home and autocracy abroad stabilizes class rule domestically by sowing the seeds of world war.

"Unusual Returns": Transnational Whiteness as Dividend

Alongside his clear concern with solidarity among the "colored world," Du Bois also theorized the failed possibilities of anticolonial solidarity between colonized peoples and white working-class movements. I show in this section how the dividends of empire as a form of transnational whiteness operate in both distinctive and similar ways as the wages of whiteness that divide the two labor movements in the United States. Du Bois first developed his understanding of the compensatory logics of transnational whiteness in essays written in the imperial contexts of World War I, which would go on to influence his account of slavery and empire in *Black Reconstruction in America*. To the extent that there are similarities between the wages of whiteness and the dividends of empire, we should read the former as an extension of the latter rather than vice versa. If so, then rather than scale the Marxist-inflected psychological wage up to the transnational level in the 1930s and beyond, Du Bois does the reverse: the psychological wage is a scaled-down version of his Fabian-inflected notion of the dividends of empire.[42] This central interpretive point provides crucial insight into the transscalar and multidimensional nature of Du Bois's transnational imaginary. Much more than simply a globalized critique of US white supremacy, the notion of the dividends of empire illustrates how Du Bois moved from the

---

41. Giddings, *Democracy and Empire*, 356–57. For a broader elaboration of the idea of democratic empire, see Adam Dahl, *Empire of the People: Settler Colonialism and the Foundations of Modern Democratic Thought* (University Press of Kansas, 2018).

42. I am grateful to Adom Getachew for highlighting this point.

outside in—that is, from a critique of European imperialism to one of racial capitalism within the United States. By emphasizing *Black Reconstruction*'s "radical intertextuality and revisionist historiographical approach," as Gary Bertholf puts it, I thus underscore the productive possibilities that arise from reading the text in a transnational and interimperial frame.[43]

Du Bois began *Black Reconstruction* by charting the divided class structure of the plantation economy. One of the distinguishing features of US political economy in the antebellum period was the presence of "two labor movements:" a movement seeking to give black laborers a modicum of rights, which would allow greater control over labor, and a movement mostly comprised of white immigrants seeking a more equitable distribution of wealth. "Thus two movements—Labor-Free Soil, and Abolition, exhibited fundamental divergence instead of becoming one great party of free labor and free land. The Free Soilers stressed the difficulties of even the free laborer getting hold of the land and getting work in the great congestion which immigration had brought; and the abolitionists stressed the moral wrong of slavery."[44] The failure of tying these two labor movements together stemmed from their myopic visions. While the abolitionists failed to grasp the significance of the subjection of labor to organized capital, the free labor movement did not adequately appreciate the exclusion of four million enslaved laborers from their program.

As the two labor movements drifted apart, poor whites gained positions in police forces aimed at the suppression of slave rebellions and as overseers and slave drivers. Such positions placed the white laborer in a position of perceived superiority over the black laborer, which Du Bois asserted "fed his vanity because it associated him with the masters. Slavery bred in the poor white a dislike of Negro toil of all sorts."[45] During and after Reconstruction, however, this wedge between the two labor movements morphed into a more pernicious form. In contrast to orthodox Marxist theory, in which solidarity among the laboring classes arose from shared economic interests and opposition to class exploitation, Du Bois emphasized how race divided the US working classes. Despite the fact that they have "practically identical interests," he wrote, the two laboring classes "hate and fear each other so deeply and persistently and . . . are kept so far apart that neither

---

43. Garry Bertholf, "Listening to Du Bois's *Black Reconstruction*: After James," *South: A Scholarly Journal* 48, no. 1 (Fall 2015): 79.

44. Du Bois, *Black Reconstruction in America*, 20–22.

45. Du Bois, *Black Reconstruction in America*, 12.

sees anything of common interest." Although the white working class received low economic wages as compensation for their labor, they also received psychological compensation in the form of "public deference and titles of courtesy," admission to public functions and superior educational institutions, and access to positions of public rank. From these political and psychological (as opposed to strictly economic) benefits, the wages of both classes were artificially suppressed by preventing the formation of cross-racial, working-class solidarities.[46]

The critical race theorist Joel Olson helpfully articulated Du Bois's notion of the public and psychological wage as a theory of democratic citizenship. To do so, Olson built on Judith Shklar's understanding of American citizenship as a form of social standing. For Shklar, the value of American citizenship is not in the material interests it helps individuals secure or in the forms of empowerment that it grants certain groups. Rather, it is in the dignity and social esteem that it affords—what she called "social standing."[47] Building on Shklar, Olson held that US citizenship is a form of racialized standing. To the extent that the privileges of citizenship were synonymous with the privileges of whiteness, the value of citizenship rights arose not despite but rather because of racial inequality. Because one's political status as citizen was so closely tied to one's status as white, Olson asserted, "the very structure of American citizenship is white."[48] In interpreting their interests as tied to their racial identity, members of the white working class receive a symbolic wage from their civic-racial status.

Despite its power in showing how the wages of whiteness constitute US citizenship as a form of racial standing, this account is limited in its methodological nationalism. Specifically, it provides no way of grasping the entwinement of the wages of whiteness with imperialism and colonial exploitation. In contrast, Marilyn Lake and Henry Reynolds track how whiteness in the late nineteenth and early twentieth centuries constituted a "transnational form of racial identification," a global project of racial rule formed in reaction to the specter of a postcolonial world. The imagined community of whiteness was not strictly a national community. It encapsulated a planetary scale, captured in the assertive yet anxiety-ridden

---

46. Du Bois, *Black Reconstruction in America*, 700–701.

47. Judith Shklar, *American Citizenship: The Quest for Inclusion* (Harvard University Press, 1991).

48. Olson, *Abolition of White Democracy*, xv. See also Dana Nelson, *National Manhood: Capitalist Citizenship and the Imagined Fraternity of White Men* (Duke University Press, 1998).

language of "white men's countries." Whiteness was "at once global in its power and personal in its meaning, the basis of geo-political alliances and a subjective sense of self."[49] Lake and Reynolds focus specifically on elite circulations of transnational whiteness in nation-building and state-building projects. For instance, in their attempts to build a white settler state, architects of Australian settler colonial rule over aboriginal peoples drew on Dunning school histories of Reconstruction that warned of the inevitable failures of experiments in multiracial democracy.

Building on Lake and Reynolds, I argue that Du Bois theorized transnational whiteness as a form of solidarity that circulated not just through elite discourses but also through shared constructions of identity among Euro-American working classes. Rather than a symbol of a "sacred union" and "fellow feeling" that sustained alliances among white settler states, transnational whiteness flourished amid competing imperial powers in the scramble for control of racially divided, global labor markets.[50] Although it thrived in a world of competing European empires, whiteness was a form of transnational identification that moved across national borders. The dividends of empire thus capture the transnational structure of white citizenship, which binds white citizens globally by membership in formally opposed imperial states. It points not simply to rights afforded white workers through national citizenship but also to shared solidarities and investments in imperial expansion and colonial exploitation that stem from their position in different (even if competing) imperial formations. As a form of transnational whiteness, the dividends of empire arise out of a geopolitical formation that Laura Doyle calls "inter-imperiality," the political and historical dynamics "created by the violent histories of plural interacting empires and by interacting persons moving between and against empires."[51] In what follows, I elaborate the dividends of empire in two Du Bois texts.

49. Marilyn Lake and Henry Reynolds, *Drawing the Global Colour Line: White Men's Countries and the International Challenge of Racial Equality* (Cambridge University Press, 2008), 3. Aileen Moreton-Robinson, Maryrose Casey, and Fiona Nicoll similarly state that "whiteness is a transnational process of racialization, which exceeds containment within fixed boundaries of identity and nation"; Aileen Moreton-Robinson et al., "Introduction: Virtue and Transnational Whiteness," in *Transnational Whiteness Matters*, ed. Aileen Moreton-Robinson et al. (Lexington, 2008), x.

50. Lake and Reynolds, *Drawing the Global Colour Line*, 3, 5.

51. Laura Doyle, "Inter-Imperiality: Dialectics in Postcolonial World History," *Interventions* 16, no. 2 (2014): 160.

THE DIVIDENDS OF EMPIRE IN "AFRICAN ROOTS"

In "The African Roots of War" (1915), Du Bois placed the African continent at the center of world history by tracing the origins of World War I to the onset of European imperialism in Africa. Arising from the carving up of Africa at the Berlin Conference (1884–85), imperialism gave rise to economic competition among empires, which in turn ignited the war. Du Bois wrote, "The present world war is, then, the result of jealousies engendered by the recent rise of armed national associations of labor and capital whose aim is the exploitation of the wealth of the world mainly outside the European circle of nations."[52] One of Du Bois's novel theoretical interventions was to grasp how these "armed national associations of labor and capital" defuse class conflict through shared commitments to imperial expansion and colonial domination. As white workers organized and developed political power to demand higher wages, the overexploitation of industrial workers led capitalists to seek new sources of exploitation. As Du Bois put it, the "dream of exploitation abroad" replaced the "boundless exploitation of one's weaker and poorer fellows at home."[53] As with the uneasy alliance between capital and abolition in *Black Reconstruction*, industrial laborers' demands for greater share in the benefits of capitalism led to a reconciliation of the white working class with imperialist captains of industry.

To the extent that colonialism alleviated social conflicts generated by the corporate concentration of capital, the racial exploitation of colonial capitalism and competition with other empires for spheres of economic influence drove capital accumulation by binding together labor and capital. Despite the necessary tendency for imperial competition over spheres of influence at the heart of the new imperialism, Du Bois nevertheless foregrounded forms of solidarity that tie white workers together across national boundaries out of a shared sense of transnational whiteness. Although the union of labor and capital at the heart of the imperial system was a national association, the white identity holding these associations together spans national boundaries, uniting "labor and capital in world-wide freebooting."[54]

In making these points, Du Bois highlighted the centrality of the racialization of finance capital to the new imperialism. Whereas Hobson treated race as incidental to this dynamic, Du Bois saw it as central. Du Bois wrote,

---

52. Du Bois, "African Roots," 711.
53. Du Bois, "African Roots," 709.
54. Du Bois, "African Roots," 711.

"Thus the world began to invest in color prejudice. The 'Color Line' began to pay dividends."[55] In grounding the language of investment and dividends in the problem of the color line, Du Bois suggested that new imperial regimes of capital accumulation politically and economically rested on the racialized division of labor produced by colonial exploitation. The metaphorical language of "dividends" and "shares" alongside that of "wages" shapes the way Du Bois understands the forms of racial compensation that Euro-American workers received from colonial expansion. The national associations of capital and labor that drove imperialism sought new outlets of expansion to increase their "division of the spoils" of the European domination of the world. By teaming with capital in imperial expansion, the "laborer at home is demanding and beginning to receive a part of his share" of the profits reaped from global regimes of capital accumulation.[56] The language of "shares" and "dividends" nicely captures the logic of imperial white compensation, what Manu Karuka has aptly called "shareholder whiteness."[57] Just as shareholders lack power over corporate decisions but receive compensation for their investments, white laborers in the metropole lack direct control over imperial ventures yet receive political and psychological dividends for their continued support.

The corporate structure of imperial whiteness—captured in the financial metaphors of shares and dividends—upends the possibilities of industrial democracy. As white laborers in the metropole trade democratic control over industry for shares in empire, they become akin to corporate shareholders lacking power and accountability. Nevertheless, Du Bois insists that white laborers in the imperial metropole cannot entirely evade responsibility for colonial exploitation. In a 1921 editorial, he wrote, "English working classes are exploiting India . . . French and Belgian laborers are raping Africa . . . the working classes of America are subjugating Santo Domingo and Haiti. . . . While the individual white employee in Europe and America is less to be condemned than the individual capitalist for the way in which the darker nations have been treated, he cannot escape his responsibility. He is co-worker in the miserable modern subjugation of over half the world."[58] Here Du Bois captures the ambiguous position of white workers

---

55. Du Bois, "African Roots," 708.

56. Du Bois, "African Roots," 709, 711.

57. Manu Karuka, *Empire's Tracks: Indigenous Nations, Chinese Workers, and the Transcontinental Railroad* (University of California Press, 2019), 149–67.

58. W. E. B. Du Bois, "Socialism and the Negro," *Crisis* 22, no. 6 (October 1921): 246–47.

in European imperial projects as both active and passive participants in colonial exploitation. Although they were not necessarily conscious of this exploitation or its direct agents, Euro-American working classes were nevertheless responsible for it insofar as they voluntarily submitted themselves to national associations headed by imperialist masters. In doing so, however, they relinquished democratic control over the economic realm of industry in exchange for returns on investment. Insofar as European working classes participated in colonial exploitation, it was both through the benefits they received from it and the relinquishment of control of the imperial political economy.

To the extent that white working classes shared in the exploitation of colonial labor, they viewed their interests and status as intricately bound to the colonial system. The "national bond" tying this coalition together was not "mere sentimental patriotism, loyalty, or ancestor-worship" but rather stemmed from the close ties between processes of wealth accumulation and racial exploitation.[59] To keep the "close union between capital and labor at home together," dynamics of capital accumulation required not just meeting "the rising demands of the white laborer" for wages and greater power in the control of industry. These dynamics also required extraeconomic forms of compensation, such as a political and psychological wage that positioned the white worker above colonially exploited laborer yet also allowed capital to keep economic wages artificially low. Yet the dividends of empire operate globally in ways that are not directly analogous to the public and psychological wage in the national context. When Du Bois later referred to "the income-bearing value of prejudice," the value that prejudice bears is not simply economic value.[60] Rather, the progress and development of the metropole maintained by European colonialism becomes itself a source of psychosocial prestige upheld by the affective investments of the white working classes.

On a more complex level, however, Du Bois shows how democratic citizenship at the national level itself operates as part of the dividends of empire: as the "white workingman" begins to share in the work of colonial exploitation, "it is no longer simply the merchant prince, or the aristocratic monopoly, or even the employing class, that is exploiting the world: it is the nation; a new democratic nation composed of united capital and labor."[61] Although white working classes lack direct control over foreign policy, their

---

59. Du Bois, "African Roots," 709.

60. Du Bois, *Dusk of Dawn*, 75.

61. Du Bois, "African Roots," 709.

greater rights of suffrage within the political order of the nation compensate for greater material inequality. The national bonds created by the democratic nation instill a sense of equality between capital and labor, granting the white working classes a degree of prestige that acquired its meaning in opposition to the exploitation of colonized labor abroad. Yet, as I will foreground later, the compensation of white workers through this national bond at once transforms the meaning and practice of democratic citizenship within the imperial metropole by increasingly domesticating claims for popular control over industry within the nation-state.

Du Bois also foregrounds rights of immigration, hospitality, and the global freedom of movement as part of the dividends of empire: "A white man is privileged to go to any land where advantage beckons and behave as he pleases."[62] Flipping liberal arguments for hospitality on their head, Du Bois illustrated how liberal-internationalist norms rose out of the racialized division of colonial labor. While the white working classes are granted freedom of movement internationally, "the black and colored man is being more and more confined to those parts of the world where life . . . is most difficult to live and most easily dominated by Europe for Europe's gain."[63] Just as the democratic rights of European working classes acquired their prestige from their denial to the colonized, the freedom of movement also became valued as a dividend of empire owing to the curtailment of the movement of the colonized part of the world. Du Bois was writing at a moment when enhanced freedom of mobility for white Europeans existed alongside the rapid closure of national borders "based on newly articulated anxiety about racial purity and invasion."[64] By 1930, almost every independent state in Europe and the Americas passed legislation restricting migration on racial grounds, and in many cases working-class organizations and socialist parties participated in the construction of these racialized migration regimes and imperial modes of labor control.[65] Thus, while differential rights of mobility were articulated through national citizenship laws, they came to symbolize forms of imperial compensation that were transnational in scope.

62. Du Bois, "African Roots," 712.

63. Du Bois, "African Roots," 712. See also Valdez, *Transnational Cosmopolitanism*, 129–34.

64. Rebecca Hamlin, *Crossing: How We Label and React to People on the Move* (Stanford University Press, 2021), 35.

65. Inés Valdez, "Socialism and Empire: Labor Mobility, Racial Capitalism, and the Political Theory of Migration," *Political Theory* 49, no. 6 (December 2021): 902–33.

THE TRANSNATIONAL STRUCTURE OF WHITE PRESTIGE IN "CULTURE OF WHITE FOLK"

In the 1917 version of "Of the Culture of White Folk," published in the *Journal of Race Development,* Du Bois more concretely theorized how the dividends of empire provide the psychological and affective glue holding together interimperial forms of transnational whiteness. The driving force of the new imperialism was not just the search for outlets of financial investment to deal with the problem of overaccumulation. It was also global competition for the control of nonwhite labor by European powers. Du Bois argued that the path to World War I emerged out of "jealousy and strife for the possession of the labor of dark millions, for the right to bleed and exploit the colonies of the world where this golden stream may be had."[66] Despite the centrality of interimperial competition for control over the terms of the racialized exploitation of labor, Du Bois emphasized bonds of transnational whiteness that connected the political consciousness of white European workers through a shared sense of superiority. During and preceding the First World War, the language of race was closely tied to that of nationalism and nationality. In the European diplomatic imagination, the war was the product of aggressive nationalism igniting conflict between, for instance, the "French race" and the "German race." In this georacial imaginary, the language of race was somewhat fluid, encompassing a series of biocultural factors such as national history, language, cultural values, and political institutions.[67]

Tethering the language of race to that of the nation, however, risked obscuring the imperial ties that bound together these warring nationalities. By portraying whiteness as a form of Pan-European identity, Du Bois upended the nineteenth-century association of racial identity with nationality. For

---

66. W. E. B. Du Bois, "Of the Culture of White Folk," *Journal of Race Development* 7, no. 4 (April 1917): 441. By 1922, the *Journal of Race Development* had morphed into *Foreign Affairs,* one of the premier intellectual outlets in Anglo-American international relations theory. Du Bois's essay partially built on a 1910 essay called "Souls of White Folk" and formed much of the second chapter of *Darkwater,* which was published in 1920. The 1910 version, however, notably does not utilize the political economy language of shares, dividends, and wages, and it exhibits no substantive attention to imperialism. See Robert Vitalis, *White World Order, Black Power Politics: The Birth of American International Relations* (Cornell University Press, 2015), 66–67.

67. Stéphane Audoin-Rouzeau and Annette Becker, *14–18: Understanding the Great War,* trans. Catherine Temerson (Hill and Wang, 2014), 153–54; Bell, *Reordering the World,* 183–84.

Du Bois, transnational whiteness was a civilizational construct constituted through the economic exploitation and political domination of colonial peoples. "In other words," Du Bois wrote, "the deeper reasons for the triumph of European civilization lie quite outside and beyond Europe, back in the universal struggles of all mankind."[68] Showing how the prestige of "modern white civilization" coalesced through common but nevertheless competing forms of imperialism provided new ways of seeing the war not simply as a product of nationalistic displays of superiority but as a complex and contradictory articulation of nationalism and international hierarchy. While national jealousies over imperial aggrandizement ignited the engine of world war, the shared pursuit of imperial domination by national associations of labor and capital generated a common sense of civilizational superiority that spanned national boundaries. Transnational whiteness stems from material structures of colonization and exploitation: "High wages in the United States and England might be the skillfully manipulated result of slavery in Africa and of peonage in Asia." Yet beyond its economic benefits in the form of higher wages, colonialism also accrues psychological and political benefits to white laborers. It not only raised material wages for white workers but also granted them a sense of "white prestige."[69]

To illustrate the transnational structure of white prestige, Du Bois offered the example of Germany, which could not economically rival England solely through exploitation of its own peasants and laborers, many of whom were already in revolt. In a desperate bid to equalize interimperial competition, Germany built its navy and secured possession of colonies in Southwest Africa. The allure of transnational whiteness was evident in the arguments of Bernhard Dernburg, the future vice chancellor and former head of the Imperial Colonial Office, who penned a 1916 essay in *The New York Times* titled "England Traitor to White Race." Illustrating what Du Bois called "the doctrine of the divine right of whites to steal," Dernburg maintained that European empires have duties to one another in the governance of colonial affairs, specifically, "the maintenance of the prestige of the white race." Dernburg continued, "In the colonial domain, every member of the white race is answerable to every other for the maintenance of his purity, culture, and prestige of the greater community." Stretching back to British policy in the Boer Wars of using Bantu warriors to fight white settlers, the British Empire, according to Dernburg, violated the transnational obligations of upholding white prestige by "lending all sorts of uncultured colored

---

68. Du Bois, "Of the Culture of White Folk," 438.
69. Du Bois, "Of the Culture of White Folk," 443–44.

men against whites, and fighting by the side of such savages."[70] More than simply a shared hegemonic status, the language of white prestige was part of an imperial grammar signaling a "reputation for power" that the white world was collectively accountable to uphold, which in turn both generated a set of transnational obligations and served as a source of strife that drove competition between imperial nation-states.[71]

While the exploitation of men for "the benefit of masters is no invention of modern Europe," Du Bois conceded, what made the new imperialism unique was its planetary scale and "elaborateness of detail which no former world ever dreamed." In exploring the uniqueness of the new imperialism, Du Bois reiterated his central point in "African Roots" that colonial expansion was a response the contradictions generated by the enhanced exploitation of white labor under industrial capitalism. "It is plain to modern white civilization that that the subjection of the white working classes cannot much longer be maintained," Du Bois wrote in "Of the Culture of White Folk." With greater education and political power, white working classes were beginning to assert greater democratic control over industry and call for a more equitable distribution of wealth and income. While such trends may augur the declining power of industrial oligarchs, "there is a loophole. There is a chance for exploitation on an immense scale; for inordinate profit, not simply to the very rich, but to the middle class and the laborers. This chance lies in the exploitation of darker peoples." Absent labor unions and working-class parties, economic exploitation in the colonies could proceed without public scrutiny and "with only one test of success: dividends." Imperialism pays psychological dividends not only to capitalists and industrial oligarchs but also to the middle classes and white laborers. Central to this form of white compensation is a "theory of human culture" wherein "everything great, good, efficient, fair and honorable is white."[72]

---

70. Du Bois, "Of the Culture of White Folk," 443–44; Bernhard Dernburg, "England Traitor to White Race," *New York Times Magazine*, January 2, 1916, 3. Dernburg also quoted in Matthew Hughey, "'The Souls of White Folk' (1920–2020): A Century of Peril and Prophecy," *Ethnic and Racial Studies* 43, no. 8 (2020): 1323–24. Alongside Dernburg, Jan Smuts also decried the arming of black African peoples in the Boer Wars, viewing it as the spark of a global crisis that ignited World War I. See Jacob Kripp, "The Creative Advance Must Be Defended: Miscegenation, Metaphysics, and Race War in Jan Smuts's Vision of the League of Nations," *American Political Science Review* 116, no. 3 (September 2022): 943–45.

71. Musab Younis, *On the Scale of the World: The Formation of Black Anticolonial Thought* (University of California Press, 2022), 89.

72. Du Bois, "Of the Culture of White Folk," 440.

Throughout the essay, Du Bois explores how the dividends of empire restrict the transnational democratic imaginary. Although socialists and the labor movement were at the forefront of the struggle for "eternal peace" and "human justice," the allure of white prestige compromised their ability to understand the true causes of war and counteract the power of capital. Du Bois noted that "in Germany and America 'International' Socialists had all but read yellow and black men out of the kingdom of industrial justice."[73] In this way, the dividends of empire restricted the construction of the "international" in socialist imaginaries by divorcing the question of the emancipation of labor from the emancipation of the colonies. Through such provincialism, socialist movements confined the "international" to the boundaries of Euro-American labor politics and ignored the central role of imperialism in shaping modern world order. As a result, anticolonial movements provided the only true hope of "peace built on world democracy, of equality of men of all races and color, and the damnation of all industrial organizations built on theft."[74]

As noted earlier, while they partake in a similar compensatory structure, the dividends of empire do not represent a direct analogy to the wages of whiteness. The distance of the racial exploitation in the colonies from the white working classes (as distinct from the proximity of the two in the US South) leads to a different set of logics from the wages of whiteness domestically. The psychological wage, for Du Bois, is an intentional and actively exercised sense of superiority that coalesces as a political force through active participation in the construction and policing of the color line. In a 1933 essay, Du Bois wrote of AFL labor leaders that they made no effort to mask their "deliberate intention to keep Negroes and Mexicans and other elements of common labor, in a lower proletariat as subservient to their interests as theirs are to the interests of capital."[75] Because white workers in the US more visibly see the effects of this psychological compensation, it is closely tied to aggressive displays of superiority (e.g., lynching). The proximity of the two working classes necessitates the violent policing of boundaries between the two to affirm the validity of white standing. Moreover, the wages of whiteness manifest through publicly institutionalized status. Because of proximity, the conferral of positions of public rank (e.g., in police departments) grants racial standing an immediate salience that leads white working classes to protect it by barring black workers from those same positions.

---

73. Du Bois, "Of the Culture of White Folk," 443.
74. Du Bois, "Of the Culture of White Folk," 446.
75. Du Bois, "Marxism and the Negro Problem," 149–50.

The dividends of empire operate somewhat differently. Because the proximity of the two systems of labor exploitation was less pronounced in the case of colonial imperialism, the conferral of public positions of rank (which would require white laborers moving to the colonies) could not serve as an immediate source of compensation. As a result, the dividends of empire manifested, oftentimes, through feelings of benevolent obligation to the colonized. In his revised version of "Of the Culture of White Folk," which appeared as the second chapter of *Darkwater* in 1920, Du Bois asserted that white working classes feel their superiority through the "burning desire to spread the gift abroad—the obligation of nobility to the ignoble." Underlying this "sense of duty" is a "possession of heritage" that is unique in the world. When the colonized receive these gifts with gratefulness and thanks, white working classes feel white prestige as "mental peace and moral satisfaction." But when the colonized reject this charity, they also "dispute the white man's title to . . . wage and position, authority and training."[76] The prestige deriving from transnational whiteness surfaces most forcefully when the colonized resist the civilizing mission. In engaging in anticolonial resistance, the agency of the colonized assaults not just the authority of imperial agents but also the prestige of white laborers and middle classes in the imperial metropole. What is crucial here is the nature of democracy implied behind each of these forms of white compensation. Under the wages of whiteness, white civic membership is produced through the performance of public and participatory spectacles of cruelty and violence.[77] Under the dividends of empire, superior civic status is produced through the more passive logics of shareholder whiteness.

While Du Bois did much to delineate the transnational structure of white prestige, it is important to recognize that he was not by any means the originator of this grammar of whiteness as a reputation for power. Indeed, the idea of transnational whiteness as a form of Pan-European solidarity can be traced back to the Haitian diplomat and anthropologist Anténor Firmin, who also attended the 1900 Pan-African Conference alongside Du Bois. Writing in 1885, Firmin envisioned Pan-European union arising out of transnational feelings of white solidarity: "Specifically, all White European nations naturally tend to unite in order to dominate the rest of the world and other human races. They may argue about who is to dominate in Europe

---

76. Du Bois, *Darkwater*, 18–19.

77. Cristina Beltrán, *Cruelty as Citizenship: How Migrant Suffering Sustains White Democracy* (University of Minnesota Press, 2020).

and which of the Slavic, Germanic, or Latin civilizations is to set the tone for the common evolution of the Caucasian race, but they unanimously recognize the right of Europe to impose its laws on other parts of the world."[78] Writing in the wake of Du Bois, the Gold Coast writer and lawyer Kobina Sekyi illustrated how anticolonial resistance threatened white prestige, noting that the hostility of white Europeans to the efforts of the National Congress of British West Africa came from the former's "amour propre, graced by him with the name of prestige." Reflecting the centrality of grammars of financial capitalism to the understanding of transnational whiteness, Sekyi similarly noted how white prestige infused the mentality of the colonized themselves, forming a "credit, that white men have acquired in the minds of most of our own people, for the material development of the Western World."[79]

Industrial Imperialism and the Global American South

In its focus on the division of the US working class, the emancipation of slaves through the general strike, and the "American Assumption," *Black Reconstruction in America* is arguably Du Bois's most quintessentially American book. Yet the dynamics of modern European imperialism and their connection to the Reconstruction era are a recurring even if at times recessive theme of the book. Moon-Ho Jung writes, "Through his apparent (and lyrical) asides and penetrating analysis, Du Bois was able to highlight the centrality of race and empire in the making of the modern world, and in the process, to deliver a searing critique of the US empire, a critique that constitutes *Black Reconstruction*'s most revolutionary and enduring insight."[80] As explored in the previous section, the notion of the psychological wage developed in *Black Reconstruction* is an extension of his analysis of transnational whiteness elaborated in his World War I–era writings, rather than vice versa. In this section, I explore how Du Bois used the language

---

78. Antenor Firmin, *The Equality of the Human Races*, trans. Asselin Charles (University of Illinois Press, 2002), 382. See also Jared Holley, "Racial Equality and Anticolonial Solidarity: Anténor Firmin's Global Haitian Liberalism," *American Political Science Review* 118, no. 1 (2024): 304–17.

79. Sekyi quoted in Younis, *On the Scale of the World*, 92–93.

80. Moon-Ho Jung, "*Black Reconstruction* and Empire," *South Atlantic Quarterly* 112, no. 3 (Summer 2013): 465.

of "industrial imperialism" to situate the problems of race and labor in the United States in a global context. In using this language, Du Bois cast the defeat of Reconstruction as a transformative moment in the global capitalist order. His central concern was not just with the racial division of the US working class and its implications for multiracial democracy but also with how the racialized division of labor at the heart of European imperialism both hindered transnational forms of labor solidarity and prevented abolition-democracy on a world scale from taking root.

One of the underappreciated threads in *Black Reconstruction* is Du Bois's argument that the rise of "the new imperialism" in the late nineteenth century not only grew out of slavery but also arose from the transformations of global capitalism necessitated by the restructuring of the global cotton economy after the Civil War. In this, Du Bois further revised Hobson's theory of the new imperialism by foregrounding its origins in the US plantation economy. Cast in terms of a labor problem rather than solely a problem of overaccumulation, the collapse of Reconstruction was directly related to the onset of the new imperialism. With slavery abolished in the United States, European industrial powers expressed a need for new systems of labor exploitation. Du Bois profoundly understood that the abolition of slavery did not end the reliance of capitalist exchange on the racialized division of labor.

Imperialism was a continuation of slavery by other means, not just through the sheer exploitation of labor but also through the landed dispossession of indigenous inhabitants, which forced them into coerced labor. In "The Hands of Ethiopia" (1920), Du Bois wrote, "Today instead of removing laborers from Africa to distant slavery, industry built on a new slavery approaches Africa to deprive the natives of their land, to force them to toil, and to reap all the profit for the white world."[81] While chattel slavery in the Americas proceeded through the "geographical alienation" of the slave trade, imperial slavery in the African colonies relied on colonial dispossession and land theft.[82] For Du Bois, this transformation in the logic of global capital accumulation from slavery to colonial imperialism propelled

---

81. Du Bois, *Darkwater*, 33. Du Bois outlined numerous means by which this process of a primitive accumulation was accomplished, which necessitated divorcing "natives" from the customary land base and disrupting tribal life to force them to work for wages: missionary conversion, land monopolies, and excessive taxation; W. E. B. Du Bois, "Black Africa Tomorrow," *Foreign Affairs* 17, no. 1 (October 1938): 100–110.

82. Patrick Wolfe, "Land, Labor, and Difference: Elementary Structures of Race," *American Historical Review* 106, no. 3 (June 2001); 868; Myers, "Beyond the Psychological Wage," 19–21.

forward because of the transformation of the US plantation economy after the American Civil War. The emancipation of enslaved peoples had global economic reverberations that destabilized the centrality of the cotton commodity in the world economy. In the wake of the abolition of slavery, the logic of imperialism transformed. Instead of transporting black labor from Africa to European colonies in the Americas, capitalists exported white capital to the European colonies in Africa.[83]

Central to Du Bois's revisionist narrative was his account of the plantation economy as an expansionist force that not only prefigured the colonial structure of European colonial empires but also provided the backbone of the European imperial system. Du Bois used imperial idioms to characterize the structures of racialized labor exploitation at the heart of the plantation economy. Although the technological force of the steam engine drove the expansion of plantation society across the western territories, it was "the black workers of America bent at the bottom of a growing pyramid of commerce and industry" that allowed this "new economic organization to expand," giving rise to "new dreams of power and visions of empire." Vast territorial expansion and conquest—the "widening stretches of new, rich, black soil—in Florida, in Louisiana, in Mexico; even in Kansas"—allowed a whole new system of culture and social philosophy based on the leisure of the master class to arise in the South. As a result, "black labor became the foundation stone" of the Southern system as well as Northern industrialism, English textile factories, and a whole new system of "buying and selling on a world-wide scale."[84]

The language of empire here was not merely incidental to Du Bois's purposes. He drew a direct analogy between the structure of Southern power and that of European imperialism in the late nineteenth and early twentieth centuries. "Like Nemesis of Greek tragedy, the central problem of America after the Civil War, as before, was the black man: those four million souls whom the nation had used and degraded, and on whom the South had built an oligarchy similar to the colonial imperialism of today, erected on cheap colored labor and raising raw material for manufacture."[85] In further accounting for the expansion of "Cotton Kingdom" into "imperial white domination," Du Bois emphasized how the exploitation of black labor intensified with the expansion of plantation society and its entrenchment in the capitalist world-system. The viability of the plantation economy, he

---

83. Sven Beckert, *Empire of Cotton: A Global History* (Vintage, 2014).
84. Du Bois, *Black Reconstruction in America*, 5.
85. Du Bois, *Black Reconstruction in America*, 237.

keenly captured, was closely bound to the expansion of territory: "For the sheer existence of slavery, there must be a continual supply of fertile land."[86] The intensified exploitation of slave labor rested on the expansion of Southern territory.

Colonial expansion enhanced the power of slaveholders in two respects by providing "more land" and "more slaves," respectively, political and economic power. The Southern "dream of empire" led planters to seek more land in Western territories and to create a "great slave empire" in Mexico and the Caribbean.[87] Absent any effective opposition from the North, the South acquired power over the navy and the army, consolidating its "imperialistic enterprise." With slavery all but abolished in Mexico, the West Indies, and South America by the 1850s, Southern planters sought to reintroduce the slave trade by projecting their power globally beyond US national boundaries. In this context, secession and the dream of empire blended together. Through an independent political and economic system, the South would rise to the status of a world power. By further expanding the domain of the plantation economy, it would "dictate its terms to the modern world on the basis of a monopoly of cotton."[88] The Southern projection of power was imperialistic not just in the sense that it embraced territorial expansion for the sake of augmenting political influence. It was also imperialistic in the sense that it sought the placement of the plantation economy at the top of global capitalist hierarchies through the consolidation of what theorists of the new imperialism called its "sphere of influence."[89]

In further delineating this process of imperial consolidation, Du Bois lik-

---

86. Du Bois, *Black Reconstruction in America*, 29.

87. Du Bois, *Black Reconstruction in America*, 41–42.

88. Du Bois, *Black Reconstruction in America*, 47. See also Matthew Karp, *This Vast Southern Empire: Slaveholders at the Helm of American Foreign Policy* (Harvard University Press, 2016).

89. Du Bois powerfully outlined a point that would become central to the "new histories of capitalism" almost eighty years before. Walter Johnson, for instance, refers to the "global reach of the cotton economy—in which millions of pounds and billions of dollars were annually traded, in which credit chased cotton from the metropolitan banks of Europe to every plantation outpost of the Mississippi valley and then back again." Johnson shows how understanding slavery in the context of antebellum ideological, economic, and political developments takes us beyond national frameworks of sectional conflict by forcing us to comprehend slavery as a global economic institution; Walter Johnson, *River of Dark Dreams: Slavery and Empire in the Cotton Kingdom* (Harvard University Press, 2013), 12.

ened the position of enslaved peoples to that of colonially subjugated workers under European colonial empires in Asia, Africa, and Latin America. In suggesting that the direct contemporary analogue of black labor is "the yellow, brown and black laborer in China and India, in Africa, in the forests of the Amazon," however, he did more than draw a metaphor for expository purposes.[90] He cast enslaved labor in the American South as a colonial system of exploitation that was intricately connected to later stages of colonial exploitation under the new imperialism. Enslaved labor was the foundation stone not just of the economic system in the nineteenth century but of the global capitalistic system as a whole. In this way, Du Bois constructed an alternative political cartography through, in Juliet Hooker's words, the "geographic reordering of the Global South within the U.S. South."[91]

From this repositioning, Du Bois ventured a more expansive set of claims regarding the role of Reconstruction's collapse in the rise of European imperialism. By the end of the second chapter on "The White Worker," he started to articulate the contradictory legacy of the Civil War. On the one hand, it represented "the first blossoming of the modern age" and engendered a "vision of democratic self-government: the domination of political life by the intelligent decision of free and self-sustaining men."[92] The Civil War was fought to determine the system of industrial organization in the United States, over whether labor and industrial productivity would be controlled by the dictatorship of capital or the dictatorship of the proletariat—what he also referred to as "industrial imperialism" and "industrial democracy," respectively. On the other hand, the failure of white labor to make a place for black labor set in motion a series of dynamics that linked the aborted experiment in industrial democracy to the world wars of Du Bois's present. Referring to the persistence of the color line in the battle between capitalists and white labor, he wrote, "And then some unjust God leaned, laughing, over the ramparts of heaven and dropped a black man in the midst. It transformed the world. It turned democracy back to Roman Imperialism and Fascism . . . it replaced freedom with slavery and withdrew the name of humanity from the vast majority of human beings."[93]

After standing for "a brief moment in the sun" during Reconstruction, the black laborer "moved back toward slavery." Du Bois's reference to the

---

90. Du Bois, *Black Reconstruction in America*, 9.

91. Hooker, *Theorizing Race in the Americas*, 143.

92. Du Bois, *Black Reconstruction in America*, 29.

93. Du Bois, *Black Reconstruction in America*, 30.

reintroduction of slavery in new form, however, was not merely to national dynamics of Jim Crow and the sharecropping economy. He encased the collapse of Reconstruction in a global frame. At the same time that the black laborer "moved back toward slavery," the "colored world went down before England, France, Germany, Russia, Italy and America" and a "new slavery arose." Du Bois continued, "The upward moving of white labor was betrayed into wars for profit based on color caste. Democracy died save in the hearts of black folk." The failure of industrial democracy in the United States was replicated at the global level. Just as white labor in the United States drew psychological and material benefits from the racial differentiation of black labor, white working-class mobility and wages globally hinged on the economic, political, and psychological profits gained from the colonial exploitation of labor. As colonial labor became subordinated to white profits, the exploitation of the colonized world "became the basis of a system of industry which ruined democracy and showed its perfect fruit in World War and Depression."[94]

Read in conjunction with the second chapter, the pivotal and penultimate chapter, "Back Toward Slavery," portends the resubjugation of black labor in the US to a new system of color caste as well as new forms of slavery and labor exploitation characteristic of the new imperialism. The road back toward slavery was paved by what Du Bois called the "counter-revolution of property," an agreement between "the Southern exploiter of labor" and the "Norther exploiter," an alliance of "imperial domination" that led to the consolidation of capital, the triumph of a "new Empire of Industry" under the "dictatorship of capital."[95] Du Bois characterized representatives of Northern capital in terms almost identical to those used by critics of the new imperialism, who sought the investment of finance capital in foreign territories to protect domestic markets and private profits. "Many of these were agents for capital and went down from the North with something of the psychology of modern investment in conquered or colonial territory: that is, they brought the capital; they invested it; they remained in charge to oversee the profits; and they acquired political power in order to protect these profits."[96] As Northern capital aligned with Southern capital in the bargain of 1876, the uneasy alliance between Northern capital and the

---

94. Du Bois, *Black Reconstruction in America*, 30.
95. Du Bois, *Black Reconstruction in America*, 596.
96. Du Bois, *Black Reconstruction in America*, 348.

abolition-democracy fractured, which involved a vast transfer of power and left the new alliance with the unbridled control of labor.

In this discussion of the counterrevolution of property, Du Bois theorized what he called "the new industrial imperialism," which reinforced "the capitalistic dictatorship of the United States" and "degraded the colored world over."[97] Despite the central role of Northern capitalists in driving the counterrevolution of property, its lasting significance was not just the consolidated ownership of land and labor in the South; it was the persistence of the intellectual and spiritual edifice of Southern civilization. Southern imperialism prior to the Civil War, in other words, struck a new key, as racial hierarchies became the basis of a globalized plantation economy operating through the control of overseas colonies. As Southern racial hierarchies fused into global imperial hierarchies, the US "became the cornerstone of that new imperialism which is subjecting the labor of yellow, brown and black peoples to the dictation of capitalism organized on a world basis."[98]

With this transformation in mind, Du Bois closed the penultimate chapter of *Black Reconstruction* by turning his critique of the South into a critique of imperialism. The failure of democracy to take root in the United States was owing to the persistence of Southern militaristic culture, which impeded the development of a full-fledged peace movement and internationalist movements that might cultivate solidarity with colonially subjugated peoples. Du Bois wrote, "The South is not interested in freedom for dark India. It has no sympathy with the oppressed of Africa or of Asia."[99] One of the primary obstacles impeding this solidarity was the persistence of the "Southern attitude," which underpinned the material structure of the new imperialism through the newly realized global power of the United States: "Imperialism, the exploitation of colored labor throughout the world, thrives upon the approval of the United States, and the United States gives that approval because of the South. World War waits on and supports imperial aggression and international jealousy."[100] The expansionism of the Southern plantocracy in the antebellum period transformed into

---

97. Du Bois, *Black Reconstruction in America*, 630.

98. Du Bois, *Black Reconstruction in America*, 631.

99. Du Bois, *Black Reconstruction in America*, 704. For a similar account that attends to the position of Asian and Indian labor in these processes, see Lowe, *Intimacies of Four Continents*, 162–75.

100. Du Bois, *Black Reconstruction in America*, 706.

a new imperial key in the wake of the compromise of 1876, consolidating the racialized division of labor at the center of global capitalism. By restoring power to former Confederates, the collapse of Reconstruction generated new sources of diplomatic power that they would use to help transform the racialized division of labor of the plantation economy into colonial imperialism.[101]

The intricate links between Southern slavery and European imperialism laid the basis for a distinctively global conception of labor solidarity among the colonially exploited populations of the world. As "the founding stones of modern industry," the "dark and vast sea of human labor" in China, India, Africa, the West Indies, and the Americas share a "common destiny." This globally exploited "dark proletariat" connected the centers of power in London, Paris, Berlin, New York, and Rio de Janeiro and laid the basis of European "universal dominion."[102] The struggles for the freedom of black workers in the South had universal resonance in their challenge to the foundation of global economic power: "The emancipation of man is the emancipation of labor and the emancipation of labor is the freeing of that basic majority of workers who are yellow, brown and black."[103] Slavery was the central episode in the global exploitation of both white and nonwhite workers throughout the world. Du Bois writes, "Indeed, the plight of the white working class throughout the world today is directly traceable to Negro slavery in America, on which modern commerce and industry was founded."[104] Despite these links between the exploitation of black and white labor, attempts to draw transnational and cross-racial class solidarities misfired because of the dividends of empire.

Instead of using Reconstruction to recenter democratic politics and history on the US experience, Du Bois's history points outward, beyond nation-state borders. He keenly grasped how capitalism after Reconstruc-

---

101. Du Bois's assertion finds support in the case of the Congo Free State. The United States was the first to grant international recognition of the Belgian colony. Diplomatic recognition of the Congo Free State was the work of Senator John Tyler Morgan of Alabama, who was a Confederate general and chair of the Senate Foreign Relations Committee; Adam Hochschild, *King Leopold's Ghost: A Story of Greed, Terror, and Heroism in Colonial Africa* (Houghton Mifflin, 1998), 79–81. See also Angela Zimmerman, *Alabama in Africa: Booker T. Washington, the German Empire, and the Globalization of the New South* (Princeton University Press, 2012).

102. Du Bois, *Black Reconstruction in America*, 15.

103. Du Bois, *Black Reconstruction in America*, 16.

104. Du Bois, *Black Reconstruction in America*, 30.

tion ignited a restructuring of global economic relations across lines of both class and color—as both formally free whites and formerly enslaved peoples struggled to maintain landed independence in reaction to the looming predominance of wage slavery. It was not just race and the wages of whiteness domestically but also the dividends of empire globally that fractured these democratic possibilities. For Du Bois, the entwined dynamics of race, capitalism, and slavery in the United States determined the scope and meaning of "democratic control." Yet this question also pushes beyond the borders of the nation-state and "still remains with the world as the problem of democracy touches all races and nations."[105] The question of the limits of democratic control—whether it would remain confined to government or extend to industry—was global in scope and became embodied in the figure of Andrew Johnson, the harbinger of Reconstruction's collapse. Exemplifying the "race provincialism" of the "Poor White South," Johnson dramatized how the failure of the white working class to develop a cross-racial class coalition with colonized labor ultimately restricted industrial democracy and delivered the world to plutocratic control.[106]

Refusing to exceptionalize the US as separate from European imperialism, *Black Reconstruction* counteracts nationalist historiography by connecting the failure of US democracy to achieve a more racially and economically egalitarian order to the rise of the new imperialism. Through this revisionist history, he highlights how the stories we tell about race, capitalism, and empire matter for how we conceptualize democratic possibilities on a world scale. Reimagining democracy along transnational lines cannot come from insulated histories that disconnect imperialism from slavery. Reconstruction within the US was thus essentially a project of decolonization that illuminates possibilities for global democratic transformation.[107] Eric Foner explains that Du Bois characterized the collapse of Reconstruction as a "splendid failure" precisely because it was no failure at all; or more precisely, because it did not fail for the reason critics predicted—that is, the

---

105. Du Bois, *Black Reconstruction in America*, 13.

106. Du Bois, *Black Reconstruction in America*, 241.

107. Angela Zimmerman, "Reconstruction Along the Global Color Line: Slavery, International Class Conflict, and Empire," in *Interpreting American History: The New South*, ed. James Humphreys (Kent State University Press, 2018), 37–62; George Lipsitz, "Abolition Democracy and Global Justice," in *Comparative American Studies* 2, no. 3 (2004): 271–86: Jesse Olsavsky, "The Abolitionist Tradition in the Making of W. E. B. Du Bois's Marxism and Anti-Imperialism," *Socialism and Democracy* 32, no. 3 (2018): 14–35.

incapacities of black democratic agency.[108] The "splendid failure" of Reconstruction was of more than national significance; it meant the demise of an incipient vision of global abolition-democracy that entailed the abolition of slavery in its colonial forms. Yet by situating Reconstruction within a "global genealogy of democratic potential and foreclosure," Du Bois recoded its history as a resurgent possibility within a new context.[109]

Reconstructing Global Democracy

In his 1945 book *Color and Democracy, Colonies and Peace*, Du Bois returned to the mutual imbrication of racial differentiation and financial capital that stand as the pillars of European imperial rule. Through imperialism, modern governments and industry have "built a tremendous financial structure upon the nineteenth-century conception of race inferiority." In this financial system, colonial possessions are a "method of investment yielding unusual returns," profits that have laid the foundation for the wealth and power of the modern industrial system as the basis for competition over colonial domination that engulfed the world in war.[110] With the end of World War II in sight, Du Bois warned that Britain and other European empires would attempt to reorganize the colonial system under the authority of international law and the United Nations, leaving the economic impulses driving war and colonialism unaddressed. Such a system not only leaves colonial peoples in a condition of poverty; it also impinges on the condition of working classes and minorities within the imperial metropole. In suggesting that the colonial system was a mode of investment that yields "unusual returns" and "high profit to investors," Du Bois hearkens the dividends of empire, a transnational form of white prestige granted to white working classes as return on investment in colonial exploitation.[111]

In this chapter, I have suggested that expanding the political-economic grammars capturing the mutual constitution of global capitalism and imperial racism has important implications for both critical theories of racial

---

108. Eric Foner, "*Black Reconstruction*: An Introduction," *South Atlantic Quarterly* 112, no. 3 (Summer 2013): 416.

109. Allison Powers, "Tragedy Made Flesh: Constitutional Lawlessness in Du Bois's *Black Reconstruction*," *Comparative Studies of South Asia, Africa and the Middle East* 34, no. 1 (2014): 106–25.

110. Du Bois, *Color and Democracy*, 275.

111. Du Bois, *Color and Democracy*, 275–76.

capitalism and critical democratic theory.[112] Moving beyond figurations of whiteness as a wage, property interest, or individual consumer investment, the notion of white prestige as a dividend or share illuminates neglected features of Du Bois's transnational democratic imaginary.[113] While a wage signifies an active service contracted in exchange for compensation, the corporate shareholder who receives a return on investment occupies a passive position marked by the relinquishment of control and responsibility over the economic activity carried out with that investment. In this sense, the idea of the dividends of empire illuminates how transnational whiteness aligns with a corporate conception of "shareholder democracy" whereby white working classes are freed from accountability for imperial expansion, resulting in a bifurcated spatial imaginary in which the wealth of European nations is disconnected from the degradation of the colonies.[114] In this process, debate and deliberation over the terms of industrial production and distribution get relegated to a corporate oligarchy insulated from popular accountability. White working classes exchange their democratic aspirations for economic control over industry for a transnational sense of white prestige centered on the amour propre of European civilization. Unusual returns indeed.

Such an account pushes critical democratic theorists to explore how transnational whiteness and colonial exploitation do not simply *bolster* popular sovereignty within the metropole but also *delimit and diminish* it by circumscribing popular control to the formalized realm of the political within the nation-state, thus shielding transnational capital from democratic forces that would arise from cross-racial class solidarities.[115] Through the bifurcation of domestic social order and international hierarchy, socialist and labor movements rely on a restricted understanding of the international that places the colonial question outside their orbit of concern.

---

112. Siddhant Issar, "Listening to Black Lives Matter: Racial Capitalism and the Critique of Neoliberalism," *Contemporary Political Theory* 20, no. 1 (March 2021): 48–71.

113. On figurations of whiteness as a wage, property interest, or individual consumer investment, see Roediger, *Wages of Whiteness*; Cheryl Harris, "Whiteness as Property," *Harvard Law Review* 106, no. 8 (1993): 1707–91; George Lipsitz, "The Possessive Investment in Whiteness: Racialized Social Democracy and the 'White' Problem in American Studies," *American Quarterly* 47, no. 3 (September 1995): 369–87.

114. For an overview of "shareholder democracy," see Adam Dahl and Joe Soss, "Neoliberalism for the Common Good? Public Value Governance and the Downsizing of Democracy," *Public Administration Review* 74, no. 4 (July/August 2014): 498–99.

115. Michael Gorup, *The Counterrevolutionary Shadow: Race, Democracy, and the Making of the American People* (University Press of Kansas, 2025).

Indeed, Du Bois emphasized how working people in Britain, France, and Belgium throughout the twentieth century effectively demanded social improvements and a rising standard of living through increased public taxation, a financial burden balanced by investment in colonialism.[116] The result of this bifurcation of democratic struggles for social democracy within the imperial metropole and struggles for democratic self-rule in the colonies was that the search for democracy in Europe and the United States will be increasingly impeded by the failure of industrial democracy to take root in the colonies.

By divorcing the pursuit of democratic control over industry from that of democratic self-rule in the colonies, the provincialism of white democratic imaginaries restricted the realization of world industrial democracy, Du Bois asserted:

> The democracy which the white world seeks to defend does not exist. It has been splendidly conceived and discussed, but not realized. If it ever is to grow strong enough for self-defense and for embracing the world and developing human culture to its highest, it must include not simply the lower classes among the whites now excluded from voice in the control of industry; but in addition to that it must include the colored peoples of Asia and Africa; now hopelessly imprisoned by poverty and ignorance.[117]

The possibilities for industrial democracy in the metropole and democratic self-rule in the colonies are connected preconditions for a new conception of democracy that embraces the world. Through his travels around the world, Du Bois realized that "so-called democracy" granted the masses only "limited voice in government" and that democratic control over the most important dimensions of social life such as labor and industry was profoundly limited.[118] Yet the failure to connect democracy in the colonies to democratic control over industry largely derived from the dividends of empire, which produced a provincial democratic imaginary. In striking an alliance with white capital in pursuit of greater shares in the exploitation of colonized peoples, white labor movements assumed the position of passive shareholders that traded democratic control over industry for the dividends

---

116. On the affective investment in imperially accumulated wealth, see Valdez, "Empire, Popular Sovereignty, and the Problem of Self-Other-Determination," 111–15.

117. Du Bois, *Dusk of Dawn*, 85–86.

118. Du Bois, *Dusk of Dawn*, 142.

of whiteness. By making these connections, Du Bois elaborated a transnational imaginary that collapsed the bifurcation of class exploitation domestically and colonial exploitation internationally.

Reconstructing world democracy after the two world wars required a new spatial imaginary that could destabilize the restrictive boundaries of socialist internationalism. With the start of World War II, Du Bois prophesized that the end of the war would bring a condition of "world-wide industrial dislocation," which would require soberly examining the relationship of white democracy to colonial peoples.[119] The central contradiction of this dislocation was that the leading countries in democratic development—Britain, France, and the United States—were also leaders in colonial expansion. Extending greater democratic control over industry and income in European metropoles beyond "mere political democracy" also meant eliminating the exploitation of labor in the colonies. The treatment of labor in the imperial metropole and in the colony were locked in a dynamic of "reciprocal influence" that was itself crucial to "the future of world democracy."[120] Central to this political imaginary was a vision of democracy within the imperial metropole as connected to and indeed dependent on self-determination in the colonies. In seeking to capture transnational whiteness as a central problem for world democracy, Du Bois turned to the language of dividends and returns in search of a spatial grammar that could convey these connections.

The dividends of empire can thus be seen as a reflection on the failures of socialist internationalism (in both its Fabian and Marxist forms) to provide for the democratic transformation of the global industrial order. In his unpublished epistolary novel "A World Search for Democracy" (1935), Du Bois challenged Marx and Engels's assumption that "when a labor class had been reduced to nadir it had nothing to lose but its economic chains."[121] In closing the *Communist Manifesto*, Marx and Engels famously proclaimed, "The proletarians have nothing to lose but their chains. They have a world to win. WORKING MEN OF ALL COUNTRIES, UNITE!" For Marx and Engels, capitalism erased national distinctions, tying together international laboring classes in a single movement opposed to the world bourgeoisie,

---

119. Du Bois, *Black Folk*, 264.

120. Du Bois, *Black Folk*, 262, 272.

121. Du Bois, *World Search*, 27. See also José Itzigsohn and Karida Brown, *The Sociology of W. E. B. Du Bois: Racialized Modernity and the Global Color Line* (NYU Press, 2020), 66–67.

which in the need to fulfill the desire for constantly expanding markets "must nestle everywhere, settle everywhere, establish connections everywhere."[122] Du Bois, however, understood that the white working classes did indeed have something more to lose than their chains: the dividends of empire that come from their membership in armed national associations in alliance with industrial imperialists.

---

122. Karl Marx and Friedrich Engels, "Manifesto of the Communist Party," in *Marx-Engels Reader*, ed. Robert Tucker (Norton, 1972), 476, 500.

[CHAPTER FOUR]

"The Voice of Colonial Peoples"
Constructing a Global Majority

> All the plans of the white people are to dominate the world. Just as sure as you do this you cannot have a democracy, you are going to have a paradox of democracy when 50 or 60 millions of people in England are ruling 460 millions of people in India and they do not have voice in the government at all.
>
> W. E. B. Du Bois, "Individualism, Democracy, and Social Control"

In 1944, W. E. B. Du Bois once again left Atlanta University and accepted a new position as director of the Department of Special Research with the National Association for the Advancement of Colored People (NAACP). After leaving the organization a decade earlier over ideological and personal differences, he returned at a somewhat auspicious moment. One of his many reasons for resigning as editor of *The Crisis* in 1934 concerned the NAACP's inattention to the transnational dimension of the race problem: "They will have nothing to do with Africa or the Negroes outside of the United States and I could not agree with them."[1] When he returned as the director of the Department of Special Research, the NAACP—like the larger African American community—had more overtly embraced the anticolonial cause. In his new role, he was tasked with preparing "material to

---

Epigraph: W. E. B. Du Bois, "Reconstruction, Seventy-Five Years After," *Phylon* 4, no. 3 (1943): 212.

    1. Du Bois quoted in Gerald Horne, *Black & Red: W. E. B. Du Bois and the Afro-American Response to the Cold War, 1944–1963* (SUNY Press, 1986), 1, 332. Against Horne, Carol Anderson explores how the NAACP embraced anticolonialism more broadly beyond the period coinciding with Du Bois's return from 1944 to 1948; Carol Anderson, *Bourgeois Radicals: The NAACP and the Struggle for Colonial Liberation, 1941–1960* (Cambridge University Press, 2015). The opening epigraph is from a speech Du Bois gave at Prairie View State College on March 14, 1944; it was not published but is on file in Du Bois Papers, box 198.

be presented to the Peace Conference or Conferences after the close of the war in [*sic*] behalf of the peoples of Africa and other colored groups so as to demand for them an assured status of security and progress in the post-war world."[2] He immediately accepted the offer and went to work researching the global condition of colonial peoples, using this research in his role as a consultant to the US delegation to the United Nations Conference on International Organization (UNCIO) in San Francisco.

In preparation for this task, Du Bois organized a "Colonial Conference" to be held April 6–7, 1945, at the Schomburg Center in Harlem. Prior to the conference, he sent invitations to activists and political leaders living in or near New York to serve as representatives of colonies as well as religious and humanitarian organizations involved in colonial policy.[3] His efforts organizing the conference came on the heels of twenty-five years of organizing the Pan-African conferences. Yet what set the Colonial Conference apart from these earlier conferences was its explicit focus on colonial populations beyond Afro-descendant peoples. Du Bois intended the conference less as a discussion of theory and opinion than as a fact-finding mission to get an accurate picture of the present and of future colonial conditions. In his invitations, he asked participants to bring petitions, resolutions, and manifestos that anticolonial movements had made since World War I. His intention was to publish these documents in a single volume titled "Colonial Demand for Democracy and Freedom in the Twentieth Century." The need for such a volume was evident, Du Bois asserted, in that "most readers and thinkers seem to have no idea that colonial peoples have ever expressed themselves in anything but vague and indefinite terms."[4]

Going into the UNCIO, Du Bois was thus expressly concerned with representing the "voice of colonial peoples" and their demands for democracy and freedom from colonial domination.[5] Yet in his self-conscious effort to act as a representative of colonial peoples on a global scale, he ran into what Lisa Disch refers to as the "constituency paradox," the fact that there was no recognizably coherent and unified constituency he could claim to represent

---

2. Marable, *W. E. B. Du Bois: Black Radical Democrat*, 162, quoting W. E. B. Du Bois to Walter White, 5 July 5, 1944, Du Bois Papers, box 103, p. 1.

3. W. E. B. Du Bois to L. D. Reddick, 8 January 1945, Du Bois Papers, box 108.

4. Du Bois pitched this volume to the MacMillan Company, which responded with a request for the manuscript, which Du Bois failed to provide. See W. E. B. Du Bois to MacMillan Company, 31 January 1945), Du Bois Papers, box 106.

5. W. E. B. Du Bois, "Postwar World Must Heed Voice of Colonial Peoples," *New York Post*, May 4, 1945, 14.

in the first place.⁶ Such efforts to represent colonial peoples entered into a contested discursive terrain and thus operated not simply as a descriptive claim but as a political and rhetorical claim that called that constituency partially into existence. As a result, the boundaries of colonial peoples in both anticolonial movements and international law were necessarily porous rather than a stable referent authorizing anticolonial claims for freedom and self-government. At stake in these debates over the boundaries of colonial peoplehood was whether racism within the United States could be understood in colonial terms. Indeed, figures as contrasting as C. L. R. James, Frantz Fanon, and James Baldwin all expressed serious skepticism.⁷

The contours of the constituency paradox surface in an exchange Du Bois had with one of the invitees to the Colonial Conference, the Baptist minister Harry Emerson Fosdick. An antiwar activist and outspoken proponent of racial equality, Fosdick was also the brother of the diplomat and prominent internationalist Raymond Fosdick. Harry Emerson Fosdick's response to Du Bois's invitation was disheartening, to say the least. Admitting that he had "not the faintest glimmering of an idea concerning what your letter means," Fosdick went on to say that Du Bois's use of the word *colony* had some special significance that evaded the ordinary meaning of the term. Repeating Du Bois's words back verbatim, Fosdick reiterated his confusion, "I cannot get even the dimmest idea as to what you mean by a colony."⁸ Fosdick declined to participate and questioned the value of his presence at the conference. Du Bois responded by enclosing a list of colonial possessions, detailing both raw population statistics and area by square miles "in order that you may realize that seven hundred fifty million people on this earth live in colonies which have rights which no white nation is bound to respect."⁹ Fosdick was skeptical that there was a singular anticolonial constituency to represent before international institutions. To bring anticolonial demands for freedom and democracy before the UN, Du Bois first had to ensure that there was a recognizable constituency to represent. Doing so

---

6. Lisa Disch, "Democratic Representation and the Constituency Paradox," *Perspectives on Politics* 10, no. 3 (2012): 599–616.

7. C. L. R. James, "The Revolutionary Answer to the Negro Problem," in *The Future in the Present: Selected Writings* (Lawrence Hill, 1977), 119–27; Frantz Fanon, *The Wretched of the Earth* (Grove, 2004), 153; James Baldwin, "Princes and Powers," in *Collected Essays* (Library of America, 1998), 143–69.

8. Harry Emerson Fosdick to W. E. B. Du Bois, 11 January 1945, Du Bois Papers, box 105.

9. W. E. B. Du Bois to Harry Emerson Fosdick, 17 January 1945, Du Bois Papers, box 105.

hinged on clearly defining terms such as *colony*, a task made all the more difficult by the inclusion in his definition formal colonies under overt political control of a foreign power as well as quasi-colonial peoples in a condition of second-class citizenship such as African Americans.

As this exchange illustrates, the linguistic and sociological boundaries of *colony* and *colonial peoples* were subjects of debate. In this chapter, I examine how Du Bois navigated these problems of constructing what Nazmul Sultan calls "colonial peoplehood" by focusing on his work in the 1940s with the UNCIO. Yet rather than focus on the "developmental incapacity for political sovereignty" imposed by imperial discourses that prevents colonized populations from claiming rights of democratic rule, I turn to a different problem of colonial peoplehood: that of representing the disconnected claims of self-determination for colonized peoples across imperial jurisdictions in international politics.[10] Through analysis of his writings, speeches, and correspondence in the 1940s, I explore the spatial grammars and rhetorical practices that Du Bois used to constitute an anticolonial constituency to bring before the newly minted institutions of global governance. Specifically, I argue that he exploited the conceptual elasticity of the meaning of *colony* to build a transnational democratic majority on a global scale. The capaciousness of such terms as *colony* and *colonial peoples* allowed Du Bois to connect disparate forms of oppression and economic exploitation across boundaries of race, nation, and empire. In connecting transnational forms of racial and colonial hierarchy, he sought to constitute a transnational and majoritarian constituency to counter the ills of global poverty, colonialism, and international inequality. His objective in this effort was not just to represent a unified set of colonial demands but also to construct a new constituency in international politics that would constitute new forms of political conflict over the colonial question.

In arguing that Du Bois seeks to call into being an anticolonial, transnational constituency, however, I do not mean to suggest he does so de novo. Historians and political theorists have long documented the networks of transnational solidarities—many of which Du Bois himself participated in—that linked African Americans with colonial peoples in a shared struggle for self-determination.[11] Inés Valdez, most significantly, shows how Du Bois,

---

10. Nazmul Sultan, "Self-Rule and the Problem of Peoplehood in Colonial India," *American Political Science Review* 114, no. 1 (February 2020): 81–94.

11. See Bush, *End of White World Supremacy*; Nikhil Pal Singh, *Black Is a Country: Race and the Unfinished Struggle for Democracy* (Harvard University Press, 2005); Hooker, *Theorizing Race in the Americas*; Bill Mullen, *Afro-Orientalism* (University of

in his editorial practices for *The Crisis* in the 1920s and 1930s, constructed a transnational public sphere that attends to "the entanglements between overarching forms of power and local social and political formations" to understand and confront transnational forms of injustice that cut across spheres of domestic and international politics.[12] While Valdez usefully attends to the transnational dimensions of Du Bois's political thinking, she elides the tensions and contestations associated with the paradoxes of representing colonial peoplehood. The task of illustrating how Du Bois theorized forms of transnational solidarity cannot assume the coherence and stability of the constituencies represented in this counterpublic sphere.

As I will reveal, Du Bois faced profound challenges in articulating such anticolonial claims that derived from the prominent place of rearticulated conceptions of national sovereignty in the UN Charter. Embodied in Article 2, liberal norms of noninterference upheld the sovereign state system by casting the claims of oppressed minorities and colonial peoples as residing within the "domestic jurisdiction" of imperial nation-states and thus outside the UN's purview. Thus, any attempt to represent colonial peoples as a transnational constituency confronted the institutional bifurcation of internal state sovereignty and international law, which separated colonial peoples as internal minorities within the sovereign domain of the nation-state rather than as a constituency with connected claims for self-determination. To overcome these constraints, Du Bois rhetorically recast the meaning of "colonial status" and "colonial peoples" by treating distinct forms of colonial domination and dependency as instantiations of an overarching process of global empire. He then demanded that any institutional model of world democracy provide deliberative avenues for the representation of colonial peoples within the decision-making bodies of the UN. In providing a new contextualization of these challenges, I show how engagements with concepts of sovereignty, jurisdiction, democratic majoritarianism, and political representation played out in the evolving spatial contexts of world politics.

Minnesota Press, 2004); Yuichiro Onishi, *Transpacific Antiracism: Afro-Asian Solidarity in 20th-Century Black America, Japan, and Okinawa* (NYU Press, 2013); Nico Slate, *Colored Cosmopolitanism: The Shared Struggle for Freedom in the United States and India* (Harvard University Press, 2017); Minkah Makalani, *In the Cause of Freedom: Radical Black Internationalism from Harlem to London, 1917–1939* (University of North Carolina Press, 2011); Keisha Blain, *Set the World on Fire: Black Nationalist Women and the Global Struggle for Freedom* (Penn Press, 2018); Penny Von Eschen, *Race Against Empire: Black Americans and Anticolonialism, 1937–1957* (Cornell University Press, 1997).

12. Valdez, *Transnational Cosmopolitanism*, 89.

I explore these dynamics in four stages. First, I sketch the outlines of Du Bois's nascent theory of "constructive minorities," developed in a paper for a 1935 conference on minority problems at Howard University. Colonial peoples, when viewed in isolation from the broader world-system of global capitalism, appear as minorities within discrete nation-states or imperial systems created by colonial policies of division and the institutional bifurcation of domestic and international politics. By expanding the scope of racial and colonial conflict beyond the nation-state, constructive minorities might become a transnational majority. The next two sections explore how Du Bois conceptually reworked the meanings of "colonial peoples" and "colonial status" throughout the 1940s and 1950s. I argue that he exploits the conceptual capaciousness of the term *colony* to connect disparate sites of colonial domination and dependency across the domains of disparate imperial formations. By condensing disconnected anticolonial claims into a majoritarian constituency that exceeded nation-state jurisdictions, Du Bois sought to a construct a transnational sense of colonial peoplehood. The fourth section shows how he used the spatial grammars of "human rights" and "minority rights" to contest the bifurcation of domestic and international politics and expand the spatial scale of democracy by placing civil rights struggles in imperial context. I conclude by reflecting on how Du Bois engages in the politics of space and scale by subjecting the background conditions of global democratic practice to critical scrutiny.

Global Majoritarianism and the Theory of Constructive Minorities

While Du Bois's involvement with the founding of the UN in the 1940s represented a unique moment in which he was in position to insert anticolonial claims into extant frameworks of international law, I argue here that much of his strategic vision surfaces in a significant but unpublished essay from 1935 called "A Pragmatic Program for a Dark Minority." Du Bois originally prepared the paper for a conference at Howard University convened by Alain Locke on "Problems, Programs, and Philosophies of Minority Groups" in April 1935.[13] The language of minority status in the conference

---

13. Du Bois, "Pragmatic Program for a Dark Minority," Du Bois Papers, box 213. In 1938, Du Bois unsuccessfully submitted the paper to *Atlantic Monthly* for publication. Despite never being formally published, it illuminates central features of his spatial framework.

title and Du Bois's paper was a clear appropriation of the language of the "minority rights regime" in the League of Nations, a series of bilateral and multilateral treaties providing collective rights of national minorities within Eastern European states after the breakup of the Ottoman and Austro-Hungarian Empires. As Robert Vitalis notes, the language of minority rights slowly emerged in the 1920s.[14] In international law, the strict definition of "national minorities" pertained to "distinct ethnic groups with an individual national and cultural character living within a state which is dominated by some other nationality." Directly invoking the minority rights treaties, however, Locke and other participants at the conference adopted a "looser definition of minorities" delineated by the League of Nations as "any people in any state differing from the majority population in either race, language or religion."[15] This expansive definition of minority status provided participants with a means of placing the problem of domestic racism in the context of international politics.[16]

Echoing this perspective, Du Bois argued in his paper that racial minorities within a nation, such as African Americans, are analogous to both formal colonies that are politically dependent on imperial powers and small nations that remain economically dependent despite formal independence. In doing so, he outlined three distinct global minority populations that shared an interconnected set of challenges in pursuing self-government: (1) formal colonies under the legal control of a foreign power that lack rights of self-rule; (2) small nations that are formally free yet have their political independence conditioned by their economic dependence on foreign capital; and (3) minority groups who face curtailed rights within larger nation-states. Although they face different forms of domination and dependence, these three distinct populations together form what Du Bois called "constructive minorities"—that is, artificially constructed minorities. Far from natural minorities, the lack of power constructive minorities face is an artifact of the spatial construction of politics. Political space, Du Bois implicitly suggests, is not naturally given but is an object of contestation itself. By confining the demands of constructive minorities for economic and

14. Vitalis, *White World Order, Black Power Politics*, 96.

15. Ralph Bunche, "A Critical Analysis of the Tactics and Programs of Minority Groups," *Journal of Negro Education* 4, no. 3 (July 1935): 308–9.

16. Attended by luminaries of the African American intellectual tradition such as Ralph Bunche, philosophers such as Sidney Hook and Horace Kallen, and foreign policy elites including Raymond Leslie Buell, participants addressed a range of topics exploring the tactics that minority groups throughout the world—from African Americans to European Jews to colonial peoples—used to agitate for equal rights.

political equality to domestic politics, colonial powers disconnect these demands through the institutional bifurcation of the domestic and international. Because of the constructed spatial context in which they operate, constructive minorities experience diminished power relative to their imperial masters, who appear as the majority: "they have little or no voice in their own government or the government of the mother country."[17]

Du Bois then outlined three options facing constructive minorities such as African Americans. One option was to seek a "separate national existence" through self-segregation. Another was to seek "eventual inclusion within mother countries" through absorption and assimilation into the majority group. Both options, however, left the underlying spatiality of politics undisturbed. That is, neither separation nor assimilation contest the coordinates of political space to reconfigure the very terrain of struggles for racial equality. A third option was to seek federation, union, and cooperation among the constructive minorities of the world. Du Bois wrote, "Minority groups, colonies and small nations occupy today an anomalous position in the world. Together they form a major part of the world's population. Separately they are dominated by majorities who wield political, economic, and social power over them. Ordinarily, they cannot hope to become majorities."[18] However, by federating with one another and by altering the spatiality of imperial politics, constructive minorities could form a transnational majority. The potential for such a majoritarian strategy is implicit within the hierarchical structure of international order. The further entrenchment of colonial hierarchies, global poverty, and statelessness all lead to the "cumulative numerical increase" of minorities. Based on his theory of constructive minorities, Du Bois envisioned a "new conception of democracy," less as an institutionalized, transnational polity than a means by which artificially separated minorities coalesce into a global majority.[19]

These ways of thinking about the relationship between minorities and majority rule had wide resonance at the Howard University conference. In his paper titled "Making the World Safe for Minorities," the philosopher T. V. Smith wrote, "So much is this so that we must, I believe, come to see the problem of safeguarding minorities as in no small measure the prob-

---

17. Du Bois, "Pragmatic Program for a Dark Minority," p. 1.
18. Du Bois, "Pragmatic Program for a Dark Minority," p. 1.
19. Du Bois, "Pragmatic Program for a Dark Minority," pp. 2, 8.

lem of creating a more democratic majority."[20] Echoing John Dewey in *The Public and Its Problems* (1927), Smith asserted that the problem of creating such a democratic majority was that there were only fractured publics with their own vested interests. There was, in other words, no unified democratic public conscious of itself as what Dewey called a "great community."[21] Until this problem of fragmented publics was resolved, the world would remain unsafe for minorities of any kind. While Smith attributed this view to Dewey, it also had clear resonances with Du Bois's broader imaginary of contested and contingent majoritarianism, which he derived from the journalist Charles Nordhoff. Nordhoff, recall from chapter 1, quipped that the primary duty of the minority was not to obey the will of the majority but to become a majority.

Where Du Bois took a step beyond Dewey and Smith was in imagining this democratic majority as transnational if not global in scope, a popular form of power that would exceed national and imperial boundaries.[22] Rather than an isolated "nation within a nation," African Americans would be part of a transnational majority on a global scale, thus altering the terrain of politics on which civil rights struggles occurred.[23] On this new terrain of politics, constructive minorities would appear as the subject of a form of majoritarian rule that cut across the boundaries of colony and empire, fusing disparate racialized and colonized populations into a single constituency. What is significant in these reflections is the way that majoritarian power on a global scale is determined not just by the demographic power of colonial peoples but also by the political space and scale within which their demands for freedom and democracy are confined. While the notion

20. T. V. Smith, "Making the World Safe for Minorities" (April 13, 1935), box 188, p. 4, Alain Locke Papers (Coll. 164), Moorland-Springarn Research Center, Howard University.

21. John Dewey, "Search for the Great Community," in *The Later Works, 1925–1953*, vol. 2 (Southern Illinois University Press, 1988), 325–50.

22. For Du Bois, this vision had distinct political implications for civil rights struggles within the US. As historian Nikhil Pal Singh puts it, "the world beyond the United States was especially important for blacks at home because it presented the possibility of wider publics—indeed a global majority—who had been denied the historic protections and benefits of nationality"; Singh, *Black Is a Country*, 53. On the global dimensions of Dewey's political thought, see John Narayan, *John Dewey: The Global Public and Its Problems* (Manchester University Press, 2016).

23. W. E. B. Du Bois, "A Negro Nation Within the Nation," *Current History* 42, no. 3 (June 1935): 265–70.

of constructive minorities signaled the sheer numerical force of colonial peoples as a sign of their democratic power, the power of such a global popular majority rested on more than demographic magnitude. As long as colonial constituencies remained insulated and disconnected because of their confinement to the national scale of domestic politics and lack of representation in institutions of global governance, they would fail to realize their numerical power.

Notably, the first two options Du Bois outlined correspond to traditional distinctions in black political thought between integration and separatism, both of which Du Bois juxtaposed with global majoritarianism.[24] His conclusion in favor of global majoritarianism is striking because it comes just a year after he broke with the NAACP for arguing for the self-segregation of African Americans into their own political, economic, and cultural enclaves as a tactic in the civil rights struggle.[25] In his arguments for racial separatism, Du Bois faced persistent criticism not just from racial liberals at the NAACP but also from younger writers such as Bunche and George Streator.[26] Bunche criticized racial separatism as "defeatism in its most extreme form," equating Du Bois negatively with both Zionism and the Garvey movement. For Bunche, the only adequate program for the masses of any minority group was "the hope that can be held out for the betterment of the masses of the dominant group."[27] Put differently, any minority group must side with the dominant working-class majority by aligning their interests, programs, and tactics. While Bunche's criticisms were directed here specifically at Du Bois's advocacy of separatism, they also stand in contrast to the global majoritarianism embedded within the theory of constructive minorities. Where Bunche presumed the boundaries of the dominant majority group and lacked a transnational account, the theory of constructive minorities contested precisely those boundaries. In contrast to Bunche, Du Bois saw any political majority as a contingent albeit durable construction, as an effect of jurisdictional mappings of space rather than as a naturalized background feature of politics. Accordingly, the first duty of any minority group is not to blindly side with the will of the dominant majority but to

---

24. Bernard Boxill, "Two Traditions in African American Political Philosophy," *Philosophical Forum* 24, no. 1 (1992): 119–35; Marable and Mullings, "Divided Mind of Black America," 69–70.

25. Lewis, *W. E. B. Du Bois: A Biography*, 335–38.

26. Vitalis, *White World Order, Black Power Politics*, 93–99.

27. Bunche, "Critical Analysis," 312, 320.

reconfigure the boundaries of that majority by contesting and transforming political space and scale.

Streator, in turn, charged Du Bois's separatist arguments with relying on the mistaken notion that a "minority group can save itself" by insulating itself from global minority struggles. Streator reminded Du Bois "that no one group can pull apart from [the] world economy, no matter how spiritual and resolved."[28] Without attending to their mutual embeddedness in global relations of capitalist exploitation, any program of minority tactics will uphold the imperial order. These criticisms clearly had an impact on Du Bois. Noting the narrowness and provincialism of this vision of self-segregation through economic cooperativism, Bill Mullen detects in this exchange Du Bois clearly "struggling to conceive an international program for economic cooperation."[29] The theory of constructive minorities appears as a partial response to such criticism. While he upheld racial separatism as "a legitimate tool but not as a final end" by the end of the paper, Du Bois argued that global majoritarianism must amend any program of voluntary segregation. Because my concern is less with Du Bois's arguments for or against racial separatism than with his rhetorical construction of colonial peoples, it is beyond the scope of this chapter to fully resolve the tensions between these countervailing features of his thought. As some scholars argue, practices of self-segregation can underlie rather than counteract transnational solidarity.[30] But it is clear here that Du Bois had doubts about the inherent capacity of racial separatism to sustain the creation of constructive minorities as a majoritarian constituency.

What I would tentatively suggest is that Du Bois turned to global majoritarianism because of his pervasive sense that self-determination for minority populations required more than the assertion of sovereignty. Du Bois did not deny the validity of national struggles and clearly upheld the ideal of national self-determination for colonial peoples. Yet he also recognized the limitations of any model of decolonization that fixated on national independence alone. According to Adom Getachew, Du Bois and

---

28. George Streator to W. E. B. Du Bois, April 8, 1935, in Du Bois, *Correspondence of W. E. B. Du Bois*, vol. 2, *1934–1944*, 90.

29. Mullen, *Un-American*, 75–76.

30. Valdez, *Transnational Cosmopolitanism*, 141–47; Hassanzadeh, "Race, Internationalism, and Comparative Political Theory," 536–42; Yuichiro Onishi and Toru Shinoda, "The Paradigm of Refusal: W. E. B. Du Bois's Transpacific Imagination in the 1930s," in *Citizen of the World: The Late Career and Legacy of W. E. B. Du Bois*, ed. Phillip Sinitiere (Northwestern University Press, 2019), 13–36.

other anticolonial figures such as George Padmore likened the structure of imperial domination to enslavement, thus linking the legacy of colonial slavery in the Americas with the new imperialism and neocolonial forms of economic domination.[31] Imperialism, in other words, was an extension of plantation slavery by other means. Although a former colony may attain national independence and end formal imperial control from outside interference, a condition of domination in international order persists as a result of entrenched racial and economic hierarchies that disproportionately distribute rights and obligations. In achieving sovereign independence without a transformation of the international order, formerly colonized nations will run the risk of sliding back toward slavery in the form of deterritorialized modes of economic imperialism. Underneath this formulation of "empire as enslavement" is a complex set of rhetorical claims that capaciously expand the meaning of colonialism to transform global minority populations into a transnational, majoritarian constituency by connecting disparate sites of imperial rule in a single analytic frame.[32]

In this task, one sees the theory of constructive minorities at work in Du Bois's rhetoric and activism in the 1940s. Indeed, the 1944 Colonial Conference itself reflected these attempts to build a global democratic majority. The conference was composed of an "all-star lineup" of anticolonial activists such as Francis Kwame Nkrumah, Kumar Goshal, Maung Saw Tung, Julio Pinto Gandia, and Amy Ashwood Garvey as well as prominent black intellectuals such as L. D. Reddick, Rayford Logan, and W. A. Hunton. By all accounts, in the words of Gerald Horne, it was "a spectacular success and may have been the most significant signpost on the road to anticolonial independence."[33] The primary objective of the conference was to present data about the status and condition of colonial peoples to draw continuities across different colonial situations into a common program of international action. After the presentations, the resolution committee, chaired by the Howard University historian Rayford Logan, selected Du Bois to present petitions demanding rights of self-determination for colonial peoples at the UNCIO in San Francisco two months later.

---

31. Getachew, *Worldmaking After Empire*, chap. 3.

32. Adam Dahl, "Self-Determination Between World and Nation," *Comparative Studies of South Asia, Africa, and the Middle East* 40, no. 3 (2020): 613–20.

33. Horne, *Black & Red*, 28–29. On the influence of the Colonial Conference on postwar anticolonial discourse, see John Munro, *The Anti-Colonial Front: The African American Freedom Struggle and Global Decolonization, 1945–1960* (Cambridge University Press, 2017), 44–48.

One of the more controversial and striking features of the petitions was their call for a "Colonial Commission" composed of all permanent members of the UN Security Council, representatives drawn from the UN General Assembly, and representatives of colonial peoples themselves. Operating under the assumption that colonialism constituted the primary threat to world peace, the petitions demanded that colonial peoples have representation on "an international body established to oversee the transition of peoples from colonial status to such autonomy as colonial peoples themselves may desire."[34] What is crucial in these demands is that participants did not necessarily see a division between the attainment of an independent and autonomous nation-state, on the one hand, and integration into the polity of the imperial mother country with full civil and political rights, on the other hand. The deciding factors were the wishes of colonial peoples themselves, yet both represented viable paths toward self-determination. In either case, participants were clearly skeptical that either solution would materialize without international oversight over the domestic affairs of imperial nation-states.

At first glance a seemingly tepid demand, the resolution harbored a radical challenge to the shape of the new international order, which upheld the sovereign state system and thus insulated the jurisdiction of imperial powers. Sam Klug has argued that the call for a colonial/trustee commission issued most prominently by Du Bois and Logan not only was a pragmatic reaction to the Atlantic Charter but also harbored a distinctive vision of decolonization premised on the anxiety that formal political independence would allow the perpetuation of neocolonial, economic dependence.[35] By placing colonies under an international commission with representation by colonial peoples, political and economic control of colonial territories would be taken from capitalist interests based in foreign nations and placed under international jurisdiction.[36] In making these demands, the petitions clearly drew on the precedent of the Permanent Mandates Commission (PMC) under the League of Nations, which Du Bois sought to extend to all colonial territories after the war. Convinced that postcolonial sovereignty would allow mere political independence, the promise of a universalized mandates commission was to take political control over colonies away not

---

34. W. E. B. Du Bois, "Report of the Department of Special Research, March 12 to April 9, 1945," Du Bois Papers, box 107, p. 2.

35. Sam Klug, *The Internal Colony: Race and the American Politics of Global Decolonization* (University of Chicago Press, 2025), 38–53.

36. Du Bois, "Future of Europe in Africa," 197.

only from European imperial states but also from business and commercial interests. The purpose of an international trustee commission would be, in Du Bois's words, "to develop native institutions for the native's good, rather than continue to allow the majority of mankind to be brutalized and enslaved by ignorant and selfish agents of commercial institutions, whose one aim is profit and power for the few."[37]

I want to suggest an adjacent though distinct reason that Du Bois and Logan called for a trustee commission: specifically, the need they felt for representation of colonial peoples within the UN. Versions of a universalized trustee commission had also been floated by international relations experts such as Raymond Leslie Buell and Henry Luce and by labor organizations on both sides of Atlantic, including the Fabian Society and the Labour Party of the United Kingdom. What distinguished Du Bois and Logan's proposal, however, was their demand that such a trustee commission include native representation and provisions for the right to petition. Here again Du Bois and Logan drew on the legacy of the PMC, which as Susan Pedersen has shown, entailed less the reform of colonial policy than of colonial discourse. "What was new" with the PMC, Pedersen argues, "was the apparatus and the level of international diplomacy, publicity, and 'talk' that the system brought into being." The mandates system was a vehicle for "internationalization"—a process "by which certain political issues and functions are displaced from the national or imperial, and into the international realm."[38] By proliferating discourse over the colonial question, new languages of international law under the League of Nations served as more than mere instruments of European imperial rule. They also provided new frameworks of articulating claims for self-determination in resistance to Western hegemony.[39]

To be sure, the connection between the idea of a trustee commission and the PMC generated significant debate. Francis Kwame Nkrumah, for instance, feared that the resolution drew too heavily on the precedent of the permanent mandates commission under the League of Nations and thus amounted to a "sell out to the colonial powers" that would place the path of self-determination under an international body dominated by those very

37. Du Bois, "To the World," 6.

38. Susan Pedersen, *The Guardians: The League of Nations and the Crisis of Empire* (Oxford University Press, 2015), 4.

39. Arnulf Becker Lorca, *Mestizo International Law: A Global Intellectual History, 1842–1933* (Cambridge University Press, 2014).

powers.⁴⁰ Nkrumah's opposition to the language of the resolutions registers debate about the extent to which the project of self-determination would be a continuation of or a break from the PMC. At both the Colonial Conference and the 1945 Pan-African Congress in Manchester, Nkrumah rejected the establishment of any mandates or trustee commission that would place the path of self-determination under an international body dominated by the imperial powers themselves.⁴¹ Nevertheless, Nkrumah compromised on the Colonial Conference resolutions by approving of the establishment of a colonial commission but rejecting that this should be called a mandates commission that extended the international authority of the League of Nations.

In this context, the insistence of Du Bois and others on a colonial commission reflected the need they perceived for a unified venue where the interconnected claims of colonial peoples could be heard in international institutions. If anticolonial struggles for self-determination were treated as wholly singular, the logic went, they would become subsumed into the domestic jurisdiction of imperial states and thus inscrutable to international oversight and criticism. As a result, they would become disconnected from one another and thus disempowered because they would ultimately be matters of internal sovereignty rather than international law. In this way, Du Bois's commitment to a colonial commission reflected his overarching project of creating a transnational majority out of the constructive minorities of the world. Yet as I show in the last section, the failure of the universalization of the trustee commission ultimately led Du Bois and Logan to turn to a different legacy of the League of Nations: the minority treaties.

Constructing Colonial Peoples

One of Du Bois's central concerns during the 1940s was theorizing the relationship between the legacies of European colonialism and the emerging conception of world democracy embodied in the United Nations. Any attempt to construct a global system of democratic institutions that did not directly address the problem of colonialism was destined for failure. In one

---

40. Horne, *Black & Red*, 29–30.

41. Rayford Logan, "The Historical Aspects of Pan-Africanism, 1900–1945," in *Pan-Africanism Reconsidered*, ed. American Society of African Culture (University of California Press, 1962), 47.

of his seminal speeches on the topic, Du Bois pronounced, "I want to indicate today that because of the colonial situation, democracy is not being practiced among most people; and without worldwide democracy applied to the majority of people, it is going to be impossible to establish a universal peace."[42] Du Bois reiterated that colonialism affects at least one-third of the world's population. When combined with forms of neocolonialism and internal colonialism, colonial peoples constituted a vast majority of the world's population. Any effort to establish world democracy that excluded such an extensive portion of the global demos would necessarily backfire because it left the underlying cause of world war—imperial competition for control of the colonies—unaddressed.

Du Bois's fear about the stillbirth of "worldwide democracy" was not mere conjecture. By failing to address the entwined problems of race and colonialism, the Dumbarton Oaks meeting in 1944—which laid out the initial framework for the UNCIO—all but promised that this political blindness would continue in San Francisco. Echoing language in Chief Justice Roger Taney's majority opinion in *Dred Scott v. Sanford* (1857), Du Bois argued, "There will be at least 750,000,000 colored and black folk inhabiting colonies owned by white nations, who will have no rights that the white people of the world are bound to respect."[43] Without accounting for the legacies of colonialism, the UN would allow a minority of white citizens to rule over a majority of colonial peoples without rights of representation and petition. Du Bois proclaimed, "It may be said that the interests of these colonial peoples will be represented in the world government by the master nations. In the same way it was said in 1787 in the United States that slaves would be represented by their masters."[44] The use of US languages of race and representation to describe the racial and colonial structure of the UN was not incidental. By refusing to grant self-rule to colonial peoples, the UN would replicate the national structure of US *herrenvolk* (master race) democracy at the global level through its domination of the Security Council.

In response to the dilemmas posed by the constituency paradox, Du Bois's conceptions of colonialism and cognate terms such as "colonial status" and "colonial peoples" were constantly shifting, undergoing persistent redefinition to connect sites of colonial domination and dependency across the domains of discrete imperial formations. The meaning of colonialism

---

42. Du Bois, "Colonialism, Democracy, and Peace," 236.

43. Du Bois, "Colonialism, Democracy, and Peace," 248–49.

44. W. E. B. Du Bois, "The Negro and Imperialism," in *W. E. B. Du Bois Speaks, 1920–1963*, 151–52.

for Du Bois and his transnational audience was by no means predetermined. Given the vast array of forms of power and domination that compose the European imperial order, the boundaries of what constituted "colonial peoples" were necessarily porous and open to question. This difficulty of constructing colonial peoplehood is immediately evident in Du Bois's masterwork from the period, *Color and Democracy, Colonies and Peace* (1945). He opened the text with the common critique that he persistently leveled at the Dumbarton Oaks meeting, which left the recurring cause of world war unaddressed; namely, the denial of "the rights of colonial peoples" and interimperial competition for control of colonies. As a consequence, the "brooding residue of colonial problems intertwined with problems of race and color" would mar the UNCIO in 1945. Without addressing this residue, the plan for global democracy designed to end war and instill universal peace would necessarily "preserve imperial power and even extend and fortify it."[45] Institutions of world democracy risked perpetuating imperial hierarchies if they left the underlying colonial issue unresolved.

In coming to discuss this residue more thoroughly, Du Bois posed the fundamental question of his inquiry: "What, then, are colonies? . . . It is difficult to define a colony precisely. There are the dry bones of statistics; but the essential facts are neither well measured nor logically articulated."[46] In attempting to answer his own question, Du Bois suggested that statistics are elusive in defining the meaning of *colony*. For instance, he collected reams of demographic data seeking to discern the size of the formally colonized population, placing it at around 750 million, roughly one-third of the world's total population. To do this, he tabulated demographic data for formally held colonial territories under the world's empires. Another numerical strategy was to account for the disproportion between the ruling class and the ruled in European empires. For example, using approximations, each British subject ruled ten colonial peoples, while each Dutch citizen ruled eight or nine colonials and each French citizen ruled two colonials. The United States was somewhat exceptional as an imperial power because it had six citizens ruling one colonial.

Although a useful starting point, "mere numbers" could not give a full picture of the extent and nature of global colonial hierarchies.[47] To get a full view of the global totality of the colonial situation, Du Bois drew connections between colonial situations across distinct imperial formations to

---

45. Du Bois, *Color and Democracy*, 245–46.

46. Du Bois, *Color and Democracy*, 253.

47. Du Bois, *Color and Democracy*, 274.

establish structural connections and similarities among them. In outlining the condition of the disenfranchised colonies, he proclaimed, "Colonies are the slums of the world. They are today the places of the greatest concentration of poverty, disease, and ignorance of what the human mind has come to know." This analogy of likening social conditions at the periphery of European imperial order to "municipal slums" at the center of metropolitan social order allowed Du Bois to cast colonialism as a global system that cut across conventional bifurcations of center/periphery, Global North/South, and West/non-West.[48] In both cases of urban slums and colonies, he contended, national economies drew their profits from the exploitation, degradation, and poverty of peripheral communities. The position of colonies and quasi colonies in the global capitalist economy resulted in a shared condition of impoverishment, and despite clear discontinuities in colonial situations, colonial peoples shared certain characteristics. "All colonies or quasi-colonies," Du Bois wrote, "do not exhibit these characteristics in the same degree. But colonial peoples are, in the first place, poor; they exhibit a degree of poverty almost unknown in civilized lands except in small depressed classes."[49]

Du Bois's challenge was to construct an understanding of colonialism as a multiplicity of diverse forms of economic dependence and political domination to account for their local specificity, yet also link them together in a global system of rule. In a 1944 lecture in Haiti called "Colonialism, Democracy, and Peace after the War," he opened the speech cueing attention to the capaciousness of colonial discourse. In his use of the word *colonial*, he admitted to investing the term with a wider meaning than is typical in ordinary language: "First of all I am deliberately using the word 'colonial' in a much broader sense than is usually given to it. A colony, strictly speaking, is a country which belongs to another country, forms a part of the mother country's industrial organization, and exercises such powers of government, and such civic and cultural freedom, as the dominant country allows."[50] In its strict meaning, a colony is a people under the legal control of a foreign power.

---

48. Du Bois, *Color and Democracy*, 253. See also Inés Valdez, "Association, Reciprocity, and Emancipation: A Transnational Account of the Politics of Global Justice," in *Empire, Race, and Global Justice*, ed. Duncan Bell (Cambridge University Press, 2019), 120–44; Hassanzadeh, "Race, Internationalism, and Comparative Political Theory," 523–29.

49. W. E. B. Du Bois, "Colonial Peoples and the Two World Wars" (April 26, 1944), Du Bois Papers, box 198, p. 1.

50. Du Bois, "Colonialism, Democracy, and Peace," 229.

Du Bois immediately moved beyond this formal definition to encapsulate a much broader set of dynamics under the rubric of colonialism: "But beyond this narrower definition, there are manifestly groups of people, countries and nations, which while not colonies in the strict sense of the word, yet so approach the colonial status as to merit the designation semicolonial." As examples, he referenced free states in the Balkans, South and Central America, and the Caribbean. Despite formal political independence and a shared sense of national identity, the self-determination of these small nations was impeded by their economic dependence on international trade and foreign investment from industrial powers. They thus comprised "the economic colonies of the owners of a closely knit world of global industry." In formally independent African states such as Liberia and Ethiopia, "there is recognized political independence, and a cultural heritage of varying strength and persistence. But on the other hand in all these cases, the economic dependence of the country on European and North American industrial organization . . . makes the country largely dependent on financial interests and cultural ideals quite outside the land itself."[51] Du Bois then added into the mix African Americans, "who do not form a separate nation and yet who resemble in their economic and political condition a distinctly colonial status."[52] The central difficulty here was the need to draw connections across sites of colonial domination and dependence without collapsing them into each other and erasing important geographic and historical specificities. By at once expanding and disaggregating the meaning of colonial status, Du Bois rhetorically called into existence a more capacious understanding of colonial peoples that attended to their mutual embeddedness in histories of slavery and empire without implying equivalence.

The central question of world peace and international cooperation after the Second World War, for Du Bois, involved the position of colonial and semicolonial peoples in the emerging global order. However, before people can "seek remedies" and construct a new conception of democracy, Du Bois called on his audience to "generalize" and "make comparisons."[53] As we see here, Du Bois's anti-imperial thought challenges how we generalize about colonial situations. Any account of colonial peoples must begin by examining local dynamics of race, inequality, and poverty as manifestations of global processes. In this effort, Du Bois spent the rest of his speech

---

51. Du Bois, "Colonialism, Democracy, and Peace," 233–34.
52. Du Bois, "Colonialism, Democracy, and Peace," 229–30.
53. Du Bois, "Colonialism, Democracy, and Peace," 230.

mapping the interconnected conditions of colonial, semicolonial, and quasi-colonial peoples. What is essential to note in this mapping of colonial peoples is the way he unmistakably drew on his earlier analysis of global minority populations in "A Pragmatic Program for a Dark Minority." He made three broad classifications of colonial peoples: (1) formal *colonial status* marked by political domination; (2) *semicolonial status* marked by economic dependence; and (3) excluded minorities and second-class citizens such as African Americans, what he calls *quasi-colonial peoples* who form part of an "internal colonial system."[54] There is thus a direct link between his theory of constructive minorities and his elastic conceptualization of colonialism.

In particular, the notion of semicolonial status, marked by the combination of formal political independence from and economic dependence on European imperial powers, allowed Du Bois to challenge the neglect of the colonial question at the Dumbarton Oaks meeting and UNCIO. Without addressing the economic legacies of colonial imperialism, small nations such as Haiti, Liberia, and some Latin American states would incorporate into the UN as "free nations which are not free." By integrating these so-called free nations into institutions of global governance without addressing forms of economic imperialism that continue to structure international hierarchy, larger nations and imperial powers would establish "spheres of influence, behind the façade of world organization" and "over the sovereign liberties of their small neighbors." For instance, Du Bois pronounced, "Haiti needs today only freedom from unjustly imposed American debt, and from industrial fetters laid upon her agriculture and commerce, to prove again to the world her ability and progress." Here again, Du Bois insisted that the realization of peace and world democracy demanded the disintegration of political, economic, and cultural hierarchies in international politics. As long as free nations continued to sink into the "spheres of influence" of wealthier imperial powers through debt and foreign investment, they would "succumb into disfranchised colonies," again raising the threat of world war brought on by interimperial competition for colonial control.[55]

Du Bois's attempts to synthesize the disparate demands of semi-, quasi-,

---

54. W. E. B. Du Bois, "Colonial Peoples and the American Negro in the United Nations" (September 25, 1946), Du Bois Papers, box 198, p. 3; W. E. B. Du Bois, "Colonies as a Cause of War" (April 20, 1949), Du Bois Papers, box 199, p. 4.

55. Du Bois, *Color and Democracy*, 283, 285–86.

and colonial peoples into a single rhetorical claim were directed at two audiences. On the one hand, he sought to instill a sense of unity of aims and strategies among global minority populations (i.e., constructive minorities) in a common program of international action, evident in his efforts organizing the 1945 Colonial Conference. On the other hand, he also directed his efforts at peace activists and civil rights activists within the US in an attempt to demonstrate that anticolonialism is central to any vision of world peace and racial equality within the nation. This attempt is clearly reflected in a 1947 speech titled "Human Rights for All Minorities," delivered before Town Hall auditorium in New York at the invitation of the East and West Association. Founded by the novelist Pearl S. Buck, the organization sought to cultivate mutual understanding between the US and Asia and agitate against colonialism and racism after World War II. Yet rather than work through state diplomats, the association adopted a transnational perspective focused on "people-to-people" relationships, direct bonds of solidarity that moved across and against the boundaries of sovereign statehood.[56] Buck had previously praised Du Bois's book *Color and Democracy* for criticizing the Dumbarton Oaks meeting for "ignoring the injustices out of which war will come." In an effort to instill this transnational sensibility, the East and West Association invited Du Bois to speak to its Peoples Congress on "Minority Peoples and Problems: A World View."[57]

In the speech, Du Bois again employed the global majoritarian discourse of "Pragmatic Program" to reconstruct the spatial boundaries of democratic politics. He said that colonial peoples throughout the world cover "a large number of people. Indeed so large that it is fair to say that minorities together form a majority, and the majority is a minority with the power to enforce its will."[58] Echoing the notion of constructive minorities, he continued, the problem is that there is "no logical nor functional unity among these minorities."[59] Du Bois went on, "We know that colonies, as centers of this frustration of democracy, are the starting point of injustice and cruelty toward all groups of people who form minority groups and who at the same time, in a sense, are the majority of the peoples of the world. And they are

56. Robert Shaffer, "Pearl S. Buck and the East and West Association: The Trajectory and Fate of Critical Internationalism," *Peace & Change* 28, no. 1 (2003): 1.

57. Buck quoted in Lewis, *W. E. B. Du Bois: A Biography*, 509. See also Lily Edelman to Du Bois, 31 January 1947, Du Bois Papers, box 113.

58. Du Bois, "Human Rights for All Minorities," 179.

59. Du Bois, "Human Rights for All Minorities," 179.

part of this majority even though unjustly treated minorities do not actually occupy colonial status. Often they occupy quasi-colonial status."[60] In such statements, Du Bois suggested that the sovereign state system itself insulates imperial jurisdictions and issues in a kind of global gerrymandering that constructs the boundaries of colonial constituencies so as to weaken their collective voice, shoring up an archipelago of minority rule within international order. As in the drawing of electoral maps, the gerrymandering of global space entails distorting the spatial distribution of colonial populations to reinforce imperial power structures.[61] In this regard, the unequal integration of colonial peoples that constitutes the imperial world order exercises its power through the construction of spatial jurisdictions formed around sovereign states.[62]

Du Bois's conception of global majoritarianism here hinges on his performative construction of colonial and quasi-colonial status. Within quasi-colonial status, he includes a wide of array of populations beyond those living in formal colonies: "Negroes in the United States who are segregated physically and discriminated against spiritually . . . South American Indians who are laboring peons, without rights or privileges . . . whole laboring classes in Asia and the South Seas who are legally part of imperial countries . . . all these people occupy what is really a colonial status and make the kernel and substance of the problem of minorities."[63] What ties internally colonized minorities together with formal colonies and semicolonial peoples, Du Bois asserted, is the way that poverty produced by global capitalism prevents them from taking "any effective part in democratic procedure." Like small nations that are unable to exercise the full rights of self-determination afforded to formally "free nations," the economic position of internally colonized populations in domestic hierarchies prevents them from exercising the formal rights of suffrage and self-rule. Structurally, internally colonized minorities within the nation are like "little nations within nations, who are encysted and kept from participation in the full citizenship of their native lands."[64] The language of nations within nations

---

60. Du Bois, "Human Rights for All Minorities," 182.

61. I adapt the language of global gerrymandering from Fraser, *Scales of Justice*, 21, 62; and James Tyner, *The Geography of Malcolm X: Black Radicalism and the Remaking of American Space* (Routledge, 2006), 128–40.

62. Getachew, *Worldmaking After Empire*, 18.

63. Du Bois, "Human Rights for All Minorities," 184.

64. Du Bois, *Color and Democracy*, 285.

as "encysted" suggests that they become both confined and concealed as domestic minorities within nation-state hierarchies.

The Temporality of Colonial Peoplehood

Throughout his work at the UN and beyond, this capacious definition of colonialism as comprising both formal colonial and semicolonial status laid the groundwork for Du Bois's understanding of the US as a neocolonial force that expanded through the global spread of purportedly self-regulating markets and liberal democratic institutions.[65] Contesting these newer forms of economic imperialism would be central to the vision of world democracy. As political independence began to spread to formerly colonized countries, there arose new forms of imperial domination spurred by the desire of US capital to dominate world markets. Du Bois wrote in 1948, "There is evident determination on the part of American capital to continue colonial imperialism in the post-war world and even expand it. Can this be accomplished without political control and military domination?"[66] Du Bois clearly captured the distinct form the new colonial order would take. While it might rely less on formal colonial status and explicit political control of colonies, US neocolonialism nevertheless required military domination through an "empire of bases" to enforce international norms that enabled the free circulation of capital.[67]

Du Bois was thus one of the first modern American intellectuals to see how US imperialism supersedes yet nevertheless continues earlier forms of European colonization.[68] US hegemony in the postwar order represented a distinctively neocolonial form of imperialism that operates through the

---

65. See Harry Magdoff, *Imperialism Without Colonies* (Monthly Review Press, 2003).

66. W. E. B. Du Bois, "Colonial Imperialism" (1948), Du Bois Papers, box 273, p. 26.

67. In a 1956 editorial, Du Bois wrote, "Direct political control and military force have in the past marked colonial imperialism. This was finally changed in economic imperialism, which ruled by investment of capital with force of course in the background"; W. E. B. Du Bois, "Colonialism and the Russian Revolution," in *Writings by W. E. B. Du Bois in Periodicals Edited by Others*, vol. 4, 276. See also James Tully, "Lineages of Contemporary Imperialism," *Proceedings of the British Academy* 155 (2009): 3–29; Chalmers Johnson, *The Sorrows of Empire: Militarism, Secrecy, and the End of the Republic* (Metropolitan Books, 2004).

68. John Carlos Rowe, *Literary Culture and U.S. Imperialism: From the Revolution to World War II* (Oxford University Press, 2000).

imposition of liberal democratic institutions and capitalist economic forms on foreign populations. In a 1951 speech on Cold War foreign policy, Du Bois succinctly proclaimed, "Colonialism has not disappeared, even though its back is broken in India and China. But American business is desperately trying to restore the essentials of colonialism under the name of free enterprise and western democracy."[69] Such analyses capture the position of the United States as an emerging imperial power during the postwar reconstruction and a formally anticolonial power, which entailed contradictory commitments to both global equality and global white supremacy. In this regard, the emerging Cold War liberal consensus enabled US ascension to global power by providing a victorious alternative to European fascism and imperialism.[70] For Du Bois, US neocolonialism constituted a deterritorialized form of imperialism forged less through occupation than webs of transnational business relationships, which then found cover in a formally anti-imperial ideology.

By presenting itself in terms of a break with formal imperialism, US hegemony over the postwar, liberal international order ideologically obscured its constitutive imperial inception. Thus, to break through liberal, anti-imperial ideology that masked the neocolonial order, Du Bois provided a deep historicization of imperial forms. Echoing Francis Kwame Nkrumah (who covered similar themes two decades later and coined the term "neocolonialism"), Du Bois argued that the new colonial order led by the US represented, in a sense, the highest stage of imperialism.[71] In the years after his work with the NAACP and the UN, Du Bois developed a stadial understanding of empire and colonialism in which imperial forms progressively developed through successive stages, building on but also dialectically superseding the previous stage. Beyond situating the emergent neocolonial order in the long context of imperial and capitalist expansion, Du Bois's stadial view of colonialism also presented a unified conception of colonial status that accounts for the dialectical entwinement of both continuities and discontinuities in discrete colonial forms across the European imperial order.

To grasp Du Bois's stadial view of colonialism and empire, it is necessary to appreciate how he explicitly drew on the grammars of colonial and semicolonial peoples in Vladimir Ilyich Lenin's analysis of imperialism and

---

69. W. E. B. Du Bois, "Peace Is Dangerous" (September 28, 1951), Speech to the National Council of Arts, Sciences and Professions, Du Bois Papers, box 227, p. 6.

70. Porter, *Problem of the Future World*, chap. 2.

71. Kwame Nkrumah, *Neo-Colonialism: The Last Stage of Imperialism* (International Publishers, 1965).

the broader discourse of the Communist International. In his 1916 theses on national self-determination, Lenin characterized China, Persia (now Iran), and Turkey as "semi-colonial countries," placing them alongside formal colonial entities. Lenin went on to proclaim that socialists must "demand the unconditional and immediate liberation of the colonies without compensation—and this demand in its political expression signifies nothing more nor less than the recognition of the right to self-determination."[72] In a similar manner as Du Bois, Lenin used numerical data to construct a majoritarian program, placing the combined population of semicolonies and formal colonies at one billion. Furthermore, Lenin also saw semicolonial status as a transitional stage in the development of global capitalism toward its highest form. In Lenin's view, the power of finance capital resides in its ability to subject "even states enjoying the fullest political independence."[73] The condition of semicolonial countries illustrated that formal independence from imperial powers did not in and of itself check the power of finance capital from recolonizing free nations. For Du Bois as well, amid one of the most dramatic transformations of international order in the modern world, the condition of semicolonial countries most forcefully indicated the shape that the new world order promised by the UN would likely take. This stadial view of imperialism, however, entailed certain elisions in the construction of colonial peoples. By casting neocolonial forms of economic domination in terms of stages of imperialism, Du Bois's language of colonial peoples risks casting aside dynamics of settler colonialism as being at a lower and less advanced stage of colonialism.

Drawing on this stadial view in a series of speeches throughout the 1950s, Du Bois traced the progressive evolution of successive phases of colonialism from the ancient Greeks and Romans through the twentieth-century neocolonial order. As we saw in the previous section, the constantly shifting meaning of the term *colony* prevented people from settling on a single meaning. In the late nineteenth and twentieth centuries, the conventional

---

72. V. I. Lenin, "The Socialist Revolution and the Right of Nations to Self-Determination: Theses," 1916, Marxists Internet Archive, https://www.marxists.org/archive/lenin/works/1916/jan/x01.htm.

73. V. I. Lenin, *Imperialism, The Highest Stage of Capitalism: A Popular Outline*, chap. 6, 1916, Marxists Internet Archive, https://www.marxists.org/archive/lenin/works/1916/imp-hsc/ch06.htm. See also V. I. Lenin, "Speech of Comrade Lenin," in *The 2nd Congress of the Communist International* ([US] Government Printing Office, 1920), 17. The language of colonial and semicolonial peoples also has precedence in the creation of the League Against Imperialism and Colonial Oppression in 1927. See Vijay Prashad, *The Darker Nations: A People's History of the Third World* (New Press, 2007), 16–30.

meaning of *colony* was a foreign land and population subject to external political control. While the rise of semicolonial status complicated this definition, Du Bois also noted another definition of "so-called colonies" that required reconsideration of the conventional definition of colonial status. Clearly referencing white settler colonies such as Australia, New Zealand, Canada, the United States, and South Africa, these other colonies were "mainly in control of white Englishmen" who came to "obtain self-rule and virtual independence within the Empire." For Du Bois, these "white colonies represented an older idea of colonial status, going back to the Greeks and Romans when groups settled in foreign regions and led independent existence with their own culture."[74]

In this regard, Du Bois argued that modern settler colonies were in key respects modeled on Greek and Roman forms of colonialism. In these ancient forms, he wrote, "a colony at one time was a settlement of immigrants from one nation in the territories of another, bringing with them their own culture, which they sought to impose on invaded land."[75] While the method of dealing with native populations greatly varied—through either subjection and elimination or association and assimilation—the effect was the dominance of what Du Bois calls "migrant masters" who governed themselves and natives through their own institutions. With the rising need for labor, migrant masters in settler colonies transferred slaves from, for instance, northern Europe to Rome or from Africa to Europe or finally, from Africa to America.[76]

After the abolition of the slave trade and slavery in the Americas, Europe then turned to what Du Bois calls "political" or "colonial imperialism" based on the external control of foreign colonies by European imperial administrators. Although the seeds of this form were in the British colonization of India starting in the eighteenth century, its pinnacle was the interimperial order to emerge after the Berlin Conference of 1884–85. Such forms of "colonial imperialism" were distinct from "economic imperialism," which corresponds to his conception of semicolonial status. Throughout the nineteenth century, these constituted two "contradictory conceptions of colonialism." While one was primarily political, the other relied primarily on

---

74. W. E. B. Du Bois, "Colonial Peoples Demand Equal Status" (May 17, 1952), Du Bois Papers, box 202, p. 1.

75. W. E. B. Du Bois, "The Status of Colonialism" (June 18, 1954), Du Bois Papers, box 204, p. 1.

76. Du Bois, "Colonial Peoples Demand Equal Status," 1–2; W. E. B. Du Bois, "Colonialism" (September 20, 1957), Du Bois Papers, box 205, p. 1.

economic control. In their economic form, "colonies were under the control of imperial nations through capital in investment and centralized control of commerce, markets, and prices." As "colonial imperialism" started to unravel with World War I, those agitating for decolonization failed to "realize the changing significance of colonialism in modern times" as colonialism morphed from early notions of colonial imperialism into economic imperialism. Economic imperialism, or "investment imperialism," whose motive was "economic gain" and not "political rule," was quickly replacing colonial imperialism.[77]

This stadial understanding of imperialism not only accounted for the rootedness of neocolonial economic institutions in the long lineage of European imperial dominance but also significantly influenced the way Du Bois constructed his conception of a transnational democratic majority. While he deliberately sought an elastic conception of colonialism to capture the shifting and expanding connections between the colonial status of political imperialism and the semicolonial status of economic imperialism, he also sought to circumscribe his conception of colonial peoples to exclude white settler colonies. In his lists of colonial possessions containing demographic data of colonial populations that he sent to potential participants in the 1945 Colonial Conference, Du Bois excluded "white self-ruling Dominions" from his definition of the British "colonial domain."[78] Likewise, in one of his major editorials on colonialism, he classified "autonomous colonies such as Canada and Australia as Free Nations," thus excluding white settlers in nominal colonial possessions of the British Commonwealth from the definition of colonial peoples.[79]

The political effects of this definition were deliberate and significant. One the one hand, Du Bois sought to prevent his definitions of colonial peoples from becoming a cloak for what L. D. Reddick called "colonial regionalism." Reddick and Du Bois were both particularly concerned with the unification of Rhodesia and the Union of South Africa into a broader "Pan-African" movement that would expand the dominion of white settler colonies.[80]

77. Du Bois, "Status of Colonialism," 3–4.

78. See Du Bois, *Color and Democracy*, 258.

79. W. E. B. Du Bois, "Imperialism, United Nations, Colonial People," *New Leader*, December 30, 1944, 5.

80. L. D. Reddick to W. E. B. Du Bois, April 5, 1945, Du Bois Papers, box 108, folder 4, p. 3. Notably, Reddick insisted that "the interest and welfare of the aboriginal people of Australia be brought within the purview of plans for world peace." This suggestion largely fell on deaf ears, though.

Stretching back into the late nineteenth century, British imperial architects had long called for an imperial federation that would unify Britain with its white Commonwealth possessions, which would then provide a model for world government.[81] The exclusion of white settler colonies from the rubric of "colonial peoples" must therefore be placed in the broader context of greater settler migration to sub-Saharan Africa, which accelerated, in Du Bois's account, through "the attempt of South Africa and the Rhodesias to increase their white population."[82] Without attending to this history of settler colonial visions of empire, any construction of colonial peoples risked reproducing the very racial and imperial hierarchies it sought to dismantle.

This issue of the expansion of white settler populations in Africa cut to the core of the conceptual meaning of "colony" and "colonialism." Many anticolonial leaders had long recognized that the designation "colonial" pertained to white settlers seeking the displacement of indigenous populations. For instance, N. G. Ranga, the leader of the All-Indian Kisan Congress, sought the blessings of Mohandas Gandhi for a "colonial and coloured people's freedom front" that would unite colonial peoples across imperial boundaries. Gandhi responded that while he supported such a movement, the term *colonial peoples* was a poorly chosen expression because *colonial* in the English language "means whites who have emigrated to the colonies."[83] Having reported on this conversation in a *People's Voice* column from 1948, Du Bois clearly realized that his appropriation of the language of "colonial peoples" as the name of this transnational constituency had to counteract the linguistic meaning of *colony* as a political body of white settlers who carried their sovereignty to new lands.[84]

On the other hand, by presenting white settler colonialism as a distant imperial form superseded by more advanced forms of economic imperi-

---

81. Mark Mazower, *No Enchanted Place: The End of Empire and the Ideological Origins of the United Nations* (Princeton University Press, 2009); Duncan Bell, *Dreamworlds of Race: Empire and the Utopian Destiny of Anglo-America* (Princeton University Press, 2020); Jeanne Morefield, *Empires Without Imperialism: Anglo-American Decline and the Politics of Deflection* (Oxford University Press, 2014).

82. Du Bois, "African Roots of Peace" (1948), unpublished manuscript, Du Bois Papers, box 214, p. 3.

83. Gandhi quoted in Peter Abrahams, "The Colonial and Coloured People's Freedom Front" (1945), box 81, p. 236, W. E. B. Du Bois Collection, Franklin Library Special Collections and Archives, John Hope and Aurelia E. Franklin Library, Fisk University.

84. W. E. B. Du Bois, "Pan Africa" (March 8, 1948), Du Bois Papers, box 218.

alism, Du Bois excluded indigenous peoples within settler colonies from his construction of colonial peoples. In some ways, this exclusion is understandable. It was not until the 1960s with intellectuals such as Vine Deloria Jr. and George Manuel that indigenous movements in the Americas drew explicit solidarities with third world decolonizing movements.[85] Nevertheless, this elision presents the tensions implicit in any attempt to build a global constituency aimed at decolonizing international order. Although Du Bois nominally included Indians in the Americas within his understanding of "colonial peoples," it was often as a laboring mass of workers exploited by capitalist powers rather than as land-based nations divorced from the territorial foundations of their societies. Furthermore, in his stadial account of colonialism, Du Bois presents settler colonialism as a past-tense injustice superseded by more advanced forms of dependence and domination characteristic of both political and economic imperialism. In this way, he reverses Patrick Wolfe's well-known characterization of settler colonialism as a structure and not an event.[86] For Du Bois, the settler phase of European imperialism is a historical event rather than an ongoing structure of power.

Human Rights, Minority Rights, and the Problem of "Domestic Jurisdiction"

Throughout his activism with the NAACP in the 1940s, Du Bois advocated three measures that he deemed essential for the United Nations to address the colonial question. First, he demanded the "representation of the colonial peoples alongside the master people" in the UN General Assembly. He deliberately left open the question of whether colonial peoples would have an equal vote or merely the right to petition the assembly, but he was adamant that the lack of colonial representation would reproduce the logics of herrenvolk representation in the US Constitution, where masters represented slaves. Second, he called for the establishment of a "colonial commission" under either the Security Council or the Economic and Social Council

---

85. David Temin, *Remapping Sovereignty: Decolonization and Self-Determination in North American Indigenous Thought* (University of Chicago Press, 2023).

86. Patrick Wolfe, "Settler Colonialism and the Elimination of the Native," *Journal of Genocide Research* 8, no. 4 (2006): 387–409. This point adds a different layer to Kevin Bruyneel's recent critique of the settler colonial dimensions of *Black Reconstruction*. See Kevin Bruyneel, *Settler Memory: The Disavowal of Indigeneity and the Politics of Race in the United States* (University of North Carolina Press, 2021), 45–75.

with defined powers to investigate complaints and petitions brought to the General Assembly and to enforce economic, social, and political standards in the administration of the colonies. In calling for "the international trusteeship" of colonial peoples, Du Bois's proposal in some ways mimicked the mandate system under the League of Nations. The difference was in his view that trusteeship extend to all colonies beyond those of the Axis powers. Third, he demanded that each imperial power make a clear statement of its intentions and plans "gradually but definitely . . . to raise the peoples of colonies to a condition of complete political and economic equality with the peoples of the master nations," either through the eventual incorporation of colonial peoples into "the polity of the master nations" or through independence.[87]

The ultimate objective of these proposals was to ensure representation and equal voice of colonial peoples in international institutions. But as I will show in this section, these demands for the representation of colonial peoples were thwarted by international discourses of "domestic jurisdiction" that separated national and international law. The effect was both to exclude colonial peoples from international institutions and to dilute the majoritarian power of anticolonial forces in international politics. In "A Pragmatic Program for a Dark Minority," Du Bois noted the difficulty of achieving minority rights: "No disadvantaged minority can successfully use force against a determined majority."[88] For this reason, he called for a form of "inter-minority unity" that would establish solidarity among global minority populations.[89] Du Bois's specific objective in redefining "colonialism" and "colonial peoples" in this more capacious way reflects a distinct spatial strategy aimed at raising the civil rights struggle from a national to a global scale through the construction of a transnational majority. By seeking to establish interminority unity, he contested and reconfigured the spatiality of democracy by disrupting settled distinctions between domestic and international politics. With rights of representation and petition before the General Assembly, colonial and quasi-colonial peoples would

---

87. Du Bois, *Color and Democracy*, 328–29; Du Bois, "Imperialism, United Nations, Colonial People"; W. E. B. Du Bois, "World Peace and the Darker Peoples" (June 1945), Du Bois Papers, box 108, p. 2; W. E. B. Du Bois, "Petition for a World Government" (January 9, 1946), Du Bois Papers, box 111, p. 1; W. E. B. Du Bois, "Colonial Conference Resolution" (April 6, 1945), Du Bois Papers, box 107.

88. Du Bois, "Pragmatic Program for a Dark Minority," 11.

89. Du Bois, "Human Rights for All Minorities," 1.

be making demands on the UN not as isolated groups but as an emerging global majority.[90]

Yet these efforts to construct such an anticolonial constituency were further impeded by Article 2, Paragraph 7 of the UN Charter, which institutionalized liberal norms of noninterference in the domestic jurisdiction clause. Article 2 stated that nothing "contained in the present Charter shall authorize the United Nations to intervene in matters which are essentially within the domestic jurisdiction of any state."[91] The domestic jurisdiction clause was largely the work of John Foster Dulles, who, as a senior advisor to member of the US delegation Senator Arthur Vandenberg, expressed concern that integrating human rights language into the UN Charter would subject the Southern United States to international scrutiny and alienate Southern Democrats. After a statement guaranteeing freedom from discrimination based on race made its way into the charter, Dulles lobbied for the addition of the domestic jurisdiction clause. This clause incensed Du Bois, who thought it jeopardized the integrity of the charter and was an instance of the South exercising its muscle in shaping the new global order in its image.[92] In a sense, it entailed the creation of a global herrenvolk democracy. Despite Du Bois's protestation, Dulles and other imperial powers insisted that human rights language could enter the UN Charter only if it accompanied the clause. In support of the domestic jurisdiction clause, colonial powers such as Britain, France, and Belgium similarly contended that allowing for representation of colonial peoples would constitute a violation of their national sovereignty.[93]

NAACP consultants such as Du Bois and Walter White embraced varied responses. White believed that because the great powers had approved the domestic jurisdiction clause, eliminating it altogether was not a possibility. In response, he advocated a pragmatic approach of clarifying and

---

90. To clarify, my argument is not simply that more numbers would automatically result in more power but that the creation of a transnational constituency would produce a different kind of politics. Du Bois hoped that it would shift the terrain of global politics by taking questions of race and colonialism out of the domestic jurisdiction of imperial nation-states and into the sphere of international law.

91. Walter White, memorandum to Roy Wilkins (May 14, 1945), Du Bois Papers, box 107, p. 1.

92. On Southern influence over US foreign policy in the 1940s, see Ira Katznelson, *Fear Itself: The New Deal and the Origins of Our Time* (Norton, 2014).

93. Carol Anderson, *Eyes Off the Prize: The United Nations and the African American Struggle for Human Rights, 1944–1955* (Cambridge University Press, 2003), 48–50.

expanding what precisely constitutes a "domestic matter."[94] Du Bois took a more radical route by contesting not so much the "boundaries of the international," in Jennifer Pitts's words,[95] but the boundaries between the international and the domestic, issuing an alternative statement to the UNCIO that he advocated in place of the domestic jurisdiction clause:

> The colonial system of government, however deeply rooted in history and custom, is today undemocratic, socially dangerous and a main cause of war. The United Nations recognizing democracy as the only just way of life for all people should make it a first statute of international law that at the earliest practical moment no nation nor group shall be deprived of effective voice in its own government. An international colonial commission on which colonial peoples shall have representation should have power to investigate the facts and implement this declaration under the Security Council.[96]

From Du Bois's perspective, the liberal norm of noninterference embedded in Article 2 had perverse effects, which shielded imperial powers from criticism by relegating colonial questions to internal matters of domestic concern. For Du Bois, Article 2 of the UN Charter directly contradicted Articles 1 and 73. Article 73 upheld the rights and well-being of non-self-governing territories as well as the obligations of UN members to ensure just treatment of colonial peoples under trust obligations, while Article 1, Paragraph 3 similarly linked the task of "international cooperation" with the promotion of respect for "human rights and for fundamental freedoms for all without distinction as to race, sex, language, or religion."[97]

The language of human rights entered the UN Charter primarily under the advocacy of the prime minister of the Union of South Africa, Field Marshal Jan Smuts, whose plea for the inclusion of human rights language struck Du Bois as "an extraordinary and confusing paradox." The fact that

---

94. White, memo to Wilkins.

95. Jennifer Pitts, *Boundaries of the International: Law and Empire* (Harvard University Press, 2018), 184–86.

96. W. E. B. Du Bois, "Winds of Time," *Chicago Defender*, July 9, 1947, in Du Bois Papers, box 216, p. 2.

97. "Memorandum to Edward Stettinius (May 7, 1945)," in *The Correspondence of W. E. B. Du Bois*, vol. 3, *1944–1963*, ed. Herbert Aptheker (University of Massachusetts Press, 1978).

the domestic jurisdiction clause in Article 2 directly followed the appeal to human rights in Article 1 only exacerbated this paradox. By upholding the norm of noninterference, the domestic jurisdiction clause effectively nullified the gesture toward human rights and self-determination made in Articles 1 and 73. In an article for a proposed (though unpublished) volume edited by L. D. Reddick called "A World View of the Negro Question," Du Bois warned that these paradoxes would bring the "United Nations under the control of the colonial powers [by preserving] the colonial system." Accordingly, the UNCIO was not a step toward peace and freedom, but a leap "backward toward war and slavery."[98] The root cause of the massive disenfranchisement of colonial and quasi-colonial peoples was the UN Charter's insistence that "international organization cannot interfere with 'domestic matters' such as colonies" and racial disenfranchisement unless in immediate cases of the threat of war.[99]

The domestic jurisdiction clause thus placed Du Bois's rhetorical claims to represent colonial peoples in a precarious position. As a racialized subject within the United States, he lacked standing to petition for the rectification of human rights abuses and other colonial injuries. In navigating this dilemma, he appropriated and recoded the meaning of extant discourses of international law such as "human rights" and "minority rights" to contest the bifurcation of international law and internal state sovereignty. This spatial strategy most vividly surfaces in perhaps his most radical and lasting legacy from this period, his authorship and editorship of *An Appeal to the World! A Statement on the Denial of Human Rights to Minorities in the Case of Citizens of Negro Descent in the United States of America and an Appeal to the United Nations for Redress* (1948). As editor, Du Bois wrote the introduction and curated a series of sociolegal studies documenting the extent of racial discrimination in the United States. Submitted to the Human Rights Council (HRC) in October 1947, the *Appeal* fed into broader anxieties on the part of dominant powers regarding the preservation of imperial state sovereignty. US officials such as Senator Tom Connally, chair of the Senate Foreign Relations Committee, worried that accepting petitions demanding

---

98. W. E. B. Du Bois, "Colonies and Peace" (December 7, 1945), Du Bois Papers, box 229, pp. 1, 13–14.

99. Du Bois, Supplementary Statement to *Color and Democracy, Colonies and Peace* (June 5, 1945), Du Bois Papers, box 219, p. 1. On these contradictions, see Thomas Borstelmann, *The Cold War and the Color Line: American Race Relations in the Global Arena* (Harvard University Press, 2001).

human rights from nonstate peoples would subject the US South to international investigations.[100] Directly invoking the domestic jurisdiction clause, Smuts objected to a similar petition brought by the Indian delegation charging South Africa with human rights violations as an act of international intervention.[101]

By invoking the notion of human rights, the *Appeal* intervened in these debates about domestic jurisdiction in two ways. First, it cast civil rights as a human rights issue to be resolved through international intervention. In appealing "to the peoples of the world" rather than to the nation, Du Bois cued attention to the spatial scope of his audience: "It may be quite properly asked at this point to whom a petition and statement such as this should be addressed?"[102] In posing this question, he rejected the notion that the petition involved a domestic question of internal concern best addressed to a national citizenry. Instead, he insisted that race in the United States is not a domestic problem but has implications for world order. Insofar as it connects to the legacies of European imperialism, it directly impinges on the question of international cooperation and world peace. As a result, "an internal and national question becomes inevitably an international question and will in the future become more and more international, as the nations draw together."[103] Because of global interconnection, "discrimination practiced in the United States against her own citizens and to a large extent a contravention of her own laws, cannot be persisted in, without infringing upon the rights of the peoples of the world."[104] In this way, the failures of US democracy are not of mere provincial concern. Rather, they jeopardized broader ideals of world peace.

Second, the *Appeal* was not simply a petition to the higher authority of international law for redress of grievances. Rather, it exposed the contradictions of a founding document of international law itself in adequately providing for human rights. In doing so, it revealed the UN as a mechanism

---

100. C. Anderson, *Eyes Off the Prize*, 3; Brenda Gayle Plummer, *Rising Wind: Black Americans and U.S. Foreign Affairs, 1935–1960* (University of North Carolina Press, 1996), 183.

101. Leland Goodrich, "United Nations and Domestic Jurisdiction," *International Organization* 3, no. 1 (1949): 23–24.

102. Du Bois, *An Appeal to the World! A Statement on the Denial of Human Rights to Minorities in the Case of Citizens of the United States of America and an Appeal to the United Nations for Redress* (NAACP, 1947), 12.

103. Du Bois, *Appeal to the World!*, 13.

104. Du Bois, *Appeal to the World!*, 13.

of continued colonial rule. Du Bois's attempt to connect racial injustice domestically with colonial injustice abroad was part of a broader framing of the United States as an imperial force on par with other European colonial empires such as France, Belgium, and Britain. Like these other colonial empires, the US had deprived millions of quasi-colonial peoples in the South of any effective voice in government in order to maintain control over labor and industrial production. Because of Southern control stemming from countermajoritarian institutions such as the Senate and the disenfranchisement of black voters, the federal government had "continually cast its influence with imperial aggression throughout the world and withdrawn its sympathy from the colored peoples and from the small nations." The US had thus become "part of the imperialistic bloc which is controlling the colonies of the world."[105] Therefore, black disenfranchisement in the South was not an isolated injustice. It was one element in a broader interimperial order whereby European powers perpetuated domination through control of international institutions. Alongside other imperial powers, the United States professed democracy with one hand but denied it to millions of people with the other.

More than just a challenge to nation-state sovereignty, the *Appeal* challenged the liberal international order itself and the authority of the UN to the extent that it relied on the norm of noninterference that bifurcated domestic and international spheres. In appealing to the world, Du Bois did not simply present a case before a free society of nations. He illuminated how the basic norms of international society embodied in the UN Charter perpetuated colonial domination. In other words, he did not make an appeal to an otherwise neutral international society. He illuminated how liberal norms of global governance disconnected minority struggles through the artificial separation of domestic and international politics.[106] For international society to act on Du Bois's *Appeal*, it would need to restructure its constitutive norms, principles, and procedures. The *Appeal* was not simply an attempt to bring global public opinion to bear on domestic practices of racial discrimination, to air the "dirty laundry" of the United States before global sentiment so as to expose the hypocrisy of US democratic ideals.[107]

---

105. Du Bois, *Appeal to the World!*, 11.

106. For further elucidation of this argument, see Adam Dahl, "Appealing to the World: Du Bois and the Transnational Politics of Petition," *South Atlantic Quarterly* 123, no. 3 (July 2024): 485–503.

107. Valdez, *Transnational Cosmopolitanism*, 109–10.

It was also an attempt to use the problem of exclusion within the United States as a vehicle for the transformation of global governance.

In this effort, Du Bois and his coauthors explicitly appropriated the language of "minority rights" surrounding the drafting of the 1948 Universal Declaration of Human Rights. Here again, the discourse of minority rights aided the authors of the *Appeal* in contesting the circumscribed spatial jurisdiction ossified by Article 2 of the UN Charter. As if to recognize its potential power, US officials deeply opposed the language of minority rights. In response to calls from the Soviet Union to establish a Subcommission on the Protection of Minorities, the US State Department sought to restrict the expansive meaning of "minority" to exclude African Americans from their purview.[108] Alongside this strategy of restricting the definition of minority status, State Department officials sought to deprive the Human Rights Commission (HRC) of authority to review petitions from "individuals and groups throughout the world protesting against wrongs."[109] Eleanor Roosevelt, who served as chairperson of the HRC and as a board member of the NAACP, openly criticized the idea of a right to petition, warning that any self-defined minority group "could get its case before the United Nations in spite of its own government."[110] If nonstate minorities had the right to petition, the argument went, they would inundate the UN with complaints regarding US human rights abuses, undermining its projected image as a democratic exemplar and moral leader in the international realm.

Yet when the General Assembly conducted its first meeting in January 1946, over one thousand petitions had been submitted by nongovernmental organizations regarding minority rights. Du Bois's petition was thus not a singular appeal to the United Nations to address racial injustice within the United States. It was part of a broader majoritarian strategy of building a transnational constituency and inserting these representative claims into official UN discourse.[111] Yet a key problem with this strategy was the restriction of representation to member states, which left nonstate minorities confined within the shackles of domestic jurisdiction and reliant on semicolonial countries with representational standing in the UN. In particular, Du Bois praised the Indian delegate and sister of Jawaharlal Nehru, Vijaya Lakshmi

---

108. Quoted in C. Anderson, *Eyes Off the Prize*, 74–75.

109. Quoted in C. Anderson, *Eyes Off the Prize*, 78–79.

110. Quoted in C. Anderson, *Eyes Off the Prize*, 87.

111. Plummer, *Rising Wind*, 170. See also Emma Stone Mackinnon, "Declaration as Disavowal: The Politics of Race and Empire in the Universal Declaration of Human Rights," *Political Theory* 47, no. 1 (2019): 65.

Pandit (who was also invited to the Harlem Colonial Conference), for her attack on Jan Smuts in the UN General Assembly for his opposition to a declaration against discrimination against Indians in South Africa. Pandit's actions garnered further praise when she extended her support to indigenous peoples in South Africa and to an assault on the color line more broadly. Lamenting the failure of semicolonial countries such as Haiti, Liberia, or Ethiopia to similarly speak up, Du Bois directed attention to the paradox that minority peoples within the United States were reliant on Indian delegates for voicing such concerns, a paradox that stemmed from a representational schematic revolving around state sovereignty: "Many American Negroes will ask how it happened that the Negroes of the world had to be defended by an Indian, while the rest of the colored world was apparently silent."[112]

What is notable in the broader debates about the definition of minority status is that the language of minority rights was largely an element of international legal discourse. The idea of a "minority rights regime" internal to the nation-state would not emerge until the 1960s.[113] Thus, when Du Bois's *Appeal* evokes "the denial of human rights to minorities" in the US, we should understand this language of minority status not in the domestic sense as an ethnic or racial minority seeking strictly equal rights within the nation but as a minority group that stands under the jurisdiction of international law. The turn to the language of "minority rights" in the *Appeal* is perplexing and virtually unnoticed by commentators. As Mark Mazower has explained, the UN's commitment to human rights was directly linked to its efforts to abandon the minority rights regime under the League of Nations. Although the Covenant of the League of Nations did contain a weaker version of the domestic jurisdiction clause, the minority rights regime allowed nonstate minorities to bring petitions forward and did at least allow for the theoretical possibility of internal intervention into member states.

In key respects, the triumph of the language of "human rights" over "minority rights" signaled the calcification of nonintervention in norms and institutions of global governance.[114] Yet in reassociating the two, Du Bois and his collaborators self-consciously turned to the older language of minority

---

112. Du Bois, "Winds of Time," *Chicago Defender*, December 30, 1946, in Du Bois Papers, box 216, p. 1.

113. John Skrentny, *The Minority Rights Revolution* (Belknap Press of Harvard University Press, 2002).

114. Mark Mazower, "The Strange Triumph of Human Rights, 1833–1950," *Historical Journal* 47, no. 2 (2004): 379–98.

rights to internationalize the problem of racial discrimination and to contest the authority of the domestic jurisdiction clause. In the sixth chapter of the *Appeal*, on "The Charter of the United Nations and its Provisions for Human Rights and the Rights of Minorities," Rayford Logan provided perhaps the clearest expression of this understanding of minority rights in international law. Based on his expertise on the operation of the mandates system in Africa, Du Bois tapped Logan as an ideal candidate to clarify both the duty and the power of the United Nations to ensure the rights of African Americans. Logan gladly accepted the charge to write the final and most important chapter of the *Appeal*, but he soon ran into obstacles. While Logan was confident that the UN had a clear duty to address racial discrimination, he confessed that he was having difficulty determining whether it actually had the power to correct the situation. The primary obstacle in doing so was the domestic jurisdiction clause of the UN Charter. At first, Logan proposed a revision of the tone and objective of the petition to focus on revising the charter.[115] By the time he finished a draft of the chapter, however, he arrived at another strategy for circumventing the constraints imposed by the domestic jurisdiction clause. Instead of requesting a revision of the UN Charter, he turned to precedents in international law that granted global governing bodies the authority to intervene and protect minority rights.

Based on his research, Logan determined that provision in international law for the protection of minority rights is a relatively modern phenomenon. He traced the first instances of minority rights in international agreements to the Treaty of Berlin (1878), which provided for the protection of Jews in Romania in the wake of the Russian defeat of the Ottoman Empire in the Balkans. Although the minority rights provision lacked enforcement, it did establish precedent followed by the League of Nations. After the Treaty of Versailles, the allied powers imposed "minority treaties" on Poland, Czechoslovakia, Yugoslavia, Austria, Bulgaria, and Hungary, among others, that took steps to protect the rights of ethnic and religious minorities after the collapse of the Ottoman and Austro-Hungarian Empires. Distinct from the Treaty of Berlin, however, the League of Nations assumed the authority to enforce the treaties and affirmed the right of any member to file petitions calling attention to violations of the treaties. Broadly construed, the petitioning provision extended to minority groups not directly represented by state interests in the league. Logan asserted, "This right of petition to a principal organ of the international machinery for the maintenance of peace and

---

115. W. E. B. Du Bois to Raymond Logan, October 1, 1946; Raymond Logan to W. E. B. Du Bois, October 12, 1946; both in Du Bois Papers, box 110.

security must be, at the very least, maintained."[116] Although the turn to the language of minority rights in the treaties was an anachronistic albeit politically generative move, in Logan's eyes it provided meaningful precedent to justify the power of the UN to address domestic abuses and the rights of minorities to petition international legal bodies.[117]

By framing the *Appeal* in the language of minority rights, Du Bois and Logan further contested the bifurcation of international order and internal state sovereignty embodied in the UN Charter, which reinforced the American assumption that race was a "static problem and had nothing to do with the dynamic development of the world."[118] In utilizing the language of minority rights, they reframed black struggles for equality by drawing an analogy with national minorities, stateless peoples, and colonial peoples similarly struggling for rights of citizenship and self-determination. In so doing, they further framed the oppression of African Americans as a form of colonial domination connected to broader claims for freedom and democracy posed by transnational, anticolonial constituencies.[119] The languages of minority rights and human rights comprised a set of spatial grammars that not only exposed the entanglement of national and international politics but also allowed Du Bois to unsettle the division of these two political spheres. Yet it is important to note that this strategy was defeated through the machinations of the UN Secretariat, the HRC, and the US State Department. By 1949, after the defeat of the *Appeal* and countless other anticolonial petitions, Du Bois would chide the UN and its "bumbling formulas on human rights" for denying "the wretched even the right to complain."[120] Du Bois thus ran up against the fact that, as Emma Stone Mackinnon puts it, "the promise of human rights was very much a promise made by nations."[121]

---

116. Rayford Logan, "The Charter of the United Nations," in Du Bois, *An Appeal to the World!*, 86.

117. Logan significantly exaggerated the capacities of the League of Nations to enforce the treaties. See Hannah Arendt, *The Origins of Totalitarianism* (Harcourt, 1976), 269–90.

118. W. E. B. Du Bois, "Is It Democracy," 5.

119. Porter, *Problem of the Future World*, 89–96.

120. Du Bois, "Colonies as a Cause of War," 7.

121. Mackinnon, "Declaration as Disavowal," 74. Here I would agree with Samuel Moyn's point that Du Bois's use of the language of human rights was perhaps a "second-best strategy," but I would maintain that this dismisses the theoretical significance of his attempt to reassociate human rights and minority rights in order to contest the juridical bifurcation imposed by the domestic jurisdiction clause. See Samuel Moyn, *The Last Utopia: Human Rights in History* (Harvard University Press, 2010), 93–107.

The Politics of Space and Scale

This criticism mounted against the UN stands in stark contrast to previous statements Du Bois made five years earlier when he proclaimed, "The United Nations is the greatest hope of abolishing colonialism and thus abolishing poverty in the world."[122] By clarifying the problems and paradoxes posed to Du Bois's transnational anticolonialism by the UN Charter, I hope to have thrown into sharper relief the significance and novelty of his alternative vision of the UN as an anticolonial force. It would be easy to read his turn against the UN as evidence of the failure of this vision, but there is a real sense in which the promise of his strategic interventions did come to belated and partial fruition. Between 1955 and 1961, as a result of decolonization, the UN General Assembly admitted thirty-nine new member states, and over the course of the next decade, it admitted thirty-three more, making formerly colonized peoples a majority-voting bloc.[123] Throughout the 1960s and into the 1970s, the UN General Assembly remained an important source of power for former colonial countries. While the UN was, as Adom Getachew notes, "a quintessentially American creation that sought to institutionalize a liberal international order," it became within twenty years of its founding an important instrument that anticolonial actors seized to pursue economic and political projects of decolonization.[124] The ability to utilize these instruments of international order rested on the consolidation of a global majority within the General Assembly.

Yet rather than close this chapter by calling for a recovery of Du Bois's alternative vision of the UN, I want to focus on the way his engagements prompt contextual attention to the politics of space and scale. For Du Bois, space and scale are not a priori features of politics and political reflection. Rather, the space and scale of democracy are themselves objects of political debate, disagreement, and contestation. Struggles for racial equality involved contesting multiple and overlapping jurisdictional boundaries of political authority at the local, national, and international levels. These scalar levels entailed distinct kinds of politics, each with their own limitations and possibilities. This strategy of contesting the space and scale of

---

122. W. E. B. Du Bois, "The United Nations and Colonies" (June 26, 1944), box 1, p. 1, W. E. B. Du Bois Papers (Sc MG 109), Schomburg Center for Research in Black Culture, New York Public Library.

123. Mazower, *Governing the World*, 258–59.

124. Getachew, *Worldmaking After Empire*, 178.

democracy was a persistent feature of his political thought stretching back to his involvement with the Niagara movement in the early 1900s, when he outlined a civil rights strategy focused on expanding the scope of racial struggles from state and local to national levels. He thus engaged in a "politics of space and scale" in which the spatial orientation of civil rights was not pregiven but was a deliberate object of political struggle.[125]

While they are ultimately inseparable, it is helpful to distinguish between the spatial and the scalar dimensions of Du Bois's transnational democratic practice. Spatially, Du Bois was concerned with the boundaries of particular political constituencies that claim representation in shifting institutional settings. As we have seen, he figured himself as a representative of colonial and quasi-colonial peoples before the UN and self-consciously navigated the constituency paradoxes of democratic representation in institutions of global governance. To assert a claim for the representation of colonial peoples at the UN, Du Bois had to construct a coherent constituency out of disparate forms of colonial domination. Yet his redefinition of colonialism to account for quasi-colonial status and semicolonial forms of economic dependence was not simply a sociological task. It was an expressly political task of working through the paradoxes of representing colonial peoples. Put another way, Du Bois was not just seeking a sociological description of colonial peoples through the tabulation of demographic data. Rather, he sought to call into being a transnational constituency out of the global conditions of colonial domination and dependence by linking the structural features of diverse colonial situations in a single set of representative claims. The effect was to transform the terrain of politics and expand the scope of political conflict, radically contesting the domestic jurisdiction of the nation-state over questions of racial and colonial domination.

In key respects, this spatial strategy of constructing a transnational democratic majority was a precondition for the scalar strategy of expanding struggles against racial and colonial domination from the national to the international. Du Bois enacted this scalar move by contesting the discourse of "domestic jurisdiction" and reassociating the international legal discourse of minority rights and human rights. In contesting national authority over the race question and shifting the political terrain to international institutions, Du Bois engaged in a practice of "scaling democracy," a thorough politicization of the processual level of engagement (e.g., local, national,

---

125. Robert W. Williams, "Politics, Rights, and Spatiality in W. E. B. Du Bois's 'Address to the Country' (1906)," *Journal of African American Studies* 4, no. 3 (September 2010): 337–58.

international) at which democratic politics occurs. This politicization of scale is itself a feature of democratic politics. As Thea Riofrancos puts it, questions concerning the "appropriate scale of democracy and its collective subject" cannot be resolved through theoretical norms or institutional design. They are resolved only through power, conflict, and contestation.[126] In his attempts to construct an anticolonial constituency, Du Bois unsettled the boundaries between domestic and international jurisdictions over the colonial question by subjecting it to democratic contestation. By grafting the international language of minority rights onto democratic claims for self-rule of colonial peoples, he destabilized settled constructions of jurisdictional authority that rested on a bifurcated division between the domestic and the international.

The problem of representing colonial claims for democracy was not just one of overcoming figurations of colonial peoples as unfit for sovereignty but of representing nonstate peoples and other colonized populations in an international order that sanctifies the domestic jurisdiction of sovereign statehood.[127] Overcoming the juridical bifurcation of international law and state sovereignty was thus integral to Du Bois's efforts to envision a democratic world order, one that would free the majority of humanity subject to Euro-American imperial rule and confined to a perpetual state of exploitation and degradation. Yet, imagining such a democratic world required calling a new constituency into existence. Much of the paradox of this worldly democratic project was that this new constituency was constitutively unrepresentable within the spatial configuration of representative bodies within the UN. Through languages of minority rights and colonial status, Du Bois conjured colonial peoples as a global, majoritarian constituency that would serve as the transformative agent of worldly democratic transformation.

126. Thea Riofrancos, "Scaling Democracy: Participation and Resource Extraction in Latin America," *Perspectives on Politics* 15, no. 3 (September 2017): 680.

127. Sultan, "Self-Rule and the Problem of Peoplehood"; Von Eschen, *Race Against Empire*, 74–78.

[CHAPTER FIVE]

"The Habit of Democracy Must Encircle the Earth"

Constellations of Democratic Peace

> I still think today as yesterday that the color line is a great problem of this century. But today I see more clearly than yesterday that back of the problem of race and color, lies a greater problem which both obscures and implements it: and that is the fact that so many civilized persons are willing to live in comfort even if the price of this is poverty, ignorance and disease for the majority of their fellowmen; that to maintain this privilege men have waged war until today war tends to become universal and continuous.
>
> W. E. B. Du Bois, "Fifty Years After"

When W. E. B. Du Bois arrived in Manchester, England, in October 1945, it was his fifth time in half a century attending and organizing a Pan-African Congress. Heralded by George Padmore, the trade unionist and primary organizer of the Fifth Pan-African Congress, as "the father of Pan-Africanism" and the symbolic embodiment of the Negro struggle in the United States, Du Bois served as presiding officer over the Congress, a role that was largely symbolic and ceremonial.[1] What set this meeting apart from the earlier ones was that it was organized primarily by African anticolonial leaders and leaders of trade unions rather than by African American intellectuals or black leaders within imperial nation-states such as French diplomat Blaise Diagne, as with previous conferences.[2] Despite this difference, Du Bois saw these efforts as integral to his broader work with the National

---

Epigraph: W. E. B. Du Bois, "Fifty Years After," bronze placard, University of Massachusetts Amherst Libraries.

1. Lewis, *W. E. B. Du Bois: A Biography*, 660–61.
2. Adi, *Pan-Africanism: A History*, 72, 125–27.

Association for the Advancement of Colored People (NAACP) and in his role as a consultant to the US delegation to the United Nations Conference on International Organization (UNCIO). Indeed, the Pan-African Congress self-consciously articulated an ideal of world peace as vitally connected to the pursuit of African self-determination.

Although his role in preparations for the congress was minimal compared with previous conferences, Du Bois was charged by Padmore with drafting the final resolutions, which were circulated in the press and issued to the United Nations (UN). The final resolution of the Pan-African Congress began by explicitly affirming the delegates' commitment to peace. Echoing the mantra popularized by Wendell Willkie, the congress called for a degree of African autonomy and independence "so far and no further than is possible in this 'One World' for groups and peoples to rule themselves subject to inevitable World Unity and Federation."[3] In this way, the call for a Pan-African federation made by congress organizers such as Padmore and Francis Kwame Nkrumah was not an obstacle but a path toward the kind of peace promised by an integrated world federation. These aspects of Pan-Africanism had long been a staple of Du Bois's transnational political thought. The "higher ideal" of Pan-Africanism, he had written in 1923, was "to bring about *the peace of world democracy* through the inclusion of all in opposition to the idea of aristocracy of races where the backward are to be permanently ruled by the forward."[4] In connecting the pursuit of peace to opposition to tutelary rule, the epistemic capacities and habits of colonial peoples for self-rule served as the foundation for the broader project of world democracy.

While in England, Du Bois took the opportunity to meet with friends and acquaintances, both old and new. One of his most eagerly awaited visits was with the novelist and famed internationalist H. G. Wells, who was lying on his deathbed. The racial views of Wells, a longtime friend of Du Bois (the two first met at the 1911 Universal Races Congress), were amorphous, to say the least, and at times downright racist, to say the most. Wells's 1901 book *Anticipations of the Reaction of Mechanical and Scientific Progress upon Human Life and Thought* openly called for "a great federation of white English-speaking peoples" as the basis for "the final peace of the world."[5] Yet by

---

3. W. E. B. Du Bois, "Fifth Pan-African Congress Final Resolution" (1945), Du Bois Papers, box 107, p. 1.

4. W. E. B. Du Bois, "High Ideals of Pan-Africanism" (1923), in *Writings in W. E. B. Du Bois in Periodicals Edited by Others*, vol. 2, 1910–1934, 214.

5. Wells, *Anticipations*, 282–83. See also Bell, *Dreamworlds of Race*, 152–202.

1920, Du Bois would approvingly cite Wells in "The Hands of Ethiopia," calling for a united African state as a key feature of the postwar reconstruction of the world: "It is the clear, common sense of the African situation that while these precious regions of raw material remain divided up between a number of competitive European imperialisms, each resolutely set upon the exploitation of its 'possessions' to its own advantage and the disadvantage of the others, there can be no permanent peace in the world."[6] On the basis of these sentiments, Du Bois invited Wells to speak to the 1921 Pan-African Congress alongside other intellectual luminaries such as Harold Laski and Ida Gibbs Hunt.

Against this backdrop of changing views and evolving friendship, Du Bois reported on his 1945 visit with Wells in his *Chicago Defender* column, "Winds of Time." Calling his visit a "pilgrimage," Du Bois recalled the celebrated novelist's socialist commitments and declaration of race prejudice as "the worst evil of modern civilization."[7] In a eulogy in the same column a year later, he turned his attention to Wells's antipathy toward war and his later prophecies of the self-destruction of the human species in nuclear war, noting that the book by Wells that he liked both "best and least" by Wells was *A Short History of the World* (1922). On the one hand, the book served as an "antidote to current conventional history" oriented around nationalist historiography. On the other hand, Du Bois lamented, "it does not do justice to the Black Race" and writes world history in a way that leaves Africa out of the picture.[8] Du Bois generously excused these limitations by making "allowances for the state of knowledge of the period," in biographer David Levering Lewis's words.[9] Wells's histories had a broad impact on historical consciousness among many anticolonial figures beyond Du Bois, clearly influencing Jawaharlal Nehru's *Glimpses of World History* (1934), which itself informed Du Bois's *The World and Africa* (1947).

That Du Bois should recall Wells's world history at a moment when he was deeply involved with the UNCIO and the Pan-African Congress was not coincidental. Written in a prophetic tone, Wells's 1922 history was born not out of the presumed triumph of the new international order represented by the League of Nations but out of frustrations with its deficiencies. Like Du Bois, Wells saw the league not as the end point but as the starting point of a new conception of international order that would transcend the

---

6. Wells quoted in Du Bois, *Darkwater*, 34.
7. Du Bois, "Winds of Time" (November 19, 1945), Du Bois Papers, box 216, p. 1.
8. Du Bois, "Winds of Time" (September 9, 1946), Du Bois Papers, box 216, p. 2.
9. Lewis, *W. E. B. Du Bois: A Biography*, 664.

violence of imperial sovereignty. Wells's history was written at the conclusion of a peace conference marking the end of world war and provided reflection on the profound limitations of the peace settlement to emerge out of war. In this regard, he sought to reconcile his readership with the evolutionary necessity if not inevitability of the extension of citizenship beyond the nation-state into a federated league not of nations but of peoples. The natural tendency of human history was toward larger social units, and the choice Wells posed was "between cosmopolitan unity and human extinction."[10] Such a cosmopolitan vision of universal progress and world citizenship required a new and common interpretation of human history. Du Bois never fully embraced this cosmopolitan vision of world citizenship. Nevertheless, I suggest that *The World and Africa* seeks to correct the blind spots of Wells's world history by providing a narrative exploration of the centrality of Africa to the search for the lasting peace of world democracy.

This chapter uses these episodes as the starting point of a new interpretation of his political thinking on Africa, especially *The World and Africa*. This work is typically interpreted as the logical culmination of a long series of books on Africa, including *The Negro* (1915), *Africa: Its Place in Modern History* (1930), and *Black Folk Then and Now* (1939). Extant accounts read these works primarily as historical narratives vindicating the "spiritual gift" of African peoples to modern civilization.[11] Within this view is a cultural conception of race wherein different racial groups, based on their positions in broader social and economic hierarchies, have specific cultural gifts to grant to the world that uniquely direct the arc of human progress. As Du Bois put it early on in "Conservation of Races" (1897), "We believe that the Negro people, as a race, have a contribution to make to civilization and humanity, which no other race can make."[12] Within this geohistorical imaginary, the history and culture of precolonial Africa are not a "primitive" imitation of European culture but are world-historical advances in their own right.[13]

Moving beyond vindicationist interpretations, I argue that *The World*

---

10. John Partington, "H. G. Wells and the World State: A Liberal Cosmopolitan in a Totalitarian Age," *International Relations* 17, no. 2 (2003): 234–35.

11. Anthony Appiah, *Lines of Descent: W. E. B. Du Bois and the Emergence of Identity* (Harvard University Press, 2014), 127. See W. E. B. Du Bois, *The Negro* (Oxford University Press, 2014); W. E. B. Du Bois, *Africa: Its Place in Modern History* (Oxford University Press, 2014); Du Bois, *Black Folk*.

12. Quoted in Appiah, *Lines of Descent*, 92.

13. Rabaka, *W. E. B. Du Bois and the Problems of the Twenty-First Century*, 57–60.

and Africa can be placed within a different problem-space than the earlier books of the series.[14] Specifically, I suggest that it was less a means of vindicating the gift of African peoples to world civilization than it was an attempt to assert the capacities of African peoples for self-government. From this perspective, the reclamation of precolonial African forms of democracy and communal ownership was much more than a form of racial vindicationism consonant with the gift theory of race. It was an attempt to historically narrate a vision of democratic peace in which world war would cease only by affirming the epistemic capacities and habits of colonized peoples for self-rule. Democracy and peace were conjoined in this vision not by preventing liberal democracies from going to war with one another but by eliminating the incentives for European empires to go to war with one another and with colonial peoples by curtailing the pursuit of profit through colonial domination and by ensuring self-determination for all peoples. Attending to these historical dimensions reveals how this anticolonial vision was a central element of Du Bois's transnational democratic imaginary.

My point here is not to say that the concern for democratic peace should displace attention to the clear vindicationist strand in Du Bois's Pan-Africanism. It is to say, though, that this democratic peace strand is adjacent to and, while connected, ultimately irreducible to the vindicationist strand.[15] There is no question that in his writings on Africa, Du Bois was, in Robert Vitalis's words, "deeply involved in a 'vindicationist' historical project that studied the vital contribution of various African cultures to

---

14. I follow Wilson Moses in defining *racial vindicationism* as a form of historical writing aimed at "defending black people from the charge that they have made little or no contribution to the history of human progress. Sometimes vindication may imply the even more basic struggle to secure recognition of the fact that black people are human at all"; Wilson Moses, *Afrotopia: The Roots of African American Popular History* (Cambridge University Press, 1998), 21.

15. As David Scott puts it, racial vindicationism is oriented around the problem of white images of colonized peoples as inhuman and thus incapable of self-government. Such rhetoric aids in romantic narratives of redemption and overcoming by proving "the humanity of blacks and their capacity for self-determination"; David Scott, "Tragedy's Time: Postemancipation Futures Past and Present," in *Rethinking Tragedy*, ed. Rita Felski (Johns Hopkins University Press, 2008), 208. Along with Scott, I question whether such romanticism is viable as a political response to the postcolonial present and, as an interpretive point, whether such a framing of the problem-space fully captures Du Bois's own response to the intertwined problems of race, war, and global capitalism.

world civilization and that refuted ideologies of racial inferiority."[16] But his focus on Africa was not solely driven by the desire to vindicate the "gift" of black folk. It involved a materially rooted analysis of the economic and political requisites for world peace in the project of decolonization and the democratization of industry. Attention to these dynamics not only corrects Du Bois's marginalization from histories of pacifism and the peace movement.[17] It also helps uncover alternative genealogies of democratic peace that overlap with, though are distinct from, its more conventional, liberal variants. Such a genealogy might reveal how the constitutive conceptual reference points—democracy, peace, war, capitalism, and race—were part of a contested discursive terrain.[18]

As suggested in chapter 1, Du Bois conceptualized democracy in its epistemic dimension not as a form of government but as a "way of life for all peoples," especially for "the mass of peoples living in colonies."[19] This chapter explores the multiple aspects of this idea of democracy as a habit that overspreads the earth. The first section examines a recurring barrier to world democracy: an intellectual disposition and habitualized mode of political practice that Du Bois called "race provincialism," which disconnected the intersecting dynamics of war, peace, capitalism, and empire. Such provincialist attitudes afflicted two constituencies that Du Bois continually engaged with from World War I to World War II—specifically, white pacifists and racial liberals. The second section provides a rereading of *The World and Africa* that centers on the Greek myth of Andromeda as providing a vision of radical democratic peace in which the denial of the democratic habits of colonized peoples poses the primary cause of world war. The final section returns to an exploration of the problem of racial provincialism in the 1950s.

---

16. Vitalis, "Graceful and Generous Liberal Gesture," 342.

17. Chiara Corazza, "By No Other Means Than Peace: W. E. B. Du Bois on Nonviolence, World Peace, and Justice," *Peace and Change* 46, no. 4 (2021): 336–52.

18. As Ido Oren has shown, the democratic peace idea that emerged in the early twentieth century is an artifact of the transformation of the meaning of democracy from its associations with the "untamed rule of mass majorities" in the nineteenth century to its normalized and liberalized version purged of any class connotations; Ido Oren, "The Subjectivity of the 'Democratic' Peace: Changing U.S. Perceptions of Imperial Germany," *International Security* 20, no. 2 (Fall 1995): 151. What I would add to this is that this association of peace with the liberalization of democracy continued to be contested by Du Bois and other anticolonial figures well into the 1950s.

19. Du Bois, "Is It Democracy," 4.

"The Problem of Problems": Deprovincializing War and Peace

Du Bois began his 1915 prose masterpiece "The African Roots of War" by quoting the Roman proconsul of Africa, Pliny the Elder, as saying "Semper novi quid ex Africa"—"Something new always comes from Africa." Targeting world histories of his own time that left Africa out of view, Du Bois took to task those who believed that the problems of colonial rule in Africa were separate from the "burning social problems" raging in Europe and the United States such as racial disenfranchisement, class inequality, and women's suffrage. He argued that such an attitude that separates problems of war and empire from domestic social problems neglects the fundamental correctness of Pliny's verdict, which remains as true today as it did twenty centuries ago. Accepting Pliny's verdict would require seeing the rise of the new imperialism of the late nineteenth century and the world war it spawned as having their roots in Africa. More prophetically, he noted, Pliny's pronouncement shows how the exploitation of Africa nourishes the roots "not simply of war to-day [sic] but of the menace of wars to-morrow [sic]."[20]

Commentators such as Amy Kaplan and Robert Gooding-Williams have astutely noted that Du Bois's turn to Pliny is meant to capture the novelty of new forms of imperialism that grew out of the Berlin Conference of 1885, which ignited the European "scramble for Africa." The newness of Africa, as Kaplan notes, is at once its "antiquity, as the source of early civilization, and its modernity in relation to the history of empires" insofar as nearly every modern empire both achieved its greatness and confronted its greatest crises in Africa.[21] Gooding-Williams similarly notes that Du Bois turned to Pliny to distinguish the new imperialism based on the *economic* exploitation of Africa from an older model of Roman imperialism predicated on a single imperial power wielding *political* control over the world.[22]

Without rejecting these important interpretations, I also suggest that they leave something equally important aside. Instead of reminding the reader of the persistence of the new imperialism after the war, Pliny's pronouncement in the final paragraph of the essay directs attention to some

20. Du Bois, "African Roots," 707.

21. Kaplan, *Anarchy of Empire*, 197.

22. Robert Gooding-Williams, "Democratic Despotism and the New Imperialism," *Abolition Democracy* (blog), October 12, 2020, https://blogs.law.columbia.edu/abolition1313/robert-gooding-williams-democratic-despotism-and-the-new-imperialism/.

"new thing" that will emerge out of the pursuit of wealth through war and luxury through murder: "a new peace and new democracy of all races: a great humanity of equal men."²³ Embodied in the figure of the Egyptian queen Nefertari, who oversaw the restoration of Pharaonic rule by expelling the Hyksos dynasty, the African continent represents not only the emergence of the new imperialism but also the redemption of the world through the spread of a new conception of peace predicated on multiracial, industrial democracy. In this view, instilling a lasting peace rested on the extension of the democratic ideal to the darker races of the world.

In this section, I trace how this vision of a democratic peace first cohered in Du Bois's critique of a habitualized mode of civic practice that he variously called "intellectual" or "race provincialism."²⁴ Du Bois's language of "provincialism" has received limited scholarly attention. Adolph Reed Jr. interprets his critique of provincialism as disdain for a kind of quotidian parochialism. Pan-Africanism, according to Reed, required the surrender of tribal particularity in favor of national union, a view that reflects Du Bois's "predatory and solipsistic optimism" in paternal rule as well as a naïve faith in "the universalist and homogenizing assumptions of social engineering."²⁵ Appiah, in contrast, traces the language to Harvard philosopher Josiah Royce's 1908 *Race Questions, Provincialism, and Other American Problems*. There Royce defines "provincialism" as the love of and pride in local culture and customs as opposed to the nation as a whole. Opposed to nationalistic patriotism that disparages the provincial and the "false sectionalism" that disunites the nation, "higher provincialism" allows modern individuals to maintain a sense of community in the face of the dislocating tendencies of modernity and mass migration.²⁶ Du Bois, according to Appiah, worried that such celebrations of provincialism would harbor the risk of black folk withdrawing from contacts across nations and relinquishing the cosmopolitan spirit necessary for racial justice struggles.²⁷

Appiah, I believe, is more on the mark here, though the language of racial provincialism cannot be reduced to Du Bois's philosophical engagements

---

23. Du Bois, "African Roots," 714.

24. W. E. B. Du Bois, "A Forum of Fact and Opinion (April 25, 1936)," in *Newspaper Columns by W. E. B. Du Bois*, vol. 1, ed. Herbert Aptheker (Kraus-Thomson, 1986), 66; W. E. B. Du Bois, "Forward," *Crisis* 18, no. 5 (September 1919): 234.

25. Reed, *W. E. B. Du Bois and American Political Thought*, 81.

26. Josiah Royce, *Race Questions, Provincialism, and Other American Problems* (MacMillan, 1908), 57–73.

27. Appiah, *Lines of Descent*, 71–73.

with Royce, nor is it necessarily indicative of cosmopolitan commitments. Instead, I seek to place his criticism of "race provincialism" in the political context of debates over the meaning of both peace and democracy in the interwar years. Provincialism, for Du Bois, was neither tribal parochialism nor the opposite of cosmopolitanism. It was rather a mode of thought and practice that confined social and political problems within a narrowly racial perspective. To be provincial is to experience "group imprisonment" where one is centered on the specific problems of a discrete racial or social group and neglects the "wider aspects" of national and world problems.[28] In this way, "race provincialism" is indicative of an intellectual tendency to disconnect the problem of the color line from social problems of peace and war, poverty and inequality, and colonialism and empire. Put another way, it is a political habit that neglects that the "present problem of problems is nothing more than democracy beating itself helplessly against the color bar."[29]

The idea that democracy crashing against the color bar constitutes "the problem of problems" suggests not that it is one political problem among others but that it is a kind of metaproblem that structures the capacity of social and political actors to perceive something as a problem at all.[30] In other words, resolving problems of race prejudice, global poverty, and world war can only be done by first comprehending the role of the color line in allowing these issues to emerge as social and political problems at all. In correspondence with Mildred Scott Olmstead, the Quaker pacifist and executive secretary of the Women's International League for Peace and Freedom (WILPF), Du Bois clarified his meaning:

> The difficulty in a problem like that of the Negro is that the problem itself gets to be provincial; that is, people do not think of it in connection with other problems, but set it entirely apart and the result is that it does not become a part of the general liberal movement and this makes it possible to be liberal concerning Negroes and reactionary on other advanced projects, and vice versa, advanced and progressive upon everything except the race problem.[31]

---

28. Du Bois, *Dusk of Dawn*, 67.

29. Du Bois, *Darkwater*, 33.

30. Here again I am indebted to Chandler, *X—The Problem of the Negro as a Problem for Thought*.

31. W. E. B. Du Bois to Mildred Scott Olmsted, 20 January 1932, in *The Correspondence of W. E. B. Du Bois*, vol.1, *1877–1934*, ed. Herbert Aptheker (University of Massachusetts Press, 1973), 449.

That these statements should be made to a leading official of WILPF is telling. Du Bois was a member of the advisory board in the 1930s and had long seen founding members of WILPF such as Jane Addams and Emily Greene Balch as crucial allies, inviting Addams to speak at the 1921 Pan-African Congress. As central figures of the peace movement, Addams, Balch, and WILPF played a key role in the movement to outlaw war.[32] Du Bois no doubt had the efforts of WILPF in mind when he demanded that any "real disarmament" in Europe and the United States required the release of yellow and black peoples from the chains of (neo)colonial rule.[33]

Du Bois's admiration for WILPF notwithstanding, he saw the white-dominated peace movement as hopelessly provincialist in its failure to comprehend the problem of war and peace as a racial problem. Without doing so, both the race problem and the peace problem would fail to reach a satisfactory settlement. In making such criticism of race provincialism, Du Bois had two specific targets. On the one hand, in setting their sights on domestic problems of racial exclusion, racial liberals in the civil rights movement (and especially at the NAACP) made the grave mistake of neglecting how ideologies of racial inferiority laid the foundation for world problems of war and peace. On the other hand, without attending to the problem of interimperial rivalry over the colonies, the white-dominated peace movement in both Britain and the United States failed to address the root causes of world war.[34] In succumbing to race provincialism, both the white peace movement and racial liberals experienced "group imprisonment" by defining social and political problems through the experiences of discrete racial

---

32. Christopher McKnight Nichols, *Promise and Peril: America at the Dawn of a Global Age* (Harvard University Press, 2011), 301–2.

33. W. E. B. Du Bois, "Peace on Earth," *Crisis* 31, no. 5 (March 1926): 215. Intellectually, Du Bois clearly echoed Addams's substitution of an active and dynamic conception of peace that requires the transformation of domestic social order for a passive ideal defined as simply the absence of war; Jane Addams, *Newer Ideals of Peace* (MacMillan, 1907). Du Bois also consistently recommended Balch's *Occupied Haiti* (1927) to others as the best book on the US occupation of Haiti. Glenda Sluga writes, "Internationalism on Balch's view was a means of weeding out the exclusivism and discrimination produced by national, imperial, and racial manifestations of political power and community"; Glenda Sluga, "From F. Melian Stawell to E. Greene Balch: International and Internationalist Thinking at the Gender Margins, 1919–1947," in *Women's International Thought: A New History*, ed. Patricia Owens and Katharina Rietzler (Cambridge University Press, 2021), 240.

34. To clarify, *race provincialism* is not simply a synonym for *nationalism* or *nation-centeredness*. More deeply, it is a way of evading the relationship between democracy and the color line as the problem of problems, as a structuring problematic for the per-

groupings. More pointedly, in doing so, they inevitably failed to address "the problem of problems," of democracy confronting the color line.

THE PROVINCIALISM OF RACIAL LIBERALISM

Race provincialism as a habitualized mode of political practice posed one of the primary barriers to the emergence of world democracy. The race provincialism of white pacifism and the racial liberalism of the NAACP, however, posed distinctive obstacles. The provincialism of racial liberalism, at best, tackled the color line domestically by detaching it from the problem of war internationally. At its worst (a tendency Du Bois himself succumbed to), it pursued racial justice at home by enlisting African Americans in the Wilsonian project of making the world safe for democracy. The limits of race provincialism as a mode of orienting civil rights struggles became most acute with the end of World War I and the solidification of postwar peace plans under the League of Nations. In the midst of the Paris Peace Conference, the NAACP focused its 1919 annual meeting on the theme of "Africa in the World Democracy." The meeting showcased an impressive lineup of intellectual forces, with the pluralist philosopher Horace Kallen speaking on "The Future of Africa and a League of Nations" and NAACP Field Secretary James Weldon Johnson speaking on the question of "Africa at the Peace Table." It was here that Du Bois first issued his call for a postwar league of nations to create a central African state out of European colonies. The opening remarks of the meeting proclaimed that the application of "the principles of self-determination to Africans" was integral to the creation of a "peace union of free peoples."[35] Central to the creation of a free African state, Kallen clarified in his opening remarks, would be the construction of an international commission composed of experts on colonial matters and representatives of racialized and colonized groups. Under such an international commission, African colonies would be "regarded as a trust, not in the hands of financiers, but in the hands of representatives of plain people of all the world."[36]

---

ception of other problems. White pacifist movements, for instance, were provincialist not in their nationalism but in their internationalism, in their tendency to disconnect problems of race and colonialism from the problems of war and peace.

35. Horace Meyer Kallen and James Weldon Johnson, *Africa in the World Democracy: Address Delivered at the Annual Meeting of the National Association for the Advancement of Colored People* (NAACP, 1919), 3.

36. Horace Meyer Kallen, "The Future of Africa and a League of Nations," in Kallen and Johnson, *Africa in the World Democracy*, 9.

The central address of the meeting, however, was not by Du Bois but by Johnson, who began his remarks by invoking the thesis offered in "African Roots" that the source of the international rivalries that ignited the Great War lay in Africa. Johnson went on to read parts of Du Bois's plan to internationalize the former German, Belgian, and Portuguese colonies by placing them under the jurisdiction of an international commission tasked with developing colonized peoples' capacities for self-government. The ultimate end of this plan to internationalize the Central African colonies was self-determination. Yet rather than continue to elaborate a justification for this proposal, Johnson spent almost the entirety of his speech clarifying the reasons that NAACP should take up the question of colonial rule in Africa. Stipulating first that "the race question in the United States is a national question" and that "the question of Africa is an international question," Johnson gave two reasons. First, to not act on sympathy for the "wrongs and sufferings" of "his blood brothers in Africa," the American Negro would indicate his own narrow self-centeredness. In this reasoning, shared racial identity instills a sense of sympathy and solidarity with colonized Africans. Second, he clarified that taking such action would correct the "criminal ignorance" of white America regarding Africa by helping to correct a "conspiracy against Africa" to strip the Negro race of all its past contributions "to the birth and growth of civilization." Reflecting the vindicationist historical imagination in which Du Bois's own writings on Africa took part, Johnson lamented that "the Negro has been raped of all credit that is due him as a contributor to civilization."[37]

On the basis of this reasoning, Johnson concluded that while African Americans should support African self-determination, "the fight for democracy for native Africans and the fight for democracy for people of African descent in the United States are not on the same plane." In rejecting that the question of democratic rights for African Americans has a place at the peace table, Johnson spatially bifurcated the question of race domestically from the questions of peace and colonialism internationally, insisting that the NAACP's "fight is here at home . . . not over there."[38] Johnson's remarks, rather than being idiosyncratic, reflected significant strands of black intellectual thought at the time. Other prominent black intellectuals—for instance, Kelly Miller, a professor of mathematics at Howard University—similarly held that African Americans could advance the

---

37. James Weldon Johnson, "Africa at the Peace Table," in Kallen and Johnson, *Africa in the World Democracy*, 17.

38. J. Johnson, "Africa at the Peace Table," 18–19.

cause of domestic civil rights by taking part in "the terrific struggle for world democracy."[39] It is in this regard that the NAACP meeting embraced race provincialism.

The question to arise from this episode concerns the differing conceptions of solidarity underlying Johnson's call for the NAACP to support African self-determination in qualified terms and Du Bois's clear frustration with the limits of this. Johnson exhibited, I submit, a conception of *expressive solidarity* whereby calls for transnational solidarity are understood as symbolic displays of affective ties with the imagined homeland of African Americans. He envisioned the NAACP cultivating symbolic support for African self-determination on the basis of shared racial identity and the need to vindicate the contributions of Africans to the progress of human civilization. Residing in the symbolic realm, where solidarity is part of a broader assertion of racial identity, Johnson's expressive solidarity nevertheless strategically bifurcated domestic struggles for civil rights from international struggles for self-determination on the part of colonial peoples.

Later reflecting on this episode, Du Bois openly criticized the NAACP for its lack of interest in Africa and its tendency to shrink back to "its narrowest program: to make Negroes American citizens, forgetting that if the white European world persisted in upholding and strengthening the color bar, America would follow in its wake."[40] Similarly recounting the NAACP's lack of interest in the Second Pan-African Congress, Du Bois attributed it to an "older liberalism" that lacked "schemes for internationalism in race problems" and was interested solely "in America and securing Americans of all and any color, their rights."[41] In his work organizing the Second Pan-African Congress in 1921, the board of directors of the NAACP believed that there were more urgent matters. As the NAACP was gearing up for a national campaign in support of a federal antilynching bill, leaders such as Johnson and Mary White Ovington contended that the organization's resources were better spent on domestic matters.[42] In these conflicts

---

39. Kelly Miller, *History of the World War for Human Rights* (A. Jenkins, 1919), 550. See also Zhang Juguo, *W. E. B. Du Bois: The Question for the Abolition of the Color Line* (Routledge, 2001), 98–99.

40. Du Bois, *Autobiography*, 185.

41. Du Bois, *Dusk of Dawn*, 137.

42. Lewis, *W. E. B. Du Bois: A Biography*, 402–3; Megan Ming Francis, *Civil Rights and the Making of the Modern American State* (Cambridge University Press, 2014); Clarence Contee, "Du Bois, the NAACP, and the Pan-African Congress of 1919," *Journal of Negro History* 57, no. 1 (January 1972): 19–20.

with the NAACP, we again see Du Bois's transscalar democratic imaginary at work as he navigates and ultimately unsettles the boundaries between seemingly discrete spatial domains of democratic practice such as the domestic/international divide and even down to microscopic level of organizational committees and boards of directors. In Du Bois's transnational political imaginary, the question of the space and scale of democratic practice within the NAACP was integral to the project of contesting the boundaries between domestic and international politics.[43]

One possibility here is that Du Bois's discontent with Johnson and the NAACP in this moment was because of his strategic sense that African struggles for self-determination could aid the civil rights movement within the United States. Political scientist Alvin Tillery has contrasted expressive solidarity with a model of *strategic solidarity*, in which black elites attempt to advance the domestic political interests of the black community rather than seek to strengthen cultural and affective ties with Africa. Within this framework, black elites engage in transnational support for anticolonial movements only when it provides an avenue to help achieve domestic political goals of serving black constituencies.[44] Indeed, Johnson held that NAACP support for African self-determination was expressively though not strategically important.

At first glance, it appears that Du Bois may have disagreed with Johnson in strategic terms, holding that emphasizing transnational connections between African self-determination and civil rights could advance domestic race struggles. Du Bois's arguments are best understood, however, in terms of a third model I would call *structural solidarity*, derived not from shared identity (expressive) or shared interests (strategic) but "the common structural conditions that lead members of a political community to

---

43. In a 1936 *Pittsburgh Courier* column, Du Bois placed this opposition to substantive internationalism on the part of the NAACP in the context of the longer "history of race provincialism," stretching back to the eighteenth and nineteenth centuries. At the center of this history was a tendency to focus on domestic rights within the nation-state at the expense of broader attention to international order and transnational forces. For instance, in their revolutionary fervor, the mulattoes of Haiti emphasized their rights as French citizens over demands for the abolition of slavery. Similarly, free Negroes in Louisiana and the US North had long agitated for their rights without reference to the rights of black slaves elsewhere; Du Bois, "Forum of Fact and Opinion," 3.

44. Alvin B. Tillery Jr., *Between Homeland and Motherland: Africa, U.S. Foreign Policy, and Black Leadership in America* (Cornell University Press, 2011), 5–6.

develop solidarity."⁴⁵ That is, solidarity between the civil rights movement and African self-determination derives from the structural interconnections between the two in broader, transnational regimes of white imperial rule. Seen through this lens, Du Bois's call for a self-determining, African state to emerge out of the Treaty of Versailles was connected to his structural view that such a lasting world peace was predicated on the extension of racial equality and democratic self-rule to the darker races of the world. In "The Hands of Ethiopia," where he most substantively developed his program for a central African state, Du Bois clarified that "the real pacifist" must necessarily embrace an anticolonial position in affirming the right of both economic and political self-determination for small nations and colonial peoples: "The real Pacifist will seek to organize, not simply the masses in white nations, guarding against exploitation and profiteering, but will remember that no permanent relief can come but by including in this organization the lowest and the most exploited races of the world."⁴⁶ Because slavery and imperialism were central to the rise of modern capitalism, the real pacifist must elaborate a program for releasing Africa from the fetters of "industrial slavery." In such a program, "a new African World State" was a means of laying the economic foundations for peace by transforming the exploitative bases of the global capitalist order.⁴⁷ Through structural solidarity that connected colonialism, economic exploitation, and war, Du Bois sought to overcome the narrow vision of race provincialism.

Nevertheless, it is important to grapple with Du Bois's own ambivalence about war during this period. Despite his frequent proclamation, "I believe in the Prince of Peace. I believe War is Murder," Du Bois notoriously affirmed black participation in and support for World War I as a means of advancing the civil rights agenda.⁴⁸ In a July 1918 editorial, he famously proclaimed, "Let us, while this war lasts, forget our special grievances and close our ranks shoulder to shoulder with our own white fellow citizens and the allied nations that are fighting for democracy."⁴⁹ Reiterating this same theme that African Americans could advance the civil rights movement by partaking in the Wilsonian project of liberal interventionism, Du Bois af-

---

45. Juliet Hooker, *Race and the Politics of Solidarity* (Oxford University Press, 2009), 38.

46. Du Bois, *Darkwater*, 35.

47. Du Bois, *Darkwater*, 37.

48. Du Bois, *Darkwater*, 1.

49. W. E. B. Du Bois, "Close Ranks," *Crisis* 16, no. 3 (July 1918): 111.

firmed that the primary means of achieving a "new democracy that shall know no color" was to take part in the war effort.[50] One explanation for this position is that Du Bois caught himself in a "practical contradiction," a position driven by strategic considerations that stood opposed to his broader global analysis of white supremacy.[51] Mark Ellis has convincingly shown that one of the most likely motivations for writing the editorial, which was significantly "accommodationist in tone," was Du Bois's pursuit of a military intelligence position within the War Department.[52]

While the historical evidence for this is quite convincing, I argue here that his "close ranks" call was not just a contradiction between his theoretical commitments and practical considerations. Rather, it was an intellectual contradiction wherein he succumbed to the very provincialism for which he criticized the NAACP. In recounting the editorial in 1940, Du Bois attributed his call to "close ranks" to the fact that black officers were finally commissioned in the army and President Woodrow Wilson was finally breaking his silence on lynching. Doubting the soundness of his "war attitude," Du Bois admitted that he did not fully understand the horrors of war nor its limits as an instrument of social reform. Tacitly evoking the language of provincialism, he confessed that in writing the editorial he was "thinking narrowly of the interest of my group and was willing to let the world go to hell, if the black man went free."[53] Attending to the role of race provincialism here can help make intellectual sense of Du Bois's widely noted "ambivalence about war" without allowing his "close ranks" position to overdetermine interpretive accounts of his thinking on war and peace.[54]

Indeed, Du Bois seems to have had his own race provincialism in mind when he solicited a message to the American Negro from the Indian poet and anticolonial leader Rabindranath Tagore for publication in *The Crisis*. Beginning by proclaiming that "the great fact of this age" is that the "human races have come out of their enclosures," Tagore's message went on:

50. Du Bois, "The Present," *Crisis* 14, no. 4 (August 1917): 165. On these themes, see Chad Williams, "In the Shadow of World War: Revisiting W. E. B. Du Bois's *Black Reconstruction*," *Du Bois Review* 20, no. 1 (2022): 43–55.

51. Jared Loggins, "W. E. B. Du Bois, the Negro Problem, and the Case Against Black Involvement in War," in *Globalizing Political Theory*, ed. Smita A. Rahman et al. (Routledge, 2023), 193.

52. Mark Ellis, "'Closing Ranks' and 'Seeking Honor:' W. E. B. Du Bois in World War I," *Journal of American History* 79, no. 1 (June 1992): 96.

53. Du Bois, *Dusk of Dawn*, 127–28.

54. On his inconsistency and ambivalence regarding war and US military interventions, see Hansen, *Lost Promise of Patriotism*, 148; Nichols, *Promise and Peril*, 14–15.

We have been engaged in cultivating each his own individual life, and within the forced seclusion of our racial tradition. We had neither the wisdom nor the opportunity to harmonize our growth with world tendencies. But there are no longer walls to hide us. We have at length to prove our worth to the whole world, not merely to admiring groups of our own people. We must justify our own existences. We must show, each in our own civilization, that which is universal in the heart of the unique.

In his commentary, Du Bois clarified that affirming the duty of racial groups to prove their worth to the world is not to deny the reality of domination and ideologies of inferiority. Rather, Tagore's message was that the universal ideal of individual growth and freedom must find manifestation in any civilization worthy of the name. Yet, Du Bois warned, both white and black America seemed incapable of hearing Tagore's message: "White America is provincial and material to the last degree. But we who criticize white America have also by our own very criticism been forced into provincialism. We are narrow by our own grievances and hate."[55]

WHITE PACIFISM AND RACIAL PROVINCIALISM

If the provincialism of racial liberalism pursued a program of domestic civil rights by detaching the problem of race from the broader problems of peace and war, the race provincialism of white pacifism did the reverse. Du Bois's experiences with the US peace movement during World War I were central to the formation of his broader vision of world democracy. Throughout the First World War, he routinely criticized how various peace societies cast "the question of peace between civilized and backward peoples" as outside their purview. The New York Peace Society (NYPS), in particular, marginalized the colonial question and explicitly envisioned peace as being between the great European powers. Recalling a meeting of the NYPS immediately before the start of the war, Du Bois lamented a comment made by an official of the organization stating that "when we want peace," it is confined to those civilized nations deemed "worthy of it."[56] Such comments were clearly emblematic of a broader tendency in nineteenth- and early

---

55. W. E. B. Du Bois, "A Message to the American Negro from Rabindranath Tagore" (July 1929), Du Bois Papers, box 183, pp. 1–2. For an extended examination of the correspondence, see Hari Ramesh, "The Politics of Peoples in Rabindranath Tagore and W. E. B. Du Bois," *History of the Present* 9, no. 2 (October 2019): 166–92.

56. W. E. B. Du Bois, "Peace," *Crisis* 6, no. 1 (May 1913): 26.

twentieth-century international law, which cast the international system as a mechanism of taming violence among civilized states. In this progressive view of international society, imperial conflicts in the colonies were "little wars" that were incidental to and ultimately inconsequential for the broader goals of achieving peace in world order.[57]

Du Bois, however, noted something more problematic in such views. In the midst of debate, the speaker at the Hotel Astor specifically referenced ongoing war in the Balkans as an example of inconsequential wars, thereby limiting peace to the great states of the world, a "peace among the big dogs of the world while they hunted the lesser ones."[58] Calls for peace among greater imperial powers thus masked the ongoing subjugation of colonial peoples. While white pacifism condemned the horror of war among European powers, it was silent "when war was confined to the Belgian Congo, to the headwaters of the Amazon, to South Africa and parts of India and the South Seas."[59] Instead of war, white pacifists viewed military actions in the colonies as a method of civilizing underdeveloped peoples. Proclaiming his disgust with white pacifists, Du Bois argued that such a vision of "peace among white folk" freed European powers to "continue their despoiling of yellow, red, brown and black folk."[60] As Murad Idris has observed, in making these arguments, Du Bois went beyond critiques of the normalization of war and the moralization of peace toward a more nuanced "critique of the boundary between war and peace" that exposed how calls for peace among Europeans were predicated on and reproduced colonial exploitation and racialized international hierarchies.[61]

Such race provincialism was broadly symptomatic of a "paradox of

---

57. Pitts, *Boundaries of the International*, 184.

58. Du Bois, "Of the Culture of White Folk," 446; Du Bois, *Color and Democracy*, 309–10.

59. W. E. B. Du Bois, "The Problem of Problems," in *Writings by W. E. B. Du Bois in Periodicals by Others*, vol. 2, 1910–1934, 119.

60. Du Bois, "The Problem of Problems," 119.

61. Murad Idris, "Peace, or, the Moral Economy of War: Between W. E. B. Du Bois and Sayyid Qutb," in *Crisis Under Critique: How People Assess, Transform, and Respond to Critical Situations*, ed. Didier Fassin and Axel Honneth (Columbia University Press, 2022), 141. Yet in making these points, Idris also dismisses attention to Du Bois's constructive discourse of peace as an idealistic vision that rests on a moralized opposition to war. Du Bois's discussion of peace, however, was not simply a deconstructive critique of white, European pacifism. As I will show in the next sections, it was also a reconstructive vision of an anticolonial and socialistic conception of peace that necessarily affirmed the right of self-determination for colonized peoples.

peace" that had grave implications for world democracy.⁶² The Anglo-American peace movement constructed the international and thus the goals of world peace as being between great powers by writing small nations and colonized peoples out of the equation. The paradox was that the imperial desire for enlarging spheres of influence through greater colonial acquisitions—premised on underlying theories of colonial peoples and small nations as inferior and developmentally lacking—was itself the driving force of world war. In neglecting the color line as "the problem of problems" and evading the problem of the economic exploitation of the colonies, white pacifism made any resolution to the problem of world war all but impossible.⁶³ Rather than a problem that is superfluous to that of peace, self-determination in the colonies was integral to achieving a "peace built on world democracy, equality of men of all races and color, and the damnation of all industrial organizations built on theft."⁶⁴

Such experiences profoundly shaped Du Bois's views on war and peace. In the moment of World War I, he never explicitly stated who it was that made such comments. But by the 1940s, when he recounted these events in the context of his work with the Pan-African Congress and the UNCIO, he singled out the philanthropist, industrialist, and ardent anti-imperialist Andrew Carnegie as the source of the comments. That Du Bois would fail to take the author of these comments to task by name during World War I is unsurprising, as he repeatedly tapped the Carnegie Foundation for funding for various projects. By World War II, however, proximity to a range of other funding sources such as the Anson Phelps Stokes Fund made such direct confrontation more feasible.

Du Bois's repeated criticisms of Carnegie's views on peace indicate the ways that he explicitly positioned his own imaginary of an anticolonial democratic peace in opposition to racialized imaginaries of peace achieved through the "transnational unification of the white race."⁶⁵ Chapter 2 argued that Du Bois positioned his alternative imaginary of interracial utopianism as a counterpoint to the racial utopianism of figures like Carnegie and Wells during the age of empire. It is unnecessary to rehash the details here. What I want to emphasize is that this explicit racialization of peace by Carnegie—where pacific imaginaries are the prerogative of and confined to

---

62. W. E. B. Du Bois, *The World and Africa*, in *"The World and Africa" and "Color and Democracy,"* ed. Henry Louis Gates Jr. (Oxford University Press, 2007), 12.

63. Du Bois, "Problem of Problems," 114; Du Bois, *Color and Democracy*, 310.

64. Du Bois, "Of the Culture of White Folk," 446.

65. Kripp, "Creative Advance Must Be Defended," 943.

civilized European states—is symptomatic of "race provincialism," a commitment to peace that both depends on and further engenders racial and civilizational hierarchies between peoples and nations. By provincializing peace and detaching it from the problems of labor and the color line, such pacific political visions both perpetuated the conditions under which global war would persist and ideologically masked the racial and colonial hierarchies on which this vision depended.

During the interwar years, as we have seen, Du Bois directed his critique of race provincialism at both white pacifists and racial liberals. By the start of World War II, however, the balance of provincialism among these two constituencies began to shift. The provincialism of white pacifism became particularly acute as the United States joined the war effort and discussions for a postwar peace settlement began to appear on the horizon. The early 1940s witnessed the proliferation of thinking about democratic federalism and alternative visions of world order beyond the nation-state.[66] In a 1942 speech called "The Future of Europe in Africa," Du Bois posed a trenchant critique of such peace plans and postsovereign visions of world politics for leaving Africa and the colonial question more broadly out of the picture. In particular, he criticized peace proposals and visions of world federalism offered by such US journalists as George Streit and Henry Luce for proposing "a domination of the world by English-speaking peoples, that is, by the peoples who have led in fostering the slave trade and color caste."[67] In *Union Now: A Proposal for a Federal Union of the Democracies of the North Atlantic* (1940), Streit held that if a "real peace" is to come at the end of the war, "it must be based on the establishment of our Inter-democracy Federal Union as the Nucleus of a world government of, by and for the people." For Streit, a federal union composed of "founder democracies" in the North Atlantic would provide the "nucleus" of democratic federalism that would then grow into a world government capable of securing peace.[68]

Streit contrasted this "method of nucleus" whereby democratic principles would diffuse around the world through the pooled power of founder democracies with two other methods of composing world government. The first, "the method of restriction," would limit membership in the democratic federation to the founder democracies, which would raise the thorny question of how to interact with nonmembers. The second, "the method of

---

66. Rosenboim, *Emergence of Globalism*.

67. Du Bois, "Future of Europe in Africa," 185.

68. George Streit, *Union Now: A Proposal for a Federal Union of the Democracies of the North Atlantic* (Harper, 1940), x, 3.

inclusion," would expand membership beyond democracies, which would erode the common political culture and shared democratic habits necessary for union.[69] The "method of nucleus" would thus allow for the navigation between the Scylla of overinclusion and the Charybdis of overrestriction by fostering the spread of liberal democracy and gradually admitting members accordingly. In "The American Century" (1941), Henry Luce clarified that the United States should join the war not to defend territory but to "defend and even promote, encourage and incite so-called democratic principles throughout the world." In this deterritorialized interpretation of national defense, Luce held it to mean not defense of territory but defense of the spread of democratic capitalism throughout the world, which would sustain US interests.[70] Luce then went on to offer Streit's democratic federalism as a means of pursuing these objectives.

Such schemes were widely criticized by prominent authors such as George Orwell for imposing civilizational hierarchies between the nucleus of the founder democracies of the North Atlantic and the underdeveloped peoples of the colonized world. The historian Or Rosenboim writes, "Streit's imagined federation was indistinguishable from the political space of imperialism, accepting the political definitions of the imperial discourse, according to which the imperial powers were 'democracies' regardless of their exploitative practices abroad."[71] Despite overlap, Du Bois's critique of Streit stood apart from that of Orwell in important respects. Admitting that Streit's plan for a "peace bloc" might achieve its objectives and might even be adopted, Orwell focused on the exclusion of the nonwhite, global majority from the nucleus of federation.[72] Du Bois went even further by suggesting that such an exclusion of colonized peoples from any vision of world democracy would in fact lay the foundation for future world war. For Du Bois, Streit's proposal was yet another episode in a broader story of white pacifism stretching back to the visions of racial peace offered by Carnegie.

If the race provincialism of white pacifism hardened in these years, that of racial liberals in the NAACP and beyond began to soften as the signing of the Atlantic Charter in 1942 laid the basis for postwar peace plans. The significant ambiguities of the document regarding the intentions of its

---

69. Streit, *Union Now*, 86–87.

70. Henry Luce, "The American Century," *Diplomatic History* 23, no. 2 (Spring 1999): 161.

71. Rosenboim, *Emergence of Globalism*, 120.

72. George Orwell, "Not Counting N**gers," July 1939, https://www.orwell.ru/library/articles/niggers/english/e_ncn.

two principal signatories—Franklin Roosevelt and Winston Churchill—provided opportunities for racial liberals within the United States to internationalize their struggle and loosen their provincialism by attaching civil rights struggles to the greater problems of peace after the war. For instance, in 1942 the Committee on Africa, the War, and Peace Aims published *The Atlantic Charter and Africa from an American Standpoint* to argue for the application of the eight points of the Atlantic Charter to the colonial situation in Africa.[73] On the one hand, Roosevelt declared, "The Atlantic Charter applies not only to the parts of the world that border the Atlantic but to the whole world; disarmament of aggressors, self-determination of nations and peoples, and the four freedoms." On the other hand, worrying that the language of the charter would jeopardize Britain's colonial holdings, Churchill clarified that it applied only to the "the extension of the sovereignty, self-government, and national life of the states and nations of Europe now under the Nazi yoke" and was thus entirely separate from the "progressive evolution of self-governing institutions" in the British colonies.[74]

For racial liberals like Walter White at the NAACP, the contradictions of the Atlantic Charter provided an opportunity to conjoin the civil rights movement with broader discussions of world peace and African decolonization, which would eventually lead to Du Bois rejoining the NAACP as director of Special Research in 1944 with the sole goal of preparing information and reports for debate at the UNCIO. Vaughn Rasberry has perceptively argued that the Allied war effort and the Atlantic Charter were at once symbols of Euro-American democracy's contradictions even as they helped demarcate democracy as a "discursive field ripe for strategic manipulation."[75] Rather than relegate black writers and activists to the discursive confines of US liberalism, the war pried open new visions of democracy and new possibilities for antifascist futures. Du Bois and other black intellectuals clearly stepped into this discursive field, imagining new articulations of democratic peace that exceeded its conventional meanings in liberal political thought. For such intellectuals, racial provincialism was it-

---

73. For an excellent overview of drafting process, see Klug, *Internal Colony*, 27–50.

74. Both Roosevelt and Churchill are quoted in Committee on Africa, the War, and Peace Aims, *The Atlantic Charter and Africa from an American Standpoint* (New York [publisher not identified], 1942), 30–31. On the broader role of the Atlantic Charter in African decolonization movements, see Bonny Ibhawoh, "Testing the Atlantic Charter: Linking Anti-Colonialism, Self-Determination, and Universal Human Rights," *Journal of Human Rights* 18, no. 7–8 (2014): 842–60.

75. Vaughn Rasberry, *Race and the Totalitarian Century: Geopolitics in the Black Literary Imagination* (Harvard University Press, 2016), 10.

self an antidemocratic habit that impeded struggles against world war and militarization. In 1943, Alain Locke proclaimed, "Of all the barriers limiting democracy, color is the greatest, whether viewed from a standpoint of national or of world democracy.... These provincialisms... now confront us as democracy's greatest practical liabilities in a time of global war."[76]

Constellations of Democratic Peace

Foregrounding this longer history of and engagement with race provincialism helps reorient new perspectives on Du Bois's writings on Africa in the 1940s, and especially *The World and Africa* (1947). In particular, it reveals the ways in which World War II and the signing of the Atlantic Charter signaled the solidification of a different problem-space that animated Du Bois's writings on Africa from the conventional interpretation of these writings as a vindication of the African gift to world civilization. The problem posed in these writings was much less that of the recovery of the genius of ancient African civilizations than it was of placing the question of self-determination for Africa at the center of broader plans for a postwar peace settlement.

By his own admission, one of Du Bois's primary purposes in writing *The World and Africa* was to expose how "the peace movement in the world before the Second World War did not envisage peace in Africa or between the imperial rulers of the world and other peoples regarded as inferior." Such claims were explicitly directed at the Concert of Europe, which ensured a degree of peace and relative stability by providing a balance of powers among Britain, France, Prussia, Russia, and Austria following the end of the Napoleonic Wars in 1815. For Du Bois, however, dominant historical narratives heralding the reign of the concert of powers as providing equilibrium among the great powers did so by writing imperial wars for the spoils of colonial exploitation out of their purview.[77] Du Bois similarly charged the modern peace movement with a kind of "colonial unknowing,"

---

76. Alain Locke, *World View on Race and Democracy: A Study Guide in Human Group Relations* (American Library Association, 1943), 1–2. See also Rayford Logan, "The Crisis of Democracy in the Western Hemisphere," *Journal of Negro Education* 10, no. 3 (July 1941): 344–52.

77. W. E. B. Du Bois, "Africa and World Peace" (1960), Du Bois Papers, box 210, p. 8. As Antonio Vazquez Arroyo has put it, "Conversely, peace, stability, and equilibrium within the European great powers meant displacing the conflict to the non-European world"; Antonio Vazquez Arroyo, "Binding Politics: Political Space, Responsibilities, and the New-Old Order," *Theory & Event* 26, no. 3 (July 2023): 539.

an epistemological orientation that occludes attention to the relational entanglements between race, war, peace, and empire.[78] Because world wars are driven by interimperial rivalries, and because Africa is currently at the forefront of this colonial competition due to decolonization in Asia, any enduring peace in the postwar world would have to be a peace both for and in Africa.

In this section, I turn to *The World and Africa* to foreground the anticolonial elements of Du Bois's vision of democratic peace oriented around a global project of eliminating the conditions enabling world war in the economic exploitation of the colonies. Such a "vision of a world organized for peace" necessarily relied on a globalized conception of "industrial democracy" that would eliminate the "incentives to war."[79] In this vision, Du Bois turned to the socialistic and democratic character of ancient African civilizations not to highlight their cultural gifts to Western civilization but to illustrate the way that five hundred years of the slave trade and European colonialism laid the basis for the catastrophes of world war in the twentieth century through the decivilization of Africa. Such a focus provides an alternative way of interpreting the developmental, civilizational, and progressive idioms in Du Bois's writings on Africa that views them as more than simple reflections of prevailing imperial ideology.

In writing *The World and Africa*, Du Bois departed from the romantic protocols of vindicationist history in stating that the purpose of the book was to remind readers of "the crisis of civilization" initiated by the world wars. The failure to see the crisis is closely connected to historical rationalizations of black inferiority that upheld the "sugar empire" and the "cotton kingdom" insofar as both rested on the omission of Africa from human history. Properly understanding the crisis of World War II required grappling with the integral role that Africa has played in world history. Deliberately distancing *The World and Africa* from *The Negro* (1915) and *Black Folk Then and Now* (1939), Du Bois clarified that neither volume was written with a critical awareness of its position in the current conjuncture of world history, the fact of existing at "the end of an age which marked the final catastrophe of the old era of European world dominance."[80] Seen in this light, this reassessment of world history from the standpoint of Africa is not a backward-

---

78. Manu Vimalassery et al., "Introduction: On Colonial Unknowing," in "On Colonial Unknowing," ed. Alyosha Goldstein et al., special issue, *Theory & Event* 19, no. 4 (2016), https://muse.jhu.edu/article/633283.

79. Du Bois, *Darkwater*, 34.

80. Du Bois, *World and Africa*, xxxi.

looking attempt to vindicate the African past but becomes the basis for reimagining new global futures.

Rather than narrate a romantic search for a triumphant precolonial past that would be rediscovered in the age of decolonization, Du Bois turns to mythological images and tropes to reorient visions of world democracy around an anticolonial project of self-determination and globalized industrial democracy: specifically, the Greco-Roman myth of Andromeda. The myth of Andromeda was intricately connected to and indeed constitutive of Du Bois's world democratic imaginary. Stretching back to the manifesto of the Second Pan-African Congress of 1921, Du Bois wrote:

> The beginning of wisdom in inter-racial contact is the establishment of political institutions among suppressed peoples. The habit of democracy must be made to encircle the earth. Despite the attempt to prove that its practice is the secret and divine gift of the few, no habit is more natural or more widely spread among primitive people, or more easily capable of development among masses.[81]

Reflecting a radical democratic faith in the capacities of colonial peoples to rule themselves, these habits of self-rule appear not as the province of white Europeans. Consistent with his position that all colonial territories should be brought under an international trustee commission, he held that local self-government could be established almost immediately in the colonies with minimal oversight. Without such a program, theories of racial inferiority that undergird colonial rule would continue to shatter dreams of peace and international cooperation.

This global democratic vision, however, was not confined to the task of widening participatory self-rule by colonized peoples. It also entailed restoring indigenous ownership of the land through respect for customary forms of communal property as well as the protection of colonized peoples' labor against the depredations of European capital. More significantly, Du Bois wrote, it required the establishment of "a great black African state" that would pursue these goals, placing Africans among the "co-rulers of the world." Such a dream is "written in the stars."[82] Which constellation specifically pointed the direction of such fantastical hopes was unclear in 1921. But by the last chapter of *The World and Africa* in 1947, it became clear: the myth of Andromeda. Andromeda appeared in Greek mythology as the

---

81. Du Bois, *World and Africa*, 150. Cf. Du Bois, "To the World."

82. Du Bois, *World and Africa*, 150–51.

black daughter of Cepheus and Cassiopeia, the king and queen of Ethiopia. Angered at Cassiopeia's boast that her daughter was more beautiful than the Nereids (sea nymphs), the god Poseidon flooded the coastlands and sent a sea monster to punish the Ethiopians. After an oracle prophesized that the sacrifice of Andromeda was required to push the waters back, she was chained and left exposed on a shoreline cliff. The demigod Perseus, while returning from decapitating the Gorgon Medusa, flew by on his winged horse Pegasus, saw the beautiful princess, and immediately fell in love with Andromeda; he then killed the sea monster and rescued her. Perseus and Andromeda married, had children, and lived happily together in Greece for the rest of her life. "After her death," Du Bois recounts, "she reigned among the stars, her arms extended and chained, together with Cassiopeia and Perseus; and anyone may see them shining upon a beautiful night."[83]

Admitting that a world stricken with war and poverty might seem to have very little to do with a Greek myth, Du Bois maintained that the legend may provide crucial guidance in the present and the future. Indeed, the release of Andromeda from bondage by Perseus (whom Du Bois portrayed as Persian) portended the emancipation of colonial peoples and "the beginning of democracy among the majority of the people of the world."[84] Suggesting that just as the world should no longer exist "half slave and half free," Du Bois depicted Africa as the center of a global struggle for world democracy in the symbolism of the release of "dark Andromeda." Europe could only survive and overcome the present calamities if Asia and Africa joined as free and equal corulers of the world. Such was "the basic hope of world democracy," embodied in the "stars of dark Andromeda" that hang in the heavens above "this tortured world."[85]

Although it is most prominent in the last chapter of *The World and Africa*, the legend of Andromeda pervades the other chapters and provides a mythic structure for the book as a whole. Exemplifying "the original sin of capitalist accumulation," the exposure and sacrifice of Andromeda points to the opening up of Africa to the expropriation of land, resources, and labor under the process of primitive accumulation.[86] The release of Andromeda is thus release not only from colonial rule but also from the oligarchic dep-

83. Du Bois, *World and Africa*, 143.
84. Du Bois, *World and Africa*, 158.
85. Du Bois, *World and Africa*, 162, 164.
86. Abdulkarim Mustapha, "Constituting Negative Geopolitics: Memoriality and Event in *The World and Africa* (1946)," *boundary 2* 27, no. 3 (Fall 2000): 183–85.

redations of global capitalism. To capture these dynamics, I interpret the myth of Andromeda as a collection of images and tropes that Walter Benjamin calls a "constellation." Benjamin proposes constellation as a means of capturing the simultaneously objective and subjective nature of ideas. Objective, historical phenomena are not simply contained in and represented by conceptual thinking. The task of studying any historical concept is not to comprehend the object represented by the idea. Rather, ideas constitute the "objective, virtual arrangement" of historical objects. By way of analogy, Benjamin clarifies that "ideas are to objects as constellations are to stars." Rather than an objective depiction of the physical essence of the stars, constellations impose an "objective interpretation" by connecting many seemingly disparate points and elements.[87]

Thinking in constellations provides a means of capturing the distinct space-time imaginaries at work Du Bois's vision of democratic peace.[88] For Benjamin, a constellation projects a "dialectical image" conjoining past, present, and future that forms in a flash in the movement of history, capturing complex historical processes at a standstill.[89] While Benjamin used constellation primarily in a temporal sense to reveal the limits of positivist historicism, the constellation of Andromeda appears in Du Bois's text in both spatial and temporal forms. Spatially, Andromeda helps overcome the distortions generated by the production and circulation of valuable global commodities produced by colonized African laborers. If Benjamin was concerned with the "commodity-on-display" in the Parisian Arcade that fulfilled the contradictory desires of the exploited European working class, Du Bois captured how the consumption of these commodities in the metropole rested on the exploitation of colonized labor.[90] As Du Bois put it, "civilized life" in Europe depended on products from colonial possessions such as coffee, tea, diamonds, ivory, peppers, spices, sugar, vegetable oils, silk, and rubber. To the extent that these commodities are necessary to

---

87. Walter Benjamin, *The Origin of German Tragic Drama* (Verso, 1998), 134.

88. I do not claim that Du Bois self-consciously thought in terms of constellations. Rather, insofar as Andromeda constitutes a structuring mytheme of the text, using constellation as an interpretive heuristic can draw out illuminating dynamics of the text that are not immediately captured through sole attention to authorial intention.

89. Walter Benjamin, *The Arcades Project* (Belknap Press of Harvard University Press, 1999), 473, 475.

90. Branwen Gruffydd Jones, "Time, History, Politics: Anticolonial Constellations," *Interventions* 21, no. 5 (2019): 599.

modern life, it is built around the spatial architecture of "colonial ownership and exploitation."[91]

The failure to see this exploitation, however, is the result of a distinctive form of commodity fetishism—a process whereby a complex set of social relations of production, distribution, and exchange are presented as an "immense collection" of things—in which the colonial relations sustaining global commodity circulation are masked through the imposition of provincialist forms of space-time perception.[92] Du Bois writes, "Because of the stretch in time and space between the deed and the result, between the work and the product, it is not only usually impossible for the worker to know the consumer; or the investor, the source of his profit, but also it is often made impossible by law to inquire into the facts. Moral judgment of the industrial process is therefore difficult, and the crime is more often a matter of ignorance rather than of deliberate murder and theft; but ignorance is a colossal crime in itself."[93] While the dependence of modern life on the production of African commodities materially tied the citizen of the European metropole closer to the exploitation of the colonies, the stretching of space-time between consumption and production masked these underlying colonial social relations.

Yet the most important of the colonial commodities at the center of this process was the commodification of black flesh. Alongside the stretching of time and space that masked the global social relations of colonial commodity production, the slave trade also "exacted a justification," one that the made of the Negro both "a half-animal [and] an article of merchandise." To aid in this process, "the notion of fetish (Portuguese *feticeiro*) was invented as a symbol of African religion," which further reinforced the image of the "barbarous Negro" at the center of the European invention of the race concept.[94] As we see here, commodity fetishism in these colonial contexts operates both to stretch space-time so as to make complex relations of exploitation appear as relations between things *and* to temporally project African religious and social practices into a barbarous, premodern past by treating those practices as a fetish. To fetishize African slave labor as a commodity is not to subject it to wage labor and the illusion of the free con-

---

91. Du Bois, *World and Africa*, 22.

92. Karl Marx, *Capital*, vol. 1, trans. Ben Fowkes (Penguin, 1990), 125.

93. Du Bois, *World and Africa*, 26. See also Itzigsohn and Brown, *Sociology of W. E. B. Du Bois*, 79.

94. Du Bois, *World and Africa*, 49. Du Bois is quoting here the German ethnologist and folklorist Leo Frobenius.

tract; it is to turn the human being into a thing through a division between civilized forms of sociality and backward, fetishized forms of sociality. Du Bois's conception of commodity fetishism thus names both forms of spatial and temporal distortion.

In many respects, the historical and temporal aspects of the Andromeda constellation constitute an attempt to produce a new spatial imaginary that overcomes these distorting effects of commodity fetishism. For Benjamin, constellation as a theoretical method operates primarily temporally, as a means of connecting disparate historical moments across time and of exploring the limits of a historicism content with establishing linear and progressive causality. The historian who takes such a historicism as the point of a departure seeks to tell "the sequence of events like the beads of a rosary" instead of grasping "the constellation which his own era has formed with a definite earlier one."[95] Rather than establish linear connections between historical moments, the method of constellation cuts through our distorted assumptions about space and time by rearranging these elements, which are otherwise separated by vast distances and durations, in new ways.[96] It is precisely in this sense that the figure of Andromeda operates as an interpretive constellation in *The World and Africa*. By rearranging the elements of African history in the broader context of world history, Du Bois reveals new conceptual interconnections among democracy, peace, war, and empire.

One of the central features of this distinctive vision of democratic peace entails Du Bois's critique of a conception of progress and historical development in which the progressive surge of European history is dependent on the regressive impoverishment of the colonized and enslaved masses of the world. The singular characteristic feature of European development and modern capitalism was a process of what Du Bois provocatively called "progress by poverty," a mode of vast wealth accumulation in which the impoverishment of "the slaves of Africa and the peons of Asia" as well as "the mass of workers in England, France, Germany and the United States"

---

95. Walter Benjamin, "Theses on the Philosophy of History," in *Illuminations*, ed. Hannah Arendt, trans. Harry Zohn (Schocken Books, 1969), 263.

96. James Martel, *Textual Conspiracies: Walter Benjamin, Idolatry, and Political Theory* (University of Michigan Press, 2011), 9–10. Also relevant here is Lisa Lowe's notion of the "intimacies of four continents," which provides a "constellation of asymmetrical and unevenly legible intimacies" that involve "considering scenes of close connection in relation to a global geography that one more often conceives in terms of vast spatial distances." In representing black Andromeda as Africa and Perseus as Persian, Du Bois tacitly invokes these asymmetrical intimacies; Lowe, *Intimacies of Four Continents*, 18.

laid the foundation the progressive economic development of European states.[97] For Du Bois, this conception of "progress by poverty" expressed the primary contradictions of European civilization, which culminated in the present catastrophe of global war. In making these claims, he deliberately fashioned his world history of Africa as a history of the present.[98]

Progress by poverty in turn required theories of inferiority and superiority to present such dynamics as the natural and inevitable result of history. If rampant poverty was the main cause of European wealth accumulation, then the outcomes of the process—disease, ignorance, and crime—needed to be "represented as natural characteristics of backward peoples." In this ideological architecture, missionary and scientific ideologies were deployed to prove the "unfitness of most human beings for self-rule and self-expression." Aspirations for democracy among colonial peoples appeared as the result of "agitators" rather than the people themselves.[99] In this way, progress by poverty rested on a profound denial of the epistemic capacities and habits of global laboring classes for popular self-rule. Out of this conception of progress thus "emerged the doctrine of the Superior Race: the theory that a minority of the people of Europe are by birth and natural gift the rulers of mankind; rulers of their own suppressed labor classes and . . . heaven-sent rulers of yellow, brown, and black people."[100]

The idea of progress by poverty powerfully condenses a number of European practices of imperial rule into one historical trope. Chief among these is the slave trade. For Du Bois, "the trade in human beings between Africa and America, which flourished between the Renaissance and the American Civil War," constitutes "the prime and effective cause of the contradictions in European civilization and the illogic in modern thought and the collapse of human culture." Echoing the gendered violence of exposing Andromeda on the cliffside, Du Bois refers to the entwined "rebirth of civilization in Europe" and the emergence of the transatlantic slave trade which sustained this rebirth during the Renaissance as "the rape of Africa."[101]

The exposure of African resources not only led to the rebirth of European civilization; it also transformed the world as a whole and fundamentally altered historical developments across the African continent. To

97. Du Bois, *World and Africa*, 16.

98. "I want to appeal to the past in order to explain the present"; Du Bois, *World and Africa*, 50.

99. Du Bois, *World and Africa*, 23.

100. Du Bois, *World and Africa*, 11–12.

101. Du Bois, *World and Africa*, 27–28.

foreground these dynamics, Du Bois takes aim at the ways that historiography of his time wrote Africa out of the history of humanity: "Africa and the Negro have been read almost out of the bounds of humanity. They lost in modern thought their history and cultures. All that was human in Africa was deemed European or Asiatic. Africa was no integral part of the world because the world which raped it had to pretend that it had not harmed a man but a thing."[102] To the extent that both pre-European African development and the constitutive role of the African slave trade in shaping modern capitalism were cast out of history, it is necessary to rewrite world history in a way that not only recenters both dynamics but also constellates them alongside each other.

The mythic image of Andromeda again powerfully captures this constellation of historical forces. In her research on "the Black Andromeda," Elizabeth McGrath has shown that ancient sources almost universally located Andromeda at the remote edges of the earth in a land south of Egypt called "Ethiopia" (which refers to "sunburnt" complexion) but also continually referred to her blackness. Ovid, who wrote the locus classicus of the myth, foregrounded the image of "dark Andromeda" who charmed Perseus with her "native color," with historians such as Pliny and Strabo following suit.[103] The historical puzzle is how, when, and why Andromeda became white. McGrath shows two key things on this front. First, while the majority of Renaissance-era artistic depictions portrayed Andromeda as white, at least three painters and engravers preserved her blackness. Second, the painters who whitened Andromeda did so not out of ignorance. Rather, Christian norms associating blackness with darkness and sin and aesthetic standards associating whiteness with beauty conspired to mask the Ethiopian roots of the mythic legend.[104]

The legend, therefore, exhibits a doubled mythological valence: the binding of Andromeda condensed a complex set of associated processes by which European civilization was built on colonialism and the slave trade; and the whitening of Andromeda arranged together the historiographical practices by which these developments as well as the civilizational development of the African continent itself were disavowed. It is in this way that the dual binding and whitening of Andromeda depicts the peculiarity of the modern conception of freedom taking root during the Renaissance: "The

---

102. Du Bois, *World and Africa*, 50.

103. Elizabeth McGrath, "The Black Andromeda," *Journal of the Warburg and Courtauld Institutes* 55 (1992): 5, 8.

104. McGrath, "Black Andromeda," 7–12.

new thing in the Renaissance was not simply freedom of spirit and body, but a new freedom to destroy freedom; freedom for eager merchants to exploit labor; freedom for white men to make black slaves."[105] Progress in Renaissance Europe was tied to "scientific enslavement of the major portion of mankind" in which the progress of Africa and Europe became mutually exclusive.[106] The whitening of Andromeda powerfully captures the racialized logics of modern historiography that read the civilizational development of Africa out of stories of modernity, in which all economic, political, and technical advancements were presented as achievements of white Europeans. In turn, any progressive steps made by Africans were attributed to either the status of those peoples as white or to intermixture with white blood or white civilization.

To illustrate these dynamics, Du Bois turned to the civilizational mythologies of Egyptology. Separated from African history more broadly, Egyptian culture and history appeared in modern historiography as the result of its Asiatic elements. The English historian Arnold Toynbee, in his twelve-volume *A Study of History*, went so far as to depict Egyptian civilization as explicitly white and European.[107] Such tactics of historical disavowal have the unmistakable imprint of Hegelian historiography, which separated "Africa proper" from the "European Africa" of the Mediterranean and the Asiatic Africa of the Nile River valley. "Africa proper," Hegel continues, "as far as History goes back, has remained—for all purposes of connection with the rest of the World—shut up."[108] Sustaining this view, the modern science of Egyptology that arose at the height of the cotton kingdom in the nineteenth century disconnected Egyptian history from African history more broadly, in turn reinforcing racial images that cast Africans as unfit for economic and political development. In doing so, Egyptology not only arose alongside modern industrial capitalism but sustained it by further rationalizing the degradation of African societies.

To correct these ongoing historical disavowals, Du Bois deliberately contests conventional space-time imaginaries of European modernity by adopting a geological perspective stretching back to "the peopling of Af-

---

105. Du Bois, *Black Folk*, 91.

106. Du Bois, *World and Africa*, 140–41.

107. Du Bois, *World and Africa*, 63.

108. G. W. F. Hegel, *Philosophy of History* (Colonial Press, 1899), 91. Against this image, Du Bois extensively recounts how the ancient Greek writers such as Herodotus viewed Egypt as both geographically and culturally African; Du Bois, *World and Africa*, 63, 77–78.

rica." Echoing the cosmological timescale of Wells's *Short History of the World*, Du Bois begins his account of African development with an image of the world emerging "two thousand million years" ago out of a "fiery mist." He further unsettles conventional space-time imaginaries of European modernity by adopting a geological perspective stretching back to the ancient supercontinent of Gondwanaland, which united Africa, South America, and Asia. Africa in its "modern form" emerged when the continents separated, and lower Egypt, once submerged in what would become the Mediterranean Sea, arose out of the water as "great rivers poured down the hills between the Red Sea, and the Nile found old and new valleys." From such a geological perspective, Du Bois expands the timescale of the "modern world" beyond the temporal frame of European modernity marked by the colonization of the Americas and the rise of globalized commercial exchange, cosmopolitanism, secularism, and liberalism.[109] It is within this temporally capacious perspective that Du Bois turns to political and economic developments in ancient Egypt as one of the first stages in the civilizational development of the African continent.

Foremost in Du Bois's mind here was the problem of building a sedentary, agricultural civilization along a powerful and wildly unpredictable river. The "first duty" of Pharaonic government was to bring the river under control, wedding "the power of the king" to "the science of the priest [and] the independence of the laborer." This made, at least to Du Bois, Egypt under the Eighteenth Dynasty (ca. 1500 BCE) "the first human example of state socialism."[110] However, Du Bois goes on to clarify that much of Egyptian culture, history, and politics is derived from Ethiopian civilization: "In Ethiopia the sunrise of human culture took place, spreading down into the Nile valley.... Ethiopia, land of the blacks, was thus the cradle of European civilization."[111] Such an interpretation overtly contradicts the theories of the natural inferiority of black folk that stands at the foundations of modern capitalism, which render them a cheap and exploitable labor force for the production of global commodities. Those who upheld an idea of progress by poverty thus sought a model of history and science that would undermine this interpretation. If Egypt had a highly advanced civilization with centralized political structures, it would contradict representations of

---

109. Du Bois, *World and Africa*, 52–53. Here I am indebted to Inder Marwah, who explores how Darwinian evolutionism accomplishes similar objectives in anticolonial contexts; "Darwin in India."

110. Du Bois, *World and Africa*, 67.

111. Du Bois, *World and Africa*, 75.

Africans as uncivilized and as natural slaves that were at the center of proslavery ideology, and so Egypt had to be written out of Africa.

At probably the most important point in the broader constellation, Du Bois mythologized the development of Western Africa from 500 to 1500 CE as a series of advanced Atlantean civilizations. Noting that the "whole culture complex of the African West Coast is native and original," Du Bois attributed the progress of the region to the presence of an "integral collectivism" that variously characterized the peoples of West Africa. "Yet on the West Coast was perhaps the greatest attempt in human history before the twentieth century to build a culture based on peace and beauty, to establish a communism of industry and of distribution of goods and services according to human need."[112] Linking progress with the extension of democracy not just to government but also to work and industry, such a narrative sought to illustrate that the polities of West Africa during the fourteenth and fifteenth centuries represented the culmination of centuries of diverse and disparate civilizational developments in Africa. For Du Bois, there was no doubt that the level of economic and political development in these polities was equal to and perhaps even greater than Europe during this time at the dawn of the Renaissance.

Such collectivist and democratic practices further laid the foundation for anticolonial agitation in the nineteenth and twentieth centuries. In examples such as the Fanti confederation movement of 1867 and the creation of the Gold Coast Aborigines Rights Protection Society in 1899 (ARPS), colonized peoples' movements for self-rule continually sought to democratize colonial governments by limiting the scope and power of commercial enterprise in the region and by seeking government recognition from colonial administrators and metropolitan officials. Such movements insisted that democracy was not a foreign import but was in many respects a native political tradition. In their demand for recognition, the National Congress of British West Africa (which evolved from the ARPS) declared in 1920, "In the demand for the franchise by the people of British West Africa it is not to be supposed that they are asking to be allowed to copy a foreign institution." Rather, the practice and principle of representative elections was deeply rooted in the political systems of British West Africa. In such systems, the congress recounted, political society is rooted in an arrangement of nested political units within larger jurisdictions ranging from the family and village councils up through provincial assemblies up to the Supreme Council, with

---

112. Du Bois, *World and Africa*, 103.

the "Paramount Chief" as the presiding authority. Such a system was "essentially a democratic one" in which chiefs are beholden to and dependent on "the will of the people."[113]

It is tempting to see these attempts to locate pre-European forms of democracy and socialism in Africa in the broader script of romantic history that seeks to vindicate the civilizational gift of black folk.[114] Yet the more overt purpose of recovering these African forms of socialism and democracy was to emphasize the way in which the slave trade and ensuing processes of colonial imperialism uprooted the social bases of these economic and political forms. Du Bois asks: "What stopped and degraded this development? The slave trade; that modern change from regarding wealth as being for the benefit of human beings, to that of regarding human beings as wealth."[115] As a space-time constellation, Andromeda exemplifies how European progress not only coincided with but depended on the economic degradation of Africa. The binding and release of Andromeda holds together both the progressive and regressive aspects of modern colonial history in a single dialectical image: the progressive history of civilizational advance in Africa and the regressive history of its decivilization. Seen in this light, Andromeda is a constellation in the sense that it expands the timescale of colonial modernity, exploding historical distinctions between modern and premodern and connecting disparate historical processes separated by millennia. Embedded in the figure of Andromeda, the idea of "progress by poverty" projects an image of history as a negative dialectic of sorts, a concept of progress that, according to Theodor Adorno, "articulates the movement of society while at the same time contradicting it."[116]

Yet it is important to appreciate how this historical constellation does not entirely eschew developmental idioms but rather appropriates and repurposes them for different use than their conventional imperial lineages would suggest. Against the popular image of Du Bois as a postcolonial thinker who entirely jettisoned progressive historical tropes, it is essential to

---

113. Du Bois, *World and Africa*, 147–48; Du Bois, "Black Africa Tomorrow," 105–6.

114. Du Bois is careful not to represent Africa in terms of an essential unity: "There is thus no one African race and no one Negro type. Africa has as great a physical and cultural variety as Europe and Asia." There are "infinitely varied inhabitants" of Africa. Du Bois, *World and Africa*, 61.

115. Du Bois, *World and Africa*, 103.

116. Theodor Adorno, "Progress," in *Critical Models: Interventions and Catchwords*, trans. Henry W. Pickford (Columbia University Press, 2005), 148.

understand the way that developmental idioms operate in his transnational thought.[117] While Du Bois clearly upholds the relevance of developmental discourses, the lack of development in West Africa is not the result of innate tribal communism but rather the slave trade and the successive waves of colonial imperialism it unleashed. Like Walter Rodney almost three decades later, Du Bois illuminated the transatlantic slave trade as the "disavowed motor" of uneven development and self-consciously "reworked developmental idioms . . . to forge new meanings of 'progress' that diverged from dominant models." For both, development is a nonlinear process that involves critical reflection on the disavowed historical trajectories that might serve as recoverable elements of a new path forward.[118]

The recovery of African capacities for socialism and democracy was vital to Du Bois's broader vision of democratic peace. In the complex constellation projected by the myth of Andromeda, it was precisely the disavowal of these capacities for development and self-rule that led to the cataclysm of world war. The question of the fitness of colonial peoples for self-rule was thus central to the question of world peace. The antidemocratic tendencies of imperial ideology, in their assumption that democracy was the unique province of European races, constituted a driving force of global conflict. Without affirming the historical and contemporary capacities of African colonial subjects for democratic rule, the conditions for world war and capitalist exploitation would continue to ripen. The release of Andromeda portends not only an image of anticolonial self-determination but also the peace obtained through world democracy. The effect is to recompose a new constellation of democratic modernity with Africa at the center, which in turn provides the foundation for a new form of democratic peace based on self-determination for colonial peoples and the disinherited masses of the European metropole.

As a vision of democratic peace, the Andromeda constellation entails an affirmation of African capacities for democratic self-rule and self-determination as well as the economic transformation of metropolitan-imperial economies. To capture this vision, it is helpful to briefly look at Du Bois's avowed influences on the final chapter on Andromeda. In the

117. See Valdez, *Transnational Cosmopolitanism*, 89–95.

118. David Temin, "Development in Decolonization: Walter Rodney, Third World Developmentalism, and 'Decolonizing Political Theory,'" *American Political Science Review* 117, no. 1 (February 2023): 240–41. See also Inder Marwah, "Provincializing Progress: Developmentalism and Anti-Imperialism in Colonial India," *Polity* 51, no. 3 (July 2019): 498–531.

foreword, he specifically notes that the final chapter of the book heavily relied on the work of the British anticolonial journalist Leonard Barnes and the political theorist Harold Laski (whom Du Bois repeatedly referenced throughout *The World Search for Democracy*). Barnes, who circulated in British anticolonial circles alongside Padmore, argued in his 1939 book *Empire or Democracy?* that the "root-defect" of liberal internationalism was its privileging of the principle of national sovereignty in such postwar peace settlements as the League of Nations.[119] From Barnes's perspective, the league failed to prevent war because it left nation-state sovereignty intact: "The roots of war reach deep down into the social structure of national societies. Before a lasting peace system can be set up, the inward character of nationhood must change."[120] According to Barnes, the "hard core of national sovereignty" in liberal thought had constituted "the main stumbling block to the organization of world peace." Insofar as corporate powers and the ruling classes use nation-state sovereignty to consolidate economic power through war, Barnes continued, peace cannot be achieved until this "hard core" is excised.[121] Although Du Bois never argued for the abolition of state sovereignty, it is clear that the excision of this "hard core" of national sovereignty is a precondition for democratic peace.

As Laski had long observed, it was precisely the hard core of national sovereignty that prevented the democratization of economic relations within the nation-state.[122] In a series of works in the 1930s, Laski characterized nation-state sovereignty as the "protective rampart of exactly those [capitalist] interests in society to which war and peace are no more than alternative ways of securing their special ends."[123] Yet he clarified that the state is the same in its internal relations as it is in its external relations, using the force of sovereignty to protect capitalist interests at home and abroad. As such, class inequality within the nation-state and colonial hierarchy

---

119. While Du Bois explicitly lists Barnes's *Soviet Light on the Colonies* (1944) in the foreword to *The World and Africa*, he elsewhere places *Empire or Democracy?* on "Africa: A selected list of books and articles published before 1945," in box 6, Du Bois Collection, Fisk University.

120. Barnes, *Empire or Democracy?*, 207–8.

121. Barnes, *Empire or Democracy?*, 211.

122. While not as deep as his friendship with Wells, Du Bois's acquaintance with Laski stretched back to the Pan-African Congresses of the 1920s where the British political theorist spoke. In England for the 1945 Pan-African Congress, Du Bois also visited Laski, who had previously helped him secure a British visa for the trip.

123. Harold Laski, "The Economic Foundations of Peace," in *The Intelligent Man's Way to Prevent War*, ed. Leonard Woolf (Garland, 1973), 533.

outside are closely linked. Insofar as the state asserts sovereignty to protect and expand capitalist interests through war, absolute sovereignty and a peaceful world order are fundamentally antithetical. If war is an expression of rampant inequality within capitalist societies and global capitalist order, then economic democracy is the only true path to peace.[124] While socialism was therefore not a sufficient condition for eliminating the monistic state as the basis of world order, the transformation of capitalist society was necessary for radically transforming an international society organized around sovereign states, which secured not a genuine peace but merely a "capitalist peace" as a "breathing-space between wars."[125]

For both Laski and Du Bois, the transformation of exploitative class relations within the state can only be pursued by attending to the deep connections between class exploitation, race, war, and empire—that is, by deprovincializing questions of war and peace. Any attempt to transform class relations from within the monistic state alone would reproduce the conditions for permanent global war rooted in an economically stratified world order.[126] The pursuit of a global industrial democracy rested on mapping the connections between the production of these stratifications within the metropole and the production of global war through colonial exploitation and interimperial competition that cut across the borders of national sovereignty. In this way, Du Bois's anticolonialism and peace activism are intricately connected. As Charise Burden-Stelly and Gerald Horne have put it, "He knew that peace activism was impossible without the eradication of imperialism; likewise, anti-imperialism made little sense without dedication to a durable peace.... Thus, the elimination of war was not merely the

---

124. Harold Laski, *The State in Theory and Practice* (Viking Press, 1935), 204, 209. It is not coincidental that, drawing on Laski, Du Bois spoke on "the economic aspects of peace" at a peace meeting held by a federation of peace organizations in New York with Harry Emerson Fosdick as chair and Jane Addams as vice-chair; W. E. B. Du Bois, "How May Another World War Be Averted" (October 25–31, 1931), box 13, Du Bois Collection, Fisk University; W. E. B. Du Bois to Seymour Waldman, 23 October 1931, box 12, Du Bois Collection, Fisk University.

125. Laski, *State in Theory and Practice*, 227–28; Peter Lamb, "Harold Laski (1893–1950): Political Theorist of a World in Crisis," *Review of International Studies* 25, no. 2 (1999): 332.

126. In this regard, Du Bois can be placed in the broader context of efforts of radical theorists to "re-conceptualize a sphere for international democracy through a critique of sovereignty" most powerfully represented by Laski; Jeanne Morefield, "States Are Not People: Harold Laski on Unsettling Sovereignty, Rediscovering Democracy," *Political Research Quarterly* 58, no. 4 (December 2005): 660.

absence of global antagonism; it was also the historical fulfillment of equality, justice, and the end of capitalist exploitation."[127]

Racial Provincialism Redux

Despite the prophetic invocations of the release of Andromeda as a dual vision of decolonization and democratic peace, Du Bois's ripening frustrations with the United Nations in the late 1940s as well as the reassertion of US neocolonial power increasingly eroded his faith in the possibility of a radical democratic peace. This last section briefly traces how this vision of democratic peace receded with the failure of the UN to secure racial equality, the consolidation of corporate oligarchy in the United States, the onset of the nuclear arms race, and the climate of hysteria and repression during the Cold War. As we saw in chapter 4, the UN's affirmation of "domestic jurisdiction" strengthened rather than eroded the primacy of nation-state sovereignty in international law, which by the onset of the 1950s had become increasingly conjoined to the neocolonial expansion of corporate power. As his faith in the UN to ensure a peaceful and democratic world order receded, Du Bois displayed a prescient sobriety that these hopes of global cooperation would give way to a world defined by endless war.

Following his departure from the NAACP over his public endorsement of Henry Wallace in the 1948 presidential race, Du Bois became a central figure of the radical peace movement and a persistent object of Cold War repression by the US national security state. In a 1949 speech to the World Peace Council in Paris, he began to challenge Cold War dichotomies pitting liberalism against totalitarianism by turning to his guiding assumption—stretching back to "The African Roots of War"—that world war is in the last instance ignited by interimperial rivalries for colonial spoils. Against the official ideology of the Cold War state, he asserted, "The real cause of the differences which threaten world war is not the spread of socialism or even of the complete socialism which communism envisages."[128] Rather, even in the post–World War II context, colonialism remained the chief cause of world war. Cold War hysteria over the spread of socialism and Soviet aggression gave US empire a new alibi that masked "the rebirth of colonialism" in

---

127. Burden-Stelley and Horne, *W. E. B. Du Bois: A Life in American History*, 206.

128. Du Bois, "Colonies as Cause of War" (April 20, 1949), Du Bois Papers, box 199, p. 1.

the form of economic neocolonialism.[129] Despite promises of postwar reconstruction, the seeds of global war continued to be sown in Africa in the efforts to "rebuild an old-world economy on slave labor." Rather than an anticolonial power, the United States was leading "this new colonial imperialism" that combined informal economic control of colonies abroad with the imposition of a "frightful militarism" at home.[130]

Emerging out of this and other meetings of the radical peace movement, Du Bois returned home and began to help organize the Peace Information Center (PIC), the aim of which was "simply to tell the people of the United States what other nations were doing and thinking about war."[131] Conceived as a transnational arbiter of information, the PIC's main activities were circulating "peacegrams" that presented the plans and proposals of various peace movements throughout the world. Foremost among these peacegrams was the Stockholm Appeal issued by the World Peace Council in 1950. In the wake of the inception of the Korean War and US President Harry Truman's announcement to pursue the development of a hydrogen bomb, the appeal called for a ban on atomic weapons and argued that any government using such weapons "will be committing a crime against humanity and should be treated as a war criminal."[132]

Shortly after recirculating the Stockholm Appeal, the PIC was indicted for failing to register as a foreign agent under the Foreign Agents Registration Act of 1938. Based on testimony from John Rogge, a founding member of the PIC, the prosecution held that whereas the express purpose of the organization was peace, "the real purpose was to promote the foreign policy of the Soviet Union."[133] Du Bois recounted these events in his 1952 memoir, *In Battle for Peace*. Partially, the book reads as what Eric Porter calls a "self-interested, extended performance of righteousness."[134] But more than that, I want to briefly read the text as a performance of transnational democratic practice and as an extended critique of resurgent race provincialism during the Cold War. Responding to the Department of Justice request that officers of the PIC register as foreign agents, the organization responded that it was entirely "American in its conception and formation. Its activities

---

129. Du Bois, "Colonies as Cause of War," p. 7.
130. Du Bois, "Colonies as Cause of War," pp. 10–11.
131. Du Bois, *In Battle for Peace*, 22.
132. Quoted in Porter, *Problem of the Future World*, 159.
133. Du Bois, *In Battle for Peace*, 89.
134. Porter, *Problem of the Future World*, 162.

were intended to and do relate only to the people of the United States."[135] The avowed purpose of the PIC in response to such accusations was the attempt to articulate the desire of the American people for peace.

It is tempting to read such reactions as the performance of patriotic duty vis-à-vis the demands for national loyalty from the Cold War state. In a public release commenting on the indictment, the defendants denied that "peace is a foreign idea," suggesting that the demand for peace comes from within the US political tradition. At the same time, they gladly admitted "that they gathered and publicized ideas and news of action for peace from everywhere they could obtain them." Resisting attempts of the US state to curtail the transnational circulation of peace discourse, the circular went on to say that "the United States has laid no embargo on the importation of ideas, or knowledge of international effort for social uplift."[136] Such an assertion suggests that the efforts of the PIC were less to foreground nationalistic commitments to peace than they were to open the nation itself up to transformation stemming from the transnational circulation of radical peace ideals. For the prosecution, ideals of peace that threatened liberal hegemony were foreign grafts imposed on the nation. Yet in asserting that the PIC was American in its conception while at once insisting that the nation cannot lay embargo on the import of ideas, Du Bois and his codefendants articulated an image of transnational citizenship in which civic practices and ideals were constituted not just within the nation but also through cross-national flows of peace activism and discourse.

In a surprising show of justice, the court agreed with the arguments of the defense that parallel views are not sufficient to establish a principal-agent relationship. Just as two parallel lines might move along the same path but never meet, the PIC could not be considered foreign agents unless the two lines intersected—that is, unless proof of a principal-agent nexus was shown.[137] The judge then chastised the prosecution, "You have to show the connection. . . . I may be in Timbuctoo and you may be in some place in South America. I may be shaving and using Gillette brushless shaving cream and you may be doing the same thing, but there is no connection except we are both using Gillette."[138] That the court acquitted Du Bois and his codefendants on this basis was remarkable, not least for the way in which it

---

135. Du Bois, *In Battle for Peace*, 34.
136. Du Bois, *In Battle for Peace*, 37.
137. Du Bois, *In Battle for Peace*, 88.
138. Du Bois, *In Battle for Peace*, 90.

gave them ammunition against the repressive strategies of Cold War liberalism. Indeed, "parallelism" was an overt "statist technology" that federal prosecutors deployed to criminalize black radical modes of anti-imperial thought and practice as consonant with Soviet ideology and aims.[139]

Yet despite the acquittal, a bright spot in an unbearably dark episode, the experience had a lasting impact on Du Bois and in many respects shaped his fluctuating understanding of the relationships among democracy, empire, and the global color line for the remainder of his life. What left such a significant impression was not just that the Cold War state would seek to repress radical peace activism but rather the way in which black liberal intellectuals failed to come to his defense. To be sure, small pockets of the black press did defend Du Bois and his codefendants. The Boston *Guardian* pronounced that in tying the problems of colonialism to the problems of war and peace, Du Bois had developed into a "world statesman." Yet on the whole, "the Talented Tenth," the black intellectual and professional classes, did not speak up.[140] The NAACP even went so far as to try to discontinue his pension after the federal indictment.[141]

This failure of the Talented Tenth on this front was the result of the racial provincialism at the center of what Burden-Stelly characterizes as "Black Cold War liberalism," which "construed Black radical demands for freedom such as the redistribution of wealth and resources, the eradication of poverty, improved labor conditions, increased living standards, and an end to capitalist exploitation as counterproductive to Black progress."[142] For black Cold War liberals, progress in the areas of increased voting rights and desegregation proceeded through support for US foreign policy imperatives. The result, Du Bois observed, was that the "color-line is yielding in the matter of voting and admission to schools." Yet these gains were indelibly tied to support for Cold War foreign policy. Black students were even sent abroad on scholarships, but always, Du Bois recounts, "with the understanding that they will defend or at least not attack the policy of this nation in regard to Negroes."[143]

The paradox of these developments was that the lessening of racial dis-

---

139. Charise Burden-Stelly, "Black Cold War Liberalism as Agency Reduction Formation During the Late 1940s and the Early 1950s," *International Journal of Africana Studies* 19, no. 2 (Fall–Winter 2018): 92.

140. Du Bois, *In Battle for Peace*, 51.

141. Porter, *Problem of the Future World*, 161.

142. Burden-Stelly, "Black Cold War Liberalism," 77.

143. Du Bois, *In Battle for Peace*, 123.

crimination did not lead to the greater embrace of socialism and democracy. Rather, Du Bois asserted, "partial emancipation is freeing [African Americans] to ape the worst of American and Anglo-Saxon chauvinism" and "to follow in the footsteps of western acquisitive society, with its exploitation of labor, monopoly of land and its resources, and with private profit for the smart and unscrupulous in a world of poverty, disease and ignorance, as the natural end of human culture."[144] Such dynamics, in which advances in civil rights were necessarily predicated on war and empire, exemplified the dynamics of "progress by poverty." Further, Du Bois explicitly noted that his experiences with the indictment had finally freed him from his own "racial provincialism" at the center of his own visions of black leadership.[145] This new freedom allowed him to fully see that black inclusion into the Cold War state not only advanced US ambitions for global supremacy but also deflected critical analysis of economic inequality and racial domination domestically.[146]

In opposition to a vision of liberal citizenship in which inclusion rested on acquiescence to the national security imperatives of the Cold War state, which Aziz Rana calls "national security citizenship," Du Bois posed peace activism as a necessary feature of transnational democratic citizenship.[147] Yet he increasingly feared that the transnational sensibilities necessary for his vision of citizenship could not be cultivated within the boundaries of nation-state alone. One of the causes of the resurgence of racial provincialism was the ideological boundaries imposed by Cold War liberalism and the climate of hysteria and repression in the 1950s, which issued in the restriction of international mobility as well as the circulation of transnational practices and habits of citizenship. In a 1958 speech called "Forty Years of American Hysteria," Du Bois proclaimed that in the face of Cold War repression, African Americans should double down not only on the right to know what socialism is and to express free opinions but also on "the right to travel, see, and know what is happening in the world, particularly in socialist countries."[148] He undoubtedly had in mind his own experiences with

---

144. Du Bois, *In Battle for Peace*, 107.

145. Du Bois, *In Battle for Peace*, 107.

146. Porter, *Problem of the Future World*, 164.

147. Aziz Rana, "Against National Security Citizenship," *Boston Review* (February 7, 2018), https://www.bostonreview.net/articles/aziz-rana-against-national-security-citizenship/.

148. W. E. B. Du Bois, "Forty Years of American Hysteria" (1958), Du Bois Papers, box 206, p. 24.

the US State Department continually revoking or delaying issuance of his passport with the intent of limiting his critical influence abroad.

But at a deeper level, he captures here how ideologies and repressive practices of racial provincialism not only violate mobility rights and freedom of expression but also consolidate the domestication of racial oppression within the borders of the constitutional nation-state. As part of the edifice that sustains US empire, racial provincialism is a habit of "empire as a way of life," pointing to the ways that "imperial politics take root in seemingly everyday habits of thought and action in modern times."[149] In casting racial provincialism as a habit of empire, Du Bois confronted forms of US exceptionalism that disconnect the race problem domestically from the broader problems of empire globally. The United States exemplifies the danger of succumbing to the illusions of sovereignty, "the image of the independent, self-contained democracy" that hides "from view its dependence on transnational relations of power," as Jennifer Pitts and Adom Getachew put it.[150] In this respect, the problem of racial provincialism ideologically masks how the domestic color line is merely the "local phase" of a broader "world problem." "The average American," Du Bois wrote, "is apt to regard the Negro problem as parochial and temporary: parochial as being largely localized in the Southern United States and temporary as being a passing phase of the slavery problem."[151] Although local manifestations of the color line both structure and reproduce imperial power, global processes also reshape the specificities of the color line at the local level. Masking these transnational connections, the impulse to provincialize the problem of the color line is symptomatic of a broader tendency to restrict democratic imaginaries to the singular scale of the sovereign nation-state.

From Racial Vindication to Human Emancipation

This chapter has sought to illuminate the vision of democratic peace as a Benjaminian constellation best represented by the figure of Andromeda.

---

149. Alexander Livingston, *Damn Great Empires: William James and the Politics of Pragmatism* (Oxford University Press, 2016), 156; William Appleman Williams, *Empire as a Way of Life* (Oxford University Press, 1980). See also Jeanne Morefield, "Harold Laski on the Habits of Imperialism," in *Lineages of Empire: The Historical Roots of British Imperial Thought*, ed. Duncan Kelly (Oxford University Press, 2009), 213–37; Dahl, *Empire of the People*.

150. Getachew and Pitts, "Disclosing the Problem of Empire," 6.

151. Du Bois, "World Problem of the Color Line," 35.

During World War I and the interwar period, Du Bois developed an enduring concern with a habit of liberal citizenship oriented around what he called "racial provincialism," which was crucial to understanding his antiwar thought and activism in the 1940s and 1950s. Race provincialism, however, was not simply a failure of intellect or theoretical insight but a failure of the broader political imaginary within which both peace activists and racial liberals operated. To make democracy a way of life that encircles the earth requires the cultivation of new habits and political capacities that would deprovincialize the problems of war, peace, race, empire, and global capitalism. To sow the seeds for the cultivation of these habituated modes of transnational citizenship, Du Bois turned to the constellation of Andromeda, which tied the affirmation of democratic capacities for self-rule in Africa and the radical restructuring of the global capitalist economy to the elimination of endless war. In envisioning democracy as a habitualized way of life that encircles the earth, the constellation of Andromeda projects new anticolonial futures of peace and economic reconstruction.

Yet, as I have argued, the myth of Andromeda signifies much more than a project of racially vindicating the gift of black folk to the progress of world civilization. It illuminates a conception of anticolonial self-determination not as a particularistic project of racial assertion but as a universalistic project of what Karl Marx, in "On the Jewish Question," called "human emancipation." Stretching back to 1925, Du Bois declared that the duty of "the New Politics" was to illustrate how the uplift of the "disinherited classes of white nations" was not only connected to but dependent on the social uplift of the colonized masses.[152] Continuing this thread in the midst of his radical peace activism and indictment by the US government for failing to register as a foreign agent in the 1950s, he proclaimed that this recent experience of political repression accelerated his continued emergence from "provincial racialism" that began after the First World War and ultimately led him toward a "world conception of human uplift" that cast ideals of peace through the elimination of interimperial conflict over economic control of the colonies as the foundation of world democracy.[153]

Despite his focus on Africa and the colonized world, Du Bois clarified that the slave trade did not simply degrade the colonial labor force. Rather, it was "the incredible accumulation of wealth based on slave labor" that

---

152. Karl Marx, "On the Jewish Question," in *The Marx-Engels Reader*, 2nd ed., ed. Robert Tucker (Norton, 1978), 30; W. E. B. Du Bois, "Africa and the New Peace" (ca. 1925), Du Bois Papers, box 215, pp. 7–8.

153. Du Bois, *In Battle for Peace*, 125.

undergirded industrialization and world trade that made the degradation of human labor both "vaster and deeper."[154] Insofar as slavery was partially the cause of rather than strictly the product of modern labor degradation in Europe, the emancipation of colonized labor in important respects indexes the emancipation of white labor. Du Bois clarified that this is not to suggest that the ancient and medieval worlds in Europe had genuine respect for labor. Rather, his point is that it was partially through the African slave trade that human labor first became commodified on a global scale. While the nineteenth century saw a substantial increase in the power of laboring classes as well as greater economic equality and expanded suffrage, labor was nonetheless associated in popular opinion with the degradation and burden of those deemed to be inferior peoples. In this respect, the "investment in human flesh" constituted "the first experiment in organized modern capitalism" and "indeed made capitalism possible."[155] Revolts by enslaved people therefore had a universalistic resonance as "the beginnings of the revolutionary struggle for the uplift of the laboring masses in the modern world."[156] Only by viewing the uplift of white and colonized labor as intricately connected could the vision of peace and world democracy signified by Andromeda be made a reality.

Uncovering these anticolonial visions of democratic peace, which fractured at precisely the moment that the liberal conceptions gained ascendance during the Cold War, can help restore the centrality of visions of peace to radical democratic theory. Indeed, the dominance of this version of democratic peace that holds that liberal democracies do not go to war with one another is symptomatic of "a troubling contracting of our political vision."[157] In living through the consolidation of this contracted liberal vision during the 1940s and 1950s, Du Bois sought to restore the centrality visions of peace to the pursuit of socialism and anticolonial politics.

154. Du Bois, *World and Africa*, 13.

155. Du Bois, *World and Africa*, 43.

156. Du Bois, *World and Africa*, 38.

157. Christopher Hobson, "Democratic Peace: Progress and Critics," *Perspectives on Politics* 15, no. 3 (September 2017): 698.

Conclusion

Democracy Out of Empire

Throughout the twentieth century and the beginning of the twenty-first, notions of "world democracy" have been indelibly tied to democracy promotion projects and the democratic imperialism of the US-led liberal international order. The inextricable links between the discourse of world democracy and US hegemony—whether it was under the guise of Wilsonian liberalism or unilateral neoconservatism—should lead us to critically question any deployment of this language. In many respects, however, the current splintering of the liberal international order presents a moment ripe for reassessing the discourse of world democracy. The invasions of Afghanistan in 2001 and Iraq in 2003, which were ideologically justified as a project of spreading liberal democratic norms and institutions throughout the world (after the realpolitik justifications failed), culminated two decades later in the humiliating retreat of the United States from Afghanistan as President Joseph Biden desperately tried to shore up the North Atlantic Treaty Organization (NATO) alliance and the liberal international order amid the Palestinian genocide in Gaza, the Russian invasion of Ukraine, and the fear of authoritarian rule at home and abroad. The unipolar vision of a liberal democratic world order embraced by US liberal internationalists has morphed into a multipolar nightmare of war, ethnonationalism, global oligarchy, ecological collapse, and authoritarian resurgence. While some radical democratic theorists and critics of US empire openly welcome this multipolar world as a pluralistic alternative to unipolar hegemony, others warn that the breakup of Pax Americana could just as easily slide into "a new multipolar order dictated by competing capitalist authoritarianisms."[1] For

---

1. Aziz Rana, "Left Internationalism in the Heart of Empire," *Dissent*, May 23, 2022, https://www.dissentmagazine.org/online_articles/left-internationalism-in-the-heart-of-empire/.

some, the aspiration to build a democratic world must be an essential part of any attempt to counteract multipolar authoritarianism, while for others the breakdown of the postwar international order is a chance to finally put the phantom of world democracy to rest.

There is a crucial sense in which this clash between a moribund liberal internationalism and a resurgent multipolar authoritarianism constitutes an interregnum in the global order. Delusional affirmations of the health and vitality of the liberal international order expressed by some of its most astute champions notwithstanding, it is undeniable that that this order is in a process of terminal decline. With its basic institutional infrastructure unraveling and no longer able to secure US interests, despite the fact that US military strength remains largely intact, the fading conceits of a globally shared commitment to liberal democratic institutions and a "rules based international order" appear as little more than hollow proclamations of the wizard behind the curtain.[2] On the flip side, the resurgence of authoritarian regimes seeking to assert control over their own spheres of influence portends the emergence of a new order marked by an all-out assault on an even nominally democratic politics. The contours of this order are yet to come fully into view, if they ever will, but one basic feature will entail a rejection of anything resembling democratic regimes of shared power, even as authoritarian populists make persistent appeals to "the people." Rather than a simple transitionary stage between two powers, this is a conjunctural crisis in which, as the famous translation of Antonio Gramsci has it, "the old is dying and the new cannot be born."[3]

If the contemporary conjuncture is defined by decay of the liberal international order, W. E. B. Du Bois lived and worked as a critic of this order at the point of its inception and consolidation. In his own time, Du Bois's universalistic vision of world democracy confronted the trenchant realism of critics of various stripes such as Carl Schmitt and Reinhold Niebuhr. Schmitt, for one, repeatedly conveyed visions of an interconnected and harmonious "one world" as a depoliticized smoke screen for the projection of Pax Americana, a new nomos of the earth that departed from the previous world order composed of territorially sovereign states.[4] Today, this opti-

---

2. Victor Bulmer Thomas, *Empire in Retreat: The Past, Present, and Future of the United States* (Yale University Press, 2018).

3. Antonio Gramsci, *Selections from the Prison Notebooks*, ed. and trans. Quintin Hoare and Geoffrey Nowell Smith (International Publishers, 1971), 276.

4. Carl Schmitt, *Theory of the Partisan* (Telos Press, 2007), 58. See also Carl Schmitt, *The Nomos of the Earth in the International Law of the Jus Publicum Europaeum* (Telos

mistic vision of "one world" (to use Wendell Wilkie's resonant phrase) that pulsed throughout Du Bois's work appears at best as a marketing phrase for world music and global arts fairs, and at worst a cynical ploy manufactured by neoliberals and global oligarchs to mask the foundations of their power in the free flow of global capital. Widely criticized by various sorts of postcolonial, realist, and agonistic political theorists as a Eurocentric conceit, the idea of world democracy appears as nothing more than an imperial imposition of Western European powers rather than as genuine aspirations of colonized, racialized, and impoverished populations. Given such critiques that expose the clear associations between discourses of world democracy and Euro-American imperial rule, how should we interpret Du Bois's repeated invocations of such language?

From a realist angle (and one explicitly indebted to Schmitt), Chantal Mouffe has criticized cosmopolitan models of democracy articulated by such figures as David Held, Daniel Archibugi, and Ulrich Beck for positing "the availability of a world beyond hegemony and beyond sovereignty, therefore negating the dimension of the political" that resides in the irreducibly agonistic character of social relations.[5] Because it is predicated on the false universalization of Western democratic norms, these cosmopolitan imaginaries of global democracy fail to give outlet for conflict between pluralistic alternatives. Imposing a single consensus around liberal democratic norms evacuates possibilities for the expression of legitimate dissent, which in turn encourages the proliferation of violent enmities. To acknowledge the irreducibly conflictual nature of the political is to recognize that the world is a pluriverse and not a universe. Such a pluralistic view requires abandoning universalistic visions of democracy on a world scale in favor of a multipolar image of the world oriented around conflicting visions of the good life. A multipolar and pluralistic world, however, will not inevitably be a democratic one insofar as it is composed of regional poles that need not be democratically organized. Still, Mouffe maintains, "we do not need to discard the possibility that democracy could one day become established worldwide."[6] For this scenario to occur, we would need to surrender the

---

Press, 2003). Yet, as Gary Wilder has noted, we should not blind ourselves to the fact that Schmitt's critique was deeply tied to the reactionary valorization of state sovereignty and permanent war; see Gary Wilder, "Decolonization and Postnational Democracy," in *Forms of Pluralism and Democratic Constitutionalism*, ed. Andrew Arato et al. (Columbia University Press, 2018), 56.

5. Chantal Mouffe, *Agonistics: Thinking the World Politically* (Verso, 2013), 20. See also Chantal Mouffe, *On the Political* (Routledge, 2005), 90–118.

6. Mouffe, *Agonistics*, 28–29.

universalization of a singular democratic model and instead appreciate how democratic ideals might be implemented differently in multipolar contexts.

From a radical democratic angle, James Tully has prominently argued that the projection of the liberal democratic model throughout the world is itself a technology of informal imperial rule. Tully contends that "the dominant forms of representative democracy, self-determination, and democratization promoted through international law are not alternatives to imperialism, but, rather, the means through which informal imperialism operates against the wishes of the majority of the population of the postcolonial world."[7] In this process of colonial imposition, the form of democracy that has been foisted on postcolonial peoples is of a "low-intensity" sort oriented around electoral and representative institutions as well as neoliberal economic arrangements that privilege protection of private property and the free mobility of capital.[8] Moreover, the imposition of these low-intensity democratic forms has proceeded without the consent and participation of colonial and neocolonial subjects. In Tully's account, this is all part of a long imperial legacy stretching back to the "civilizing mission" of nineteenth-century empires and the "duty to civilize" under the Mandate System of the League of Nations. Although the words for these imperial arrangements have shifted—for example, from civilization to modernization to democratization—the underlying "grammatical structure" remains the same.[9] As such, the anti-imperial pursuit of high-intensity and participatory democratic forms must break with these lineages through radical democratic modes of contestation and negotiation.

From a postcolonial perspective, David Scott similarly notes continuities in how democracy itself has, in the post–Cold War moment, come to stand in as "the new standard of civilization" that structures the unipolar order.[10] "In short," Scott argues, "the new post-Cold War/post 9/11 world of Pax Americana, is, at once, a civilizational and an imperial project that articulates itself in the political idiom of democracy and the acceleration of global democracy promotion."[11] The basic assumption of "democracy promotion"

---

7. James Tully, *Public Philosophy in a New Key*, vol. 2, *Imperialism and Civic Freedom* (Cambridge University Press, 2008), 158.

8. Tully, *Imperialism and Civic Freedom*, 156–58.

9. Tully, *Imperialism and Civic Freedom*, 263.

10. David Scott, "Norms of Self-Determination: Thinking Sovereignty Through," *Middle East Law and Governance* 4, no. 2–3 (2012): 198.

11. Scott, "Norms of Self-Determination," 200–201.

projects, whether in a liberal or neoconservative guise, is that both sovereign legitimacy and self-determination are tied most closely not to *external* dynamics of recognition and territorial integrity but to *internal* questions of political and economic form.[12] Understood in this way, the normative presumption of a universal entitlement to democratic self-rule has attended a process whereby the rights of sovereignty and self-determination in the Global South are contingent on the acceptance of the liberal democratic model. The situation presents a peculiar inversion of the problem of domestic jurisdiction that Du Bois tackled in the 1940s. Where Du Bois contested the juridical bifurcation of state sovereignty and international law that insulated racialized domination and colonial rule from scrutiny in global politics, the bifurcation of democracy promotion discourses has served to absolve the role of international order in perpetuating dedemocratizing tendencies within the internal borders of postcolonial states.

While such critiques touch upon almost the entirety of US foreign policy in the twentieth century, they are particularly resonant in the post–Cold War moment that ran from the humanitarian interventions of the 1990s and the US-backed coups in Venezuela and Haiti to the invasions of Iraq and Afghanistan as well as President Barack Obama's interventions in the Middle East of the post-9/11 era. This moment, arguably, has come to pass, even as the ghosts of its limits and colossal failures haunt the present conjuncture. In midst of the current global interregnum, the declining saliency of these critiques, precisely *as* a critique of the present, opens new opportunities to reassess the semantic politics of alternative visions of world democracy. As I have shown throughout this book, Du Bois offers a world democratic imaginary in which such an integrated vision is not reducible to a mask for US police power and neoliberal economic integration. Especially in the last decades of his life, Du Bois was deeply critical of projects of democracy promotion in which "American business is desperately trying to restore the essentials of colonialism under the name of free enterprise and western democracy."[13] While the spread of democratic ideals throughout the world has been indelibly tied to either Wilsonian liberalism or neoconservatism, Du Bois and the intellectual networks he was enmeshed in offer an alternative grammar of world democracy that is more than an ideological mask for US imperial interests. In connecting the language of world democracy to anticolonial struggles for self-determination, constituencies overtly excluded from Wilsonian conceptions of self-determination, these alternative

12. Scott, "Norms of Self-Determination," 223–24.

13. Du Bois, "Peace Is Dangerous," 6.

discourses evaded hegemonic meanings of the term *world democracy* and instead sought to instantiate a new, universalistic vision of democratic habits encircling the earth.

Nevertheless, this attempt to conceptually rework and repurpose world democracy gave rise to significant tensions and contradictions in the way in which Du Bois so often tied this vision to a simultaneous affirmation and critique of US leadership. On the one hand, he deliberately enlisted domestic racial domination in a broader critique of US foreign policy and claims to world leadership. Spearing the aspirations of liberal internationalists to make the "World Safe for Democracy," he satirically mocked the image of the United States spreading human rights and democracy abroad while remaining silent about white vigilante mobs in Chicago and St. Louis. Refusing the tendency to separate distinct dynamics of racial and colonial domination into discrete national histories, he provocatively asked, "What is the black man but America's Belgium?"[14] By mapping the interconnections of white racial violence in the industrial centers of the United States to the colonial violence of the Belgian Congo, he powerfully stripped US liberal internationalists of their claims to global leadership. Liberal internationalism was an extension of the new imperialism, Du Bois asserted, indistinguishable from "the current theory of colonial expansion.... Bluntly put, that theory is this: It is the duty of white Europe to divide up the darker world and administer it for Europe's good."[15]

On the other hand, Du Bois tied this familiar critique to the possibility that the United States might someday live up to its self-proclaimed status as a democratic exemplar. In *Color and Democracy* (and as we saw in chapter 4), he cast the confinement of thirteen million African Americans to a status of second-class citizenship as a form of quasi-colonial status that positioned them as colonial subjects in the broader European imperial order. As a consequence, racial oppression "forces the United States to abdicate its natural leadership of democracy in the world and to acquiesce in a domination of organized wealth which exceeds anything elsewhere in the world."[16] Yet he went on to say that if the United States really wishes to seize leadership of world democracy, it will attempt to make "the beneficiaries of the new economic order not simply a group, a race, or any form of oligarchy but, taking advantage of its own wealth and intelligence, will try to put democracy in control of the new economy." It is only with this program of uplift for the

---

14. Du Bois, *Darkwater*, 20.

15. Du Bois, *Darkwater*, 23.

16. Du Bois, *Color and Democracy*, 297.

majority of colonial peoples of the world that "American industrial democracy" will triumph over "the oligarchical technocracy of Neuropa" (Adolf Hitler's vision of a new European order).[17] The triumph of democracy over fascism is dependent on the overthrow of imperialism and the affirmation of democratic methods and popular intelligence in the colonies.

In these statements, the affirmation of US democratic leadership did not involve a nostalgic invocation of American exceptionalism but rather a futuristic vision of political reconstruction and economic transformation that would extend democracy from the political to the economic dimension. As we saw in chapter 3, the lateral extension of popular control from the formal realm of political rule into the economic realm of industrial production was dependent on and indeed proceeded from the vertical extension of democratic struggles beyond the realm of the nation-state into the realm of transnational, anticolonial solidarity between the working classes of the metropole and those of the colonies. Here, the affirmation of US democratic leadership and thus a transformation of world order necessarily entailed the extension of popular self-rule to the arena of the postwar political economy. If democracy is to be a just way of life for all people, democratic imaginaries must move beyond a simple demand for voice in government and embrace demands for popular control of the economy.

It is important to appreciate that this wavering hope in US democratic leadership is a subset of a broader problem with world democracy, specifically regarding the role of state leadership. Du Bois's celebration of other antidemocratic formations beyond the United States, such as the Soviet Union and Japanese imperialism, has received wide and in-depth commentary. Regarding Japanese imperialism, the rise of the nonwhite world especially was an integral aspect of the transnational political imaginary. In 1917 Du Bois explicitly wrote that "the escape of Japan, and the rise of India and the unrest of Africa and black America all give hope of real peace: of peace built on world democracy, of equality of men of all races and color, and the damnation of all industrial organizations built on theft."[18] The inclusion of Japan as an agent of world democracy alongside India and Africa performs a "persistent parallax" that displaces from view the ongoing structures of Japanese imperialism through metonymic association with anticolonial struggles elsewhere.[19] Typically, Du Bois's support for Japanese

---

17. Du Bois, *Color and Democracy*, 301. See also Du Bois, "Neuropa: Hitler's New World Order," *Journal of Negro Education* 10, no. 3 (July 1941): 380–86.

18. Du Bois, "Of the Culture of White Folk," 446.

19. Chandler, "Persistent Parallax."

imperialism is attributed to a romanticized and essentialist form of Afro-Orientalism.[20] But it also points to broader limits of world democracy as a political imaginary. Despite his failure to critique non-Western forms of imperialism, Du Bois's writings on Japan exhibit a theorization of "transnational democratic leadership" that would be accountable to the masses of the nonwhite world. Such leadership would only be upheld insofar as it directly empowered and enabled the uplift of the masses. Such a commitment to state-led democratic leadership was fluid insofar as democratic exemplars such as the United States or even Japan could, in Alex Haskins's words, "lose the mantle of democratic leadership, as the mantle could shift to other actors who better embodied a commitment to the masses."[21]

This view of a flexible and fluid form of transnational democratic leadership helps partially explain the shifting location and site of such leadership, moving back and forth as it did throughout Du Bois's life from the United States to the Soviet Union and Japan and even to Ghana. It also highlights a pervasive limit of the discourse of world democracy. As I suggested in chapter 1, Du Bois is a peculiar kind of radical democrat insofar as he weds a radical democratic affirmation of the popular judgment of the masses and the democratic habits of colonial peoples to a custodial vision of politics as rule and leadership. While this commitment to sovereign state-leadership in the movement for world democracy represents a continuation of the custodial notion of politics as leadership, it also conflicts with his skepticism of state sovereignty and domestic jurisdiction as a structuring principle of international law and institutions. World democracy, paradoxically, can only emerge for Du Bois through state leadership, even as a dogmatic commitment to state sovereignty and domestic jurisdiction undercuts the very possibility of radical democratic transformation. What is fundamentally at stake here is the way that any vision of world democracy requires, for Du Bois, a catalyzing agent for its realization, a kind of political agency that only sovereign states can provide. And it is this search for a political agent of worldly democratic transformation that leads to his troubling embrace of authoritarian powers as a counterweight to European imperial hegemony.

A related tension is Du Bois's willingness to work within liberal internationalist institutions such as the League of Nations and the United Nations (UN), which often proceeds alongside a critique of the imperial entanglements of those very same institutions. As we saw in chapter 4, Du Bois cast

20. Mullen, *Afro-Orientalism*; Onishi, *Transpacific Antiracism*.

21. Alex Haskins, "Leaders Fit for the Masses: W. E. B. Du Bois and Japan's Transnational Democracy Leadership," *Du Bois Review* 21, no. 1 (Spring 2024): 183.

the UN in the 1940s as harboring potential to become an anticolonial instrument insofar as it provided an institutionalized venue for colonial peoples as a global majority to take shape. Crucial to this process was loosening the hold of domestic jurisdiction over international law, which would help constitute colonial peoples as an interconnected constituency in international politics rather than as separate movements operating within the singular domains of imperial states. More than twenty years earlier, Du Bois similarly called for engagement with the League of Nations, noting that "the worst Internation is better than the present anarchy in international relations."[22] The anarchy he warned of, however, was not simply that of the power politics of sovereign states competing in the absence of a unifying international order. It was "the anarchy of empire," a hierarchical order built on interimperial rivalries over colonial supremacy.[23] To overcome the anarchy of empire, building a more democratic "inter-nation" required working with and against liberal institutions such as the League of Nations "with all its autocracy and ... for Democracy of all races and men."[24]

Such a vision of the UN and the League of Nations as anticolonial instruments, however strategic and realistic it might be, is unlikely to continue to inspire anticolonial movements. But it is important to appreciate the ways that Du Bois acted as an "immanent critic" of these arrangements who sought to elicit future political possibilities from within the existing arrangements of the imperial world order.[25] Any vision of world democracy will emerge out of empire, not as a phoenix rising from the ashes but as a dialectical entwinement with its institutional forms of domination. As Adom. Getachew puts it, European imperialism was "itself a world-constituting

22. W. E. B. Du Bois, "The League of Nations," *Crisis* 19, no. 1 (November 1919): 336–37.

23. Du Bois, *Darkwater*, 162. See also Kaplan, *Anarchy of Empire*, 171–212; Edward Keene, *Beyond the Anarchical Society: Grotius, Colonialism and World Order in Politics* (Cambridge University Press, 2002).

24. Du Bois, "League of Nations," 336–37.

25. Gary Wilder, "Reading Du Bois's Revelation: Radical Humanism and Black Atlantic Criticism," in *The Postcolonial Contemporary: Political Imaginaries for the Global Present*, ed. Jini Kim Watson and Gary Wilder (Fordham University Press, 2018), 117. See also Joshua Simon, "Overcoming the Other America: José Martí's Immanent Critique of the Unionist Paradigm," *Review of Politics* 84, no. 1 (Winter 2022): 55–79. In a similar vein, Ira Katznelson notes Du Bois's "insurgent incorporation of mainstream language and concepts"; Ira Katznelson, "Du Bois's Century," *Social Science History* 23, no. 4 (Winter 1999): 460.

force that violently inaugurated an unprecedented era of globality."[26] If Du Bois operated within and exemplified a global consciousness marked by worldly interconnection, then it was a consciousness created by empire itself. And if race and empire constitute modern globality, then any vision of world democracy will entail a complex negotiation with and contestation of that legacy. Indeed, Du Bois often drew on and refashioned imperial discourses in his arguments and activism against empire. In using the discourse of liberal internationalism embedded in the League of Nations and the UN, he found a set of spatial grammars by which to contest the sovereign state order that those very institutional arrangements upheld and thereby transnationalize democratic struggles against war, racial domination, and class rule within the United States. What is crucial to this account, though, is that these forms of immanent critique were not just within an abstract set of ideas and discourses. They were embedded within institutional infrastructures and concrete political predicaments.

To the extent that Du Bois can be seen as decolonizing democratic theory, it was not simply by exposing the Eurocentrism of Western democratic thought. It was by engaging in a kind of "conceptual reanimation" of world democracy—that is, repurposing it to transform the European dominated interimperial order.[27] In this regard, this book dovetails with recent efforts of historians of international thought to "explore alternative spatial imaginaries of political order" in the twentieth century that do not issue in the nation-state as the presumed telos of anticolonial thought and resistance.[28] Yet rather than recommend these spatial imaginaries for retrieval as alternatives in the present, my goal has been to raise new questions about how to study the spatial contexts of global political thought. An essential part of this is attending to how perceptions of space and scale are insinuated

26. Getachew, *Worldmaking After Empire*, 3.

27. Adom Getachew and Karuna Mantena, "Anticolonialism and the Decolonization of Political Theory," *Critical Times* 4, no. 3 (December 2021): 359–88.

28. Or Rosenboim, "The Spatiality of Politics: Cesare Battisti's Regional and International Thought, 1900–1916," *Modern Intellectual History* 19, no. 2 (June 2022): 397; Bell, *Dreamworlds of Race*; Gary Wilder, *Freedom Time: Negritude, Decolonization, and the Future of the World* (Duke University Press, 2015); Frederick Cooper, *Citizenship Between Empire and Nation: Remaking France and French Africa, 1945–1960* (Princeton University Press, 2014); Merve Fejzula, "The Cosmopolitan Historiography of Twentieth-Century Federalism," *Historical Journal* 64, no. 2 (2021): 477–500; Duong, "Universal Suffrage as Decolonization"; Getachew, *Worldmaking After Empire*; Theo Williams, *Making the Revolution Global: Black Radicalism and the British Socialist Movement Before Decolonization* (Verso, 2022), 216–52.

into political concepts. Or Rosenboim highlights the category of "political space" as a useful one for the historical study of political thought, which prompts reflection on "the midcentury perceptions of the physical geographical conditions of the world and their impact on political and social order."[29] David Armitage similarly argues, "When conceptions of space expand, webs of significance ramify and networks of exchange proliferate to create novel contexts and unanticipated connections among them. . . . Changing conceptions of space expanded the contexts for ideas and, with them, the very possibilities for thought."[30] The role of changing spatial contexts is most evident in Du Bois's use of a broad array of technoscientific tropes (i.e., the fourth dimension, evolution, the color line belt) to capture the shifting relationship between democracy and the color line on a world scale. Attention to these expanded spatial contexts places the veil as one among many conceptual figurations he deployed to convey the partitioning and connections of racialized spatial orders.

But if the proliferation of global spaces created new possibilities for political thought, something like the reverse is also true. What I propose here is a shift from understanding *the spatiality of politics* (the way that spatial discourses and contexts shape political thinking) to *the politics of space* (the way that political actors use spatial grammars to act politically). Grasped in these terms, political space is not simply a concealed or latent metaphysics that is implicit within political concepts and categories. Rather, perceptions about the proper ordering of political space as well as codified constructions of space in both domestic and international law are contested dynamics of political, economic, and ideological conflict.[31] The politics of space thus requires attention not just to how perceptions of space and scale influence political concepts but also to how the deployment of spatial grammars and imaginaries figures into radical democratic strategy. Put otherwise, spatiality figures into democratic politics not simply as an end goal but also as a strategic means.[32]

---

29. Rosenboim, *Emergence of Globalism*, 5.

30. David Armitage, "The International Turn in Intellectual History," in *Rethinking Modern European Intellectual History*, ed. Darrin McMahon and Samuel Moyn (Oxford University Press, 2014), 241.

31. I take this notion of spatial politics from Henri Lefebvre, who argues that spatiality is both a precondition and effect of social relations: "so there is no sense in which space can be treated solely as an *a priori* condition of these institutions and the state which presides over them"; Lefebvre, *Production of Space*, 60, 85.

32. R. Williams, "Politics, Rights, and Spatiality," 338.

None of this is to ignore the rich even if inchoate normative vision implied by the language of world democracy but to provide for an apprehension of the political and spatial imaginaries that allow for a better grasp of the background conditions and pregivens of normativity. Within a transscalar democratic imaginary, the normative association between democratic politics and the appropriate space and scale can never be fixed in advance as a matter of a priori theoretical principles. Rather than normatively fix the proper scale of democratic politics, Du Bois conjures an image of world democracy as a transscalar endeavor that would confront the recursions of class rule, racial domination, and militarism across boundaries of the sovereign state and through their intricate circulations at multiple levels of political contestation. In doing so, he enacts a performative embodiment of what Sheldon Wolin calls the "multiple civic self," a political actor engaged across polyspatial settings.[33] A central feature of this multiple civic self resides in the contestation and negotiation of the spatial and temporal imaginaries that comprise the background conditions of democratic politics.

As we saw in the shifting valence of dimensional language outlined in chapter 2, Du Bois increasingly engaged in the political contestation of space-time conceptions to envision new horizons of democratic possibility on a world scale. As such, we can reconceptualize political action as partially composed of the speech acts and motivated grammars by which political actors seek to contest and decontest (i.e., lock in) space-time imaginaries.[34] Self-consciously stepping into this domain of contestation, he sensed that the semantic politics of democracy was closely bound to spatial and temporal grammars. In intervening at the level of the political imaginary, Du Bois sought to reconfigure the background space-time conceptions through which we imagine the possibility of democratic collectivity. In this reconfiguration, his deployment of the discourse of world democracy resonates with what Tully has called "public philosophy," the aim of which is to "disclose the historically contingent conditions of possibility of this singular set of practices of governance and the range of characteristic

---

33. Sheldon Wolin, *The Presence of the Past: Essays on the State and Constitution* (Johns Hopkins University Press, 1989), 190.

34. Blake Ewing, "Conceptual History, Contingency and the Ideological Politics of Time," *Journal of Political Ideologies* 26, no. 3 (2021): 22–45. On decontestation, see Michael Freeden, *Ideologies and Political Theory: A Conceptual Approach* (Oxford University Press, 1998), 75–95.

problems to solutions to which it gives rise."[35] Du Bois's search for world democracy displays a "critical orientation to the background conventions" of contemporary problematizations in seeking to break loose from reigning strictures of dominant political vocabularies oriented around race provincialism.[36] Through the discourse of world democracy and its semantic chains of meaning, he enacted a range of critical practices of subjecting the spatiotemporal background conventions of democratic thought and practice to negotiation, contestation, and transformation. My goal has thus been to provide a genealogy of how he conceptualized the problem of world democracy not just in theoretical discourse but in a variety of imaginative terms and spatial grammars.[37]

In the words of Kari Palonen, Du Bois shifts from "a politics of answers to given questions to a politics of thematizing the questions themselves."[38] The questions and problems to which political theory addresses itself are at once sites of contingency and controversy. In his declaration of "the world problem of the color line," we see that contesting spatial and temporal imaginaries is central to his formulation of the relationship between race and democracy as a distinct political and theoretical problem.[39] These practices of spatiotemporal contestation entail ascertaining not just how Du Bois articulates a political vision of world democracy but also, more significantly, how he poses the problem of democracy as a world problem. Throughout his life, he continually grasped for spatial grammars by which to reconfigure the problematic relationship between race, empire, and democracy in transscalar terms. In this understanding of world democracy as a distinct problem-space, the question of democracy moves beyond the singular scale of the nation-state and spans outward in its connection to questions of war and peace, global capitalism, international order, and empire and colonialism. By remapping the terrain of the problem, he illustrates that the failed attempt to transcend the color line is intricately connected to the problem

---

35. Tully, *Imperialism and Civic Freedom*, 16.

36. James Tully, *Public Philosophy in a New Key*, vol. 1, *Democracy and Civic Freedom* (Cambridge University Press, 2008), 34.

37. In this regard, part of my methodological orientation is to provide a history of problematizations (or *problématiques*) informing Du Bois's transnational political visions. See Colin Koopman, *Genealogy as Critique: Foucault and the Problems of Modernity* (Indiana University Press, 2013).

38. Kari Palonen, "The Politics of Conceptual History," *Contributions to the History of Concepts* 1, no. 1 (March 2005): 50. See also R. G. Collingwood, *An Autobiography* (Oxford University Press, 1982), 37.

39. Du Bois, "World Problem of the Color Line," 35.

of attempting to achieve democracy while remaining confined within the scale of the sovereign state or the bounded space of the interstate order. In Du Bois's transnational imaginary, transforming the United States into a multiracial democracy requires also transforming and reconstructing the imperial world order.

If Du Bois's transnational vision of world democracy failed to take root in any meaningful sense, it was not necessarily the failure of deficient imagination (if anything, there was a surplus of imagination!) but because of the repressive apparatus of the US national security state. After his indictment in 1951, the US State Department revoked Du Bois's passport, only to return it more than half a decade later. In the last few years of his life, he and his wife Shirley Graham Du Bois famously became citizens of Ghana, the first independent black nation in Africa. This repression was certainly part of the reason that ultimately led W. E. B. Du Bois to announce his decision not to vote in the 1956 US presidential election pitting Dwight Eisenhower against Adlai Stevenson. In his editorial for *The Nation* titled, "I Won't Vote," he explained that he had voted in every other presidential election since he was eligible in 1889 based on strategic considerations of the particular candidates' attitudes toward African Americans even if it meant voting for the "lesser of two evils" in the absence of a third-party candidate. Yet by 1956, in the wake of the *Brown v. Board of Education* decision, and undoubtedly because of the rampant militarism of the national security state, the repressive clampdown on socialism, and the consolidation of corporate power, Du Bois pronounced that there are no longer "two evils" that exist in the US party system, but instead "one evil party with two names." He then closed the editorial by stating, "Democracy is dead in the United States. Yet there is still nothing to replace real democracy. Drop the chains, then, that bind our brains. Drive the money-changers from . . . the halls of Congress. Call back some faint spirit of Jefferson and Lincoln, and when we can again hold a fair election on real issues, let's vote, and not till then. Is this impossible? Then democracy in America is impossible."[40]

Posing the question of the impossibility of democracy in America is startling, not least of all because of the striking similarity in the language to one of Du Bois's most hopeful paeans to world democracy in "The African Roots of War," wherein he pronounced, "We must extend the democratic ideal to the yellow, brown, and black peoples. . . . We shall not drive war

---

40. W. E. B. Du Bois, "I Won't Vote," *Nation*, October 20, 1956, https://www.thenation.com/article/archive/i-wont-vote/.

from this world until we treat them as free and equal citizens in a world-democracy of all races and nations. Impossible? Democracy is a method of doing the impossible."[41] As I have argued, the utopian dream of world democracy was intricately linked to Du Bois's efforts to transcend the color line and achieve a democracy of all races and nations throughout the multiple dimensions of political space. If the first half of the twentieth century revolved around an oscillation between a utopian faith and despair in the face of global cataclysm, the onset of the twentieth century's second half—defined by the Korean War, the rise of NATO, the economic tyranny of the Marshall Plan, the consolidation of corporate oligarchy, and the specter of atomic warfare—had finally shattered that faith. Tracing this long arc of Du Bois's career poses a troubling question: What does it mean to suggest that democracy is at once impossible and a method of doing the impossible? It partly registers how Du Bois's transnational thought was always responding to shifting historical conditions and the changing dynamics of empire.

But more significantly, this duality of the impossibility of democracy speaks to the problem generated by the fact that the sources of democratic transformation would not and could not come from within the United States alone. Read alongside the impossibility of world democracy, the impossibility of democracy in America suggests that more than "Jefferson and Lincoln" is needed for radical democratic transformation. Rather, any radical transformation of the United States into a multiracial democracy would also require an equally dramatic transformation of the imperial lineages of world politics.

---

41. Du Bois, "African Roots," 712, 714.

Acknowledgments

I came to writing this book quite reluctantly. I was initially (and still am) working on a project that explores narrative and rhetorical claims to transnational citizenship in US political thought. At first, I avoided writing a chapter on W. E. B. Du Bois, knowing that it would be difficult to contain. Eventually, somewhere around 2017, I started to compose early drafts of chapter 3 as part of this broader project. A bit later, one chapter became two, and before I knew it, I was writing an entire book rather than a single chapter on Du Bois. I recount this only to foreground the hesitancy, humility, and trepidation with which I came to this project. I am indebted to the many people and organizations that helped me along the way. The project would have never been possible without the support of Dr. Whitney Battle-Baptiste and Adam Holmes of the Du Bois Center at the University of Massachusetts Amherst. A fellowship in 2019 from the center gave me time to orient myself to the Du Bois Papers at UMass. The Du Bois Center remains among the most vibrant and welcoming intellectual spaces I have found in academia. Conversations and talks from fellows at the center have exposed me to unfamiliar texts that have profoundly shaped the contours of this project. I am especially indebted to the research and insights of Jingjing Zhang, Lisa McLeod, Freeden Blume Or, Phillip Luke Sinitiere, and Agustin Lao-Montes. Phil, in particular, has been a steadfast champion of Du Bois scholarship who has generously shared archival documents with me and has helped me find my way through multiple archives.

Several colleagues have provided in-depth comments on various chapters (in many cases, multiple chapters) that helped me reorient my argument and saved me from needless mistakes: Begum Adalet, Ali Aslam, Nick Brommell, Stephen Clingman, Théophile Deslauriers, Rebecca Dingo, Lisa Gilson, Jane Gordon, Lewis Gordon, Rachel Green, Peter Haas, Jennie Ikuta, Anne Kerth, Agustin Lao-Montes, Fred Lee, Toussaint Losier, Emma Stone Mackinnon, Rob Martin, Liz Markovits, Inder Marwah, Sam Ng, Erin Pineda, Svati Shah, George Shulman, Joshua Simon, Corrine

Tachtiris, David Temin, Inés Valdez, Liz Wingrove, Kevin Young, and Mariah Zeisberg. The project has benefited from comments from audience members at the Human Rights in Comparative Perspective symposium at Wesleyan University; the University of Michigan Political Theory Workshop; the University of Connecticut Political Theory Workshop; the Race and Representation faculty seminar at the Institute for Holocaust, Genocide, and Memory Studies; the Crossroads in the Study of the Americas faculty seminar at the Five College Consortium; and the Pioneer Valley Political Theory Workshop. I am deeply indebted to Jennifer Pitts and Adom Getachew, both of whom provided helpful suggestions on early versions of chapter 3 and graciously invited me to a 2019 workshop at the Chicago Center for Contemporary Theory on their anthology of Du Bois's writings on international politics, which was recently published by Cambridge University Press. At the workshop, I was fortunate to learn from a range of social and political theorists and eminent Du Bois scholars: Lawrie Balfour, Derrick Darby, Andrew Douglas, Julian Go, Robert Gooding-Williams, Daragh Grant, Sarah Johnson, Jared Loggins, Bill Mullen, Christopher Taylor, Inés Valdez, and Robert Vitalis.

Like many scholars who experienced significant disruptions in their research during the COVID-19 pandemic, I am grateful to countless individuals who helped me overcome the obstacles of conducting archival research through the shutdowns. My thanks to staff at the following archival sites: the Special Collections and University Archives at the University of Massachusetts Amherst; the Schomburg Center for Research in Black Culture; the Franklin Library Special Collections and Archives at Fisk University; the Manuscript Division of the Library of Congress; and the Moorland-Springarn Research University at Howard University. Funding from the following sources provided me with the resources to travel to these various sites and to hire research assistants: the Department of Political Science; the College of Social and Behavioral Sciences; and the Office of Research Development. I am grateful to Ben Nolan, Ricardo Vega Leon, and Samantha Davis for their excellent research assistance, whether it was exploring archives, organizing documents, or writing bibliographies.

I want to give especial thanks to Sara Doskow at the University of Chicago Press for her enthusiasm about the project and for garnering two incredibly helpful reviews. Thanks to the anonymous reviewers for their generative feedback. Any author can only hope to be read in such a generous and productive though honest and critical way. An earlier version of chapter 3 was published with the same title in *Constellations*, and an earlier version of chapter 4 was published as "Constructing Colonial Peoples: W. E. B. Du Bois, the United Nations, and the Politics of Space and Scale," in

Modern Intellectual History. Thanks to these journals for allowing reprinted material from the articles. I am also grateful to the editors at *Constellations*, Duncan Kelly at *Modern Intellectual History*, and the anonymous reviewers at both journals for helpful feedback on what would become chapters 3 and 4.

Thanks to my political theory colleagues at UMass—past and present—for their collegiality and support: Roberto Alejandro, Angélica Bernal, Barbara Cruikshank, Andrew March, and the late Nick Xenos. A shout-out to the ESC crew for holding space to keep my mind off all this.

Finally, and most importantly, I thank my family. A good portion of the book was written during the pandemic, when my own sense of space and time was profoundly altered. Confined to the small, domestic spaces of family life because of vast, global forces beyond our control was a bewildering experience. But I couldn't imagine a better bunch to have done it with. My twin daughters, Lola and Phoebe, were born just as I started the project. Writing almost the entirety of it has coincided with watching them grow into thoughtful, caring, and fun-loving children. I take great pride in the fact that they are hardly aware I even wrote this book and surely don't care. My thanks and love go out to my biggest supporter, Laura Attanasio. I would not have made it through any of this without her grace and resoluteness. She is our rock. On top of her own important research, Laura was supportive of the project at every turn, allowing me time to write and travel to archives. She even took interest in some of the ideas in the book.

Bibliography

Archival Sources and W. E. B. Du Bois's Writings

ARCHIVAL SOURCES

Alain Locke Papers (Coll. 164). Moorland-Springarn Research Center, Howard University.
Hugh and Mabel Smythe Papers (MSS57505). Manuscript Division, Library of Congress.
W. E. B. Du Bois Collection. Franklin Library Special Collections and Archives, John Hope and Aurelia E. Franklin Library, Fisk University.
W. E. B. Du Bois Papers (Sc MG 109). Schomburg Center for Research in Black Culture, The New York Public Library.
W. E. B. Du Bois Papers (MS 312). Special Collections and University Archives, University of Massachusetts Amherst Libraries.

W. E. B. DU BOIS'S PUBLISHED WRITINGS

"Address to the Nations of the World." In *W. E. B. Du Bois Speaks: Speeches and Addresses, 1890–1919*.
"The African Roots of War." *Atlantic Monthly*, May 1915, 707–14.
Africa: Its Place in Modern History. Oxford University Press, 2014.
Against Racism: Unpublished Essays, Papers, Addresses, 1887–1961. Edited by Herbert Aptheker. University of Massachusetts Press, 1985.
An Appeal to the World! A Statement on the Denial of Human Rights to Minorities in the Case of Citizens of the United States of America and an Appeal to the United Nations for Redress. NAACP, 1947.
The Autobiography of W. E. B. Du Bois. Oxford University Press, 2007.
"Black Africa Tomorrow." *Foreign Affairs* 17, no. 1 (October 1938): 100–110.
Black Folk Then and Now. Oxford University Press, 2007.
Black Reconstruction in America. 1935. Reprint, Free Press, 1998.
"The Class Struggle." *Crisis* 22, no. 4 (August 1921): 151–52.
"Close Ranks." *Crisis* 16, no. 3 (July 1918): 111–12.
"Colonialism and the Russian Revolution." In *Writings by W. E. B. Du Bois in Periodicals Edited by Others*, vol. 4.
"Colonialism, Democracy, and Peace After the War." In *Against Racism*.
Color and Democracy. In *"The World and Africa" and "Color and Democracy."*

"The Color Line Belts the World." *Collier's Weekly*, October 20, 1906, 30.

"Coming of the Lesser Folk (1911)." In *Writings by W. E. B. Du Bois in Periodicals Edited by Others*, vol. 2.

The Correspondence of W. E. B. Du Bois. Vol. 1, *1877–1934*. Edited by Herbert Aptheker. University of Massachusetts Press, 1973.

The Correspondence of W. E. B. Du Bois. Vol. 2, *1934–1944*. Edited by Herbert Aptheker. University of Massachusetts Press, 1976.

The Correspondence of W. E. B. Du Bois. Vol. 3, *1944–1963*. Edited by Herbert Aptheker. University of Massachusetts Press, 1978.

Dark Princess. Oxford University Press, 2007.

Darkwater: Voices from Within the Veil. 1920. Reprint, Verso, 2016.

Dusk of Dawn. 1940. Reprint, Oxford University Press, 2007.

"Editorial." *Crisis* 1, no. 1 (1910): 10–11.

"The Evolution of the Race Problem." In *W. E. B. Du Bois Speaks: Speeches and Addresses, 1890–1919*.

"A Forum of Fact and Opinion (April 25, 1936)." In *Newspaper Columns by W. E. B. Du Bois*, vol. 1, edited by Herbert Aptheker. Kraus-Thomson, 1986.

"Forward." *Crisis* 18, no. 5 (September 1919): 234–35.

"The Future of Europe in Africa." In *Against Racism*.

"High Ideals of Pan-Africanism (1923)." In *Writings by W. E. B. Du Bois in Periodicals Edited by Others*, vol. 2.

"Human Rights for All Minorities." In *W. E. B. Du Bois Speaks: Speeches and Addresses, 1920–1963*.

"I Won't Vote." *Nation*, October 20, 1956. https://www.thenation.com/article/archive/i-wont-vote/.

"Imperialism, United Nations, Colonial People." *New Leader*, December 30, 1944, 5.

In Battle for Peace. Oxford University Press, 2007.

"Is It Democracy for Whites to Rule Dark Majorities?" In *Writings by W. E. B. Du Bois in Periodicals Edited by Others*, vol. 4.

"The League of Nations." *Crisis* 19, no. 1 (November 1919): 336–37.

"Marxism and the Negro Problem." In *African American Political Thought, 1890–1930*, edited by Cary Wintz. M. E. Sharpe, 1996.

"Memorandum to the Secretary for the NAACP Staff Conference (October 10, 1946)." In *Against Racism*.

The Negro. Oxford University Press, 2014.

"The Negro and Imperialism." In *W. E. B. Du Bois Speaks: Speeches and Addresses, 1920–1963*.

"The Negro Mind Reaches Out." In *The New Negro*, edited by Alain Locke. Simon & Schuster, 1997.

"A Negro Nation Within the Nation." *Current History* 42, no. 3 (June 1935): 265–70.

"Neuropa: Hitler's New World Order." *Journal of Negro Education* 10, no. 3 (July 1941): 380–86.

"Of the Culture of White Folk." *Journal of Race Development* 7, no. 4 (April 1917): 434–47.

"Peace." *Crisis* 6, no. 1 (May 1913): 26.

"Peace on Earth." *Crisis* 31, no. 5 (March 1926): 215–16.

"Postwar World Must Heed Voice of Colonial Peoples." *New York Post*, May 4, 1945, 14.

"The Present." *Crisis* 14, no. 4 (August 1917): 165.

"The Present Outlook for the Dark Races of Mankind." In *The Problem of the Color Line at the Turn of the Twentieth Century: The Essential Early Essays*, edited by Nahum Chandler, 111–38. Fordham University Press, 2014.
"The Problem of Problems." In *Writings by W. E. B. Du Bois in Periodicals Edited by Others*, vol. 2.
"Races." *Crisis* 2, no. 4 (August 1911): 157–59.
"The Races Congress." *Crisis* 2, no. 5 (September 1911): 200–209.
"The Races in Conference." *Crisis* 1, no. 2 (December 1910): 16–17, 20–21.
"Reconstruction, Seventy-Five Years After." *Phylon* 4, no. 3 (1943): 205–12.
"The Relations of the Negroes to the Whites in the South." *Annals of the American Academy of Political and Social Science* 18 (July 1901): 121–40.
"Socialism and the Negro." *Crisis* 22, no. 6 (October 1921): 245–47.
"The Souls of White Folk." In *Writings by W. E. B. Du Bois in Periodicals Edited by Others*, vol. 2.
"To the World: Manifesto of the Second Pan-African Congress." *Crisis* 23, no.1 (November 1921): 5–11.
"A Vacation Unique." In *Dark Voices: W. E. B. Du Bois and American Thought, 1888–1903*, by Shamoon Zamir. University of Chicago Press, 1995.
W. E. B. Du Bois Speaks: Speeches and Addresses, 1890–1919. Edited by Philip Foner. Pathfinder Press, 1970.
W. E. B. Du Bois Speaks: Speeches and Addresses, 1920–1963. Edited by Philip Foner. Pathfinder Press, 1970.
"The World and Africa" and "Color and Democracy." Edited by Henry Louis Gates Jr. Oxford University Press, 2007.
"The World Problem of the Color Line." In *W. E. B. Du Bois on Asia: Crossing the World Color Line*, edited by Bill Mullen and Cathryn Watson. University Press of Mississippi, 2005.
"World War and the Color Line." *Crisis* 9, no. 1 (November 1914): 28–30.
"Worlds of Color." *Foreign Affairs* 3, no. 3 (April 1925): 423–44.
Writings by W. E. B. Du Bois in Periodicals Edited by Others. Vol. 2, *1910–1934*. Edited by Herbert Aptheker. Kraus-Thomson, 1982.
Writings by W. E. B. Du Bois in Periodicals Edited by Others. Vol. 4, *1945–1961*. Edited by Herbert Aptheker. Kraus-Thomson, 1982.

Other Sources

Abbott, Edwin. *Flatland: A Romance in Many Dimensions*. Penguin, 1998.
Adalet, Begum. "Infrastructures of Decolonization: Scales of Worldmaking in the Writings of Frantz Fanon." *Political Theory* 50, no. 1 (2022): 5–31.
Addams, Jane. *Newer Ideals of Peace*. MacMillan, 1907.
Adi, Hakim. *Pan-Africanism: A History*. Bloomsbury, 2018.
Adorno, Theodor. "Progress." In *Critical Models: Interventions and Catchwords*, translated by Henry W. Pickford. Columbia University Press, 2005.
Alombert, Anne. "Towards a Bifurcation: Internation and Interscience in the Twenty-First Century." In *Bernard Stiegler: Memories of the Future*, edited by Bart Buseyne, Georgios Tsagdis, and Paul Willemark. Bloomsbury, 2024.
Anderson, Benedict. *Imagined Communities: Reflections on the Origin and Spread of Nationalism*. Verso, 1983.

Anderson, Carol. *Bourgeois Radicals: The NAACP and the Struggle for Colonial Liberation, 1941–1960*. Cambridge University Press, 2015.
Anderson, Carol. *Eyes Off the Prize: The United Nations and the African American Struggle for Human Rights, 1944–1955*. Cambridge University Press, 2003.
Appiah, Anthony. *Lines of Descent: W. E. B. Du Bois and the Emergence of Identity*. Harvard University Press, 2014.
Arendt, Hannah. *The Origins of Totalitarianism*. Harcourt, 1976.
Armitage, David. "The International Turn in Intellectual History." In *Rethinking Modern European Intellectual History*, edited by Darrin McMahon and Samuel Moyn. Oxford University Press, 2014.
Audoin-Rouzeau, Stéphane, and Annette Becker. *14–18: Understanding the Great War*. Translated by Catherine Temerson. Hill and Wang, 2014.
Aydin, Cemil. *The Politics of Anti-Westernism in Asia: Vision of World Order in Pan-Islamic and Pan-Asian Thought*. Columbia University Press, 2007.
Bair, Barbara. "Pan-Africanism as Process: Adelaide Casely Hayford, Garveyism, and the Cultural Roots of Nationalism." In *Imagining Home: Class, Culture and Nationalism in the African Diaspora*, edited by Robin Kelley and Sidney Lemelle. Verso, 1994.
Bakhtin, Mikhail. "Forms of Time and of the Chronotope in the Novel." In *The Dialogic Imagination*, edited by Michael Holquist, translated by Caryl Emerson and Michael Holquist. University of Texas Press, 1981.
Baldwin, James. "Princes and Powers." In *Collected Essays*. Library of America, 1998.
Balfour, Lawrie. "*Darkwater*'s Democratic Vision." *Political Theory* 38, no. 4 (August 2010): 537–63.
Balfour, Lawrie. *Democracy's Reconstruction: Thinking Politically with W. E. B. Du Bois*. Oxford University Press, 2011.
Balfour, Lawrie. "Unreconstructed Democracy: W. E. B. Du Bois and the Case for Reparations." *American Political Science Review* 97, no. 1 (February 2003): 33–44.
Barder, Alexander. *Global Race War: International Politics and Racial Hierarchy*. Oxford University Press, 2021.
Barnes, Leonard. *Empire or Democracy? A Study of the Colonial Question*. V. Gollancz, 1939.
Barnett, Clive. *The Priority of Injustice: Locating Democracy in Critical Theory*. University of Georgia Press, 2017.
Basevich, Elvira. *W. E. B. Du Bois: The Lost and the Found*. Polity, 2021.
Basevich, Elvira. "W. E. B. Du Bois's Socialism: On the Social Epistemology of Democratic Reason." *Philosophical Topics* 48, no. 2 (Fall 2020): 23–50.
Becker Lorca, Arnulf. *Mestizo International Law: A Global Intellectual History, 1842–1933*. Cambridge University Press, 2014.
Beckert, Sven. *Empire of Cotton: A Global History*. Vintage, 2014.
Bell, Duncan. "Before the Democratic Peace: Racial Utopianism, Empire, and the Abolition of War." *European Journal of International Relations* 20, no. 3 (September 2014): 647–70.
Bell, Duncan. "Beyond the Sovereign State: Isopolitan Citizenship, Race and Anglo-America Union." *Political Studies* 62, no. 2 (2014): 418–34.
Bell, Duncan. *Dreamworlds of Race: Empire and the Utopian Destiny of Anglo-America*. Princeton University Press, 2020.
Bell, Duncan, ed. *Empire, Race, and Global Justice*. Cambridge University Press, 2019.

Bell, Duncan. "Founding the World State: H. G. Wells on Empire and the English-Speaking Peoples." *International Studies Quarterly* 62, no. 4 (December 2018): 867–79.

Bell, Duncan. "Making and Taking Worlds." In *Global Intellectual History*, edited by Samuel Moyn and Andrew Sartori. Columbia University Press, 2013.

Bell, Duncan. *Reordering the World: Essays on Liberalism and Empire*. Princeton University Press, 2019.

Beltrán, Cristina. *Cruelty as Citizenship: How Migrant Suffering Sustains White Democracy*. University of Minnesota Press, 2020.

Benjamin, Walter. *The Arcades Project*. Belknap Press of Harvard University Press, 1999.

Benjamin, Walter. *The Origin of German Tragic Drama*. Verso, 1998.

Benjamin, Walter. "Theses on the Philosophy of History." In *Illuminations*, edited by Hannah Arendt, translated by Harry Zohn. Schocken Books, 1969.

Bennett, Nolan. *Claims of Experience: Autobiography and American Democracy*. Oxford University Press, 2019.

Bentley, Nancy. "The Fourth Dimension: Kinlessness and African American Narrative." *Critical Inquiry* 35, no. 2 (Winter 2009): 270–92.

Bernasconi, Robert. "Our Duty to Conserve: W. E. B. Du Bois's Philosophy of History in Context." *South Atlantic Quarterly* 108, no. 3 (2009): 519–40.

Bertholf, Garry. "Listening to Du Bois's *Black Reconstruction*: After James." *South: A Scholarly Journal* 48, no. 1 (Fall 2015): 78–91.

Bhabha, Homi. "Global Minoritarian Culture." In *Shades of the Planet: American Literature as World Literature*, edited by Wai Chee Dimock and Lawrence Buell. Princeton University Press, 2007.

Blain, Keisha. *Set the World on Fire: Black Nationalist Women and the Global Struggle for Freedom*. University of Pennsylvania Press, 2018.

Borstelmann, Thomas. *The Cold War and the Color Line: American Race Relations in the Global Arena*. Harvard University Press, 2001.

Bourne, Randolph. "Trans-National America." In *War and the Intellectuals: Collected Essays, 1915–1919*, edited by Carl Resek. Hackett, 1999.

Boxill, Bernard. "Two Traditions in African American Political Philosophy." *Philosophical Forum* 24, no. 1 (1992): 119–35.

Briggs, Charles. "Genealogies of Race and Culture and the Failure of Vernacular Cosmopolitanisms: Rereading Franz Boas and W. E. B. Du Bois." *Public Culture* 75, no. 1 (January 2005): 75–100.

Bromell, Nick. "Honest and Earnest Criticism as the 'Soul of Democracy': Du Bois's Style of Democratic Reasoning." In Bromell, *Political Companion to W. E. B. Du Bois*.

Bromell, Nick. *A Political Companion to W. E. B. Du Bois*. University Press of Kentucky, 2018.

Brown, David Luis. *Waves of Decolonization: Discourses of Hemispheric Citizenship in Cuba, Mexico, and the United States*. Duke University Press, 2008.

Bruyneel, Kevin. *Settler Memory: The Disavowal of Indigeneity and the Politics of Race in the United States*. University of North Carolina Press, 2021.

Bunche, Ralph. "A Critical Analysis of the Tactics and Programs of Minority Groups." *Journal of Negro Education* 4, no. 3 (July 1935): 308–20.

Burden-Stelly, Charise. "Black Cold War Liberalism as Agency Reduction Formation During the Late 1940s and the Early 1950s." *International Journal of Africana Studies* 19, no. 2 (Fall–Winter 2018): 77–130.

Burden-Stelly, Charise, and Gerald Horne. *W. E. B. Du Bois: A Life in American History*. ABC-CLIO, 2019.
Bush, Roderick. *The End of White World Supremacy: Black Internationalism and the Problem of the Color Line*. Temple University Press, 2009.
Buzan, Barry, and George Lawson. *The Global Transformation: History, Modernity, and the Making of International Relations*. Cambridge University Press, 2015.
Cajori, Florian. "Origins of Fourth Dimension Concepts." *American Mathematical Monthly* 33, no. 8 (October 1926): 397–406.
Carnegie, Andrew. *The Reunion of Britain and America: A Look Ahead*. Andrew Elliot, 1898.
Castoriadis, Cornelius. *Figures of the Thinkable*. Stanford University Press, 2007.
Castoriadis, Cornelius. *The Imaginary Institution of Society*. MIT Press, 1998.
Chandler, Nahum. *Beyond This Narrow Now: Or, Delimitations, of W. E. B. Du Bois*. Duke University Press, 2022.
Chandler, Nahum. "A Persistent Parallax: On the Writings of W. E. Burghardt Du Bois on Japan and China, 1936–1937." *CR: The New Centennial Review* 12, no. 1 (Spring 2012): 291–316.
Chandler, Nahum. *X—The Problem of the Negro as a Problem for Thought*. Fordham University Press, 2013.
Claeys, Gregory. *Imperial Sceptics: British Critics of Empire, 1850–1920*. Cambridge University Press, 2010.
Collingwood, R. G. *An Autobiography*. Oxford University Press, 1982.
Committee on Africa, the War, and Peace Aims. *The Atlantic Charter and Africa from an American Standpoint*. New York [publisher not identified], 1942.
Conrad, Sebastian. *What Is Global History?* Princeton University Press, 2016.
Contee, Clarence. "Du Bois, the NAACP, and the Pan-African Congress of 1919." *Journal of Negro History* 57, no. 1 (January 1972): 13–28.
Coopan, Vilashini. "Move on Down the Line: Domestic Science, Transnational Politics, and Gendered Allegory in Du Bois." In *Next to the Color Line: Gender, Sexuality, and W. E. B. Du Bois*, edited by Susan Gillman and Alys Eve Weinbaum. University of Minnesota Press, 2007.
Cooper, Frederick. *Citizenship Between Empire and Nation: Remaking France and French Africa, 1945–1960*. Princeton University Press, 2014.
Corazza, Chiara. "By No Other Means Than Peace: W. E. B. Du Bois on Nonviolence, World Peace, and Justice." *Peace and Change* 46, no. 4 (2021): 336–52.
Dahl, Adam. "Appealing to the World: Du Bois and the Transnational Politics of Petition." *South Atlantic Quarterly* 123, no. 3 (2024): 485–503.
Dahl, Adam. *Empire of the People: Settler Colonialism and the Foundations of Modern Democratic Thought*. University Press of Kansas, 2018.
Dahl, Adam. "Self-Determination Between World and Nation." *Comparative Studies of South Asia, Africa, and the Middle East* 40, no. 3 (2020): 613–20.
Dahl, Adam, and Joe Soss. "Neoliberalism for the Common Good? Public Value Governance and the Downsizing of Democracy." *Public Administration Review* 74, no. 4 (July/August 2014): 496–504.
Darby, Derrick. "Du Bois's Defense of Democracy." In *Democratic Failure: NOMOS LXII*, edited by Melissa Schwartzberg and Daniel Viehoff. New York University Press, 2020.

Davari, Arash. "On Democratic Leadership and Social Change: Positioning Du Bois in the Shadow of a Gray To-Come." In Bromell, *Political Companion to W. E. B. Du Bois*.
Dawson, Michael. "Hidden in Plain Sight: A Note on Legitimation Crises and the Racial Order." *Critical Historical Studies* 3, no. 1 (Spring 2016): 143–61.
de León, Cedric, and Michael Rodríguez-Muñiz. "The Political Sociology of W. E. B. Du Bois." In Morris et al., *Oxford Handbook of W. E. B. Du Bois*.
Dernburg, Bernhard. "England Traitor to White Race." *New York Times Magazine*, January 1916, 3–4.
Deudney, Daniel. *Bounding Power: Republican Security Theory from the Polis to the Global Village*. Princeton University Press, 2007.
Dewey, John. "Search for the Great Community." In *The Later Works, 1925–1953*, vol. 2. Southern Illinois University Press, 1988.
Dietz, Mary. "Between Polis and Empire: Aristotle's Politics." *American Political Science Review* 106, no. 2 (May 2012): 275–93.
Disch, Lisa. "Democratic Representation and the Constituency Paradox." *Perspectives on Politics* 10, no. 3 (2012): 599–616.
Douglas, Andrew J. "Du Bois and Marx's Influence: Black Reconstruction." In Morris et al., *Oxford Handbook of W. E. B. Du Bois*.
Douglas, Andrew J. *W. E. B. Du Bois and the Critique of Competitive Society*. University of Georgia Press, 2019.
Doyle, Laura. "Inter-Imperiality: Dialectics in Postcolonial World History." *Interventions* 16, no. 2 (2014): 159–96.
Duong, Kevin. "Universal Suffrage as Decolonization." *American Political Science Review* 115, no. 2 (May 2021): 412–28.
Elia, Adriano. "W. E. B. Du Bois's Proto-Afrofuturist Short Fiction: 'The Comet.'" *Il Tolomeo* 18 (December 2016): 173–86.
Ellis, Mark. "'Closing Ranks' and 'Seeking Honor:' W. E. B. Du Bois in World War I." *Journal of American History* 79, no. 1 (June 1992): 96–124.
Emerson, Ralph Waldo. "The Young American." In *Complete Works of Ralph Waldo Emerson*, vol. 1. Houghton Mifflin, 1904.
Esmeir, Samera. "On Becoming Less of the World." *History of the Present* 8, no. 1 (Spring 2018): 88–116.
Ewing, Blake. "Conceptual History, Contingency and the Ideological Politics of Time." *Journal of Political Ideologies* 26, no. 3 (2021): 22–45.
Fanon, Frantz. *The Wretched of the Earth*. Grove, 2004.
Fejzula, Merve. "The Cosmopolitan Historiography of Twentieth-Century Federalism." *Historical Journal* 64, no. 2 (2021): 477–500.
Femia, Joseph. *Against the Masses: Varieties of Anti-Democratic Thought Since the French Revolution*. Oxford University Press, 2001.
Ferguson, Kathy. "Theorizing Shiny Things: Archival Labors." *Theory & Event* 11, no. 4 (2008): https://muse.jhu.edu/article/257578.
Firmin, Anténor. *The Equality of the Human Races*. Translated by Asselin Charles. University of Illinois Press, 2002.
Foner, Eric. "*Black Reconstruction:* An Introduction." *South Atlantic Quarterly* 112, no. 3 (Summer 2013): 409–18.
Foucault, Michel. *Archaeology of Knowledge and the Discourse on Language*. Pantheon, 1972.

Francis, Megan Ming. *Civil Rights and the Making of the Modern American State*. Cambridge University Press, 2014.
Fraser, Nancy. *Scales of Justice: Reimagining Political Space in a Globalizing World*. Columbia University Press, 2009.
Freeden, Michael. *Ideologies and Political Theory: A Conceptual Approach*. Oxford University Press, 1998.
Galli, Carlo. *Political Spaces and Global War*. University of Minnesota Press, 2010.
Getachew, Adom. *Worldmaking After Empire: The Rise and Fall of Self-Determination*. Princeton University Press, 2019.
Getachew, Adom, and Karuna Mantena. "Anticolonialism and the Decolonization of Political Theory." *Critical Times* 4, no. 3 (December 2021): 359–88.
Getachew, Adom, and Jennifer Pitts. "Democracy and Empire: An Introduction to the International Thought of W. E. B. Du Bois." In *W. E. B. Du Bois: International Thought*, by W. E. B. Du Bois, edited by Adom Getachew and Jennifer Pitts. Cambridge University Press, 2022.
Getachew, Adom, and Jennifer Pitts. "Disclosing the Problem of Empire in Du Bois's International Thought." In Morris et al., *Oxford Handbook of W. E. B. Du Bois*.
Giddings, Franklin. *Democracy and Empire: With Studies of Their Psychological, Economic, and Moral Foundations*. MacMillan, 1900.
Go, Julian. *Postcolonial Thought and Social Theory*. Oxford University Press, 2016.
Go, Julian, and George Lawson. "Introduction: For a Global Historical Sociology." In *Global Historical Sociology*, edited by Julian Go and George Lawson. Cambridge University Press, 2017.
Gooding-Williams, Robert. "Democratic Despotism and the New Imperialism." *Abolition Democracy* (blog), October 12, 2020. Columbia Center for Contemporary Critical Thought, Columbia Law School. https://blogs.law.columbia.edu/abolition1313/robert-gooding-williams-democratic-despotism-and-the-new-imperialism/.
Gooding-Williams, Robert. *In the Shadow of Du Bois: Afro-Modern Political Thought in America*. Harvard University Press, 2009.
Gooding-Williams, Robert. "Philosophy of History and Social Critique in *The Souls of Black Folk*." *Social Science Information* 26, no. 1 (1987): 99–114.
Goodrich, Leland. "United Nations and Domestic Jurisdiction." *International Organization* 3, no. 1 (1949): 14–28.
Gong, Gerrit. *The Standard of "Civilization" in International Society*. Clarendon Press, 1984.
Gorup, Michael. *The Counterrevolutionary Shadow: Race and the Making of the American People*. University Press of Kansas, 2025.
Gramsci, Antonio. *Selections from the Prison Notebooks*. Edited and translated by Quintin Hoare and Geoffrey Nowell Smith. International Publishers, 1971.
Gruffydd Jones, Branwen. "Time, History, Politics: Anticolonial Constellations." *Interventions* 21, no. 5 (2019): 592–614.
Habermas, Jürgen. *The Postnational Constellation: Political Essays*. MIT Press, 2001.
Hamlin, Rebecca. *Crossing: How We Label and React to People on the Move*. Stanford University Press, 2021.
Hansen, Jonathan. *The Lost Promise of Patriotism*. University of Chicago Press, 2003.
Harris, Cheryl. "Whiteness as Property." *Harvard Law Review* 106, no. 8 (1993): 1707–91.

Hartman, Saidiya. "The End of White Supremacy, an American Romance." *Bomb*, June 5, 2020. https://bombmagazine.org/articles/the-end-of-white-supremacy-an-american-romance/.
Harvey, David. "Globalization and the Spatial Fix." *geographische revue* 2 (2001): 23–30.
Harvey, David. *Justice, Nature, and the Geography of Distance*. Blackwell, 1996.
Haskins, Alex. "Leaders Fit for the Masses: W. E. B. Du Bois and Japan's Transnational Democracy Leadership." *Du Bois Review* 21, no. 1 (Spring 2024): 182–200.
Hassanzadeh, Navid. "Race, Internationalism, and Comparative Political Theory." *Polity* 50, no. 4 (October 2018): 519–46.
Hegel, G. W. F. *Philosophy of History*. Colonial Press, 1899.
Heidegger, Martin. "The Age of the World View." Translated by Marjorie Green. *boundary 2* 4, no. 2 (Winter 1976): 340–55.
Held, David. *Democracy and the Global Order: From the Modern State to Cosmopolitan Governance*. Stanford University Press, 1995.
Henderson, Linda. *The Fourth Dimension and Non-Euclidean Geometry in Modern Art*. Rev. ed. MIT Press, 2018.
Herman, Arthur. *The Idea of Decline in Western History*. Free Press, 1997.
Hinton, Charles Howard. *The Fourth Dimension*. Swan Sonnenschein, 1906.
Hinton, Charles Howard. "What Is the Fourth Dimension?." In *Speculations on the Fourth Dimension: Selected Writings of Charles H. Hinton*. Dover, 1980.
Hobsbawm, Eric. *The Age of Empire, 1875–1914*. Pantheon Books, 1987.
Hobson, Christopher. "Democratic Peace: Progress and Critics." *Perspectives on Politics* 15, no. 3 (September 2017): 697–710.
Hobson, J. G. A. *Imperialism*. James Nisbet, 1902.
Hobson, John. *The Eurocentric Conception of World Politics: Western International Theory, 1760–2010*. Cambridge University Press, 2012.
Hochschild, Adam. *King Leopold's Ghost: A Story of Greed, Terror, and Heroism in Colonial Africa*. Houghton Mifflin, 1998.
Holley, Jared. "Racial Equality and Anticolonial Solidarity: Anténor Firmin's Global Haitian Liberalism." *American Political Science Review* 118, no. 1 (February: 2024): 304–17.
Hooker, Juliet. *Race and the Politics of Solidarity*. Oxford University Press, 2009.
Hooker, Juliet. *Theorizing Race in the Americas: Douglass, Sarmiento, Du Bois, and Vasconcelos*. Oxford University Press, 2017.
Horne, Gerald. *Black & Red: W. E. B. Du Bois and the Afro-American Response to the Cold War, 1944–1963*. SUNY Press, 1986.
Hughey, Matthew. "'The Souls of White Folk' (1920–2020): A Century of Peril and Prophecy." *Ethnic and Racial Studies* 43, no. 8 (2020): 1307–32.
Ibhawoh, Bonny. "Testing the Atlantic Charter: Linking Anti-Colonialism, Self-Determination, and Universal Human Rights." *Journal of Human Rights* 18, no. 7–8 (2014): 842–60.
Idris, Murad. "Peace, or, the Moral Economy of War: Between W. E. B. Du Bois and Sayyid Qutb." In *Crisis Under Critique: How People Assess, Transform, and Respond to Critical Situations*, edited by Didier Fassin and Axel Honneth. Columbia University Press, 2022.
Ikuta, Jennie. "A Matter of Long Centuries and Not Years: Du Bois on the Temporality of Social Change." *Political Theory* 52, no. 2 (2024): 289–316.

Issar, Siddhant. "Listening to Black Lives Matter: Racial Capitalism and the Critique of Neoliberalism." *Contemporary Political Theory* 20, no. 1 (March 2021): 48–71.

Itzigsohn, José, and Karida Brown. *The Sociology of W. E. B. Du Bois: Racialized Modernity and the Global Color Line*. New York University Press, 2020.

Ivie, Robert. *Democracy and America's War on Terror*. University of Alabama Press, 2005.

James, C. L. R. *The Life of Captain Cipriani: An Account of British Government in the West Indies*. Duke University Press, 2014.

James, C. L. R. "The Revolutionary Answer to the Negro Problem." In *The Future in the Present: Selected Writings*. Lawrence Hill, 1977.

Jameson, Frederic. *Archaeologies of the Future: The Desire Called Utopia and Other Science Fictions*. Verso, 2005.

Jerng, Mark. *Racial Worldmaking: The Power of Popular Fiction*. Fordham University Press, 2018.

Jerome, Fred, and Rodger Taylor. *Einstein on Race and Racism*. Rutgers University Press, 2006.

Johnson, Chalmers. *The Sorrows of Empire: Militarism, Secrecy, and the End of the Republic*. Metropolitan Books, 2004.

Johnson, James Weldon. "Africa at the Peace Table." In Kallen and Johnson, *Africa in the World Democracy*.

Johnson, Walter. *River of Dark Dreams: Slavery and Empire in the Cotton Kingdom*. Harvard University Press, 2013.

Joo, Hee-Jung Serenity. "Racial Impossibility and Critical Failure in W. E. B. Du Bois's *Darkwater*." *Science Fiction Studies* 46, no. 1 (March 2019): 106–26.

Juguo, Zhang. *W. E. B. Du Bois: The Question for the Abolition of the Color Line*. Routledge, 2001.

Jung, Moon-Ho. "*Black Reconstruction* and Empire." *South Atlantic Quarterly* 112, no. 3 (Summer 2013): 465–71.

Kallen, Horace Meyer. "The Future of Africa and a League of Nations." In Kallen and Johnson, *Africa in the World Democracy*.

Kallen, Horace Meyer, and James Weldon Johnson. *Africa in the World Democracy: Address Delivered at the Annual Meeting of the National Association for the Advancement of Colored People*. NAACP, 1919.

Kaplan, Amy. *The Anarchy of Empire in the Making of U.S. Culture*. Harvard University Press, 2020.

Karenga, Maulana. "Du Bois and the Question of the Color Line: Race and Class in the Age of Globalization." *Socialism and Democracy* 17, no. 1 (2003): 141–60.

Karp, Matthew. *This Vast Southern Empire: Slaveholders at the Helm of American Foreign Policy*. Harvard University Press, 2016.

Karuka, Manu. *Empire's Tracks: Indigenous Nations, Chinese Workers, and the Transcontinental Railroad*. University of California Press, 2019.

Katznelson, Ira. "Du Bois's Century." *Social Science History* 23, no. 4 (Winter 1999): 459–74.

Katznelson, Ira. *Fear Itself: The New Deal and the Origins of Our Time*. Norton, 2014.

Keene, Edward. *Beyond the Anarchical Society: Grotius, Colonialism and World Order in Politics*. Cambridge University Press, 2002.

Kern, Stephen. *The Culture of Time and Space, 1880–1918*. Harvard University Press, 2003.

Kincaid, Paul. "On the Origins of Genre." *Extrapolations* 44, no. 4 (Winter 2003): 409–19.
Klug, Sam. *The Internal Colony: Race and the American Politics of Global Decolonization.* University of Chicago Press, 2025.
Knox, Robert. "Valuing Race? Stretched Marxism and the Logic of Imperialism." *London Review of International Law* 4, no. 1 (March 2016): 81–126.
Kocka, Jürgen. "Comparison and Beyond." *History and Theory* 42, no. 1 (February 2003): 39–44.
Koopman, Colin. *Genealogy as Critique: Foucault and the Problems of Modernity.* Indiana University Press, 2013.
Koselleck, Reinhart. *Futures Past: On the Semantics of Historical Time.* Translated by Keith Tribe. Columbia University Press, 2004.
Koselleck, Reinhart. "Introduction and Prefaces to *Geschichtliche Grundbegriffe.*" Translated by Michaela Richter. *Contributions to the History of Concepts* 6, no. 1 (Summer 2011): 1–37.
Koselleck, Reinhart. *Sediments of Time: On Possible Histories.* Edited and translated by Sean Franzel and Stefan Ludwig-Hoffmann. Stanford University Press, 2018.
Kripp, Jacob. "The Creative Advance Must Be Defended: Miscegenation, Metaphysics, and Race War in Jan Smuts's Vision of the League of Nations." *American Political Science Review* 116, no. 3 (September 2022): 940–53.
Lake, Marilyn, and Henry Reynolds. *Drawing the Global Colour Line: White Men's Countries and the International Challenge of Racial Equality.* Cambridge University Press, 2008.
Lamb, Peter. "Harold Laski (1893–1950): Political Theorist of a World in Crisis." *Review of International Studies* 25, no. 2 (1999): 329–42.
Landemore, Hélène. "An Epistemic Argument for Democracy." In *Routledge Handbook of Political Epistemology,* edited by Michael Hannon and Jeroen de Ridder. Routledge, 2021.
Laski, Harold. "The Economic Foundations of Peace." In *The Intelligent Man's Way to Prevent War,* edited by Leonard Woolf. Garland, 1973.
Laski, Harold. *The State in Theory and Practice.* Viking Press, 1935.
Lavender, Isiah. *Race in American Science Fiction.* Indiana University Press, 2011.
Lefebvre, Henri. *The Production of Space.* Translated by Donald Nicholson-Smith. Wiley-Blackwell, 1991.
Lenin, V. I. *Imperialism, The Highest Stage of Capitalism: A Popular Outline.* 1917. Marxists Internet Archive. https://www.marxists.org/archive/lenin/works/1916/imp-hsc/ch06.htm.
Lenin, V. I. "Preface to the French and German Editions." In *Imperialism, The Highest Stage of Capitalism: A Popular Outline.* July 6, 1920. Marxists Internet Archive. https://www.marxists.org/archive/lenin/works/1916/imp-hsc/pref02.htm.
Lenin, V. I. "The Socialist Revolution and the Right of Nations to Self-Determination: Theses." 1916. Marxists Internet Archive. https://www.marxists.org/archive/lenin/works/1916/jan/x01.htm.
Lenin, V. I. "Speech of Comrade Lenin." In *The 2nd Congress of the Communist International.* [US] Government Printing Office, 1920.
Lewis, David Levering. *W. E. B. Du Bois: A Biography.* Henry Holt, 2009.
Lipsitz, George. "Abolition Democracy and Global Justice." *Comparative American Studies* 2, no. 3 (2004): 271–86.

Lipsitz, George. "The Possessive Investment in Whiteness: Racialized Social Democracy and the 'White' Problem in American Studies." *American Quarterly* 47, no. 3 (September 1995): 369–87.

Liss, Julia. "Diasporic Identities: The Science and Politics of Race in the Work of Franz Boas and W. E. B. Du Bois, 1894–1919." *Cultural Anthropology* 13, no. 2 (May 1998): 127–66.

Livingston, Alexander. "The Cost of Liberty: Sacrifice and Survival in Du Bois's *John Brown*." In Bromell, *Political Companion to W. E. B. Du Bois*.

Livingston, Alexander. *Damn Great Empires: William James and the Politics of Pragmatism*. Oxford University Press, 2016.

Locke, Alain. "Color: Unfinished Business of Democracy." In *The Works of Alain Locke*, edited by Charles Molesworth. Oxford University Press, 2012.

Locke, Alain. *World View on Race and Democracy: A Study Guide in Human Group Relations*. American Library Association, 1943.

Logan, Rayford. "The Charter of the United Nations." In *An Appeal to the World! A Statement on the Denial of Human Rights to Minorities in the Case of Citizens of the United States of America and an Appeal to the United Nations for Redress*, edited by W. E. B. Du Bois. NAACP, 1947.

Logan, Rayford. "The Crisis of Democracy in the Western Hemisphere." *Journal of Negro Education* 10, no. 3 (July 1941): 344–52.

Logan, Rayford. "The Historical Aspects of Pan-Africanism, 1900–1945." In *Pan-Africanism Reconsidered*, edited by the American Society of African Culture. University of California Press, 1962.

Loggins, Jared. "W. E. B. Du Bois, the Negro Problem, and the Case Against Black Involvement in War." In *Globalizing Political Theory*, edited by Smita A. Rahman, Katherine A. Gordy, and Shirin S. Deylami. Routledge, 2023.

Lowe, Lisa. *The Intimacies of Four Continents*. Duke University Press, 2015.

Luce, Henry. "The American Century." *Diplomatic History* 23, no. 2 (Spring 1999): 159–71.

Mackinnon, Emma Stone. "Declaration as Disavowal: The Politics of Race and Empire in the Universal Declaration of Human Rights." *Political Theory* 47, no. 1 (2019): 57–81.

Magdoff, Harry. *Imperialism Without Colonies*. Monthly Review Press, 2003.

Makalani, Minkah. *In the Cause of Freedom: Radical Black Internationalism from Harlem to London, 1917–1939*. University of North Carolina Press, 2011.

Mampilly, Zachariah. "The Du Bois Doctrine: Race and the American Century." *Foreign Affairs* (September/October 2022): 156–67.

Manela, Erez. *The Wilsonian Moment: Self-Determination and the International Origins of Anticolonial Nationalism*. Oxford University Press, 2007.

Marable, Manning. *W. E. B. Du Bois: Black Radical Democrat*. Twayne, 1986.

Marable, Manning, and Leith Mullings. "The Divided Mind of Black America: Race, Ideology, and Politics in the Post–Civil Rights Era." *Race & Class* 36, no. 1 (1994): 61–72.

Markell, Patchen. "Education, Independence, and Acknowledgement." In *Debating Moral Education: Rethinking the Role of the Modern University*, edited by Elizabeth Kiss and Peter Euben. Duke University Press, 2009.

Martel, James. *Textual Conspiracies: Walter Benjamin, Idolatry, and Political Theory*. University of Michigan Press, 2011.

Marwah, Inder. "Darwin in India: Anticolonial Evolutionism at the Dawn of the Twentieth Century." *Perspectives on Politics* 21, no. 3 (September 2023): 880–95.
Marwah, Inder. "Provincializing Progress: Developmentalism and Anti-Imperialism in Colonial India." *Polity* 51, no. 3 (July 2019): 498–531.
Marx, Karl. *Capital*. Vol. 1. Translated by Ben Fowkes. Penguin, 1990.
Marx, Karl. *Grundrisse*. Translated by Martin Nicolaus. Penguin, 1973.
Marx, Karl. "On the Jewish Question." In *The Marx-Engels Reader*, 2nd ed., edited by Robert Tucker. Norton, 1978.
Marx, Karl, and Friedrich Engels. "Manifesto of the Communist Party." In *Marx-Engels Reader*, edited by Robert Tucker. Norton, 1972.
Mazower, Mark. *Governing the World: The History of an Idea, 1815 to the Present*. Penguin, 2013.
Mazower, Mark. *No Enchanted Place: The End of Empire and the Ideological Origins of the United Nations*. Princeton University Press, 2009.
Mazower, Mark. "The Strange Triumph of Human Rights, 1833–1950." *Historical Journal* 47, no. 2 (2004): 379–98.
McClelland, J. S. *The Crowd and the Mob: From Plato to Canetti*. Routledge, 1989.
McGrath, Elizabeth. "The Black Andromeda." *Journal of the Warburg and Courtauld Institutes*, 55 (1992): 1–18.
McLeod, Lisa. "Du Bois's *A World Search for Democracy*: The Democratic Roots of Socialism." *Socialism and Democracy* 32, no. 3 (2018): 105–24.
Miller, Kelly. *History of the World War for Human Rights*. A. Jenkins, 1919.
Mommsen, Wolfgang. *Theories of Imperialism*. Translated by P. S. Falla. Random House, 1980.
Morefield, Jeanne. *Empires Without Imperialism: Anglo-American Decline and the Politics of Deflection*. Oxford University Press, 2014.
Morefield, Jeanne. "Harold Laski on the Habits of Imperialism." In *Lineages of Empire: The Historical Roots of British Imperial Thought*, edited by Duncan Kelly. Oxford University Press, 2009.
Morefield, Jeanne. "States Are Not People: Harold Laski on Unsettling Sovereignty, Rediscovering Democracy." *Political Research Quarterly* 58, no. 4 (December 2005): 659–69.
Moreton-Robinson, Aileen, Maryrose Casey, and Fiona Nicoll. "Introduction: Virtue and Transnational Whiteness." In *Transnational Whiteness Matters*, edited by Aileen Moreton-Robinson, Maryrose Casey, and Fiona Nicoll. Lexington, 2008.
Morris, Aldon D., Michael Schwartz, Cheryl Johnson-Odim, et al. *The Oxford Handbook of W. E. B. Du Bois*. Oxford University Press, 2022.
Moses, Wilson. *Afrotopia: The Roots of African American Popular History*. Cambridge University Press, 1998.
Moses, Wilson. *Creative Conflict in African American Thought*. Cambridge University Press, 2004.
Mouffe, Chantal. *Agonistics: Thinking the World Politically*. Verso, 2013.
Mouffe, Chantal. *On the Political*. Routledge, 2005.
Moyn, Samuel. *The Last Utopia: Human Rights in History*. Harvard University Press, 2010.
Mullen, Bill. *Afro-Orientalism*. University of Minnesota Press, 2004.
Mullen, Bill. *Un-American: W. E. B. Du Bois and the Century of World Revolution*. Temple University Press, 2015.

Munro, John. *The Anti-Colonial Front: The African American Freedom Struggle and Global Decolonization, 1945–1960.* Cambridge University Press, 2017.

Mustapha, Abdulkarim. "Constituting Negative Geopolitics: Memoriality and Event in *The World and Africa* (1946)." *boundary 2* 27, no. 3 (Fall 2000): 171–97.

Myers, Ella. "Beyond the Psychological Wage: Du Bois on White Dominion." *Political Theory* 47, no. 1 (February 2019): 6–31.

Narayan, John. *John Dewey: The Global Public and Its Problems.* Manchester University Press, 2016.

Narayan, John. "The Wages of Whiteness in the Absence of Wages: Racial Capitalism, Reactionary Intercommunalism and the Rise of Trumpism." *Third World Quarterly* 38, no. 11 (2017): 2482–500.

Naresh, Vatsal. "Problems of an Other's Making: Ambedkar, Caste, and Majoritarian Domination." Preprint, *American Political Science Review*, December 17, 2024. https://doi.org/10.1017/S0003055424001126.

Nelson, Dana. *National Manhood: Capitalist Citizenship and the Imagined Fraternity of White Men.* Duke University Press, 1998.

Nichols, Christopher McKnight. *Promise and Peril: America at the Dawn of a Global Age.* Harvard University Press, 2011.

Nkrumah, Kwame. *Neo-Colonialism: The Last Stage of Imperialism.* International Publishers, 1965.

Nordhoff, Charles. *Politics for Young Americans.* Harper, 1875.

Obst, Anthony. "'Revolution of Thought and Action': W. E. B. Du Bois's World Search for Abolition Democracy," *Lateral: Journal of the Cultural Studies Association* 11, no. 2 (Fall 2022), https://csalateral.org/issue/11-2/revolution-thought-action-du-bois-world-search-abolition-democracy-obst/.

Olsavsky, Jesse. "The Abolitionist Tradition in the Making of W. E. B. Du Bois's Marxism and Anti-Imperialism." *Socialism and Democracy* 32, no. 3 (2018): 14–35.

Olson, Joel. *The Abolition of White Democracy.* University of Minnesota Press, 2004.

Ong, Aihwa. *Flexible Citizenship: The Cultural Logics of Transnationality.* Duke University Press, 1999.

Onishi, Yuichiro. *Transpacific Antiracism: Afro-Asian Solidarity in 20th-Century Black America, Japan, and Okinawa.* New York University Press, 2013.

Onishi, Yuichiro, and Toru Shinoda. "The Paradigm of Refusal: W. E. B. Du Bois's Transpacific Imagination in the 1930s." In *Citizen of the World: The Late Career and Legacy of W. E. B. Du Bois*, edited by Phillip Sinitiere. Northwestern University Press, 2019.

Oren, Ido. "The Subjectivity of the 'Democratic' Peace: Changing U.S. Perceptions of Imperial Germany." *International Security* 20, no. 2 (Fall 1995): 147–84.

Orwell, George. "Not Counting N**gers." July 1939. https://www.orwell.ru/library/articles/niggers/english/e_ncn.

O'Tuathail, Gearoid. *Critical Geopolitics: The Politics of Writing Global Space.* Routledge, 1996.

Pagden, Anthony. *Peoples and Empires: A Short History of European Migration, Exploration, and Conquest, from Greece to the Present.* Random House, 2007.

Palonen, Kari. "An Application of Conceptual History to Itself." *Redescriptions: Political Thought, Conceptual History and Feminist Theory* 1, no. 1 (1997): 39–69.

Palonen, Kari. "The Politics of Conceptual History." *Contributions to the History of Concepts* 1, no. 1 (March 2005): 37–50.

Partington, John. "H. G. Wells and the World State: A Liberal Cosmopolitan in a Totalitarian Age." *International Relations* 17, no. 2 (2003): 233–46.

Pedersen, Susan. *The Guardians: The League of Nations and the Crisis of Empire.* Oxford University Press, 2015.

Philips, Anne. "Global Justice: Just Another Modernisation Theory?" In Bell, *Empire, Race, and Global Justice.*

Pitts, Jennifer. *Boundaries of the International: Law and Empire.* Harvard University Press, 2018.

Plummer, Brenda Gayle. *Rising Wind: Black Americans and U.S. Foreign Affairs, 1935–1960.* University of North Carolina Press, 1996.

Pocock, J. G. A. *Politics, Language, and Time.* University of Chicago Press, 1989.

Porter, Eric. *The Problem of the Future World: W. E. B. Du Bois and the Race Concept at Midcentury.* Duke University Press, 2010.

Powers, Allison. "Tragedy Made Flesh: Constitutional Lawlessness in Du Bois's *Black Reconstruction.*" *Comparative Studies of South Asia, Africa and the Middle East* 34, no. 1 (2014): 106–125.

Prashad, Vijay. *The Darker Nations: A People's History of the Third World.* New Press, 2007.

Rabaka, Reiland. *W. E. B. Du Bois and the Problems of the Twenty-First Century: An Essay on Africana Critical Theory.* Lexington, 2007.

Ramesh, Hari. "The Politics of Peoples in Rabindranath Tagore and W. E. B. Du Bois." *History of the Present* 9, no. 2 (October 2019): 166–92.

Rana, Aziz. "Against National Security Citizenship," *Boston Review*, February 7, 2018, https://www.bostonreview.net/articles/aziz-rana-against-national-security-citizenship/.

Rana, Aziz. "Left Internationalism in the Heart of Empire." *Dissent*, May 23, 2022. https://www.dissentmagazine.org/online_articles/left-internationalism-in-the-heart-of-empire/.

Rana, Aziz. "Renewing Working-Class Internationalism." *New Labor Forum* 28, no. 1 (2019): 30–38.

Rasberry, Vaughn. *Race and the Totalitarian Century: Geopolitics in the Black Literary Imagination.* Harvard University Press, 2016.

Reed, Adolph, Jr. *W. E. B. Du Bois and American Political Thought: Fabianism and the Color Line.* Oxford University Press, 1997.

Rieder, John. *Colonialism and the Emergence of Science Fiction.* Wesleyan University Press, 2008.

Riofrancos, Thea. "Scaling Democracy: Participation and Resource Extraction in Latin America." *Perspectives on Politics* 15, no. 3 (September 2017): 678–96.

Robinson, Cedric. *Black Marxism: The Making of the Black Radical Tradition.* University of North Carolina Press, 1983.

Roediger, David. *Wages of Whiteness: Race and the Making of the American Working Class.* Verso, 2007.

Rogers, Melvin. "The People, Rhetoric, and Affect: On the Political Force of Du Bois's *The Souls of Black Folk.*" *American Political Science Review* 106, no. 1 (February 2012): 188–203.

Rosenboim, Or. *The Emergence of Globalism: Visions of World Order in Britain and the United States, 1939–1950.* Princeton University Press, 2019.

Rosenboim, Or. "The Spatiality of Politics: Cesare Battisti's Regional and International Thought, 1900–1916." *Modern Intellectual History* 19, no. 2 (June 2022): 397–420.

Rowe, John Carlos. *Literary Culture and U.S. Imperialism: From the Revolution to World War II*. Oxford University Press, 2000.

Royce, Josiah. *Race Questions, Provincialism, and Other American Problems*. MacMillan, 1908.

Saman, Michael. "Du Bois and Marx, Du Bois and Marxism." *Du Bois Review* 17, no. 1 (Spring 2020): 33–54.

Saward, Michael. "The Representative Claim." *Contemporary Political Theory* 15, no. 3 (2006): 297–318.

Schmitt, Carl. *The Nomos of the Earth in the International Law of the Jus Publicum Europaeum*. Translated by G. L. Ulmen. Telos Press, 2003.

Schmitt, Carl. *Theory of the Partisan*. Translated by G. L. Ulmen. Telos Press, 2007.

Schrader, Stuart. *Badges Without Borders: How Global Counterinsurgency Transformed American Policing*. University of California Press, 2019.

Scott, David. *Conscripts of Modernity: The Tragedy of Colonial Enlightenment*. Duke University Press, 2004.

Scott, David. "Norms of Self-Determination: Thinking Sovereignty Through." *Middle East Law and Governance* 4, no. 2–3 (2012): 195–224.

Scott, David. "Tragedy's Time: Postemancipation Futures Past and Present." In *Rethinking Tragedy*, edited Rita Felski. Baltimore: Johns Hopkins University Press, 2008.

Seigel, Micol. "Beyond Compare: Comparative Method After the Transnational Turn." *Radical History Review*, no. 91 (Winter 2005): 62–90.

Shaffer, Robert. "Pearl S. Buck and the East and West Association: The Trajectory and Fate of Critical Internationalism." *Peace & Change* 28, no. 1 (2003): 1–36.

Shklar, Judith. *American Citizenship: The Quest for Inclusion*. Harvard University Press, 1991.

Simon, Joshua. "Overcoming the Other America: José Martí's Immanent Critique of the Unionist Paradigm." *Review of Politics* 84, no. 1 (Winter 2022): 55–79.

Singh, Nikhil Pal. *Black Is a Country: Race and the Unfinished Struggle for Democracy*. Harvard University Press, 2005.

Singh, Nikhil Pal. "On Race, Violence, and So-Called Primitive Accumulation." *Social Text* 34, no. 3 (2016): 27–50.

Sinitiere, Philip Luke. "'An Impressive Basis for Research': Arna Bontemps' Co-Creation of the W. E. B. Du Bois Collection at Fisk University." *Black Scholar* 52, no. 2 (2022): 50–62.

Sinitiere, Philip Luke. "'There Must Be No Idle Morning:' W. E. B. Du Bois's Legacy as a Black Radical Intellectual." *Socialism and Democracy* 32, no. 3 (2018): 207–30.

Skrentny, John. *The Minority Rights Revolution*. Belknap Press of Harvard University Press, 2002.

Slate, Nico. *Colored Cosmopolitanism: The Shared Struggle for Freedom in the United States and India*. Harvard University Press, 2017.

Sluga, Glenda. "From F. Melian Stawell to E. Greene Balch: International and *Internationalist* Thinking at the Gender Margins, 1919–1947." In *Women's International Thought: A New History*, edited by Patricia Owens and Katharina Rietzler. Cambridge University Press, 2021.

Smith, Thomas. *Emancipation Without Equality: Pan-African Activism and the Global Color Line*. University of Massachusetts Press, 2018.

Son, Kyong-Min. *The Eclipse of the Demos: The Cold War and the Crisis of Democracy Before Neoliberalism*. University Press of Kansas, 2020.

Spiller, Gustav, ed. *Papers on Inter-Racial Problems: Communicated to the First Universal Races Congress*. P. S. King & Son, 1911.

Steger, Manfred. *The Rise of the Global Imaginary: Political Ideologies from the French Revolution to the Global War on Terror*. Oxford University Press, 2008.

Stiegler, Bernard. *States of Shock: Stupidity and Knowledge in the 21st Century*. Polity, 2015.

Stoddard, Lothrop. *The Rising Tide of Color Against White-World Supremacy*. Scribner, 1920.

Streit, George. *Union Now: A Proposal for a Federal Union of the Democracies of the North Atlantic*. Harper, 1940.

Sultan, Nazmul S. "Self-Rule and the Problem of Peoplehood in Colonial India." *American Political Science Review* 114, no. 1 (February 2020): 81–94.

Sundquist, Eric. *To Wake the Nations: Race in the Making of American Literature*. Harvard University Press, 1994.

Taylor, Charles. *Modern Social Imaginaries*. Duke University Press, 2004.

Temin, David. "Development in Decolonization: Walter Rodney, Third World Developmentalism, and 'Decolonizing Political Theory.'" *American Political Science Review* 117, no. 1 (February 2023): 235–48.

Temin, David. *Remapping Sovereignty: Decolonization and Self-Determination in North American Indigenous Thought*. University of Chicago Press, 2023.

Thomas, Victor Bulmer. *Empire in Retreat: The Past, Present, and Future of the United States*. Yale University Press, 2018.

Throesch, Elizabeth. *Before Einstein: The Fourth Dimension in Fin-de-Siècle Literature and Culture*. Anthem Press, 2017.

Tillery, Alvin B., Jr. *Between Homeland and Motherland: Africa, U.S. Foreign Policy, and Black Leadership in America*. Cornell University Press, 2011.

Toscano, Alberto. "America's Belgium: W. E. B. Du Bois on Race, Class, and the Origins of World War I." In *Cataclysm 1914: The First World War and the Making of Modern World Politics*, edited by Alexander Anievas. Brill, 2016.

Tully, James. "Lineages of Contemporary Imperialism." *Proceedings of the British Academy* 155 (2009): 3–29.

Tully, James. *Public Philosophy in a New Key*. Vol. 1, *Democracy and Civic Freedom*. Cambridge University Press, 2008.

Tully, James. *Public Philosophy in a New Key*. Vol. 2, *Imperialism and Civic Freedom*. Cambridge University Press, 2008.

Tyner, James. *The Geography of Malcolm X: Black Radicalism and the Remaking of American Space*. Routledge, 2006.

Valdez, Inés. "Association, Reciprocity, and Emancipation: A Transnational Account of the Politics of Global Justice." In Bell, *Empire, Race, and Global Justice*.

Valdez, Inés. "Empire, Popular Sovereignty, and the Problem of Self-and-Other Determination." *Perspectives on Politics* 21, no. 1 (March 2023): 109–25.

Valdez, Inés. "Socialism and Empire: Labor Mobility, Racial Capitalism, and the Political Theory of Migration." *Political Theory* 49, no. 6 (December 2021): 902–33.

Valdez, Inés. *Transnational Cosmopolitanism: Kant, Du Bois, and Justice as a Political Craft*. Cambridge University Press, 2019.

Vázquez-Arroyo, Antonio. "Binding Politics: Political Space, Responsibilities, and the New-Old Order." *Theory & Event* 26, no. 3 (July 2023): 531–58.

Vimalassery, Manu, Juliana Hu Pegues, and Alyosha Goldstein. "Introduction: On Colonial Unknowing." In "On Colonial Unknowing," edited by Alyosha Goldstein, Juliana Hu Pegues, and Manu Vimalassery. Special issue, *Theory & Event* 19, no. 4 (2016). https://muse.jhu.edu/article/633283.

Vitalis, Robert. "The Graceful and Generous Liberal Gesture: Making Racism Invisible in American International Relations." *Millennium* 29, no. 2 (2000): 331–56.

Vitalis, Robert. *White World Order, Black Power Politics: The Birth of American International Relations*. Cornell University Press, 2015.

Von Eschen, Penny. *Race Against Empire: Black Americans and Anticolonialism, 1937–1957*. Cornell University Press, 1997.

Waligora-Davis, Nicole. "W. E. B. Du Bois and the Fourth World." *New Centennial Review* 6, no. 3 (Winter 2006): 57–90.

Walling, William English. "Socialists and Imperialism." In *Towards an Enduring Peace: A Symposium of Peace Proposals and Programs, 1914–1916*, edited by Randolph Bourne. American Association for International Conciliation, 1916.

Webb, Sidney, and Beatrice Webb. *Industrial Democracy*. Longmans, Green, 1897.

Weeks, Kathi. "Scaling-Up: A Marxist Feminist Archive." *Feminist Studies* 47, no. 3 (2021): 1–29.

Weinbaum, Alys Eve. *Wayward Reproductions: Genealogies of Race and Nation in Transatlantic Modern Thought*. Duke University Press, 2004.

Wells, H. G. *Anticipations of the Reaction of Mechanical and Scientific Progress upon Human Life and Thought*. Harper, 1901.

Wells, H. G. *In the Days of the Comet*. Century, 1906.

Wells, H. G. *The Time Machine*. In *Three Prophetic Science Fiction Novels of H. G. Wells*. Dover, 1960.

Werner, Michael, and Bénédicte Zimmermann. "Beyond Comparison: *Histoire Croisée* and the Challenge of Reflexivity." *History and Theory* 45, no. 1 (February 2006): 30–50.

White, Christopher, and Matthew Hughey. "Above the Color Line: W. E. B. Du Bois's Otherworldly Perspective and a New Racial Order." *Journal of the Academy of American Religion* 91, no. 3 (September 2023): 605–620.

Wilder, Gary. *Concrete Utopianism: The Politics of Temporality and Solidarity*. Fordham University Press, 2022.

Wilder, Gary. "Decolonization and Postnational Democracy." In *Forms of Pluralism and Democratic Constitutionalism*, edited by Andrew Arato, Jean Cohen, and Astrid Von Busekist, 52–71. Columbia University Press, 2018.

Wilder, Gary. *Freedom Time: Negritude, Decolonization, and the Future of the World*. Duke University Press, 2015.

Wilder, Gary. "Reading Du Bois's Revelation: Radical Humanism and Black Atlantic Criticism." In *The Postcolonial Contemporary: Political Imaginaries for the Global Present*, edited by Jini Kim Watson and Gary Wilder. Fordham University Press, 2018.

Williams, Chad. "In the Shadow of World War: Revisiting W. E. B. Du Bois's *Black Reconstruction*." *Du Bois Review* 20, no. 1 (2022): 43–55.

Williams, Chad. *Torchbearers of Democracy: African American Soldiers in the World War I Era*. University of North Carolina Press, 2010.

Williams, Melissa. "Deparochializing Democratic Theory." In *Deparochializing Political Theory*, edited by Melissa Williams. Cambridge University Press, 2020.

Williams, Robert W. "Politics, Rights, and Spatiality in W. E. B. Du Bois's 'Address to the Country' (1906)." *Journal of African American Studies* 4, no. 3 (September 2010): 337–58.

Williams, Theo. *Making the Revolution Global: Black Radicalism and the British Socialist Movement Before Decolonization*. Verso, 2022.

Williams, William Appleman. *Empire as a Way of Life*. Oxford University Press, 1980.

Wilson, Peter. "Fabian Paternalism and Radical Dissent: Leonard Woolf's Theory of Economic Imperialism." In *Imperialism and Internationalism in the Discipline of International Relations*, edited by David Long and Brian Schmidt. SUNY Press, 2005.

Wilson, Peter. *The International Theory of Leonard Woolf*. Palgrave MacMillan, 2003.

Wilson, Woodrow. "Address to a Joint Session of Congress Requesting a Declaration of War Against Germany: April 02, 1917." American Presidency Project. https://www.presidency.ucsb.edu/node/207620.

Wolfe, Patrick. "Land, Labor, and Difference: Elementary Structures of Race." *American Historical Review* 106, no. 3 (June 2001): 866–905.

Wolfe, Patrick. "Settler Colonialism and the Elimination of the Native." *Journal of Genocide Research* 8, no. 4 (2006): 387–409.

Wolin, Sheldon. *Politics and Vision: Continuity and Innovation in Western Political Thought*. Princeton University Press, 2004.

Wolin, Sheldon. *The Presence of the Past: Essays on the State and Constitution*. Johns Hopkins University Press, 1989.

Yaszek, Lisa. "Afrofuturism, Science Fiction, and the History of the Future." *Socialism and Democracy* 20, no. 3 (2006): 41–60.

Younis, Musab. *On the Scale of the World: The Formation of Black Anticolonial Thought*. University of California Press, 2022.

Younis, Musab. "United by Blood: Race and Transnationalism During the Belle Époque." *Nations and Nationalism* 23, no. 3 (2017): 484–504.

Zamir, Shamoon. *Dark Voices: W. E. B. Du Bois and American Thought, 1888–1903*. University of Chicago Press, 1995.

Zimmerman, Angela. *Alabama in Africa: Booker T. Washington, the German Empire, and the Globalization of the New South*. Princeton University Press, 2012.

Zimmerman, Angela. "Reconstruction Along the Global Color Line: Slavery, International Class Conflict, and Empire." In *Interpreting American History: The New South*, edited by James Humphreys. Kent State University Press, 2018.

Index

abolition-democracy, 90, 112, 117, 120
abolitionist movement, 29, 99
Aborigines Rights Protection Society (ARPS), 200
Addams, Jane, 176
"Address to the Nations of the World" (Du Bois), 56
Afghanistan invasion by US (2001), 213, 217
Africa: commodity fetishism and, 194; development and, 198–202; Du Bois on, 125, 196–97, 201; Du Bois's writings on, 171–72, 178, 189–91; marginalization in history of humanity of, 197; modern conception of, 199; precolonial traditions of democracy and communal ownership in, 38, 170–71, 191, 200–202; racial vindicationist approach to, 171–72, 178; roots of anticolonialism in, 200; self-determination and, 168, 178–81, 189; spiritual gift of African peoples to modern civilization, 37–38, 170–71, 201; world history and, 190–91, 197; world peace and, 172, 174. *See also* African Americans; "African Roots of War, The" (Du Bois); anticolonialism; colonial imperialism; colonial peoplehood; decolonization; imperialism; neocolonialism; Pan-Africanism; settler colonialism; slavery; South Africa; *World and Africa, The* (Du Bois)
Africa: Its Place in Modern History (Du Bois), 170

African Americans: anticolonialism and, 180; constructive minorities and, 132–34; Du Bois on, 143, 209; human rights and, 14; imperialism's connection to, 6, 14, 53, 128, 131, 143–44, 163, 178, 218; liberal interventionism and, 181–82; Marxism and, 85; minority rights and, 160, 162; race provincialism and, 177; self-determination and, 128, 168, 178; self-segregation and, 134; solidarity and, 128, 133, 179. *See also* black laborers
"African Roots of War, The" (Du Bois): capitalism in, 76, 108; dividends of empire in, 102–5; economic imperialism in, 79; imperialism as cause of war in, 76, 108, 178, 205, 226–27; world democracy in, 226–27; World War I in, 102
America. *See* United States
"American Century, The" (Luce), 187
American Federation of Labor (AFL), 85, 109
American Negro Academy, 51
American South. *See* South, the
Anderson, Benedict, 58
Anderson, Carol, 125n1
Andromeda: anticolonialism and, 202, 205, 211; commodity fetishism and, 194–95; constellation of, 193, 195, 197, 201–2; decolonization and, 205; definition of, 191–92; democratic peace and, 172, 205; developmental idioms and, 201–2; self-determination and, 202–3, 211; whitening of, 197–98;

Andromeda (*continued*)
  world democratic imaginary and, 191, 195, 210–12
Anglo-Saxon union, 59–60, 65
annihilation of distance, 38, 42, 55, 57, 63–64, 79, 82
Anson Phelps Stokes Fund, 185
Anticipations of the Reaction of Mechanical and Scientific Progress (Wells), 168
anticolonialism: colonial commission proposal and, 139; colonial peoplehood and, 37, 127–30, 155, 164, 166, 171; democratic peace and, 171, 190, 212; dividends of empire and, 109–10; domestic jurisdiction and, 139; Du Bois's approach to, 7, 34–35, 83, 98, 125, 164; peace activism's intimate connections with, 204–5; self-determination and, 149, 181, 191, 202–3, 211, 217; solidarity and, 89, 98, 219; transnational democratic imaginary and, 171, 185; white laborers and, 23, 89, 98, 110; white privilege and, 111; world democracy and, 109, 217; world peace and, 145
anti-imperialism, 16, 80, 89–94, 143–44, 148, 185, 204, 208, 216
Appeal to the World!, An (Du Bois), 157–63
Appiah, Anthony, 174
Aristotle, 3, 25, 81
Armitage, David, 223
Atlantic Charter (1942), 137, 187–89
Autobiography (Du Bois), 58

Bakhtin, Mikhail, 38, 40–41, 45, 50–51
Balch, Emily Greene, 176
Balfour, Lawrie, 8n17, 29, 69–70, 89n14
Barnes, Leonard, 203
Battle of Tours (732), 74
Bell, Duncan, 59
Benjamin, Walter, 193
Berlin Conference (1884–85), 90, 102, 150, 173
Bertholf, Gary, 99
Biden, Joseph, 213
Black Americans. *See* African Americans

Black Folk Then and Now (Du Bois), 37, 170, 190
black laborers, 85–86, 99, 109, 113–16, 118
Black Reconstruction in America (Du Bois), 1, 98–99, 102, 111–17, 119
Boas, Franz, 63
Boer Wars, 107–8
Bourne, Randolph, 71
Britain: anti-imperialism in, 93; color line in, 53–54; democracy in, 21–22; domestic jurisdiction and, 155; Du Bois's experiences in, 168; empire of, 52, 107, 159, 188; "Greater Britain," 58; imperial federation proposals for, 152; imperialism of, 125; laborers in, 122, 195–96; neocolonialism and, 120; peace movement in, 176; popular sovereignty in, 80; US relations with, 59; white prestige and, 107–8; world democracy and, 123; World War I and, 73
Bromell, Nick, 26–27
Brown v. Board of Education (1956), 226
Buck, Pearl S., 145
Buell, Raymond Leslie, 138
Bunche, Ralph, 134–35
Burden-Stelly, Charise, 204, 208
Burke, Edmund, 35

capitalism: black laborers and, 113–14; dividends of empire and, 36, 87–89, 95–96; Du Bois on, 34–35, 79, 88–89, 146, 212; financial capitalism, 36, 71–72, 86, 88, 92, 111, 120; global color line and, 71–73, 79; imperialism and, 13, 16, 34, 79, 95, 108, 112, 130, 149, 181; industrial capitalism, 23, 79, 86, 108, 198; labor's relation to capital in, 24, 77–79, 96, 102–5, 107; Marxism and, 23, 85–86; racial capitalism, 86–89, 120–23; racial inferiority and, 199; slavery and, 72, 181, 197, 212; sovereignty and, 203–4; technological development and, 79; transnational whiteness and, 87, 111; wages of whiteness and, 86–87; world democracy and, 36–37, 119, 211

Carnegie, Andrew, 59–60, 65, 185
chronotopes, 38, 40–45, 51–52, 64, 82–84
Churchill, Winston, 188
citizenship: cosmopolitan vision of, 170; dividends of empire and, 100–101, 104–5; minority rights and, 163; national security citizenship, 209; race provincialism and, 211; self-determination and, 32–35; transnational forms of, 56, 59, 207–9; wages of whiteness and, 100–101, 110; world peace and, 209
civil rights movement, 176, 180–81, 188
Civil War (US), 112–13, 115, 117, 196. *See also* Reconstruction
civilization. *See* European civilization
civilizing mission, 74, 94, 110, 216
Claeys, Gregory, 92n20
class conflict, 6, 85, 92, 102, 119
class inequality, 173, 203–4
class solidarity, 77, 82, 84–85, 89
class structure, 85–86, 99
classes, laboring. *See* black laborers; labor; white laborers
Cold War (1947–91), 6, 30, 148, 205–10, 212, 216
colonial commission proposal, 137–39, 153–54, 156
Colonial Conference (1945), 126–27, 136–39, 145, 151
colonial imperialism, 22–23, 110, 112–13, 118, 144, 147, 150–51, 201–2, 206. *See also* imperialism
colonial peoplehood: anticolonialism and, 37, 125–30, 155, 164, 166, 171; classification of colonial peoples and, 144–46; colony's meaning and, 127–30, 141–43, 149–52; constituency paradox and, 126–27; construction of, 128–47; constructive minorities theory and, 130–39; definition of, 128; domestic jurisdiction and, 153–63, 166; Du Bois on, 144–46, 150; human rights and, 153–63; minority rights and, 131, 153–63; politics of space and scale and, 164–66; settler colonialism and, 149–53; temporality of, 147–53; transnational political imaginaries and, 219; UN and, 127–29, 153–55, 165; world democracy and, 129, 147
colonial regionalism, 151
colonialism. *See* anticolonialism; colonial imperialism; colonial peoplehood; decolonization; imperialism; neocolonialism; settler colonialism
"Colonialism, Democracy, and Peace after the War" (Du Bois), 142
Color (Locke), 40
Color and Democracy (Du Bois), 120, 141, 145, 218
color line. *See* global color line
"Color Line Belts the World, The" (Du Bois), 53
"Comet, The" (Du Bois), 69–72
commodity fetishism, 194–95
Communist International, 149
Communist Manifesto (Marx and Engels), 123
Congo Free State, 118n101
"Conservation of Races" (Du Bois), 170
constellations, 193–95
constituency paradox, 126–27, 140, 165
constructive minorities, 130–40
cosmopolitanism, 9–10, 27, 71, 170, 174–75, 199, 215
Crisis, The (journal), 64, 66, 68–69, 85, 182
critical democratic theory, 90, 121

Darby, Derrick, 8–9
Dark Princess (Du Bois), 80–81
Darkwater (Du Bois), 69–70, 110
Darwinism, 45, 61–63, 82, 97
Davis, Jefferson, 47
decolonization, 7, 33, 35, 64, 119, 135–37, 151, 153, 172, 191, 222
Deloria, Vine, Jr., 153
democracy: control in, 2, 21–24, 37, 79, 89, 103–4, 108, 119, 122–23; definition of, 19–20; demophobia and, 35; Du Bois as a radical democrat, 15–16, 19–20, 31, 220; Du Bois on, 19–34, 55, 77, 172, 211, 217. *See also* abolition-democracy; democratic peace;

democracy (*continued*)
  economic democracy; industrial democracy; world democracy
Democracy and Empire (Giddings), 97
democratic despotism, 77, 95–97
democratic empire, 22, 97–98, 213
democratic federalism, 186–87
democratic imperialism, 22, 97–98, 213
democratic peace, 167–212
Dernburg, Bernhard, 107
Deudney, Daniel, 57n43
development, 34–35, 54–56, 185, 190–91, 195–202
Dewey, John, 32, 63, 133
Diagne, Blaise, 167
Disch, Lisa, 126
disenfranchisement, 13, 21–22, 25, 28, 142, 144, 157–59, 173, 200
dividends of empire, 36, 87–90, 97–110, 118–24
domestic jurisdiction, 13, 37, 129, 139, 153–66, 205, 217, 220–21
Doyle, Laura, 101
Dred Scott v. Sanford (1857), 140
Du Bois, Shirley Graham, 226
Du Bois, W. E. B.: context of, 30–31; education of, 19–20, 46; indictment against, 206–9, 211, 226; influences on, 20, 46, 63, 72, 76, 82–83, 91, 97, 203; location of democratic theorizing of, 11–16; Niagara movement involvement of, 165; overview of, 1–9, 36–39; poetry of, 68–70; political orientation of, 3, 15–16, 26, 31; as radical democrat, 15–16, 19–20, 31, 220; scholarship on, 8–10, 12–13, 27, 31, 201–2; science fiction writings of, 45–47; world travels of, 1. *See also* League of Nations; National Association for the Advancement of Colored People; United Nations; world democracy; *specific subjects and writings*
Dulles, John Foster, 155
Dumbarton Oaks (1944), 140–41, 144–45
Duong, Kevin, 25n68

East and West Association, 145
economic democracy, 12, 22–23, 37, 204
economic exploitation, 12, 22, 80, 95, 107–8, 128, 173, 181, 185, 190. *See also* labor
economic imperialism, 2, 12, 36–37, 77, 93–94, 144, 147, 150–53
economies, capitalist. *See* capitalism
education, 19–20, 28, 31–33, 46, 100, 108
Egyptology, 198–200
Einstein, Albert, 40–41, 45, 45n13, 48–50
elitist conception of democracy, 30–33, 55
Ellis, Mark, 182
Empire and Commerce in Africa (Woolf), 93
Empire or Democracy? (Barnes), 203
England. *See* Britain
"England Traitor to White Race" (Dernburg), 107
Ethiopia, 143, 161, 192–99
Eurocentrism, 215, 222
European civilization, 79, 97, 107, 121, 197–99
evolution, 38, 41, 45, 49, 60–64, 82
"Evolution of the Race Problem, The" (Darwin), 62

Fabian Society, 20, 89–94, 97–98, 138
Fanti confederation movement (1867), 200
Firmin, Anténor, 110
Flatland (Abbott), 48
Foner, Eric, 119
"Forty Years of American Hysteria" (Du Bois), 209
Fosdick, Harry Emerson, 127
Fosdick, Raymond, 127
fourth dimension, 38, 45–51, 55, 64, 82–83
France, 73, 116, 123, 155, 159
Fraser, Nancy, 14
free nations, 144, 146, 149, 151
Free Soilers, 99
freedom, 20, 23, 35, 47–48, 126–29, 152, 155–57, 197–98, 208–10
"Future of Africa and a League of Nations, The" (Kallen), 177
"Future of Europe in Africa, The" (Du Bois), 40, 186

Galli, Carlo, 15n37, 18
Gandhi, Mohandas, 152
Germany, 73, 85, 107, 109, 195
Getachew, Adom, 13, 135–36, 164, 210, 221
Giddings, Franklin, 97
Glimpses of World History (Nehru), 169
global color line: annihilation of distance and, 57–64; chronotopes and, 38, 40–47, 51–55, 64, 82–84; democratic imaginary and, 41, 71–82; dividends of empire and, 90–98, 103; evolution and, 45, 61–64, 82; imagined communities and, 58–59; interracial utopianism and, 41–45, 54–64, 82–84; modern worldview constituted by, 78; race provincialism and, 175–77, 210
global majoritarianism, 28, 130–39, 145–46, 166
globalization, 44, 57–58, 64
Gooding-Williams, Robert, Jr., 31, 173
Gramsci, Antonio, 214

"Hands of Ethiopia, The" (Du Bois), 112, 169, 181
Harcourt, Alfred, 1
Harlem Colonial Conference, 83, 161
Harvey, David, 92
Haskins, Alex, 220
Hegel, G. W. F., 3, 198
Heidegger, Martin, 78
Hinton, Charles Howard, 49
Hobhouse, Leonard, 63
Hobsbawm, Eric, 91
Hobson, J. G. A., 63, 76, 82–83, 91–98, 102–3, 112
Hooker, Juliet, 61n59, 70n81, 115
Horne, Gerald, 136, 204
hospitality, 88, 105
human rights, 153–65
Human Rights Council (HRC), 157, 160, 163
"Human Rights for All Minorities" (Du Bois), 145
humanitarian interventions, 217
Hunt, Ida Gibbs, 169
"Hymn to the Peoples, A" (Du Bois), 68–69, 72

"I Won't Vote" (Du Bois), 226
Idris, Murad, 184, 184n61
immigration, 75, 88, 99, 105
imperialism: abolition of, 6–7, 12; African Americans' relation to, 6, 14, 53, 128, 131, 143–46, 163, 178, 218; capitalism and, 13, 16, 34, 95, 108, 112, 130, 142, 149, 181; classification of peoples in, 144–46; colony's meaning and, 127–30, 141–43, 149–52; constituency paradox and, 140–41; constructive minorities and, 131–34; democracy and, 22–23, 33–35, 94–96; democratic imperialism, 22, 97–98, 213; democratic peace and, 173–74; Du Bois on, 2, 7, 12, 22, 33–34, 53, 61, 63, 80, 102, 108, 120, 140, 142, 150–51; industrial imperialism, 24, 87–88, 90, 111–20; internal colonialism, 140, 144; labor and, 2, 21–23, 76–77, 92–93, 102, 108, 110, 112–15, 116, 118; Marxism and, 23; new imperialism, 76, 90–92, 98, 102, 103, 106, 108, 112–19, 136, 173–74, 218; overaccumulation as cause of, 76–77, 92–93, 95, 112; quasi-colonialism, 128, 144, 146, 154, 157, 159, 165, 218; semi-colonialism, 148–49; slavery and, 112–14, 119, 136, 181; sovereignty and, 121, 152, 188; stadial understanding of, 148–51; UN and, 13–14, 33, 37, 158–59, 164; war and, 35, 73, 76–77, 79, 141, 204–5; world democracy and, 2, 6–7, 11–12, 16, 34–35, 54, 80, 119, 139–40, 213–27; world peace and, 77, 137, 143, 158. *See also* "African Roots of War, The" (Du Bois); anti-imperialism; colonial imperialism; colonial peoplehood; decolonization; dividends of empire; economic imperialism; industrial imperialism
Imperialism (Hobson), 76, 91
Imperialism (Lenin), 5, 90
In Battle for Peace (Du Bois), 206
In the Days of the Comet (Wells), 72
India, 35, 103, 115, 118, 148, 150, 161, 219
"Individualism, Democracy, and Social Control" (Du Bois), 125

industrial democracy: coining of, 96n36; definition of, 21–23, 115; dividends of empire and, 36, 88–89, 122–23; Du Bois on, 7, 82, 89, 96, 122, 119, 190, 204; global color line and, 77
industrial imperialism, 24, 87–88, 90, 111–20
industrial peace, 92, 98
inter-nation, 27–28, 37, 58, 66, 221
International Labor Organization, 5
international law, 14–15, 74, 131, 157–59, 161–62, 216
interracial utopianism, 38, 41–45, 55–60, 64–65, 70–73, 77, 80–84, 185
intraracial utopianism, 80–82
Invisible Man, The (Wells), 47
Iraq invasion by US (2003), 213, 217
Island of Dr. Moreau, The (Wells), 47

James, Henry, 50
James, William, 46, 50
Japan, 74, 81, 219–20
"Jefferson Davis as a Representative of Civilization" (Du Bois), 47
Jim Crow, 61–62, 116
Johnson, Andrew, 119, 178–80
Johnson, James Weldon, 177–80
Johnson, Walter, 114n89
Jung, Moon-Ho, 111

Kallen, Horace, 71, 177
Kaplan, Amy, 53, 173
Karuka, Manu, 103
Keynesian-Westphalian sovereignty, 14–15
Kidd, Benjamin, 97
Klug, Sam, 137
Koselleck, Reinhart, 38, 41n2, 43–44, 43n9
Kropotkin, Peter, 63

labor: abolitionism and, 99; bifurcation of democratic struggles and, 121–22; capital's relations with, 24, 77–79, 96, 102–5, 107; commodification of, 194, 211–12; Du Bois on, 76–77, 79, 99–100, 103; imperialism and, 2, 76–77, 79–80, 92–93, 102, 108, 110, 112–13, 116, 118; interracial utopianism and, 80–82, 84; Marxism and, 85–86; racialized division of, 87, 89, 103, 112, 118; slave labor, 114, 194, 206, 211–12; slavery and, 107, 114, 118, 194, 206, 211–12; wages of whiteness and, 86–87; working class, 23, 54, 76–77, 79, 86, 88, 96, 99, 123, 146, 196, 212. *See also* black laborers; dividends of empire; wages of whiteness; white laborers
Lake, Marilyn, 100–101
Laski, Harold, 169, 203–4
Le roman de l'avenir (Bodin), 64
League of Nations: Du Bois's work with, 5, 12, 27, 177, 203, 220–21; mandate system of, 35, 137–39, 154, 169, 216; minority rights regime in, 131, 161–62
Lenin, V. I., 5, 90–93, 148–49
Lewis, David Levering, 169
liberal internationalism, 20, 39, 105, 148, 159, 164, 203, 213–14, 218, 222
liberalism, racial, 134, 172, 176–83, 186–88, 211
Lippmann, Walter, 30–32
Locke, Alain, 130, 189
Locke, John, 34–35
Logan, Rayford, 136, 162–63
Lowe, Lisa, 86, 195n96
Luce, Henry, 138, 186–87
Luxemburg, Rosa, 93

Mackinnon, Emma Stone, 163–64
Madison, James, 30
"Making the World Safe for Minorities" (Smith), 132–33
Manuel, George, 153
Marable, Manning, 8n17
Marx, Karl, 3, 57, 85, 211
Marxism, 2, 21–24, 85–86, 91, 123–24
"Marxism and the Negro Problem" (Du Bois), 85
Mauss, Marcel, 27
McGrath, Elizabeth, 197
"method of nucleus," 186–87
Miller, Kelly, 178–79
Minkowski, Hermann, 50

minorities, constructive. *See* constructive minorities
"Minority Peoples and Problems" (East and West Association conference), 145
minority rights, 29, 131, 153–63, 165–66
modernity, 44, 78–79, 173–74, 198–99, 201–2
Moses, Wilson, 171n14
Mouffe, Chantal, 215–16
Mullen, Bill, 134–35
multipolarity, 39, 213–16
Myers, Ella, 87

National Association for the Advancement of Colored People (NAACP), 5, 26, 125–26, 134, 153, 167–68, 176–80, 187–88
National Congress of British West Africa (formerly ARPS), 111, 200
NATO (North Atlantic Treaty Organization), 213, 227
Nefertari, 174
Negro, The (Du Bois), 170
"Negro Mind Reaches Out, The" (Du Bois), 43, 77
Nehru, Jawaharlal, 160, 169
neocolonialism, 136–37, 140, 147–49, 151, 205–6, 216
neoconservatism, 213, 217
New York Peace Society (NYPS), 183
Niagara movement, 165
Niebuhr, Reinhold, 214
Nkrumah, Francis Kwame, 138–39, 148, 168
non-Euclidean geometry, 40, 49
noninterference, 129, 156–59
Nordhoff, Charles, 28–29, 133

Obama, Barack, 217
"Of the Culture of White Folk" (Du Bois), 89, 106–11
"Of the Ruling of Men" (Du Bois), 8–9, 20, 28–29, 31–32
Olmstead, Mildred Scott, 175
Olson, Joel, 100
"On the Jewish Question" (Marx), 211

Oren, Ido, 172n18
Orwell, George, 187
Ovid, 197
Ovington, Mary White, 179–80

Padmore, George, 136, 167–68
Palonen, Kari, 225
Pan-African Congresses, 34–35, 46, 56, 60, 139, 167–69, 179, 191, 203n122
Pan-Africanism, 20, 38, 58, 151, 167–68, 171, 174
Pandit, Vijaya Lakshmi, 160–61
Paris Peace Conference (1919), 69, 177
Peace Information Center (PIC), 206–7
peace movement, 117, 172, 176, 183, 185, 189, 205–6
Permanent Mandates Commission (PMC), 35, 137–39
Pitts, Jennifer, 13, 156, 210
Plato, 30, 49
Pliny the Elder, 173
political space, 9, 16–19, 41, 78, 82, 132–35, 187, 223, 227
Politics for Young Americans (Nordhoff), 28
politics of space, 7, 16–19, 130, 164–66, 223
Porter, Eric, 206
"Pragmatic Program for a Dark Minority, A" (Du Bois), 130, 144–45, 154
"Present Outlook for the Dark Races of Mankind, The" (Du Bois), 51, 54, 73–74
provincialism. *See* race provincialism
Public and Its Problems, The (Dewey), 133
public philosophy, 224–25

race provincialism, 38, 119, 122, 172, 174–89, 205–11
Race Questions, Provincialism, Other American Problems (Royce), 174
racial discrimination, 5–6, 12–13, 25–27, 34, 155, 157–62. *See also* Jim Crow; segregation
racial equality, 35, 64–65, 127, 131–32, 145, 164, 181, 205

racial inferiority, 23, 34, 73, 80, 120, 172, 176, 183, 190–91, 196, 199
racial liberalism, 134, 172, 176–83, 186–88, 211
racial separatism, 134–35
racial vindicationism, 170–72, 189–90, 210–12
Ranga, N. G., 152
Rasberry, Vaughn, 188
Reconstruction, 7, 31, 33, 64, 86, 90, 99–100, 111, 115–17, 119–20. See also *Black Reconstruction in America* (Du Bois)
Reddick, L. D., 151, 157
Reed, Adolph, Jr., 90, 174
Renaissance, 196–200
Reynolds, Henry, 100–101
Rhodes, Cecil, 59
Riofrancos, Thea, 166
Rodney, Walter, 202
Roediger, David, 86
Roosevelt, Eleanor, 160
Roosevelt, Franklin, 188
Rosenboim, Or, 187, 223
Royce, Josiah, 174–75
Russo-Japanese War (1904–5), 74

scaling democracy, 165–66
Schmitt, Carl, 214
Schumpeter, Joseph, 30
science fiction, 45–47, 69
Scott, David, 171n15, 216
segregation, 5–6, 42–43, 52, 61–62, 132, 134–35, 208. See also racial discrimination
Sekyi, Kobina, 111
self-determination: African self-determination, 168, 178–81, 189; anticolonialism and, 149, 181, 191, 202–3, 211, 217; citizenship and, 32–35; colonial commission proposals and, 191; colonial peoplehood and, 128–29, 135–39, 143, 146; constructive minorities and, 132, 135; debates over meaning of, 5; democracy and, 32; democratic peace and, 171, 177–78; domestic jurisdiction and, 37; Du Bois on, 31–32; equality and, 185; ignorance as greatest challenge to, 31–32; imperialism and, 6–7, 11, 34, 88, 123, 146, 149, 216–17; industrial democracy and, 122–23; masses and, 30–31; mob and, 31; precolonial traditions of, 191; race provincialism and, 122; racial discrimination and, 11, 31; racial provincialism and, 122; solidarity and, 179; spatial imaginaries and, 80; transscalar conception of, 12–13; UN and, 140, 153–55, 163; world democracy and, 5, 11–13, 64, 168, 185, 191, 217, 219; world peace and, 35, 168, 185, 202
settler colonialism, 101, 149–53
sharecropping, 116
shareholder whiteness, 103, 110
Shklar, Judith, 100
Short History of the World, A (Wells), 169, 199
Singh, Nikhil Pal, 86, 133n22
slavery: abolition of, 99, 112–16, 150; capitalism and, 72, 181, 197, 212; civilization and, 194–95; Du Bois on, 112, 194, 196, 200–202, 206, 211–12; economic slavery, 33, 107, 119, 136; imperialism and, 112–14, 118–19, 136, 181
Sluga, Glenda, 176n33
Smith, T. V., 132
Smuts, Jan, 108n70, 156, 161
social Darwinism, 45, 61–63, 82
Socialist Party, 85
solidarity: anticolonialism and, 89, 98, 219; civil rights movement and, 180–81; class solidarity, 77, 82, 84–85, 89, 118–19; colonial peoplehood and, 128–29; dividends of empire and, 89, 96–97; expressive solidarity, 179–80; strategic solidarity, 180; structural solidarity, 180–81; transnational solidarity, 81, 88, 129, 135, 179; transnational whiteness and, 88, 101–2, 110–11
Souls of Black Folk, The (Du Bois), 46
South, the: disenfranchisement in, 159; dividends of empire and, 111–20; Du Bois on, 90, 113–17, 155. See also Reconstruction

INDEX › 261

South Africa, 62, 150, 152, 158, 161
sovereignty: capitalism and, 203–4; colonial peoplehood and, 128–29, 135–36; democracy and, 28, 217; democratic peace and, 203–4; imperialism and, 121, 152, 188; interracial utopianism and, 60; liberal internationalism and, 203; minority rights and, 163; popular sovereignty, 14, 30, 80, 121; postcolonial sovereignty, 80, 137–38; world democracy and, 14–15. *See also* domestic jurisdiction; international law
spatial imaginaries, 3–6, 13–19, 43, 57–58, 80, 83, 121–23, 222–24
spatiality of politics, 9, 132, 223
spatiotemporal grammars, 5, 16, 18–19, 41, 64, 82, 123, 128, 130, 163, 222–25
spheres of influence, 22, 93, 102, 144, 185, 214
Spiller, Gustave, 65
Stockholm Appeal, 206
Stoddard, Lothrop, 74–75
Streator, George, 134
Streit, George, 186–87
Study of History, A (Toynbee), 198
submerged tenth, 31
suffrage, 2, 11, 25, 31, 54, 105, 146, 173, 212
Sultan, Nazmul, 128

Tagore, Rabindranath, 182–83
Talented Tenth, 31, 208
Taney, Roger, 140
Taylor, Charles, 16
technological development, 49, 55–61, 63, 75, 113
techno-optimism, 57
Teutonism, 46–48
Throesch, Elizabeth, 48
Tillery, Alvin, 180
Time Machine, The (Wells), 50
Tocqueville, Alexis de, 97
Tolstoy, Leo, 97
Toynbee, Arnold, 198
transnational democracy, 10–16, 220. *See also* world democracy

transnational political imaginaries: anticolonialism and, 171; bifurcation of class exploitation collapsed in, 123; central elements of, 20, 66; colonial peoplehood and, 219; confinement of democracy contested by, 15; constructed and contingent majoritarianism in, 28, 180; definition of, 7–16; dividends of empire and, 98–99, 109, 121; global color line and, 41–43, 51–54, 64, 77–84; industrial democracy and, 24; world democracy and, 5–17, 19–22, 41, 73, 82, 98, 109, 121–22, 171, 180, 185, 191, 213, 217–19, 224
transnational solidarity. *See* solidarity
transnational whiteness, 36, 87–89, 98–102, 107, 110–11, 121, 123
Treaty of Berlin (1878), 162
Treaty of Versailles (1919), 162, 181
Truman, Harry, 206
Tully, James, 216, 224

UNCIO. *See* United Nations Conference on International Organization
Union Now (Streit), 186
United Nations (UN): Charter of, 13–14, 37, 155–60, 162–64; colonial commission proposals for, 137–40, 153–54; colonial peoplehood and, 127–29, 153–55, 165; debates on founding of, 83; domestic jurisdiction and, 13, 129, 154–61, 205, 221; Du Bois on, 2, 12, 26–27, 33–34, 37, 126, 130, 140, 153–59, 161, 163–66, 205, 221; human rights and, 155–61, 163; minority rights and, 160–61; racial discrimination as domestic issue in charter of, 13–14; sovereignty and, 129, 163; Universal Declaration of Human Rights and, 160; world democracy and, 129, 139–40, 220–21. *See also* United Nations Conference on International Organization
United Nations Conference on International Organization (UNCIO), 126, 128, 136, 140–41, 144, 156–57, 168–69, 185, 188

United States (US): Afghanistan invasion of, 213, 217; bargain of 1876 in, 116; capitalism furthered by, 117–19, 187; Civil War in, 112–13, 115, 117, 196; class structure of, 85–86; democracy promotion by, 6, 213, 216–17; democratic possibility in, 19, 42, 120, 218–19, 224–27; Du Bois on, 6, 53, 95, 147, 218–19, 226; exceptionalism of, 210, 219; hegemony of, 147–48, 213, 217–18, 226; Iraq invasion of, 213, 217; labor movements in, 98–99; neocolonialism of, 147–48, 205–6; Pax Americana, 213–16; race question in, 52–54, 125, 165, 174–76, 178–79, 210; wages of whiteness in, 87–88; white supremacy in, 13, 98. *See also* Cold War (1947–91); Reconstruction; slavery; South, the

Universal Races Congress (1911), 38, 42, 45, 60, 63–69, 73

utopianism. *See* interracial utopianism; intraracial utopianism

"Vacation Unique, A" (Du Bois), 45–48

Valdez, Inés, 8n17, 128–29

Vandenberg, Arthur, 155

veil, 38, 45, 52

vindicationism, racial, 170–72, 189–90, 210–12

Vitalis, Robert, 131, 171–72

wages of whiteness: capitalism and, 86–87; citizenship and, 100–101, 109–10; definition of, 36; dividends of empire distinguished from, 87–88, 98, 109–10, 121

Wallace, Henry, 26, 205

Walling, William English, 93

war: abolishing of, 59–60, 65–66, 176; causes of, 35, 42–43, 61, 65, 73–74, 76–77, 79, 141, 156, 204–5; democracy's relation to, 35, 77; deprovincializing of, 173–83; Du Bois on, 55, 61, 74, 181, 205; race provincialism and, 176, 182; race war, 42–43, 72–74, 76–77; racial utopianism and, 59–60; world wars, 190, 205. *See also* "African Roots of War, The" (Du Bois); Cold War (1947–91); Russo-Japanese War (1904–5); World War I; World War II

Webb, Beatrice, 96n36

Webb, Sidney, 96n36

Weinbaum, Alys Eve, 80

Wells, H. G., 47, 50, 59–60, 65, 72, 168–70, 185, 199

Westphalian conception of sovereignty, 14

"What Is the Fourth Dimension?" (Hinton), 49–50

What the Negro Wants (Logan), 83

White, Walter, 155, 188

white dominion, 59, 75, 87–88, 113

white global hegemony, 62, 75, 80

white laborers, 23, 80, 86, 87, 89, 98, 99, 103–10

white pacifism, 177, 183–89

white prestige, 87–88, 96, 104, 106–11, 120–21

white supremacy, 13, 16, 75, 98, 148, 182

Wilder, Gary, 83–84

Willkie, Wendell, 168

Wilson, Woodrow, 5, 182

Wilsonianism, 5–6, 20, 177, 213, 217

Wolfe, Patrick, 153

Wolin, Sheldon, 17–18, 224

Women's International League for Peace (WILPF), 175–76

Woolf, Leonard, 89, 93–94

World and Africa, The (Du Bois): aims of, 37–38, 169, 189–90; Andromeda myth and, 191–95; context of, 169, 189–90; as corrective to Wells, 170; problem-space of, 170–71

world democracy: aims of current volume on, 5–8, 14–19; anticolonialism and, 109, 217; capitalism and, 36–37, 119, 211; colonial peoplehood and, 129, 147; conceptual genealogy of, 5–7, 9–16; decolonization and, 7, 33, 64, 119, 191, 222; definition of, 3–4, 6, 11; democratic theory's relation to, 26–27; development of, 1–7, 40–45, 224–25; dividends of empire and, 88–89, 120–24; Du Bois on, 1, 7, 34, 43, 191, 226–27; early vision of, 38; fourth dimension and, 38; global color

INDEX › 263

line and, 40–45, 54, 64; imperialism and, 2, 6–7, 11–12, 16, 34–37, 54, 80, 119, 139–40, 147, 213–27; industrial democracy and, 7, 80, 191; interracial utopianism and, 42–43, 64; obstacles to realization of, 6–7, 11–13, 16, 33, 34, 80, 119, 139–40; outline of current volume on, 36–39; overview of, 1–9, 36–39, 213–27; race provincialism and, 184–85, 211; restructuring of, 120–24; self-determination and, 5, 11–13, 64, 168, 185, 217, 219; sovereignty and, 14–15; spatial imaginaries and, 3–6, 13–15, 222–24; transscalar perspective and, 12–13, 15, 224; UN and, 129, 139–40, 220–21

world order, 3–4, 9, 42, 75, 146, 149, 204–5, 213–14, 219, 221, 226

world peace: anticolonialism and, 145; citizenship and, 209; decolonization and, 35, 172; democratic peace and, 176; global color line and, 76; imperialism and, 77, 137, 143, 158; industrial democracy and, 24, 77; interracial utopianism and, 38, 41–42, 82; paradox of peace, 184–85; peace movement, 117, 172, 176, 183, 185, 189, 205–6; race provincialism and, 176, 184–87; racial equality and, 65, 181; racial utopianism and, 59–61; self-determination and, 35, 168, 185, 202; white pacifism and, 177, 183–89. *See also* democratic peace

World Peace Council (1949), 205–6

"World Search for Democracy, A" (Du Bois, unpublished): aims of, 1–5, 11; colonialism in, 2–3; elitist conception of democracy in, 32; epistemic problem of ignorance in, 33; epistolary structure of, 2–4; industrial democracy in, 21; Keynesian-Westphalian frame and, 14–15; Marxism challenged in, 123; political and human emancipation in, 21; question of democracy in, 15

"World View of the Negro Question, A" (Reddick), 157

World War I: black participation in, 181; Du Bois on, 32, 73, 75, 102, 106, 181–83; Du Bois's thought impacted by, 43, 45; economic explanations of, 93; global color line and, 64, 73, 77, 82–83; imperialism as cause of, 73, 102, 106–7, 178, 190, 205; interracial utopianism and, 42–43, 70, 73, 83; nationalist interpretation of, 106–7; transnational whiteness and, 106–7, 111–12; Wilsonian moment of, 5; world democracy and, 5, 43. *See also* "African Roots of War, The" (Du Bois)

World War II: Du Bois on, 85, 123, 189; imperialism and, 120, 190, 205; interracial utopianism and, 83; race provincialism and, 186; racial discrimination and, 6

"Worlds of Color" (Du Bois), 43, 77, 79

Younis, Musab, 58–59

Zamir, Shamoon, 46, 49
Zimmerman, Angela, 10n25
Zimmern, Alfred, 74

www.ingramcontent.com/pod-product-compliance
Lightning Source LLC
Chambersburg PA
CBHW022043290426
44109CB00014B/958